W9-BPM-369

WISE MEN AND THEIR TALES

Portraits of Biblical, Talmudic, and Hasidic Masters

ELIE WIESEL

Schocken Books, New York

Copyright © 2003 by Elirion Associates, Inc.

All rights reserved under International and Pan-American Copyright
Conventions. Published in the United States by Schocken Books, a division
of Random House, Inc., New York, and simultaneously in Canada
by Random House of Canada Limited, Toronto. Distributed
by Pantheon Books, a division of Random House, Inc., New York.
Originally published in hardcover by Schocken Books,
a division of Random House, Inc., in 2003.

Schocken and colophon are registered trademarks of Random House, Inc.

Library of Congress Cataloging-in-Publication Data

Wiesel, Elie, 1928–
Wise men and their tales: portraits of biblical, Talmudic, and Hasidic masters /
Elie Wiesel.
p. cm.
ISBN 0-8052-1120-9
1. Bible. O.T.—Biography. 2. Bible. O.T.—Legends. 3. Talmud—Biography.
4. Talmud—Legends. 5. Hasidim—Biography. 6. Hasidim—Legends. I. Title.
BS571.W5485 2003
296'.092'2—dc21
[B]   2003045576

www.schocken.com

Book design by Virginia Tan

Printed in the United States of America

First Paperback Edition

4 6 8 9 7 5 3

This volume is dedicated with love to
Elisha Wiesel and Steve Jackson
who, each in his own way, carries on the tradition of
his grandparents, my parents.

Contents

Contents

IN HASIDISM

Preface

FOR TRYING to precipitate the redemption, the Baal Shem Tov was punished. Exiled to a faraway land, he was deprived of his powers and his knowledge. He turned to Reb Tzvi-Hersh Soifer, his faithful servant and disciple, who never left him. Help me, said the Baal Shem Tov, do you remember *anything*—a prayer, even a *word*, from before? No, Tzvi-Hersh did not. He too had forgotten everything. Everything? Really? No, said Tzvi-Hersh, I still remember the alphabet. Then what are you waiting for, exclaimed the Master of the Good Name, start reciting! *Aleph-Bet-Gimmel-Daled*, Tzvi-Hersh began. And with great fervor they both recited all twenty-two letters, repeating them again and again until their memory was restored to them.

This tale is among the most beautiful in Hasidic literature, because it emphasizes the virtues of both faith and learning. An obligation as well as a passion, it is study that marks my own endeavors as both teacher and writer. From my teachers I learned to read and reread our sacred texts with constant amazement and eagerness. But "read" is not really the proper word. *Mikra*, which is Hebrew for "read," can also be translated as "appeal." To approach a biblical passage is to respond to its call, its interpretation, while exploring the depths of its multiple meanings, some of which are immediately understandable, and some enveloped in dazzling mysteries.

This applies equally to my love for the Talmud. An eternal source of inspiration and wonder, the Talmud has accompanied the Jewish people for more than two thousand years of exile, almost as if to alleviate their suffering. Just as the Torah has no beginning, the Talmud has no end. Each succeeding generation of scholars contributes to its growth and its power.

Oh yes, the Talmud and the strength of its dialogue. One can say that the Talmud is nothing more than an endless series of debates between masters and their disciples, and among the masters themselves. But the beauty lies in the respect they all show for one another, particularly when two camps disagree on matters of the law and its application. In the world of the Talmud, the majority and the minority have the same right to be heard. And discussed. And admired.

Whether it involves a pilgrimage to biblical sources or simply celebrates the joy of learning, the act of studying always evokes for me the warm ambiance of the yeshiva. Through this new volume of readings and commentaries, collected over the course of many years, I offer the reader an invitation to come and study together with me.

Prophetic warnings, midrashic stories, Rashi's interpretations, and Hasidic tales—within the context of an uninterrupted present, even those stories that at first glance seem worn by the sands of time continue to guide and enlighten us, and to teach us how to deal with contemporary challenges and eternal dreams. And even when we are not governed by the answers, we remain affected by the questions that are raised, and by the tales which become part of our own.

All this—provided our passion for learning is not diminished.

Elie Wiesel
April 2003

Introduction:
And What Does Rashi Say?

I LOVE RASHI.
   Why? Because.

Because of a question I used to hear and repeat for years and years. *"Un vos zogt Rashi?"* And what does Rashi say?

Like most Jewish children in my town, in all Jewish towns in the vanished world of Eastern Europe, I had a soft spot in my heart for Rashi. For Jewish children and adolescents in exile, he was a learned and wise companion on a journey that took us first through the Humash or the Pentateuch and then through the concise realm of the Mishna and the enchanting world of the Gemara. Did I love him because he commented on the Babylonian but not on the Palestinian Talmud? Did *he* favor Diaspora Jewry, for whom study served as a nostalgic attachment to an invisible but inviolate homeland? He was there, always, ready to help us decipher a difficult word, comprehend a complex situation, assimilate a complicated idea. Rashi was the beacon, the simplifier. Without him, the road before us was often dark and threatening.

That's what I thought in those days and evenings when I was a small *kheider yingel* or yeshiva pupil. I thought I loved Rashi because he made my life easier.

Today—I still love Rashi, I love him even more than before, but for a different reason. I love him because of *his* taste for questions.

Listen to how he opens his masterly commentary on the Torah:

Amar Rabbi Itzhak—said Rabbi Itzhak. The Torah should have begun with the first law handed down to the people of Israel (which deals with the calendar). For what reason, then, does it begin with a story about the creation of the universe? Here is the reason, says Rashi. Should the nations of the world one day tell the people of Israel, "You are thieves, for you have conquered lands that belonged to seven nations," the people of Israel would answer, "The whole world belongs to God; and He gives it to whomever he wants. He had given this land to the other nations first but took it back and gave it to us."

I know: this commentary could be interpreted in political terms. As if Rashi (a fervent nationalist?) were telling the whole world that the land of Israel belongs neither to Christians nor Muslims but to the people of Israel. Without this legal ownership of the land, there would be no *mitzvot*—no commandments—related *to* the land and the Temple for Jews to obey.

However, we must be careful. Here, Rabbi Shlomo ben Itzhak, who is known by the acronym Rashi, speaks neither as a politician, nor as a theologian. Then what does he speak as? We shall return to this question later.

But who is this Rabbi Itzhak whom he is quoting? Rashi does not identify him. One commentator claims that he wanted to pay homage to his father, Rabbi Itzhak, by referring to his rich commentary on Scripture, thus dispelling rumors depicting him as an ignorant Jew. True or not, the theory is touching but not necessarily informative. For not much is known of the Rabbi Itzhak except that he was Rashi's father and that Rashi adored him.

The problem is that in Midrash Tanhuma, we find a Rabbi Itzhak offering us the same explanation of the opening verse of the Bible. Chances are that Rashi took it from there.

Furthermore, a renowned scholar, the nineteenth-century Kabbalist-traveler Rabbi Haim David Azulai, wrote that Rashi's father *was* a great scholar and did not need his son to defend his reputation. Hence the conclusion that the reference is not of a personal nature?

I suggest we stay out of this dispute.

For the moment, may I simply declare my gratitude to the father for giving us a son of such grandeur and generosity. For the last eight or nine centuries we have all been in Rashi's debt.

Rabbi Nahman of Bratzlav called him "the brother of the Torah." Indeed, the Torah and Rashi's commentary seem inseparable to teachers and pupils alike: he remains the companion of all those who study and all those who teach. Without him, how often would I have lost my way in the great labyrinth of the Talmud? At times, when confronting an obscure passage, I hear myself murmur, *"Un vos zogt Rashi?"* What does Rashi say? Instantly, light is shed upon the words and their meaning.

RASHI IS CELEBRATED and beloved to this day because his approach to what we now call textual analysis represents precision and clarity.

And yet one may safely say that his biography is far from precise or clear.

How is one to explain the mystery that surrounds some aspects of his life? We don't even know whether he was Ashkenazi or Sephardi—not that it matters much. His birthdate itself is subject to debate among scholars. The year usually cited is 1040. Why? Because that is when the celebrated Rabbeinu Gershom Meor Hagolah, "the Light of Exile," passed away. And we believe that no generation could sustain itself without a great teacher in its midst: when the sun sets, another sun must rise. Two other years, 1030 and 1037, also figure in Rashi's file as possible birth years. But not the month or the day. We do know, however, the exact date of his death: July 13, 1105, or, in the Hebrew calendar, the twenty-ninth day of Tammuz in the year 4865 since creation. This piece of information was found in a manuscript quoted by a French-Israeli scholar, Shimon Schwarzfuchs. It reads as follows:

The divine arc, the holy of holies, the great Master Rabbeinu Shlomo—may the name of this Just Man be a blessing and protection for us all—son of the holy Rabbi Itzhak the French, was taken from us Thursday, the 29th day of Tammuz, in the 4,865th year since the creation of the world. He was 65 years old when he was recalled to dwell in the celestial academy.

Where did he die? Unfortunately, his grave has not been found. Where was he born? In Troyes? In Mainz? In Worms perhaps? As is the case with Homer, more than one city claims him as its native son.

Several legends circulated about his birth. It seems that his parents owned a precious stone filled with rare light which the Church was eager to acquire at any price. They were offered huge sums of money. They refused. Faced with coercion, and fearing temptation, they chose to throw the stone in the sea. Their reward? A son whose light was even more radiant than that of the precious stone.

It is said that Rashi's pregnant mother was walking in a narrow street when a carriage came from the opposite direction and nearly crushed her. As she pressed her belly against the wall, the wall receded—and to this day, we are told, one can see the niche created by her stomach.

Another legend maintains that his father Rabbi Itzhak was worried that he would not have a minyan for the circumcision of his only son. He need not have worried. The prophet Elijah or Abraham—or both—were happy to oblige. Because of the son? Because of the father, too. When his contemporaries referred to him later as *ha'kadosh,* the holy man, it was because he died as a martyr of the faith.

Troyes then had a Jewish community of only a hundred or so families.

That the child was precocious is fact, not fiction. Still young, he left Troyes and traveled to Mainz, where he studied with the three great masters of the land, all disciples of the late Rabbeinu Gershom. They gave Rashi access to their notes and through them to Rabbeinu Gershom's teaching.

It is difficult today to imagine the impact Rabbeinu Gershom had on his contemporaries. He was *the* Halakhic and spiritual authority in Diaspora. His word was law. It was he who prohibited polygamy and the repudiation of a wife without her consent. He also forbade the embarrassment of penitents by reminding them of their old sins. Another prohibition that bears his name: the opening of someone else's mail.

Rabbeinu Gershom's life was shadowed by tragedy. His son was forced to convert and the father sat shiva. But he never became bitter. He was too much of a humanist for that.

Rashi's principal teacher was Rabbi Ya'akov ben Yakar. The other two were Rabbi Itzhak Halévy and Rabbi Itzhak son of Rabbi Yehuda, whose recently discovered headstone reveals that he died in the year 4824 since creation—which is 1063 or 1064 in the Gregorian calendar. Thus, Rashi was his disciple to the end. All three rabbis were leaders of Talmudic academies or yeshivot. In those times, they were small in size and located in the rabbi's house. Fund-raising was not necessary for the upkeep.

At the age of twenty-five, Rashi returned to Troyes. He married and had three or four daughters—but no son—and accepted a position as rabbi and head of his own yeshiva. But this brought many responsibilities. Though the rabbi received no salary, he was expected to subsidize his school and his pupils, who came from all over France and the Rhineland.

Fortunately, Rashi could afford this. Was he wealthy? Did he marry into a wealthy family? Thanks to his vineyards, which, in the province of Champagne, were among the best, he must have lived comfortably. But what about dowries for his daughters? Miriam married Rabbi Yehuda ben Nathan and Yokheved married Rabbi Meir ben Shmuel. As for Rachel, her marriage to a certain Eliezer ended in divorce. Known for her beauty, Rachel was nicknamed "Belle Assez," which means Beautiful Enough. Rashi's grandchildren became his fervent students and influential tossafists. Among them were the Rashbam and Rabbeinu Tam, who got his income from money-lending and money-changing.

Rabbeinu Tam was too young to study with his grandfather: he was four years old when Rashi passed away. But, in more ways than one, he may be included among his disciples.

Rashi was close to his students. He corresponded with them as well as with other masters; no letter remained unanswered. In matters of Responsa, 334 of his decisions were recorded. One question that was put to him makes one smile. In a community that has only one synagogue, what is the *din,* the law, if two *kohanim,* or priests, both *hatanim,* or grooms, want the honor of being called first to the reading of the Torah? Who should get it? Of course, it is inconceivable to imagine a community with only one synagogue. But Rashi thought of all possible situations. In general, he sided with Hillel the Elder, whose moderation and tolerance appealed to him. In this respect, he followed the line of Rabbeinu Gershom. Like Rabbeinu Gershom, he allowed *anusim*—involuntary converts to Christianity—to return to their Jewishness and forbade anyone to remind them of their past. If the convert was a descendant of Aaron, a *kohen,* Rashi ordered his priestly status be restored to him. Thus, on holidays, the former convert could bless the congregation.

All that has been historically established. But, as frequently happens with great personalities, Rashi had his share of hagiographers. Some imaginative commentators maintain that he traveled all over the world, that he visited the poet Rabbi Yehuda Halévy in Spain, the Duke of Prague in his castle, and that Godfrey of Bouillon appeared before him before embarking on the First Crusade to free Jerusalem.

His admirers were convinced that he spoke all the languages, mastered all the sciences, and possessed all the mystical powers needed to make himself invisible.

Hasidic literature nourishes a profound affection for Rashi, whom they call *der heiliger Rashi*—the saintly Rashi. They believe that his work was inspired by the Shekhina herself. One Hasidic text goes so far as to claim that Rashi did not die a natural death. In simpler words, he did not die at all. Rather, he ascended to heaven alive.

Said Rabbi Yitzhak-Eizik of Ziditchoiv: When God, blessed be His name, put an end to Abraham's trial and ordered him to spare his son, who was already bound to the altar, Abraham refused to listen to the angel who transmitted the divine order. He yielded only when God promised Abraham that among his descendants would be a certain Shlomo son of Isaac or Itzhak of Troyes.

But Rashi had followers not only in the Jewish scholarly community. Christian theologians also fell under his influence. Nicholas de Lyre, a priest of the late thirteenth and early fourteenth centuries, quotes Rashi so often in his translation of the Bible that a certain Jean Mercier of the Royal College of Paris was said to have called him "Simius Solomonis"—Shlomo's ape. And through Nicholas de Lyre, Rashi influenced Martin Luther, whose own translation of the Bible owes much to his. Today, linguists study Rashi for different reasons. Thanks to him they have the opportunity to rediscover ancient French words. The ones used by Rashi in his various commentaries—the *be'la'az*—number three thousand.

What do *we* owe Rashi? We owe him a commitment to the intriguing and indispensable art of commentary.

To comment on a given text means first of all to establish between oneself and the text a relationship of intimacy: I explore its depths so as to seize its transcendental meaning. In other words, in commenting on a text, I abolish distances. I read a sentence that was formulated on the other side of oceans and centuries, by Rabbi Akiba perhaps, and in order to penetrate its original intent, I let it pass through other sentences to surface in my mind.

To comment on a text, preferably an ancient text, is to know that though I am not always capable of attaining truth, I may come closer to its source. It is to go back to the origins of a word or a name that is rooted in the Revelation at Sinai. Frequently, the Talmud uses the expression *Halakha le' Moshe mi' Sinai*—that is the Law as it was spoken to or by our teacher Moses at Sinai. Maimonides uses it as well. It has special significance because it stops the debate. The moment we identify the genesis of a decision, we ought to be satisfied. And all the rest is commentary.

Commentary in Hebrew is *perush*. But the verb *lifrosh* also means to separate, to distinguish, to isolate—that is, to separate appearance from reality, clarity from complexity, truth from its disguise. Discover the substance, always. Discover the spark, eliminate the superfluous, push back obscurity. To comment is to reclaim from exile a word or notion that has been patiently waiting outside the realm of time and inside the gates of memory.

When you pray, said the late Louis Finkelstein, you speak to God; when you study, God speaks to you. If study is discovery, commentary is adventure. As I begin to dig into the recesses of a text, uncovering layers after layers, I encounter predecessors who lead the way. Will I dare to go farther and deeper than they? Is it possible? Is it possible for a modern commentator to leave Rashi behind? No—and yet we are encouraged to go beyond him. Any student is allowed to comment on Rashi's commentaries so as to better understand a biblical verse or a Talmudic passage. Thus the process of commentary will never end.

But how are we to know which interpretation is correct? The answer lies in the one that enriches memory. If it distorts it, the interpretation is wrong. In other words, an excess of imagination risks harming the original thought. To understand Isaiah, I must look for him in the majestic and often brutal poetry of his public addresses. To receive Hillel's precepts, I must plunge into his lessons and remain loyal to them. As in everything else, the key word in commentary is loyalty.

Rashi's greatness springs from the fact that he is forever loyal to the text before him—and before us.

He never lets his erudition weigh upon the reader. He does not try to impress us with the originality of his mind. To quote ancient sources and to reconcile them with the text, that is sufficient for him.

His commentary is never an end but a beginning, an eternal beginning. It begs for more, always more. Thus the student, the reader becomes his associate, his partner, his fellow seeker. Together they go deeper and deeper into the secret workings of seemingly simple words in complicated sentences.

He is never petty. He recognizes what he owes his predecessors and his peers. Often he would accompany a thought by giving credit to his "father and teacher," his masters of the yeshiva in Mainz. He would say, *"shamati,"* I heard from . . . , *"kibalti,"* I received from, I learned from . . . Or *"nireh li,"* it seems to me that . . .

A personal illustration of his humility is given to us by his grandson, the Rashbam, who together with Shmaya served as his secretary. Listen: "Rabbeinu Shlomo, my mother's father who has been the light of the Diaspora, composed many commentaries on the Bible and the Prophets; at times, he gave oral interpretations, too. . . . I, his grandson, talked with him about some of them, and he admitted that had he had enough time, he would have written them in a different spirit. . . ."

On occasion, in his own writings, he does not hesitate to admit that he doesn't know the answer to a question—or that he doesn't understand a biblical passage, a Talmudic decision. Scholars have come up with more than thirty such instances.

Example: in the Book of Genesis—chapter 28, verse 5—the text tells us that "Isaac sent Jacob off, and he went to Paddan-aram, to Laban the son of Bethuel the Aramean, the brother of Rebecca, mother of Jacob and Esau." It is a long, convoluted sentence, and Rashi comments with utter candor, "I don't know what it is telling us." The author of *Siftei Hakhamim* responds with tongue in cheek: "There are those who wonder why Rashi felt the need to inform us that he doesn't know. If he doesn't know, let him keep quiet." But Rashi believes in truth. If he doesn't know something, he must acknowledge it. In this case, he doesn't see why the text repeats itself. At this stage in the narrative, doesn't everybody know who Rebecca is? Admit it, the question is valid. But what is the answer? Must there be one? Now you have one more reason for my infinite affection for the man. Like him, I believe that some questions are more important than answers.

Also, I remember, as a child, I would be so happy to stumble on one of Rashi's confessions of not knowing. For then, in turn, I could avoid the tutor's question by saying: if Rashi doesn't know, how can I know?

In truth, it is with a sense of awe that I study Rashi's life and work.

His output is so immense that one cannot help but wonder how he managed to write so much, on so many subjects. He wrote commentaries, letters, litanies. He also taught classes, examined students, wrote or dictated replies to opinions. Were there no distractions in Troyes? And what about his family? He had to watch over the education of three little daughters. We know that they were learned: who taught them if not he? He also had to make a living; he must have been busy in his vineyards. After all, he didn't produce wine only for religious purposes. He had to sell it. When did he find time for business?

Furthermore, he must have been politically active. He must have taken a role in communal Jewish affairs. Did he? After all, things were happening in the world . . .

The new millennium began with trouble and turbulence. Much like today, many wars were about conquest—both spiritual and political. Christendom and Islam continued their prolonged ideological conflict through various territorial battles: Norway, Sweden, Burgundy, Spain, France. Too many kings wanted to rule over too many people. Romanus III, the Byzantine emperor, added Syria to his list of conquests. In Constantinople, the patriarch was excommunicated by Rome, thus marking the beginning of a lasting schism in Christianity between East and West. In Rome, Benedict—a corrupt and cruel man—was elected pope only to be unseated and later reinstated. Eventually he sold his title and position to Gregory VI, who would also be deposed. In the Islamic world, the Shiites and Sunni lived in constant fear of and desire for bloodshed leading to supremacy. The Battle of Hastings, the capture of the Byzantine emperor by the Turks, the appearance of anti-popes on the stage, Rome's efforts to limit and weaken the authority of local princes, the excommunication of Emperor Henry IV by Pope Gregory VII, who forced him to come on his knees and ask for forgiveness at Canossa, the opening battles for the Reconquest of Spain from the Almoravids, the burning of Rome by the Norman troops of Robert Guiscard, the tumultuous reign of William the Conqueror . . .

What a century that was! Ten years before it ended, Rashif en-din

Sinam created the clandestine society called the Assassins, whose fanaticism continues to be practiced to this day. Its leaders gave hit lists to its secret members, who were as efficient in eliminating rivals then as they are now.

What about the Jewish situation? While Gentiles were busy fighting one another, they usually found time to vent their anger on Jews. But for the better part of the eleventh century, chroniclers recorded no major catastrophe. Jews dwelled in relative peace, which meant in relative danger in Europe and in the Holy Land. In Spain, for instance, Jews savored the fruits of a golden age of interreligious harmony. The great thinker Rabbi Shmuel Hanagid served as commander in chief of the Catholic king's armies and played a major role in defeating the Muslims on various battlefields. Shlomo Ibn Gabirol and Yehuda Halevy paved the way for Maimonides. Nothing special happened, meaning nothing especially evil befell Jews in France and the Rhinelands. It was too good to last.

For the Jews of western Europe the eleventh century ended in terrifying events filled with fear, brutality, and death—all in the name of a man, born Jewish, whose dream was to allow love to penetrate the hearts of men everywhere.

The Crusades.

One cannot read the chronicles of those tragic times of religious hatred on the one hand and spiritual courage on the other without feeling heartbroken.

It all began on November 27, 1095, at Clermont-Ferrand in France, when Pope Urban II issued a call to Christians to go to Jerusalem and free its holy sites from Muslim domination. Those who headed his appeal put crosses on their garments, thus becoming the Crusaders.

At first, the operation had only to do with Muslims. But there were Jews who knew better. Jewish communities in France dispatched emissaries to their sister communities in Mainz and Worms, warning them to prepare for trouble. Strangely, those communities in the Rhinelands also sent messengers to the French Jews, warning *them* of the impending threats, since the march began on their territory. Eventually, the Rhineland Jews proved to be in greater danger. Indeed, as the Crusaders began their journey along the Rhine and Danube rivers, they inflicted suffering and death upon thousands of Jews in Cologne, Mainz, Worms, and Speyr, in their effort to convert them by force.

In some places the Crusaders met with armed Jewish resistance. In others, the majority of Jews chose martyrdom. The first to prefer death to conversion was a woman. Others followed. The tales of their heroic deeds make unbearable reading. In the courtyards of synagogues, men recited the blessing of slaughter before stabbing their wives, then their children, and finally themselves. There were stories of parents who sacrificed daughters who were about to get married, and of small children who tried to hide. In some places, the martyrs sang the prayer that concludes every office: "Praise be given to the Lord of all that exists and to the Creator of beginnings." "Accept baptism and you will live," the Crusaders repeatedly told their tortured prisoners and victims. "We believe in God, the only God," men and women replied, and died.

In his masterpiece on the *akedah,* the late Shalom Spiegel quotes a passage from Rabbi Eliezer bar Nathan's book on the disasters of 1096. When the Crusaders entered Mehr, a village on the Rhine, the local prince handed over its Jews. Some were slain, others forcibly converted. A certain Shemaria bribed a bursar, who helped him flee with his wife and three sons. Then the bursar betrayed them. During their last night together, Shemaria

slaughtered his wife and their three sons, then plunged the knife into himself. He fell unconscious but was still not dead. The next morning, when the enemy came upon him, they found him lying on the ground: "Will you convert from your faith to ours? Do so and you will live." But Shemaria replied: "God forbid that I should forswear the Living God." So the townspeople dug a grave and he, Rabbi Shemaria the saint, walked into it himself; he took his three sons and laid them to his left, and placed his wife to his right. Then the people began to throw upon him the earth from the graveside. But all that day, till the following morning, he wept out loud, weeping and keening over himself, his sons, his wife-helpmeet lying beside him. Upon hearing him, the enemies of the Lord came back and removed him, still alive, from the grave. Again they asked him: "Do you want to give up your God?" But the saintly Rabbi Shemaria refused to barter the great and glorious. He held fast to his integrity till his last breath. So they put him into the grave a second time and threw earth upon him, and there the saint died for the unity of the glorious and awesome Name, and there he remained steadfast in his trial like Father Abraham. Oh how fortunate he was, Oh his fortunate lot. . . .

Why did so many of them, in the Rhine provinces, choose suicide and martyrdom, whereas in Sephardi lands, during the Jihad, their brothers and sisters did not? Read Gershon Cohen's essay on this question, and you will be rewarded. I will not reveal the answer, since it is unrelated to Rashi.

But the Crusades are related to our master.

When the Crusaders, led by Godfrey of Bouillon, finally reached Jerusalem, they ransacked the city and brutalized its inhabitants. Jews and Muslims combined forces and fought them with great vigor, but were outnumbered. At one point, the Crusaders locked a group of Karaites and Jews in a synagogue and set it on fire. All were burned alive.

Poems, prayers, and litanies were composed to remember these tragedies. They survived the centuries and are recited in many communities to this very day.

But . . . what did Rashi say about them?

At the beginning of the First Crusade, Rashi was fifty-five years old. He had ten more years to live. Busy as always, he was more productive than ever. His creativity was boundless. He wrote *kuntrassim* and pamphlets, answered questions related to Halakha, continued to work on his commentaries.

But how did he manage to go on studying and teaching in spite of the violence around him? How did he manage to write? Were his powers of concentration so strong that he could shut out the suffering of his people? True, his family was unharmed, his community remained intact, and Troyes was miraculously spared, at least for a while. Later, in 1288, thirteen Jews were burned alive after a Jewish dignitary, Isaac Chatelain, was accused of ritual murder. All died while sanctifying God's Name. But in Rashi's time, Troyes was quiet, whereas Mainz and Worms were not, and they were not that far away. Echoes of the massacres and scenes of martyrdom must have reached his community. It is inconceivable that he was not informed. In fact, there is proof that he was. Indeed, some of his commentaries on Psalms resonate with his pain over the tragedies that befell his people in his own time.

In some of his penitential prayers, the "Selihot," he implores God to "gather in his cup the tears of His children." He also pleads with the Torah to intercede on behalf of those who give their lives for its glory. Here too the presence of the tragic events is clearly felt.

Is his beautiful introduction to the Song of Songs his response to them? It is a moving appeal meant to bring comfort and consolation to his persecuted people. He says that there are numerous readings of this text in the midrashic sources, but "I say that King Solomon foresaw the time when the people of Israel will be sent from exile to exile, from one catastrophe to another. And they will lament while recalling their past glory, and the love that made them different from others. And they will remember the promises He made them." And God, says Rashi, quoting prophetic verses, "will reassure them, saying that He too remembers, and that their marriage is still in force: he has not sent them away. Israel is still God's spouse—and He will return to her."

Does it follow that Rashi turned to the Song of Songs so late in his life?

In a wider context, this question has not been answered with true precision: What did Rashi compose first, his commentary on the Talmud or that on Scripture?

Conventional wisdom wants us to believe that the Torah came first—just as it did at Sinai. Without the Bible, there would be no Talmud. Furthermore, Rashi succeeded in finishing his work on Torah but not on the Talmud, whose commentary remains incomplete—his disciples picked up where he left off.

The expression *kan niftar rabbeinu*—here, at this precise point, our master died, or *kan hifsik rabbeinu*—here, our master interrupted his work, appears three times in his writings on Talmud. In Baba Batra the text says, "What preceded was the commentary of Rashi; what follows is that of his grandson the Rashbam." In the Pizzaro edition of the Talmud, the note is more explicit: "Here Rashi passed away." In the Treatise of Makkot, the flow of the text is brutally interrupted: "Our Master who lived and died with purity of body and soul stopped his work here. From now on, it is his disciple Rabbi Yehuda ben Nathan who speaks." In Pesakhim or Passover, the note merely says: "This is the commentary of Rabbeinu Shmuel, Rashi's disciple." Nothing of this kind occurs in Rashi's commentary on Scripture. So—we must conclude that his work on the Talmud came later, since it includes words about his death.

But is this a valid argument? Not really. It is quite possible that Rashi interrupted his work three times, but not that he died three times. In other words, it is conceivable that he worked on several treatises at once, and even on both projects at the same time.

If I could rely on my intuition, I would say that Rashi's introductory thoughts on Genesis were written at the time of the First Crusade. In order to reassure his fellow Jews and teach Christians, he felt the need to declare as an opening thought: "Peoples of the world, beware! Christians and Muslims are waging war over a piece of land? That land belongs not to either of you, but to the people of Israel."

But here it is we who must beware, lest we prejudice readers against our hero: he might be accused of dealing with politics.

So Rashi *did* react to Jewish suffering during those terrible events. Was it enough to write poetry when, around him, men and women endured tragedy? But then, what else should a writer do? As scholar, commentator, and teacher, did he respond to the upheavals by continuing his work?

If the answer is yes, some critics may be disapproving. From the purely personal and human viewpoint, how could he devote his intellectual energy to the elucidation of an obscure ancient term or phrase while Jerusalem was being ransacked, its synagogues reduced to cinders, their worshipers tortured and shamed?

But perhaps therein lies his greatness. From Rabbi Akiba he learned—as we do—that for us there is no better refuge than Torah. Wasn't the Mishna written during the national disasters that shook up Jewish history for three centuries? Rashi too knew how to transcend the present by conferring upon it the indispensable dimension of timelessness.

Later, during pogroms and persecutions, in houses of prayer and study, old teachers and their fervent disciples, with their last breath, immersed themselves in the study of Talmud. Meanwhile, a few steps away, excited hooligans, drunk with hate and blood, sharpened their knives and readied their clubs. That was our way of handing down a message to future generations: the killers have done their job, and we have done ours.

The Crusaders proclaimed the reign of death? Rashi celebrated that of life. And of memory.

So let us go back to the beginning: *Vos zogt Rashi?* What does Rashi say?

I remember: as a child, his round cursive letters scared me; more than the biblical ones, they suggested a world that only adults could enter.

Each time the teacher asked "What does Rashi say?" I felt like answering: I don't know what he says for others; I want him to speak to me personally. Later, I was grateful to him. When I failed to grasp the meaning of a problem or a word, I would look into his commentary; and it was to me, personally, that he spoke: Look here, child; this way; do not be afraid; all ideas must be communicated, shared in simple words. You stumble upon some? Some words are obstacles? Well, start again. It happened to me too at times. I started again.

And I loved him. I could not study without him. Naturally, I have studied other commentaries—Abrabanel, Ibn Ezra, Sforno, Or Hahaim. But Rashi's is different; it radiates friendship. At times I feel as if he had been sent into this world mainly to help Jewish children overcome their fear of ancient texts.

Rashi, a celebration of faith, clarity, and knowledge?

He is, above all, a celebration of memory.

To both God and Israel he says: Remember the past, remember the times when both worked together, to attain the same goal.

The future of humankind itself is rooted in memory.

In the Bible

Ishmael and Hagar

A MAN, A WOMAN. Abraham and Sarah. Who has not heard of them? Everyone loves them. They radiate goodness, nobility, human warmth. Who doesn't claim kinship with them? Humankind is what it is because they shaped our destiny. He is the father of our people, she the mother. Everything leads us back to them. The promised land bears their seal. Faith—our faith—was kindled by theirs. A couple unlike any other, they inspire joy and hope. Tormented by our own troubles, we recall theirs, which give ours a transcendent meaning. Abraham, the first to be chosen, the first to choose God and crown him God of the universe; Abraham, synonymous with loyalty and absolute fidelity, a symbol of perfection. And yet . . . a shadow hovers over one aspect of his existence. In his exalted life, we encounter a painful episode that cannot but puzzle us, if not cause us to recoil. I refer, of course, to his behavior toward his maid, concubine, or companion, Hagar, and their son, Ishmael.

Let us read the text, shall we? It tells us that Sarah, poor Sarah, is barren. She cannot conceive. Unhappy above all for her husband, who desires a son and heir, she proposes that he have this child with his Egyptian servant, Hagar. Jewish women being good matchmakers, the *shiddukh* is successful. Abraham and Hagar are together, Hagar

3

becomes pregnant—and that is when the problems start: the servant becomes disrespectful toward her mistress, who takes offense. Eventually, a persecuted Hagar takes flight. Proud, she prefers to die in the desert rather than remain a slave in Sarah's house. By chance, an angel notices her and advises her to return home. Hagar obeys, goes back to Abraham, and gives birth to Ishmael. Fourteen years later, Sarah finally gives birth to her own son: Isaac. What must happen, happens: When Ishmael, like any other boy, plays tricks on his young sibling, Sarah arranges for Hagar and her son to be sent away for good.

The text, of course, is more detailed and contains some astonishing descriptions: Sarah's state of mind, Hagar's character, Abraham's behavior—it's all there. Sometimes a single word suffices to paint a vivid picture; a silence conveys the ambiguity of a situation. The more we reread the story, the more it troubles us. It makes us feel ill at ease. We wish it had happened somewhere else, in another book, in someone else's memory. It has no place in ours. How is it possible? Can Jewish history really begin with a domestic quarrel between an elderly matron and her young maid? And if so, why did the Bible preserve it?

Naturally, none of this would have happened had Sarah not been childless for so many years. But then, why was she? Why did she have to be so afflicted?

Actually, there are those who answer that Sarah has this in common with other matriarchs who had the misfortune of being barren at first. The reason? One midrashic author offers a generous explanation—generous, that is, to the husbands, the patriarchs. This author says that pregnant, the most beautiful wives appear less attractive because they lose their figures. So to be desirable to the patriarchs for as long as possible, the matriarchs had no children for years and years. A compassionate and courteous Midrash adds that Sarah, when she became a mother at the age of ninety, still had the looks of a young bride on her wedding night.

In other words, the entire tragedy of Hagar and Ishmael would not have happened if God—or the text—had not decided to cater to the masculine pride of our forefather Abraham. Is it possible? Is it plausible? Let us not forget: if Sarah had given birth to a son earlier, immediately after her marriage, Hagar would have remained a servant, Ishmael would not have been born—and Israel, today, would not have an Arab problem.

But let's be serious: this story unfolds on a higher level; it has a deeper meaning. Nothing in Jewish destiny is frivolous. All doors open on metaphysical dilemmas and conflicts.

Let us begin at the beginning. Abraham is not yet called Abraham, but Abram. Sarah is known as Sarai. They are a lonely couple whose life seems rather turbulent. Abraham has left the home of his parents to follow the path leading to God—a dangerous path, full of obstacles and traps. Famine and wars succeed each other, as do divine promises. Except the earthly troubles are more real. Abraham does not stop: his life is one long battle. Against neighboring kings, against the powerful unbelievers, against the cruel nature of some people, against drought. Nothing comes easy to him. Everywhere he must fight, but everywhere he wins. After all, isn't God on his side? And yet, on one front, he feels beaten: he has no child. But God has made promises—solemn promises! We can imagine his grief: with no son, no heir, what kind of future is there? Who will continue his work? We can understand Sarah's grief: when they were young, they had hope—each day, each night could bring good news. Now, after so many years, it is more and more difficult to imagine, more improbable, and—why not?—even impossible. Uncertainty, anguish, agony without end.

Then Sarah, in a characteristic gesture of empathy, offers to lend her servant Hagar to her old husband. Hagar is young, she will bear him a child. Perhaps a son. Thus Abraham will be the father of a child even if she, Sarah, will not be the mother. Abraham does not refuse. Hagar, with pregnancy, becomes arrogant; Sarah makes her pay dearly. Hagar flees, returns, gives birth to Ishmael, and remains for fifteen years—long enough to witness the birth of Isaac, whose arrival overshadows all else. Then comes the final drama: the breakup, the explosion between the two women, the two brothers, and, above all, between father and son. Sarah demands that her husband expel Hagar and Ishmael, who provoke her. Abraham hesitates. Ishmael is his son; he feels he has neither the right nor the strength to drive him away into the unknown. Divine intervention is needed to make him decide. But what about pity in all this? And compassion? And the human heart and Jewish morality?

These are troubling, painful, baffling questions. And there are others, many others. All of them inevitable. They call into question the actions of the entire cast of characters. Who are they? A father—Abraham. Two mothers—Sarah and Hagar. Two sons—Ishmael and Isaac. Is that all? Surely not. For God—yes, He too—plays an essential role in the evolving plot. Except for Him, all the characters seem to be real, living beings, so detailed and colorful are their features.

Abraham: submissive in his relationship to God, sure of himself in his relationship with those around him. He obeys heaven but is obeyed on earth. We perceive him as moody, impulsive, used to giving orders. Strong, invincible. He appears vulnerable only with Sarah. Inflexible with others, he is patient with his wife. He was able to resist his father, Terah, but Sarah is irresistible. Whatever she desires, she obtains. It is Sarah, not Abraham, who comes up with the idea of a match with Hagar. Abraham never would have dreamed of living with another woman. He loves Sarah. Too much perhaps. She is his strength and perhaps his weakness as well.

At this point, an obscure incident ought to be recalled. It happened in Egypt which the two visited as tourists—though their interest was not tourism, but food. At home, in Canaan, people were starving. An unexpected problem confronted Abraham and Sarah in Egypt: the king Avimelekh fell in love with her. It was love at first sight. And Abraham knew that kings usually get their way. Avimelekh could easily eliminate the cumbersome husband and keep the widow. So Abraham, with her consent, introduced Sarah everywhere as his sister. She spent a whole night with the king who, lo and behold, thanks to heavenly intervention, was struck by some illness and was unable to touch her.

This strange episode smacks of unpleasantness; it has always left me uneasy. Yet instead of separating the couple, it strengthens their bond. Bravo, but we still don't understand Abraham: Fearful? For his life? And what about his honor? How could he abandon his wife—his adored, beloved wife—to the whims of a king who has an eye for women, especially strange women, other men's women? How could a hero like Abraham—who had defeated *five* kings—yield to a single one without so much as a fight? How is it possible that a man of his stature thinks only of saving his own skin? Admittedly, he is preoccupied with theological questions, but is there no loyalty in him, not to mention chivalry?

We shall ask these same questions with regard to Hagar and Ishmael. Abraham drives them away? He who is famous for his hospitality? For love of his wife he sacrifices his son? For sacrifice is what we are talking about! He sends them into the desert, where death surely awaits them. How can he be so cruel toward a woman who has loved him, be it for one night only—and toward a child, his own child at that! Sarah doesn't like them—good, let them stay at a neighbor's. Let them go and live with some distant tribe! But why condemn them to death? How are we to explain these flaws in Abraham's character? To what shall we attribute them? Is this the same Abraham whose faith and goodness remain models for all time? Could *he* have committed such acts of heartlessness?

Let us read again the passage about the second character in the drama—Sarah. We shall see that she too doesn't come off too well in a second reading. Negative traits appear. In Egypt, she is a willing accomplice in her husband's play-acting. Like a couple illegally crossing some dangerous border, together they try to cheat the police. But have the police nothing better to do than wait for Sarah? Thousands upon thousands must be pouring into the region in search of food—and Sarah alone is threatened? The answer is yes, and Abraham tells us why. She *is* very beautiful. Agreed. But to whom does Abraham say that? To his wife. And she accepts the compliment without protesting? And what about humility? Modesty? Couldn't she, shouldn't she, answer her husband: Really, you are very sweet, but there are women more beautiful, more attractive; let's not play such a charade. We are married, let's remain so in the eyes of the whole world! Besides, what good is such a game? Why not ask God to protect us? No, Sarah's behavior in Egypt does not become her.

This grows even more evident later on, in the conflicts with Hagar. No sooner has Sarah persuaded Hagar to try to conceive Abraham's child, than she seems to regret it. She is jealous, keeps close watch over her servant, and looks for quarrels. She slaps her face with her bedroom slippers, says the Midrash. As soon as Hagar is pregnant, Sarah finds her arrogant. What if she is mistaken? What if the servant's behavior is simply due to her pregnancy? Pregnant women have strange desires, impulses, whims—everybody knows that—everybody but Sarah! It is quite possible that the text is mistaken, and we are mistaken, because Sarah herself is mistaken: Hagar may have meant no disrespect toward her mistress. Sarah may have imagined all sorts of terrible things. In other words, in this story, Hagar is Sarah's victim! Sarah was wrong to impose a role upon her and then resent her for playing it too well.

Later on, things become even more inflamed: Hagar comes back with her son, and then Sarah has a son of her own. But instead of making peace with the servant, instead of being grateful to fate— after all, her greatest wish has come true, she *has* become a mother— Sarah continues to torment Hagar and *her* child. The servant acts with restraint and watches her every step, every gesture, every word— that's clear, since Sarah no longer complains. Then, suddenly, Abraham's wife picks on little Ishmael! Now it is he whom she scrutinizes and suspects! This too is clearly indicated in the text: she sees Ishmael playing with Isaac and she gets upset! Why does that upset her? What could be more natural, more beautiful than to see two children—two brothers!—playing together? Sarah finds this neither beautiful nor touching. Had Ishmael done otherwise, had he avoided his little brother, had he chosen not to play with him, Sarah surely would have accused him of something else—of duplicity, of selfishness. Of childish cruelty. She seems to hate him. Nothing about him pleases her. She dislikes the way he dresses, eats, speaks, and sleeps.

She resents his joy. Finally, she turns to her elderly husband and demands that he expel the servant and her son. She does not even refer to them by name. "Send *them* away," she says, "for I refuse to let the son of the servant share my son Isaac's inheritance." Her son has a name, the other does not. The apparent reason for this request? Abraham's wealth. The text says so, and most commentators emphasize the point. What? Sarah is concerned with earthly possessions? Sarah, a materialist who wants everything for her son alone? A mother for whom no one else exists in the world? No, her behavior toward Ishmael is not appealing. Our empathy—our sympathies—go instead to her victims: Hagar and Ishmael.

Only there, too, we meet obstacles. In rereading the text, our enthusiasm is dampened for the servant and her son. Hagar and Ishmael are no saints, either.

Let's take a closer look at Hagar. She has an unpleasant side, that much is certain. She is young and vibrant—and she *knows* it. She knows of her mistress's misfortune. But instead of showing some gratitude to the family that has taken her in, she sows discord between husband and wife. The text confirms it. There is muffled anger in Sarah's tone—not only against Hagar, but also against her own husband. *"Hamasi alekha"*—this rudeness to me is your fault . . . May God judge which one of us is right. Some Talmudic commentators agree with Sarah, who reproaches Abraham for his silence. Oh yes, Sarah says to her husband, You have seen Hagar behave badly toward me and you have *said* nothing, *done* nothing to put her in her place. You didn't take my side; you remained silent . . . Because of Hagar, the couple seems no longer united.

Instead of humoring her childless mistress, Hagar irritates her. In his commentaries Rashi says in no uncertain terms that Hagar lacked respect for Sarah. She gossiped about her, she said that Sarah was a hypocrite and that this was why she was not allowed to have children. Is that the way to repay kindness and generosity? Let us listen to the Midrash: At first, Sarah introduced Hagar to her neighbors and friends, saying, "Look at this poor girl, let's help her to adjust, to find her bearings." Later, Hagar visited those same neighbors and friends to tell them malicious stories about her mistress. No wonder Sarah felt she had to take measures.

Later on, we see Hagar and her son in the middle of the desert. There is no water, and Ishmael becomes ill. What does Hagar do? She casts her son far away from her so as not to see him die. Is this the attitude of a mother? Surely, she loves him and cannot bear his illness or his agony. But why doesn't she think of *him*, of *his* needs? Doesn't Ishmael need her? To emphasize the generally negative side of Hagar, the Midrash interprets the expression "she went astray in the desert" in this way: she strayed far from the faith and the customs she had learned in Abraham's house; she returned to her pagan ways and to her pagan gods. According to the Midrash, this was her way of protesting against her fate. It was her personal response to what she had suffered: to reject faith in God. In this too she is different from our ancestors, who were able to draw greater strength from their trials, and to find through them additional reasons to believe in God. As for Hagar, she bends in the face of suffering, so much so that one almost understands why the Torah turns against her.

Now for the fourth character—Ishmael. No one can fault him: he is almost outside the drama. Object rather than subject of a story that is beyond him, he could have remained uninvolved. He is there by accident. A model victim, there is no way he can be happy. One could say that happiness escapes him. He knows very well that he is not the son his father desired. And if he didn't know this instinctively, it is constantly being told to him by others. What is he called at home? The son of the servant. Not the son of Abraham. Yet he too is linked to a divine promise, one that his mother received from an angel during her pregnancy. But the same angel had predicted the nature and the social standing of the son to be born: *"Pere adam"*—he would be wild. *"Yado ba'kol, ve'yad kol bo."* He would have his fingers in everything. The commentators did not hesitate to explain: he would be a vagabond. A thief. Violent. Poor thing—he isn't even born yet, and already he is being accused of crimes and sins as vague as they are unfair. Already he is being described as an antisocial ele-

ment. From the moment he arrives, what does he see? Helpless, he is
witness to some painful scenes: his mother is humiliated without
end. What must he think of the system in which he grows up? What
must he think of the patriarch Abraham whose reputation transcends borders? Or of his God who permits so much injustice within
His human family? And later, in the desert, what must he think of his
own mother who casts him far away to let him suffer alone, agonize
alone, die alone?

However, Ishmael, too, has a bad press among the commentators
who cannot admit that Abraham and Sarah are capable of gratuitous
cruelty toward him. And when the text says that Sarah saw Ishmael
"metzahek"—having fun—the Talmudic commentators (always suspicious of fun) say that *metzahek* means something worse: that Ishmael indulged in idolatry, and even murder. In other words, *metzahek*
means that Ishmael ridiculed the faith and the laws of Abraham. He
indulged in debauchery by word and deed. And he had a bad influence on Isaac by pushing him to run after young girls and married
women. Worse: he showed a taste for hunting. He was never without
his bow and arrows, the most deadly weapons of the time. Did he
try to teach Isaac how to use them? Sarah caught him shooting an
arrow in the direction of her son without hurting him. Frightened,
Sarah decided to get rid of Ishmael. A more charitable commentator
translates *metzahek* as "he discussed with Isaac the question of the
inheritance," saying that as the firstborn he would receive the larger
portion of Abraham's estate. In any case, Ishmael's role is less benign
than one might have thought. A victim himself, he also victimized
Isaac, who indeed was the only innocent figure in this whole drama—
he was too young.

But there remains one more character about whom not much
has been said: God. What is His role in all of this? Is He also innocent? Why did He prevent Sarah from conceiving? And why did He
advise—no, *order*—Abraham to obey his wife and banish Hagar and
her child? He could have abstained. He didn't have to be directly
involved in this business. In fact, Abraham and Sarah could have put
the whole blame on Him! It's His fault, and human beings could

do nothing! It is He who holds the secret of human suffering, He who dispenses joy and happiness, He who takes them away from whomever He wishes, whenever He wishes. If Abraham and Sarah have committed an injustice toward Hagar and Ishmael, it is because they were caught in a situation willed and ordered by God.

In other words: in this drama, none of the characters is entirely without guilt. All are wrong, because every one of them finds himself at a certain moment and for various reasons in conflict with the others.

But at which crossroad does this tragedy begin? Who committed the first mistake, and when? Hagar, when she accepted Sarah's suggestion? Sarah, in making it? Abraham, when he submitted with surprising passivity? God, as it were, when He made too many promises to too many people at the same time?

In going deeper into the text, we realize that the tragedy unfolds on more than one level. At first sight, it's the drama of a childless couple. On a more social level, the text tells us about a servant's troubles. A third reading gives psychological implications: a couple is affected by the presence of a stranger. And then, on a theological level, God appears and disappears in order to endow simple gestures and words with a hidden meaning that justifies exaltation or despair. Here everything is complicated. The angel orders Hagar to name her son Ishmael, but it is Abraham who gives him the name. Hagar weeps, but it is the voice of her silent son that God hears. First it is an invisible angel who speaks to Hagar, but she speaks of a vision. Miracles play an important part in this tale. By a miracle, Sarah becomes a mother; by a miracle, Ishmael is saved from death. One might say that God, in a good mood, has decided to help everybody, to ward off evil from everywhere, to intervene in favor of all His creatures and lead them toward a bright future.

But there is another way to read the story: one relating to historical facts. In the eyes of secular scholars, the plot is natural and accurate, for it reflects the spirit and the law of the Code of Hammurabi, as illustrated by documents originating with the Nuzzi in the northeast of Iraq. For example: "If Gilimninu bears her husband Shennima children, he will not take another wife. But if Gilimninu is unfruitful, it is she who will choose a woman for her husband." Which is what Sarah did in giving Hagar to Abraham. The Code of Hammurabi adds another provision to this law: "If the woman chosen by the wife becomes arrogant, she loses her new status and becomes a slave again." Here again is exactly what happened to Abraham's family. Seen from this angle—that of the ancient culture and environment to which Abraham belonged—the biblical story evolves according to the logic and the law of the time. And all the characters are right— except, of course, for Hagar. On the simplest level, she is guilty. She got what she deserved. She had only to respect the rules of the game. Arrogance must get its due. Social transgressions must be punished. Had Hagar not shown disdain toward her mistress, she would have remained in her home, respected and happy. By violating the customs, she put herself in jeopardy. And Sarah was right when she turned to Abraham—the master of the house, the supreme and all-powerful judge—to mete out just punishment to the guilty woman. Since she knew the law, she also knew the nature of the punishment, and she was right to remind him of it. We therefore have here a clear and simple situation: dramatic, no doubt, but without any problems.

Only we prefer to follow our own tradition. A story is studied in terms of its own cultural values. The Code of Hammurabi is of interest to us, but the Torah alone can explain the Torah. *"Moshe kibel Torah misinai"* is what characterizes Judaism: everything connects us to Sinai, because everything comes *from* Sinai. The light must come from the text itself. *"Hafokh ba ve'hafokh ba dekula ba,"* the questions and the answers are all in the text.

I therefore suggest that we read the story once more, taking a closer look at Hagar. The Code of Hammurabi aside, Hagar seems to us the most attractive of the characters on stage. She is beautiful, young, dynamic, and proud. The moment she feels offended by her mistress, she goes away. It has nothing to do with the fact that she spent a night with Abraham. That's the way she is: proud by nature— I would almost say, by birth. She is not a nobody, our Hagar. There is, in fact, a midrashic legend that describes her as an Egyptian princess. This legend links the adventures of the biblical couple in Egypt to the drama of Hagar. When Abraham misled the Egyptian king Avimelekh by presenting Sarah as his sister, Avimelekh, we remember, fell ill and could not approach Sarah. Learning the truth the next day, he apologized to Sarah and gave her his daughter as a gift. *Her* name? Hagar. Lest we judge the royal father too harshly, the Midrash attributes this comment to him: "It is better, my daughter, that you be a servant in the house of Sarah and Abraham, than a princess in some other palace." Even though her father considers this a consolation or even a reward, Hagar's servitude was a terrible humiliation for this young woman in love with freedom.

That is why she at first refuses to yield to Sarah's wishes. In fact, Sarah had to make considerable efforts to persuade her to accept Abraham as a lover. For Hagar had no taste for such an arranged—and hasty—match. Once persuaded, she continues to bear herself with dignity. Although a servant and a "stand-in," she does not forget that she is a princess. And when Sarah is too hard on her, she chooses freedom. She goes into the desert—the desert she knows—her homeland. To her it means total freedom—for her imagination, her dreams, her memories. Better to die in the desert—in freedom—than to live in security—in servitude.

Imagine her—alone with her anger, her wounded pride—in the desert, near a well. In Hebrew the word is *ayin,* which also means eye. Because images are reflected in it? And because the eye, like the well, attracts friend as well as stranger? One cannot live without water—or without light. Or without hope. Thus, the eye and the well: cry of hope and hope itself. Hagar, in her extremity—with no hope left—gazes at her image in the well. Suddenly a voice calls to her. An angel has found her. It is a beautiful line: "She fled her mistress and was found by an angel of God." This is not one of those wandering angels who roam the cities looking for surprises, or who crisscross the desert measuring its wonders. No, this angel is on a special mission. He must find the fugitive. To save her? Not exactly. Rather, to bring her home first—that is, back into servitude—and then to console her. Listen to the dialogue: "Hagar," says the angel, "servant of Sarah, where do you come from, and where are you going?" And she answers: "I am running away from my mistress Sarah." Our commentators try to explain this answer by emphasizing Hagar's slave mentality: she ought not to have said "I am running away from my mistress Sarah," but simply "I am running away from Sarah." The Talmud comments: "When you call someone an ass, at least let him use a saddle." *I* prefer to see in this answer evidence of frankness, of sincerity: Hagar does not lie. She is a slave and she says so. If the slave feels ashamed, her owner must feel even more so. Hagar's response is therefore an accusation pointed at Sarah: she treats me as a servant, she humiliates me. That is why I decided to run away! But listen carefully: she answers the first part of the question and not the second. She says where she is coming from, but not where she is heading. Comments the Malbim: this is the fate of the fugitive; he knows where he comes from, but not where he may go. In this respect, nothing has changed since then: in our time refugees do not know if they will find a place to rest and establish roots. With this difference: the refugees of my generation did not even know where they had come from; they came from so many countries, persecuted by so many oppressors, tormented by so many destructive angels. Unlike us, Hagar had but one enemy—and had been exiled from only one place.

But her divine messenger surprises us with his answer: he sends her back into servitude and at the same time predicts that she will continue to suffer. But he finds a way of reassuring her: her suffering will have a purpose. She is pregnant, she will bear a son whom she must call Ishmael, because "God has heard your pain." Moved, overwhelmed, Hagar suddenly expresses herself as a poet, a mystic: she seems to refute the angel. Surely God hears, but that's not all: God sees. And Rashi adds: God sees the pain of the afflicted. "You are the God who sees all," says Hagar, "and I myself have seen it here." That is why she calls the well—or the spring—*"be'er lahai ro'ii."* The well of the living vision? Of one who sees life? Yes, she is somebody, this Hagar.

So much so that the great sage Rabbi Shimon bar Yohai envies her and says so in public. When he is in Rome on behalf of his brethren in occupied Judea, he exclaims: "Hagar, a servant of my ancestors, was three times privileged to see an angel bearing a blessing—and I here on a humanitarian mission have seen no angel at all! Is that fair?"

Actually, the promise given to Hagar recalls the one given Abraham. Hagar, too, receives the assurance that her offspring would be numerous, even innumerable. According to the Midrash, Balaam, poor prophet that he was, understands it very well: of the seventy nations created by God, only two will bear His name: Israel and Ishmael. And at the end of days, says the Midrash, it will be the sons of Ishmael who will wage wars in the Holy Land against the sons of Isaac.

Stimulated and encouraged by the angel of God, Hagar returns to Abraham and Sarah. She has a son, and Abraham names him Ishmael. He is an old man, our patriarch, when his son is born—eighty-six years old. Thirteen years later God tells him that he will soon become a father again. Abraham laughs. Sarah laughs. God changes their names: Abram becomes Abraham, Sarai is called Sarah. Meanwhile, things are happening in the world. Sodom attracts a little too much attention; Sodom disappears. Lot and his two daughters are saved; his wife, too curious, is unwittingly discovering sculpture: she turns into one herself. Abraham again leaves for Egypt and returns from Egypt. Isaac is born—and the second chapter of the drama marks the return of Hagar, who during these last years has dwelled offstage. The plot unfolds during the great feast Sarah and Abraham are giving to celebrate the weaning of Isaac. While the adults are drinking, eating, singing, and storytelling, Ishmael *"metzahek"*—literally, he laughs—with Isaac, or "makes him laugh." Sarah gets angry, and the servant and her son are thrown out of the house. For good. Let us add another interpretation of the word *metzahek:* Ishmael tries to pervert Isaac by initiating him into idolatry. This is Rabbi Akiba's view. His disciple Rabbi Shimon bar Yohai takes the liberty of contradicting him: "This is one of the rare times when I disagree with my Master," he says. It is inconceivable that Ishmael,

Abraham's son, could have practiced idolatry in the house of his father—of our father.

But whatever the relations between the two brothers, more important is the fact that Hagar and Ishmael become exiles—refugees, uprooted. We imagine them abandoned, in danger, on the threshold of death. Ishmael is ill, he has a fever, and his mother is sick with despair. So she leaves her child in the bushes. Cruel behavior? Let us not judge her too severely. She distances herself so she can cry out loud. As long as she is near her son, she manages to hold back her tears—so as not to frighten him, not to distress him. What could be more natural, more human, on the part of a mother? An interesting detail: in her speech, Ishmael is always a *yeled,* a child; for the angel, and the text, Ishmael is a *na'ar,* a boy. Though he is seventeen years old, he is, in his mother's eyes, a child—a sick and unhappy child. We love Hagar in the Bible, and also in the Talmud. We cannot help but love her. With all her faults, she remains a perfect mother—though not a Jewish mother.

Abraham is another story: Ishmael is his son, yet he banishes him. What kind of father is he, this father of the Jewish people? But let us not be too hasty. Who are we to judge Abraham? Caught between his duty as a husband and his responsibilities as a father—between two loves—he wavers. For the first time in his life he cannot make up his mind. Also for the first time, we detect a misunderstanding between Abraham and Sarah. A painful rift. Sarah calls Ishmael "the servant's son," Abraham continues calling him his son. In the end, it is God Himself who must prompt him to act—to act against his own heart, his own conscience. "Listen to the voice of your wife," God tells him. Had God not insisted, Abraham would not have given in to Sarah. Even so, he feels uncomfortable. He *knows* that he is making a mistake. Let us read the text: *"Va'yashkem Avraham ba'boker,"* and Abraham rose very early in the morning; he took some bread and a pitcher of water and handed them to Hagar. Like a thief, one might say. Why so early in the morning? For two reasons. First, he wanted Hagar and Ishmael to set out before sunrise, before the great heat, when it is still possible to walk on the sand. Second, Abraham wanted to say farewell to his son and to the boy's mother while Sarah was still asleep. This was the right moment to see Ishmael off. What if he were to get too emotional? If he were to burst into tears? Worse: what if Sarah were to look for a quarrel and say that he was giving them too much bread, too much water? No, it is better that she not be there.

Our Talmudic sages are extremely generous and understanding with regard to Abraham. They find a lot of excuses for him. Besides, they are convinced that Abraham continued to think lovingly of Ishmael even after he and Hagar had left.

One midrash says that Abraham tied the heavy pitcher to Hagar's hip so it would drag in the sand and leave tracks. Thus Abraham would be able to find his son. He often thought of him, and Sarah did not like that. Three years after the dramatic separation, Abraham could bear it no longer, and he decided to find Ishmael. Sarah must have made a scene, because she exacted from Abraham a promise to go only as far as Ishmael's house, but not to enter it. In fact, he promised Sarah that he would not get down from his camel. So Abraham set out, following the tracks in the sand. He reached his destination toward noon. A woman—Aissa, the Moabite wife of Ishmael—welcomed him. "Where is your husband?" he asked. "He has gone to gather fruit and dates." "I am thirsty and hungry," said Abraham, "and exhausted from the journey. Please give me some water and a bit of bread." "I have neither bread nor water," said Aissa. Then Abraham said to her: "When your husband comes home, tell him that an old man came to see him from the land of Canaan, and the old man was displeased with the threshold of his house."

When Aissa gave Ishmael the message, he understood what it meant and at once repudiated his wife. Hagar then sent him to Egypt to find a new one. And he did. Fatima. Three years later, Abraham, overwhelmed with yearning, came back. "Where is your husband?" he asked Fatima. "He is not here," she said. "His mother and he went to look after the camels in the desert." "I am hungry, I am thirsty," said Abraham, "and exhausted from the journey." "Of course," she answered, and she went quickly to bring bread and water. Then Abraham prayed to God on behalf of his son, and at once Ishmael's home was filled with every possible delicacy. "When your husband gets home," said Abraham to Fatima, "give him this simple message. An old man came from the land of Canaan. He very much liked the threshold of your house." The moral of this tale? Abraham cared for his son, he loved him, but he never saw him again.

Some sages believe that he even cared for Hagar. The proof: after Sarah's death, he married a woman named K'turah who bore him six sons. Who was this K'turah? Rashi reveals her identity: Hagar. K'turah and Hagar are one and the same. To quote the Midrash: "Abraham took Hagar back, for she was a woman of distinguished bearing." Of distinguished bearing? A former servant? Well, she *had* been a king's daughter. By marrying her, Abraham rehabilitated her. And the Midrash adds that during all those years in exile, Hagar had remained faithful to him—to the only man in her life. And so the circle was closed. Abraham and Hagar were reunited—and were happy, perhaps. Did they ever think back to their first encounter? Let us do it for them. It took place in Egypt, when Hagar was a young girl and Abraham a young man. When Abraham and Sarah pretended to be brother and sister. Because of their lie, Avimelekh, king of Egypt, is punished: he and his entire royal house become sick. That night, they are all victims of Abraham and Sarah. And what was *their* punishment? The tragedy of Hagar and Ishmael. Had they not lied, the king would not have felt the need to offer his daughter to Sarah. And the history of the Jews—and of Islam—might have been different.

The *Akedah*, the binding of Isaac, a high point of Jewish experience throughout the ages, is also considered a punishment for the sufferings of Ishmael. Here again we find a midrashic text that says Abraham was wrong when he preferred Isaac to Ishmael: no father has the right to favor one child over another. Thus, when God orders Abraham to take Isaac and bring him to Mount Moriah, the sentence reads: *"Kakh na et binkha, et yehidkha, asher ahavta, et Yitzhak."* Take your son, your only son, the one you have loved, Isaac. But that is wrong! Isaac is not his only son! The punctuation needs to be changed. As I see it, the sentence should read as follows: *"Kakh na et binkha* (comma)—take your son—*et yehidkha asher ahavta* (comma)—the only one you have loved—Isaac." Thus the command contains a reproach as well as an explanation.

The *Akedah*—the supreme test a father and a people can face—is therefore the result, the consequence, of the injustice committed by Abraham and his wife toward the unloved son, Ishmael. Sarah hated him? Abraham should have explained the situation to her. God sided with Sarah? Abraham should have argued with Him as he had done for Sodom. But Ishmael did not bear a grudge against his father at all. That is clear from the text itself. Having lived a rich and full life, Abraham died at the age of 175. And his two sons Isaac *and* Ishmael came to bury him in the cave of Makhpela. Yes, Isaac *and* Ishmael were both there for the funeral. Together. Reconciled. For the Talmud, this is proof that Ishmael had "repented." Additional proof: he allowed his brother to precede him in the biblical description. Had Ishmael seen his father again while he was alive? No doubt he had. After all, Abraham did marry Ishmael's mother. But the text says nothing of such meetings. Ishmael reappears only at Abraham's death, as if to remind us of the eternal truth: Death often resolves the most difficult problems. In the face of death, most conflicts look childish. But that's not all. The reunion of the two brothers before their father's grave also reminds us of a truth too many generations have tended to forget: Isaac and Ishmael—both of them—are Abraham's sons.

It is sad to say—and even sadder to repeat—but a possible villain in this story is Sarah, our beautiful and noble matriarch, so warm toward strangers, so hospitable to the needy, so welcoming to all women seeking faith. Too intense, too jealous a mother? Of course she desired a glorious future for her son! But she was wrong to do so at the expense of another mother, another son. Mind you, it is not I who says so—it was said by the great Rabbi Moshe ben-Nahman—the Ramban—Nahmanides. When Sarai, as she was then known, persecuted Hagar, she committed a sin, said the Ramban. And Abraham, by not preventing her, became an accomplice to that sin. That is why God heard the lament and the tears of Hagar and gave her a wild son whose descendants would torment the descendants of Abraham and Sarah. The sufferings of the Jewish people, said the Ramban, derive from those which Sarah inflicted on Hagar.

And the Radak—Rabbi David Kimhi, the great exegete and philosopher of the twelfth century—also does not hesitate to blame Sarah for her immoral behavior, for her lack of charity and compassion. The term *vate'aneha*—and she, Sarah, made her suffer—was to haunt our history for centuries to come.

Of course, one could invent all kinds of excuses to whitewash our matriarch. We have mentioned a few. Hagar's arrogance, the bad influence Ishmael had on his little brother, the fate and future of Israel: if we try hard, we can exonerate Sarah. But apologies no longer have a place in our tradition. We are sufficiently mature to admit our shortcomings—especially since Scripture itself chooses not to conceal them. The patriarchs are neither infallible saints nor angels. They are human beings with impulses of grandeur and weakness. They love, they know fear, they hate and say so, they try to go beyond their condition and share in God's vision of creation. When Sarah is hurt, she admits it; when she is jealous, she shows it. Whatever she is, she is no hypocrite. Hagar is unfair toward her mistress: Sarah was never two-faced. She loved her husband and therefore gave him Hagar; she believed in God and in His promise, therefore she suffered for her own kindness. And because she suffered, she inflicted suffering. Was she wrong? Maybe, but we love her nonetheless. In fact, I would say that we love her even more. In other words: Because she was wrong and knew it but could not help it, it becomes our duty to do the impossible and correct her fault without diminishing her. We are her children; that is the least we can do for our mother.

If only she could have shared her love between Isaac and Ishmael. If only she could have brought them together instead of setting them apart. Would today's tragedies have been avoided? The Palestinian problem? As always, it is the mother's fault. And yet, and yet . . .

Having read the text and all its commentaries, having studied the question and all its ramifications, we cannot but feel sorry for Hagar—but we love Sarah.

We love Isaac and we feel empathy for Ishmael, but if only he had learned to overcome suffering and turn it into a desire to fight suffering—wherever it exists.

Our story? A story in which all participants are profoundly human. Their present is not only our past; it is also *our* present.

Lot's Wife

TWO CELESTIAL BEINGS, angels disguised as men, have come to bring good news to Abraham and Sarah, to inform them that in spite of their advanced age, they will become parents.

On hearing their improbable, implausible prediction, Sarah, who in her youth was famous for her beauty as well as for her piety, burst out laughing—and then denied that she had laughed. Naturally, a family quarrel ensued. You did laugh, her husband told her, why then pretend that you didn't? Perhaps because they were embarrassed at having provoked a dispute, the angels left while looking toward Sodom.

"And they looked towards Sodom." What an ominous, disquieting sentence. It surely portends misfortune and evil. One feels in it a distant threat. Something serious, even terrible, will soon happen to Sodom—and Sodom is not aware of it. Even Abraham is in the dark. This is clearly indicated in the text. God asks, "Am I going to hide from Abraham what I am about to do?" Which is, of course, the destruction He was about to inflict upon the most sinful of cities. Then, suddenly, God decides to shift direction, to make a detour. He opens parentheses. Forgetting Sodom, He begins to speak about His closest friend and associate, Abraham: "Abraham will surely become a great, powerful nation; all others will be blessed in him. For I have chosen him to teach his children and theirs the path leading to Almighty God, to practice justice so as to allow God to fulfill the promises made to him. . . ." Then, suddenly, God closes the parentheses and comes back to the subject that seems to be at the forefront of His mind: "And the Almighty said: The outcry of Sodom and Gomorra is mounting towards me. Enormous are their sins. Thus I shall go down and see for myself if the scandalous sounds below are true; if they are not, I shall know it."

And so we are plunged into the heart of the drama. Sodom is already lost, no doubt about it. The mechanism of its destruction has been set in motion; nothing can stop it, nothing will. Nothing? No. Not even Abraham's intercession. But—what about *teshuvah*? What about repentance and its extraordinary power? Is it too late for Sodom's citizens to mend their ways and be saved? Hasn't tradition told us again and again, since the beginning of history, that it is never too late for *teshuvah,* never too late to turn toward heaven and beg for forgiveness? Granted, it is not the angels' role to urge human beings to improve their behavior. But it is man's responsibility to his fellow man. And so what about Abraham? Why didn't he rush to Sodom to sound the alarm? Rather than argue with God over the hypothetical number of *Tzaddikim,* of righteous men, in Sodom, why didn't he share his knowledge of the impending catastrophe with its future victims? And furthermore: didn't he know from the outset that this debate was a waste of time? Can one win victories over God? The same question may be addressed to God: why did He allow Abraham to go on arguing, when He knew that there were no righteous men in Sodom? He could have said to His friend and ally: Really, Abraham, save your strength; it is of no use; it is too late . . . These are troubling questions.

LET US GO to Sodom, that singular city where everything is expensive except life and human dignity.

Is it dangerous to go there? Well, literature tells us that it is sometimes necessary, if not fruitful, to live dangerously. In Sodom, danger is selective: it threatens only foreigners. Never mind, let's go there anyway.

A fascinating spectacle has been prepared for us. A spectacle in five acts: the daily life in Sodom, the arrival of the three emissaries, the dialogue between Abraham and God, the destruction of the city, and the rescue of Lot. The pace of events is as breathless as the tale is devastating. At the end, everything will be reduced by fire; the most beautiful edifices will lie in ashes. Few managed to escape; fewer emerged unscathed. Lot and his family? Only some members of his family survived—his wife and their two unmarried daughters. Having survived an immense tragedy, they became its main characters. The others, the angels, for instance, played a secondary role.

Lot and his wife are at the center. May I publicly admit my sympathy for Mrs. Lot? Poor woman, she dies on the day she is liberated. First she enjoys God's support in the form of a miracle, then she is deprived of the chance to reap its reward: she dies without experiencing the joy inherent in the act of liberation. She does not even have time to speak about it to her grandchildren. Why such harsh punishment? Only because she looked where it was forbidden to look? So what! If our own gaze could kill us, there would not be enough room for all the cemeteries on our planet. All right, she *did* disobey the angels' injunction, and *did* deserve a punishment—but why death? Wouldn't it have been enough for her to lose her sight? I feel sorry for Lot's good wife, who arrived in the desert, only to stay there forever: Josephus Flavius writes that he had seen her statue with his own eyes.

Well, let her rest a bit while we do what she shouldn't have done: look at her native town. Do not worry, at this point in our journey, Sodom is still intact. Flourishing, in fact: the evil was flourishing.

When we visit Sodom we realize that it is not only the scene of its collective tragedy that we are about to witness, we will also encounter one of its protagonists. Sodom has its own temperament, its own mentality, its own personality. All of its inhabitants, with some rare exceptions, think and behave the same way. One would say that Sodom is inhabited by one person alone, but copied and imitated a thousand times. The slogan "One for all and all for one" could apply to Sodom, with a minor change: all are like one, and the one is selfish, violent, cruel, cynical, corrupt, almost inhuman. That is why God has decided to annihilate the city: its population had pushed its taste for sin, its thirst for injustice too far. Its people have caused too much harm to too many men and women. The Midrash is full of legends illustrating the moral depravation that reigned in that city, which had become the world—or cosmic—capital of crime.

Look at the social picture: everybody was a thief, a liar, a swindler, a sadist, a narcissist, a monster. The people respected nothing and obeyed no one. They believed in no spiritual force and followed no ethical precept; they feared neither man nor their Creator. Nothing was sacred and no one was safe in their eyes. Legend has it that once a year they gathered in a certain place to celebrate their right to free pleasure. How? Through orgies that the most fervent hedonists would find exaggerated and obscene: fathers slept with their daughters, husbands borrowed their friends' wives for one hour or one night—with the consent of their own wives—and all of this was carried out in public.

Still, their behavior toward strangers was worse: they saw in every stranger an enemy to be vanquished and robbed of his fortune and of his hope. One might say that they did everything to give tourism a bad name. To see Sodom meant to be exposed to ridicule, humiliation, and death—the worst, most violent kind of death.

A visitor who happened to enter Sodom could easily die of hunger: the inhabitants would sell him or even offer him anything but food. If he had food in his bag, they would torture him by making him lie in a bed that was either too big or too small. If it was too small, they would mutilate his body to fit the bed. If it was too big, they would pull him by the hands, by the feet, by all his limbs, deaf to his shrieks and laments.

What they did was bad enough. But then they would pretend that this torture was for the visitor's own sake: to allow him to sleep more comfortably.

Worst of all: they pretended to act in accordance with the law of the land.

Whatever they undertook was ordered, or at least approved, by local courts. Strange as it may sound, there were four or five sitting judges in Sodom, says the Midrash. All had names that suited them perfectly: one was called Man of Deceit, another Man of Falsehood, the third was Head of Liars. With judges such as these, the plaintiff never had a chance. He was condemned even before presenting his case, before opening his mouth. And Abraham's nephew Lot was their leader. The chief justice. But they listened to him only when he spoke their language and expressed their ideas; then they applauded him. When he disagreed with their decisions, they interrupted him and shouted: What! A foreigner comes to dwell in our midst and he wants to rule over us?

In other words, there *was* a system in Sodom. Air-tight and self-locked, it functioned with brutal and calculated efficiency. The system crushed any outsider who dared to challenge it. All trips to Sodom were one-way. It was possible to enter the city but not to leave it. Actually, according to one midrashic source, it wasn't as easy to enter Sodom as one might think. The Sodomites saw to it that all roads leading to their city were flooded. Was it an expression of their xenophobia? Or their idea of public relations? Did they think that if word got around that their city was inaccessible, more and more people would be attracted to it? Possibly. But there is a simpler explanation: since the ground of Sodom was made of pure gold, its citizens wanted all of the riches for themselves. Didn't they have enough? They did. But such is the nature of the selfish man: not only does he wish to be wealthy and happy, he needs to know that others are not.

If and when a foreign visitor did manage to enter the city, its inhabitants knew how to deal with him—legally: they assaulted him and deprived him of his possessions, but each person took only small things. Thus, they could tell the judge: look, your honor, it's nothing. For this I am to face charges?

It was a game, nothing else. The Sodomites needed not fear justice. The courts existed only to condemn and punish the victim—

even if he or she was one of their own tribe. For example: if a Sodomite struck his neighbor's pregnant wife and caused her to lose her baby, her husband was told to give his wife to the man who hit her so that he could make her pregnant again. If a man wounded his fellow man and made him bleed, the wounded man was told to pay his aggressor for the blood-letting.

Cruel to human beings? The Sodomites were equally cruel toward animals and birds, in other words, toward any living creature whose life and movement escaped their authority. And eventually the Sodomites manifested cruelty toward one another. In spite of their plentiful natural resources, the Sodomites envied one another and stole from one another. Is that why God grew angry and said: "I have given you more than I gave others, and you use my blessings to make others suffer"? Is this why He chose to annihilate Sodom? We stumble here upon a serious and disturbing issue, that of collective guilt: does it exist within the framework of Jewish tradition? Could there be no innocent person within a community of sinners? What about the children, the infants? Are they, too, guilty? Guilty of what? Of having been born? And even if the guilt was all-pervasive, why were Lot and his wife and their children spared? Only because they were Abraham's relatives? Is nepotism a valid defense? If the answer is yes, why were Aaron's children punished by death for their sin?

Let's stay a moment with Lot—the permanent winner of Sodom's nicest citizen award. In the biblical text, he is introduced in flattering terms. Unlike his compatriots, he was kind and hospitable toward strangers. Is that why he deserved to survive? It seems so. Didn't he welcome the three celestial emissaries, even though he ignored their identity and was unaware of their mission? Both Scripture and its commentaries make much of this episode. He invited the three angels into his home, he offered them food and shelter, and when the Sodomites—all of them, young and old, rich and richer—came to besiege his house and demand that he hand them over, he refused: a perfect host, he protected his guests to the end. He went so far as to propose a deal to the aggressors: instead of his three visitors, he would give them his two young daughters, both virgins: "Do with them whatever your heart desires," Lot told the Sodomites. His plea fell on deaf ears. What they wanted was to sodomize and lynch the three foreigners; nothing less would satisfy their vile instincts. They were about to break down the doors when, finally, the three angels—who until now were rather passive—decided to take action: they blinded the attackers, thus rendering them harmless. At this point one feels like yelling: Bravo, Lot, well done, you are indeed special. But . . . wait. Let us not be too hasty. That the angels deserve our praise, that goes without saying; angels are by definition praise-worthy. But Lot? What kind of a father was he, ready to hand his own daughters over to a bloodthirsty and sex-thirsty mob? Did he even consult with his daughters?

Is it possible they they agreed to be sacrificed? One somewhat per-verse theory maintains that this is what they subconsciously desired. The reason? They weren't that young any more. And they never knew the mysterious joys of physical love. It is a fact that, following their escape, they abused their father's fatigue and made use of his vigor while he remained asleep . . . All right, suppose they *were* con-senting adults when Lot offered them to the populace—does this necessarily exonerate him?

Admittedly, the angels were grateful. So much so that they revealed to Lot the true nature of their mission: the entire city was doomed. "Take your family," they told him. "Your sons, your daughters, their husbands, take them and flee, for this place will be destroyed." Lot took the warning seriously. Quickly, he ran to meet with his sons-in-law; he repeated the precise words he had heard from the angels and urged them to pack and leave. But it was in vain. They refused to believe him; they mocked him for his fears and ridiculed his visions of horror. In the meantime, the angels grew impatient and began press-ing Lot to leave; time was running out. "Do not linger," they told Lot. It's later than you think. Your sons-in-law refuse to join you; leave them behind. Take your wife and your two unmarried daugh-ters, and come with us. Those who were unwilling or unable to hear your warning, those who refused to be saved, too bad for them. Growing more anxious by the minute, the angels led them out of town by hand. "Do not look back," they warned them. "To look back means instant death."

We are shocked by the behavior of the angels. That they were in a hurry was understandable. But since they could perform miracles, why didn't they perform one last miracle and save all the members of Lot's family—even against their will?

And since we have come upon such a perplexing point, may we extend it to humbly ask our grandfather Abraham something about his own whereabouts during this phase of the tragedy? Where was he when his nephew fled Sodom? Granted, he argued with God and debated with Him point by point on the unjust fate of the sinful city. Trying to save it, he bargained with God. His courage was evident, no doubt about that. But . . . why did he, all of a sudden, vanish from the stage? At a certain point in the debate, Abraham gave up. He picked up his marbles, so to speak, and went home. *"Va'yelekh Ha-shem ka'asher kila ledaber el Avraham, ve'Avraham shav limkomo."* Having told Abraham that He accepts his challenge, and that Sodom will be saved if it had ten righteous men in its midst, Abraham returned to his dwelling place.

What is this? God was ready to annul His devastating decree if only Abraham could designate ten righteous men—and Abraham didn't even try to locate them? To identify them? He didn't knock at doors, didn't consult friends and experts? He simply went home and did nothing? He, who knew how to fight, who loved to fight for his fellow man? What happened to him? What made him yield to passivity? What made him so resigned?

And, the question of questions whenever we confront someone else's tragedy, what about God in all this? How is one to explain His attitude? Before the destruction of Sodom, He seemed to play a game with His favored Jew—a game totally unfair to Abraham who had no control over its outcome.

Clearly, Abraham bargained with God in good conscience. He couldn't have known whether there were ten or ten hundred righteous men in the city. But God knew! So why did He force Abraham to play such a ridiculous game? Why didn't He stop him right away and say: Look, my dear fellow, do not waste your energy! It's no use! What is bound to happen will indeed happen! And there is nothing you can do about it . . . Why did He let Abraham sink deeper and deeper into his own inevitable defeat? Is it possible, is it conceivable that God actually wanted to demonstrate to Abraham something that Abraham already knew, namely that the Creator is superior to His creation, that God's knowledge lies beyond that of man?

Admit it. All the protagonists here seem, at certain moments, determined to move us to dismay, as if to tell us: Wait, you haven't seen everything yet; there are other surprises in store for you . . .

Lot's wife? Is she also going to surprise us? Yes, even she is full of surprises. We plan to question her—later. Do not worry. We know where to find her; she won't run away.

Let us retrace our steps and revisit the place of no return: Sodom. We had the familiar and doubtful pleasure of meeting its sinners. Was there really no honest citizen, no charitable woman, no decent individual in that entire city that was cursed by itself and punished by destiny? Wait: there was one. One person. One soul. A member of Lot's family. Himself? No. His wife? No. His daughter. We even know her name: Paltit. True, her name does not appear in Scripture, but she does play a rather significant role in the Midrash.

The Midrash offers us some interesting details about her personality. As the wife of an influential Sodomite, she lacked nothing, needed nothing to enjoy life and its blessings. Like the young Cakya Muni or Buddha, she must have thought that everybody under the sun was as happy and healthy as she was. Then, one day, she noticed a hungry beggar and couldn't help but feel sorry for him. Unfortunately, that was forbidden in Sodom, where human responses were outlawed. So she brought him food under cover of night. At first the Sodomites failed to understand how the beggar managed to survive. Eventually they figured it out. Paltit was arrested, tried, judged, and sentenced to die at the stake. In her agony she screamed to heaven: "Master of the Universe, be my judge and the Judge of Sodom." That is when God decided to leave His celestial throne and pass judgment upon her tormentors and executioners. This is suggested in the biblical text: *"Erada-na ve'ereh ha'ketzakata haba'a elai"*—I must go down below and see what is happening, for her outcry has reached me. One outcry only? Or the outcry of a single woman? Indeed, it happened that the suffering inflicted upon one person moved God more than the pain endured by multitudes.

Does this mean that Paltit was the only righteous person in Sodom? There was another one, claims the Midrash, which tells the story of two girlfriends who would go together to draw water from the fountain. You look bad, said the one. The other did not answer. But the first one was so persistent that her friend had to explain: We have no food at home. The first girl came from a wealthier family and could have helped her friend, but again: compassion was considered a crime in Sodom. The rich girl had an idea. She filled her jug with grain. The two friends exchanged jugs. The generous one also ended up on the stake. And it is because of her suffering that God destroyed Sodom.

Another midrashic text describes another sinful town (there were five of them) where a nice young girl also felt sorry for a stranger. She too was arrested, judged, and sentenced to death: this time not by fire, but by the sting of thousands of bees. And it was because of her that Sodom was punished.

Thus the Midrash seems to emphasize the importance of individual suffering. I like such an attitude. I like to think that when a victim, any victim, feels pain, God listens. When a person, any person, is tortured, God is moved to bring justice. But . . . wait a minute. Any person? Any victim? God was unable to bear the pain of a charitable Sodomite girl. But what about the pain of the strangers who happened to visit Sodom? Am I to conclude that their tears left God indifferent? Does the agony of a Sodomite weigh more heavily upon God than that of the others? Does God practice discriminatory love toward victims of different ethnic groups?

Good questions? They prove that the divine meaning of human justice or injustice has often eluded its victims. This is true even to a higher degree for Lot's wife. She has been saved—correction: she was meant to be saved. Look at the list of the survivors; she is there.

Why? Because Lot was her husband? Was she better than other wives in Sodom? The midrashic answer is a resounding no. She was no less wicked than her peers. If she became a pillar of salt, it was not because she had looked back, but because of what she had done before. It was because of her that Lot's three celestial guests were discovered. Listen: Upon their unexpected arrival, Lot turned to his wife and asked her to offer them the customary bread and salt. Right away, she said, and she went to knock at the door of her neighbors. Could she please borrow some salt? They were curious: why did she need salt all of a sudden? It's for our guests, she replied. That is how the inhabitants of Sodom learned of the presence of strangers in their midst. And since the punishment must fit the crime, she was turned into salt.

LET US STOP again. We need respite from this tale of evil and misfortune. With the notable exception of two local girls, none of the protagonists seems irreproachable. Not even the supreme Judge? He could have issued earlier warnings to Sodom telling its citizens of their impending fate; he could have incited them to repent. Did He? The Midrash says yes, He did. According to one source, many natural and unnatural catastrophes had struck Sodom during the fifty-two years preceding the biblical story. All of these upheavals, wars, and earthquakes were meant to awaken the Sodomites. A nice try, but there is no hint of this in the biblical text. Did God do nothing because He knew all along that Sodom would remain Sodom? But . . . haven't we learned from Rabbi Akiba that *"ha'kol tzafui,"* everything is foreseen on the human level, but on the level of God, everything is still possible?

Do I appear to want to be Sodom's legal defender? Don't I realize that such efforts, however valiant and selfless they might be, would end in failure? If Abraham lost, how could I expect to win? Still, may I be allowed to have a closer look at the file? It seems to me that one question ought to dominate our tale: Is collective punishment compatible with the Jewish tradition? Regrettably, the answer is yes. The

Bible speaks of an *"Ir ha'nidah'at"*—a rebellious, sinful, isolated, and doomed city which must, according to the law, be annihilated. Totally. The law seems cruel? Yes, but . . . it is one of those laws that exist on the page but have never yet been implemented. Sodom's case is an exception, and what's more, it is predated—hence illegal? Abraham believes so. And doesn't hesitate to say so. For him, there is no collective punishment. Remember Abraham's celebrated outburst: *"Hashofet kol ha'aretz lo ya'aseh mishpat"*—Can you, the Judge of all that exists, commit an injustice? He continues: "Are you really going to punish, to kill the righteous and the wicked together?" In other words, whether someone does good or evil will have no effect on your decision? Does it mean that the righteous may not be rewarded, or worse, that they may be punished? For what? For being righteous? (By the way, the problem of theodicy is only half-articulated here. Usually, we protest the happiness of the wicked and the unhappiness of the righteous; only the second part of the enigma is touched upon in this biblical passage.) What pains and shocks Abraham is that *all* people could be equal in the eyes of the Almighty. We understand Abraham's perplexity. If the wicked and the righteous are equal, on any level, how is one to differentiate between them? Isn't Judaism a desire, a need to distinguish good from evil, the sacred from the profane?

And what is God's answer to Abraham's objections? He simply states that there is no righteous man left in Sodom. In other words, do not worry, Abraham, nothing bad will happen to the righteous; there are no righteous persons over there. If there were, I would save them. Better yet: I would save everybody else as well . . .

And so—the case may be closed. Everything is settled. Abraham has nothing to reproach himself for, nor does God. Abraham has done his duty. As has God. Could Abraham have pushed the debate a bit further? He could have said: Please, God, save Sodom even if it is for the sake of a single righteous citizen. But Abraham realized that it was pointless to continue. He had lost and he knew it. That is why he picked himself up and went home. What else could he have done? At least his close relatives would be saved . . .

And yet if Lot and his children were saved, Abraham could not take credit for it. Uncle Abraham didn't even mention them in his plea bargaining. It was God's idea, or His angels', not Abraham's. Aren't we entitled to ask: Why didn't Abraham intercede on their behalf? Did he suddenly understand that they too were sinners? Lot's wife too, and their children? But then, why were they worthy of being spared?

The midrashic commentaries tend to be harsh toward the entire family. Not only was Lot part of Sodom's corrupt system, he was said to have been a sex maniac. Whatever he did, wherever he went, he looked for women. The verse "And Lot lifted his eyes and saw the entire Jordan valley" is interpreted by Rabbi Nahman bar Hanina in a purely erotic way.

The other members of the family? Better not talk about them. Well, let's. Lot's wife? She betrayed the three guests. The children? Two daughters were married, the two others were not. When Lot told them of the impending catastrophe, his two sons-in-law snapped back at him: "Are you crazy? Poor Lot, do you really expect us to believe that our city is on the edge of disaster? Don't you hear the music, the songs that come from its streets and houses? A city that sings is about to perish, is that what you are telling us?" And so they stayed behind. And their wives too. And their children. The two sons-in-law were fools. After all, their father-in-law was not just anyone. He had access to important people. If he was panicking, they should have listened. Naturally, Lot should have insisted on their departure, but time *was* running out. The angels told him so. Every minute could have been the last. Soon flames would come down from heaven and . . .

Escorted by the angels, Lot and his wife and their two unmarried daughters fled the burning city. At that moment, the midrashic tale dramatically changes course. Suddenly, the mother appears as a positive figure. Disobeying the angels' order, she looked back, and what she saw filled her with . . . with what? With fear, says one source: she saw the magnitude of the catastrophe and died. She was filled with light, claims another source: she saw the Shekhina with impunity.

(Incidentally, looking back was severely judged in antiquity. When Orpheus rescued Eurydice from the land of the dead, he received a similar warning. Unable to resist his curiosity, he lost his beloved forever.)

But why did Lot's wife transgress this prohibition? The midrashic explanation is charitable. It was her maternal instinct that made her look back. She wanted to see the place where she had left her two daughters behind. She was a mother, after all. A compassionate mother. Sodom had not hardened her heart. She continued to love her children and grandchildren. She loved them even more knowing that they were dead. How could she have abandoned them without even looking at what was left of them?

The two surviving daughters? They were granted extenuating circumstances. Convinced that their immediate family represented the entire human species (as in the time of the Flood), they felt an obligation to perpetuate it. It's a normal impulse, isn't it? They did it with their father—so what? They had to leave SOMETHING for future psychoanalysts . . . Anyway, there were no other men around. And didn't Noah's daughters do the same thing with THEIR father? Anyway, Lot's daughters may have felt like strangers to their father: didn't he treat them as strangers when he offered them to the mob that had besieged their house back in Sodom?

A midrashic text goes even further. It suggests that the two single daughters had no choice: they had to bear Lot's children so as to allow King David to be born—David, a descendant of Ruth the Moabite, who was herself a descendant of Lot's daughter. In other words, in this case, incest seemed necessary if not unavoidable. Without it, Jewish history would not have moved toward messianic redemption.

So all were rehabilitated. All? Almost all. Not Lot. He is a difficult case. As a character, he is not too appealing. Why did he flee Sodom in such haste? Once out of town, he didn't even look back. How can a father detach himself from his children with such ease? Granted, the angels ordered him not to look back—so what? Was he so pious that he couldn't disobey them? His wife seems more sensitive, more vulnerable, more human. Having lost, in one minute, all her belongings, having been separated from some of her children, she felt irresistibly drawn to them, she *had* to look back one last time before confronting the future. Frightened and tormented by guilt for having survived, she was looking for her two married daughters: where were they? Is it possible that, being unable to locate them, she *wanted* to stay behind, even as a statue? Had she been alive, would she have permitted the incestuous act? And what about her husband? Why did he permit it?

The only thing that Lot could say in his defense was that he was . . . drunk. Still, at least one text maintains that he wasn't *that* drunk while his daughters . . . Lot? An egocentric hedonist. How could *he* be exonerated? Well, he was.

LISTEN TO THE next phase of the tale. When Lot escaped from the burning city, he made a request to the angels. On whose behalf? On behalf of unknown people. Look, he told them. Look at that little town; its name is Mitzar. I implore you: spare it from destruction. I want to go and find refuge there. Naturally, I could try the mountains, but I prefer cities. I prefer that city. Let it live. And lo and behold, the angels heeded his plea.

Astonishing, isn't it? Lot succeeded where Abraham failed. He saved human lives. He saved an entire community. An entire city.

Thus, at last we find ourselves ready to be reconciled with Lot. And his daughters. And their mother.

But what about Abraham? He taught us an important lesson: It is always good to argue. Even if the debate seems pointless, continue to fight. And to bargain.

WELL, it is time for us to leave Sodom. What is the meaning of its history? Victory or defeat? Or both perhaps? Ultimately, Sodom means the failure of a society, and the triumph of a few individuals. What was the Sodomite society guilty of? It condemned itself by rejecting and humiliating and oppressing the poor, the stranger, the refugee—who more than anyone need compassion and generosity. The story of Sodom is the story of a warning to each of us for all time.

The lesson? A society that violates the humanity of its weaker human components is in fact bequeathing if not producing its own misfortune and malediction. Sodom is not only a place of long ago; its flames rushed through our recent past and tore its buildings apart.

Our history is reflected in Lot's story. Questions about him apply to us as well. Must I articulate them? Why did my contemporaries in Europe refuse to believe that death was near? Why did so many children fall victim to murderers? Where was divine justice? Why did one survive while so many others did not? Why did my generation lack intercessors, while even Sodom did not? These questions are troubling and eternal. The answers? I do not know them.

All I know is that I understand Lot's wife better than him. For at times one must look backward—lest one run the risk of turning into a statue. Of stone? No: of ice.

Aaron and His Problem
of Innocence

MAY I BEGIN with a confession? I do not understand Aaron, nor do I understand the attitude our tradition has shown toward him. Why does it pay him homage alongside his younger brother, whose stature and destiny are surely worthier and more elevated than his? Why are their names forever bound together in the Psalms as well as in our prayers? *Moshe ve'Aharon,* Moses and Aaron: you rarely mention the first without the other. Is it to remind us, again, and again, that the two were different but brothers nevertheless? What did Aaron *do* to deserve the honor of remaining in our collective memory as the founder of the priestly dynasty?

From what you have just read, you must already understand, I have problems, serious problems with this hero.

Something is wrong with this character and with his part in the eternal story of Israel. I expected more, or something else, from this leader, from a spiritual guide of his caliber. In other words, one senses an abyss between the person and the image, between the man and the legend surrounding him—almost an abyss one finds it difficult to bridge.

Remember, in the entire turbulent history of Exodus, it is the chapter dealing with the Golden Calf that disturbs and saddens us most.

Our forefathers had just been freed from Pharaoh's bondage, they had just witnessed the grandiose miracles of the crossing of the Red Sea and of survival in the desert, they had just heard the Almighty God's voice ordering them to shape for themselves a national destiny anchored in the ethics of faith—and they have already rejected, repudiated, and forgotten everything?

Forty days earlier, they had an appointment with God at Sinai. Freed from slavery, free and proud, they declared as one man, *"na'asseh ve'nishma,"* submitting body and soul to His will, to His Law—and, all of a sudden, they could not resist the temptation of old demons embodied by the magic of idolatry? How could they fall from such heights to such depths in such a short period of time?

No. I do not understand them.

But in truth, I understand even less the man who, in Moses' absence, was their undisputed leader: Aaron, the elder son of the family. How could *he* join the excited mob? And why with such haste, without any resistance? If, at least, he had tried, with words or deeds, to reprimand them, to calm their unholy enthusiasm; if he had tried to slow them down, to win time in order to reflect on what was happening, to get advice and find allies; if he had made an effort to drag things, long enough to implore Heaven to come to his rescue, to perform another miracle, to hasten Moses' return. But no, Aaron adjusted quickly to the ill-fated uprising, did nothing to stop it. How is one to explain this absence of character, this ethical shortcoming on the part of the future first High Priest? Better yet: how did he manage to be anointed High Priest? Does it mean that his sin was forgiven? Then why only his, and not others'? Is there one law for important persons and another for ordinary citizens? Isn't it incumbent upon a leader to be more ethical—and more resolute in matters of principle—than the simple members of his or her community? Logically, he should have been condemned before the others, and harsher than the others . . .

Again: I fail to understand the personal history of Aaron if not his place in Jewish history.

IN SCRIPTURE, Aaron appears on the stage almost unannounced, as if by sheer accident. We meet him through his younger brother. Better yet: as if to provide God with a convincing example in his bitter and exhausting argument with Moses.

For runaway Moses—remember?—is both timid and obstinate. He is in the desert when God offers him a choice appointment. God gives him an assignment—and what an assignment! But he politely yet stubbornly says no. God offers him a central role in Jewish history, and he answers: thank you, but . . .

The scene, filled with beauty and awe, takes place near the burning bush which burns and burns and is never consumed. Moses, a solitary dreamer, hears God's voice ordering him to remove his sandals, for "sacred is the ground" under his feet. And the voice continues: "I am the God of your father. God of Abraham, God of Isaac and God of Jacob." Then, says the text, Moses hides his face, for he is afraid of looking at the face of the Lord. Moses is no doubt shaken. What next? Soon after, the celestial monologue goes on: "I have seen, seen well, the affliction of my people in Egypt. I have heard their outcry."

Moses hasn't uttered a word yet. Impressed, deeply moved, he waits. God informs him of a critical situation, so he listens. For the moment, it is his only duty: to be there and open his ears. Perhaps he wonders why the Master of the universe has chosen him, a poor shepherd, to be his privileged confidant. Suddenly he understands. God wants something from him. He wants him to do something— something urgent, something dangerous. He wants him to go back to his native Egypt, where a death sentence is hanging over his head. "I am sending you to Pharaoh," says God; "the children of Israel must leave Egypt." Moses' reaction seems somewhat bizarre: though he hasn't lived among Jews for a long time, he begins to argue like them. He asks God: "Why me? Who am I to go to Pharaoh and free the children of Israel from Egypt?" Patiently, God tries to reassure him: "I shall be with you." That's good news, but Moses is not satisfied. "All right, says he. Suppose I accept. I do go there. I meet the Jews, I tell them that the God of their ancestors has sent me. What if they ask me, what is His name? What am I to answer?"

Isn't it strange? Moses worries over what Jews, not Pharaoh, may ask him. Still patient, God gives him a cryptic answer: his name? Not I am who I am but *"eh'yeh asher eh'yeh"*—I shall be who I shall be. And he tells him what other words to use. They sound like bribery: "I shall strike the Egyptians. . . . And you shall leave but not empty-handed. . . ." Unconvinced, Moses complains further: "They will not believe me." So God, in a good mood, accomplishes a few miracles, just to prove his point and lend him courage. Changing tactics, Moses becomes more personal: "I am not an orator, I am not good at speech-making, I am a stutterer; my tongue is heavy when I speak." Nothing doing. God too is stubborn. "Who gives you speech? I shall be your speech writer." In despair, one can hear Moses' outburst: "Please . . . Send someone else." Now God gets angry and summons Aaron to enter the narrative: "I knew perfectly well that your brother Aaron will do the speaking . . . By the way, he is on his way; he saw you and his heart is rejoicing."

Aaron? Who is he? What is he doing here? It is the first time we hear his name mentioned. Up to this moment the text ignored his very existence. Where was he hiding until now? What was his occupation in Egypt? Was he married? Did he live with his parents? Were they still alive? Was he thinking about his younger brother, who was to become Pharaoh's public enemy number one? Who told him to hurry to the desert and meet him again? As for Moses, was *he* aware of the fact that he had left behind an elder brother and their parents?

Clearly, the biography of Aaron's earlier years is astonishingly scanty. Scripture is of no help to us. The Midrash is more generous—several pious legends, that's all. They stress the point that, already in Egypt, under Pharaoh's rule, Aaron served as a Jewish prophet. And that it was God Himself who ordered him to go and meet Moses in the desert.

In the text, his fame is sudden, his career dazzling. As soon as he appears he is appointed by the highest authority to serve as Moses' companion and God's official spokesman.

In the Midrash, Moses is punished for resisting the Almighty's will. At first, God had intended to make him the first High Priest. In view of Moses' timidity, God changed his mind. The honor of founding the exalted priestly dynasty was given to his older brother instead.

But is the punishment fair? Was Moses wrong in arguing with God? Some of you may guess my answer: No, Moses was not wrong. I would go as far as suggesting that whenever he argued with God, he emerged enhanced. Unlike Moses, Aaron did not argue. He never does. He accepts everything from everybody. How different the two brothers are. Moses is the man of action, Aaron the man of words. Moses is subject to frequent mood changes, Aaron is more solid. Moses gets angry, Aaron never. Moses fights battles and loses some but never gives up or gives in, whereas Aaron runs away from any violent confrontation. Moses is a fervent believer in truth, just as Aaron is in peace—in peace above all. What he really desires is to be left in peace.

It is not that he constantly remains in the shadows. A public figure cannot *not* be seen in public. Aaron is seen only when he has no choice. Endowed with a mission, he fulfills it. Given a task, he accomplishes it. But he never takes the initiative. He does not ask for anything. He does what he is supposed to do. He accompanies Moses and speaks for him. And he speaks well. But he says only what God wants him to say to the Pharaoh on one hand, to the Jewish slaves on the other.

His first leadership task is, according to Scripture, to share the platform with Moses, who summons the elders of the community to an urgent meeting. It is he, Aaron, who transmits God's will, as formulated by Moses. The two brothers try to persuade the elders to join them in the march to Pharaoh's royal palace. Neither brother is young any more. Aaron is eighty-three, Moses eighty. Aaron, comments Rashi, endures here his first defeat. His efforts at persuasion end in failure. It's simple: the elders are afraid. One after the other, they all retreat and disappear. Moses and Aaron are alone when they find themselves face to face with the cruel Pharaoh, who dismisses them with disdain. They are humbled and sad—sad because, as a result of their intervention, Jewish slaves are made to endure harsher oppression.

Well—we know what follows. God's threats, His miracles, Pharaoh's promises and withdrawals, the suffering of the Jews, who oscillate between anguish and hope—we acquaint ourselves once more with the amazing convulsions of Jewish history. The script remains forever the same: God speaks to Moses, who speaks to Pharaoh, who, dismayed and struck by the tremendous power of the Jewish God whose name he has never heard, promises everything and gives nothing. With a few exceptions, God addresses His words to Moses, whom He considers His unique interlocutor. Aaron's role? The text defines it with great clarity: he is his brother's "prophet"; from Moses' lips he receives the divine message and communicates it to Pharaoh. At the end, Moses feels he no longer needs an intermediary. He speaks directly to the enemy leader. Short, biting sentences: "Shelah et ami"—Let my people go! In parentheses, some commentators explain, not without humor, that it was fortunate for Jewish history that Moses was such a poor speaker; otherwise he would have launched into long lectures about philosophy, sociology, and human rights. Thanks to his stuttering, he had to be brief. There was no time left for debates. It was yes or no, now or never. A difficult task to convince Pharaoh? Aaron's was no less difficult. His task was to persuade the Jews to give up slavery and to leave on a long journey. Destination: the desert.

At the end, both brothers may claim victory: the text invites drama and ecstasy. We are witnessing the end of the beginning. Collective slavery is succeeded by a general exodus. We read about the nocturnal escape, the flight toward the Red Sea. The spectacular miracle of the parting of the waves. The rescue of the weak, the death of the mighty. The Song at the Sea as Moses gives thanks to God. One can breathe now. The children of Israel are free and out of danger. Here is the desert. Six hundred thousand men, women, and children begin a wandering that, after forty years, will lead their descendants to the promised land.

It is still not easy. True, the Egyptian threat has vanished. But there are others. Thirst. Hunger. People are exhausted. They need a scapegoat, someone to blame. Whose fault is it if nights are dark and cold? Moses'. Whose fault is it that food is insufficient and probably tasteless? Moses'. Everything is always *his* fault—never Aaron's.

Already before crossing the Red Sea, they attacked Moses and shouted at him with anger: Why have you brought us here? Weren't there enough graves for us in Egypt? For us it would have been better to work as slaves in Egypt than to perish in the wilderness.

Three days after being rescued, they turned on Moses with a new complaint: they were thirsty and had no water. There was a fountain nearby, but its water was bitter. Commented the celebrated Rebbe of Kotzk: it was not the water but the people that were bitter. And who was their wrath directed against? Moses.

The moment they are dissatisfied, the moment things don't look good, they attack Moses—always Moses. Why do they never protest against Aaron, or at least against Aaron *also*? Isn't he the official and officially anointed co-leader or associate leader of this community in transformation? Isn't he number two, the closest aide to the military and political chief? Why is nobody ever angry at him? What makes him a kind of "Teflon leader" whom people never criticize personally but only, if at all, together with Moses? At a station called Refidim, the thirsty crowd is ready to stone Moses—yes, Moses, not Aaron.

Is it because Moses is always—to quote the French Romantic poet Alfred de Vigny—"lonely and solitary," as if separated from the people by a column of clouds, dwelling always in the shadow of God, in the *ohel mo'ed,* the special sacred tent where he receives God's voice? And because Aaron, on the other hand, stays all the time with the people? Is it because ordinary men and women see in Aaron someone they can identify with, whereas they sense in Moses a superior being, chosen and condemned by God for a destiny of isolation and solitude known to special leaders alone? Is it possible that the people fear Moses but love Aaron?

Oh yes—the two brothers *are* different.

Aaron has almost no power; Moses does. Moses delegates authority, but his is the supreme authority. Moses is inaccessible, Aaron is not. To receive the Law, Moses ascends alone into heaven. Aaron, Joshua, and seventy elders, all in positions of leadership, stay behind, below. Together. Typical: Aaron is always surrounded by people. Moses will forever use a harsh voice issuing orders, decrees, commandments, prohibitions; not so Aaron, who wears a smile on his face even when sin seems to prevail. Moses personifies the rigor of the Law and its inflexibility. Aaron incarnates warmth, goodness, kindness, indulgence. One could almost state, not without some reticence, that Moses wants to be closer to God, and Aaron to people. No wonder that people love him. But . . . why does God look upon him with grace, since he has done nothing heroic, nothing out of the ordinary for the sake of His eternal glory?

Furthermore, God is so fond of Aaron, and so desirous of pleasing him, that he orders Moses to personally take care of his brother's career and happiness. It is Moses who must procure for Aaron his special vestments. Only Aaron? No, his sons too. As if Moses wasn't busy enough; as if he had no other worries. But Moses complies. In fact, he is happy for his brother and nephews. Aaron, Eleazar, Ithamar, Nadab, and Abihu receive from Moses their priestly clothes. Does Moses think of his own sons, who do not benefit from his high position? If both the function and the title of priests are hereditary, those of the teacher are not. Moses' sons are treated in the Book of Books as ordinary mortals. At the end, they simply and quietly vanish from the stage. Why doesn't Moses, a good Jewish father, after all, see to it that their future is assured? Moses has other worries. God, the Law, the collective destiny of his people, its place in history and in the vision of God. Individual everyday problems are Aaron's domain:

it is he who will wear the *hoshen mishpat*, the pectoral of judgment with its twelve precious stones symbolizing the names of the twelve tribes. Aaron represents the external aspect of leadership, all that is visible and tangible: form, style, and protocol. Moses, on the contrary, personifies the substance of authority: an inner power that remains secret and inviolate. Here too one understands the popularity of Aaron among Jews—but how is one to explain the multiple favors he receives from God?

Does he but deserve them? Naturally, one may say: who are we to judge him? But . . . following a short passage about the laws of Shabbat, almost immediately after the long weekly portion of the Bible, *parshat Tetzaveh,* where the role, vestments, and responsibilities of the priests are described in great detail, we come in the next portion, that of *Ki Tissa,* upon the harrowing episode of the Golden Calf. Why are the two events chronologically so closely linked? Is it to teach us that one was the result of the other? That when spiritual leaders pay too much attention to their external outlook, and when simple laws of Shabbat are violated, idolatry may not be too far away?

Obviously, it is the people, or a malicious segment of the people, and not Aaron, who came up with the idea of producing a Golden Calf. The biblical narrative is worth rereading. As Moses' absence grew inexplicably long—when he had left forty days earlier he had told nobody that he was ascending into heaven to receive the Law— impatient skeptics and cynics exploited the people's discouragement. They ran to Aaron and implored him to produce an idol, a god, a new god to lead them. And lo and behold, Aaron agrees. He doesn't even try to change their minds. He doesn't say: Look, you are exhausted; go to your tents, sleep on it; tomorrow we shall see together what needs to be done. No: his instant reaction is to be on their side. He joins their ranks. He asks them to bring him the golden rings belonging to their wives and children. Not their own? Does he think that that would be too great a sacrifice? He's wrong: all of the people bring him their golden rings. And Aaron, rather than say: "Now leave, please; this is a delicate job; let me work alone; it may take a few hours, several days perhaps," seizes the rings, places them in a mold, and fabricates a calf or a mask of a calf. And all the people present, in a sudden outburst of frenzy, shout: *"Eyleh elokekha!"* Israel! Look, Israel! This is thy god, the god that brought you out from Egypt!

Is he shocked by the blasphemy? Does he feel the need to shout, to weep, to act to defend the honor of the God of Israel? If so, he does not show it. Quite the contrary: he seems to be in total harmony with the rebels. He goes even further than they: he erects for them an altar—an item that did not figure in their demands. Then he cries out: *"Hag la'shem mahar"*—Tomorrow is a holiday, a holy day dedicated to the Lord. Did he mean the Lord with a capital *L*? The populace did not hear it that way. For them, it meant a holiday named for the idol they could see and touch.

Well! Here is Aaron, a leader at last! People obey *him*. All of them rise early and come to celebrate with him: they eat, drink, bring offerings, they rejoice, they are exuberant and happy, they laugh . . .

What happened to Aaron, God's emissary and first High Priest? How could he transgress the fundamental Jewish law prohibiting idolatry? Is he so weak, so frightened that he does not dare to antagonize the hysterical mob, thirsty for sinful adoration? He, the celebrated speaker, could have used his oratory talent to convince some if not all the Jews to wait, to think it over, not to go overboard. He could have at least broken the unanimity, provoked dissension, a useful split perhaps . . . Why didn't he?

Aaron's conduct is indeed incomprehensible.

But Moses' and God's are more so.

STUDYING THE SOURCES we realize that tradition, in general terms, has done everything possible to exculpate, whitewash, and rehabilitate Aaron. Most midrashic and medieval commentators are so charitable that they make him a victim of a misunderstanding. Aaron emerges as the most misunderstood character in the Bible. But what about his misdeeds? Oh, it is a matter of perception. In spite of what the story tells us, he did nothing wrong, nothing bad—or surely not consciously.

Listen to the image a Midrash offers us of the situation: Anguished by Moses' being late—he should have been away forty days only, and it's already the fortieth—the people are agitated. Aaron enlists the help of his nephew, Khour, son of Myriam and father of Caleb, to calm their fear, saying: be patient, Moses will return, he is on the way back, wait a few hours . . . The exhortation does have an effect on the crowd. This is clear since Satan is getting worried. Satan is troubled. If the High Priest is successful in his endeavors to abort the Golden Calf, his own plan is doomed. As God's enemy, and Israel's, he needs a Jewish spiritual surrender. And so, to counteract Aaron's efforts, the sorcerer Satan shows the people a mortuary bed suspended in the clouds—and who is in it? Moses. Moses on his deathbed. At that moment forty thousand men, the Egyptian sorcerers Younous and Yombrus among them, surround Aaron and demand that he provide them with a new leader, a visible and concrete god . . . In other words, it is not Aaron's fault but Satan's.

Better yet: Khour and Aaron, knowing that the image is false and diabolically misleading, try to preach the good word, the word of truth and moral courage. For a while the two relatives are alone, facing the exalted mob. Alone? But where are Aaron's four sons? And Moses'? Why don't they rush to join forces with those few who fight in the name of faith? Are they asleep? Hiding perhaps? Have they escaped? For the moment, Aaron and his nephew are the only ones to defend God's name. Soon Aaron will be alone: the mob kills Khour. Aaron is now alone against thousands and thousands of infuriated, fanatic idol worshipers. No wonder he is afraid. Afraid also of being assassinated. It's human. God has not ordered him to die for His sake. Neither did Moses. In fact, nobody has revealed to him the future law according to which idolatry is one of the three prohibitions one must not transgress, even at the price of one's self-sacrifice. That is why, suggests a midrash, Aaron yields to the crowd's dangerous, illicit, and obscene passions.

That's all? Certain apologists are not satisfied with presenting attenuating circumstances. They view Aaron as an excellent tactician and a keen psychologist. If he proposed to the people to bring him their wives' jewels, it is because he knew wives' mentality. He knew they would refuse. First because they love jewels. But more important, because unlike their husbands, they know the meaning of gratitude: having witnessed the miracles accomplished by God, they would not repudiate Him just like that, for a silly little calf, even one made of pure gold. In the end, claims the Midrash, the men are forced to bring their own jewels to the High Priest so that he can make a Golden Calf. However, it is not Aaron but the two Egyptian anti-Pharaoh sorcerers who make the calf. And if Aaron tells the crowd to come back next day for a fiesta, it is because he hopes Moses will reappear during the night. That is why, says Rashi, he had the idea to build an altar: to give himself time. So—if the fiesta did take place, it is because Moses was *really* late: six hours late. A midrashic commentator, in Vayikra Raba, goes as far as praising Aaron for building the altar: he did it to prevent the people from doing it. He thought to himself: if they do the construction, they will do it fast; I will be slow. Furthermore, Aaron thought: it is better if the guilt falls on me than the entire community. Differently put: in taking the blame on himself, Aaron sacrificed his honor for the sake of Israel. And in his invitation to the feast for next day, he did not say, *"Hag la'egel"* but *"la'shem mahar."* He invited them to celebrate not the calf but God.

Even in heaven, Aaron receives a friendly reception. God is angry with his people but not with his High Priest. Worse: God is annoyed at Moses, but not at Aaron. God's voice sounds severe, harsh, as he speaks to his favorite prophet: *"Leikh reid ki shiheit amkha . . ."*—Go, go down, for your people have engaged in corruption! *Shiheit* is a terrible word. It implies violence and adultery. In this case it also includes idolatry. Which of the three sins has most angered God? Several answers exist, but clearly God seems disappointed with Moses— poor Moses, who wasn't even present at the crime! In the Midrash, God informs him of his demotion: *"Reid,* go down in rank, for your people have engaged in corruption!" Practically speaking, Moses is expelled from heaven. Deeply hurt, he is compelled to defend himself: "My people, Lord? Isn't it also yours?" At that moment, says the Midrash, five destructive angels are ready to kill him. But Moses invokes the memory of Abraham, Isaac, and Jacob. And God consents to take him under his protection.

Analyze these tales and you will admit that they are intriguing. Why has Moses rather than his brother become the culprit? Isn't he on assignment, in heaven? Hasn't he been summoned by God Himself? Why then is he held responsible for something that has been done by someone else? Is it that God's ways, in matters of justice, have always been inscrutable?

Perhaps we ought not to be too harsh with the Supreme Judge over creation. He knows what he is doing, and why. Isn't Moses the chief, and isn't the chief always responsible? If the people, under his leadership, stray from the good way, it is also his fault. But who is *mainly* to be blamed? The people. And so God abruptly has a change of heart; now he is determined to chastise the people of Israel. To Moses he gives a detailed report of what happened and declares: "I am going to annihilate this people. And I shall make you the founder of a great nation." Which means: of another nation. But everything is clear: God is disappointed, offended by, disgusted with his chosen people. Instead of changing prophets, he will change peoples.

We know the next phase. In an extreme situation, Moses rises to even greater and nobler heights. *"Va'yehal Moshe,"* and Moses prayed, or, according to the Rebbe of Kotz, *"zei hobben im krank gemacht,"* they made him sick. He pleads for the children of Israel, all descendants of Abraham, Isaac, and Jacob. And he succeeds in softening the Lord's position. Then he leaves heaven with the two Tablets of the Law in his arms. Down below, at the foot of Sinai, he sees Joshua, who has been waiting for him. They go to the encampment. Moses has no idea of what he will find there. From a distance, he perceives sounds of the noisy celebration. Then he sees the Golden Calf, the dancers, the idol worshipers. In his wrath he throws to the ground the Tables of the Law, breaks them, burns the calf, and then, only then, does he turn to his brother and speak to him. He addresses him with emotion, even with surprising tenderness. He doesn't ask him, "What did you do, and why did you do it? How could *you* have taken part in something so silly and so vile?" Instead he says, "What did the people do to *you* to make you commit such a terrible sin?!"

Aaron's answer? Sadly disappointing. Instead of taking the blame upon himself—as the Midrash suggests he did earlier—he seizes the opportunity offered by Moses and lays all the guilt on the anonymous people: "You know," he says to his brother, "you know what the people are capable of. They made me act under duress." He does not deny having asked for the golden jewels, and that he threw them in the fire, but he maintains that the Golden Calf was not his doing. Whose then was it? He does not know. He threw the golden jewels in the flames—and out came the Golden Calf, just like that, by itself. In his statement he also omits referring to the altar which he built with his own hands. And also his invitation to the crowd to come back and take part in the fiesta the next day . . .

Is this the proper behavior of a leader?

As for Moses, he seems to hold no grudge against his brother. He does love him—and his love is tender, fraternal, and shielding. Full of understanding, it is he who put the proper words in Aaron's mouth to better defend himself as if in plea-bargaining: yes, he has lit a fire and placed golden objects in its flames—but that was all he has done; and even this he did because he had no choice; had he refused, the mob would have killed him.

Better yet: Moses seems to imply that Aaron only served as an instrument in the hands of the crowd, which needed to give vent to its repressed frustrations. The Golden Calf episode actually revealed the base instincts that the people carried in their subconscious. Thanks to the complicity of the High Priest, all that was hidden appeared on the surface. Now the situation became healthier: in the full light of reality Moses would be able to take the necessary steps to cleanse the soul of the people of Israel.

His first move is to order a collective catharsis. A true bloodbath. Done by whom? By the tribe of Levites. They attack the culprits. But . . . isn't Aaron one of them? He enjoys singular privileges of total immunity. The High Priest is untouchable. The Levites, some Levites, affirms Rabbi Abraham Ibn Ezra, armed with spears, hurl themselves upon the sinners and slay them. Moses' orders are executed without restraint or pity: even the relatives—half-brothers and uncles—are not spared. That day saw the death of three thousand men and women. Then, determined to close that chapter once and for all, Moses turned to God and implored him to do the same: "If you forgive them," he said, "good; if not, erase my name from your book."

There is Moses in his true grandeur! God's messenger is threatening God! He issues him an official ultimatum! It's either-or. Forgiveness or separation. And God yields. He cannot nor does he want to continue his work with Israel without a man like Moses.

And so everything falls back in order. Though diminished, the Jewish people will proceed on their long and exhausting journey toward the promised land. And Aaron will serve as he did before in his exalted functions as High Priest.

AGAIN, I do not understand. How could a leader who followed rather than led, a man who has betrayed his calling, how can he remain the spiritual guide of an entire community, as if nothing had happened? How is it possible that the people did not voice their anger? Was there no one to say openly what many must have thought privately, that something was wrong in those high official circles?

If no one thought about it or said it, Aaron did. Secretly, in his heart, he must have carried guilt. Not only for having collaborated with idolatrous insurgents, but also for having been, though indirectly, the cause of the death of so many people.

At times I wonder whether he forgave himself. I wonder because I remember the tale of his two unfortunate sons, Nadab and Abihu, who died tragically and untimely in the sacred tent. *"Va'yidom Aharon."*

Aaron was mute. Faced with the catastrophe that struck his family, he said nothing. Numerous texts conduct the exegesis of and offer praise for his silence. They speak of his dignity, his moral strength, the depth of his faith in divine justice. One might conclude that that was the most meaningful, the truest moment in his life.

Well—I would humbly suggest a different hypothesis. I would connect the death of Aaron's sons with the episode of the Golden Calf. And I ask myself: what if the two stories were related? Let us elaborate: imagine Aaron feeling guilty and thinking that the death of his two sons was nothing but punishment for his role in the degrading affair of the Golden Calf. Is it too far-fetched? And what if we were told that he kept quiet *because* he felt guilty? He knows that no transgression goes unpunished. Except that, occasionally, it takes time for the punishment to strike the sinner. Is such a reaction on the part of Aaron absolutely inconceivable?

Having said that, I must add that if he felt guilty, he was the only one to feel guilt. After the death of Nadab and Abihu, God speaks to him directly, and not through Moses. God has not only overlooked his error, He seems to have elevated him. As for the people, they mourned Aaron's death for thirty days.

Tradition attributes to him many virtues. The Midrash does not stop praising his love for his younger brother. He was happy, he was exuberant when learning of Moses' appointment as God's messenger to Egypt. He was never jealous of Moses' achievements. If, in Scripture, brothers do not enjoy favorable reviews, Moses and Aaron constitute the exception to the rule. Never was there a moment of discord in their relations. Sharing their official functions, together they led their people to its national and religious destiny. Together they are punished, not for the Golden Calf, but for having struck the rock when the people were in need of water: neither entered the land of Canaan. At the end, when Aaron's hour is near, it is Moses who, alone, accompanies him up the mountain; it is Moses who prepares him, dresses him in mortuary shrouds, and stays with him until he breathes his last breath. One could always lean on the other; one was to the other a presence.

IN TRUTH, the image kept of Aaron is that of a humanist, forever ready to help anyone in need. He is called *"Ohev shalom ve'rodeph shalom"*: he loved and pursued peace. Had there been then a Peace Prize, he would have been the ideal candidate. Whenever a fight broke out, among family or friends, he was there to reconcile spouses, associates, friends, and rivals. In legend, that is his specific greatness: he devoted his entire life to reuniting broken hearts, to restoring harmony among human beings as well as between them and their Creator.

Is this the reason for his being forgiven his role in the Golden Calf affair? Because he was always on the side of the people, even if it meant not being on the side of God? I do not know.

All I would venture to say, in conclusion, is this: if God and history have forgiven him, why should we be more rigorous than they?

Miriam the Prophetess and Her Melancholy Fate

THE TALE UNFOLDS in the wilderness. It's about a woman, a very special woman. Of all the women who dwell in the turbulent universe of the Bible, she seems the most elusive, the most obscure. And perhaps the most underestimated.

We know many things about vivacious grandmother Eve, perhaps too many. We are told whom she chatted with when her husband was away from home, which fruit she preferred, and how she wheedled a man named Adam who thought he was free . . .

We are also given considerable detail about the life of Sarah, who became a mother much too late, and the life of Rebecca, who was a little young to marry a distant cousin, Isaac. We are told about the suffering of pale Leah, her eyes always weary, and the misery of her younger sister Rachel, who had to wait fourteen years to wed the only man she ever loved.

Each of these women is vivid, fully realized. But the Bible is less informative about Miriam, who, given the role she played in our people's destiny, should interest us much. After all, while the four matriarchs—Sarah, Rebecca, Rachel, and Leah—were involved in domestic dramas some might call almost trivial, Miriam occupies a singular place in the story of the very birth of a nation whose experience would profoundly affect history.

She is intriguing, to say the least.

Why is she always away from the limelight? Why does she seem veiled in shadow?

We are not told when she was born: one might say she existed only in relation to her brothers. The text is explicit on this: Pharaoh condemned all the male Jewish children to death. As a result, says the Talmud, husbands were separated from their wives so as not to bring children into a hostile world. Then "there went a man of the house of Levi, who took to wife a daughter of Levi." The text continues: "And the woman conceived, and bore a son. And when she saw that he was a goodly child, she hid him for three months. . . . And when she could no longer hide him, she took for him a wicker basket, and daubed it with slime and pitch, and put the child therein; and she laid it in the reeds by the bank of the Nile River. And his sister stood far off to observe what would be done to him."

What? The baby had a sister?

No names are given but we understand perfectly. The baby was of course Moses, and his sister Miriam. This is the first time she is mentioned, though unnamed at this point. Clearly she was intelligent and daring. "Then said his sister to Pharaoh's daughter, shall I go and call to thee a nurse of the Hebrew women, that she may nurse the child for thee?" And whom did she call? The child's mother, thus her own. "And the woman took the child, and nursed it. And the child grew and she brought him unto Pharaoh's daughter, and he became her son." A brilliant, imaginative scenario: Moses is saved, nursed by his own mother, adopted, and presumably launched on a great career, all because his sister Miriam handled a difficult situation so intelligently.

Still, in the text she is not named. Why was there no mention of her birth? Could the Bible be antifemale? Fortunately, we can refute this charge of gender discrimination, since Aaron, the elder brother, is not yet mentioned either. Later he will be Moses' ally and companion; the two will be inseparable.

And their sister Miriam? Often unknown, invisible, we sense her presence in the wings. But her name is set down only seven times in Scripture. Should we pity her for the modest role assigned her in the text? Let us admit it: she deserves more respect and more recognition.

WAS SHE GRACIOUS, beautiful, sociable? We do not know. We do not even know with certainty whether she was married. The text is so reticent about her that we are compelled to wonder if it is trying to hide something.

First, she appears as a self-effacing anonymous figure of secondary importance. Later, she is given the honorific title of prophetess, but we have no idea what she may have prophesied. Then the text suggests that she talked a bit too much and a bit too rashly.

Yet it is impossible not to love Moses' big sister, his protector. Courageous, devoted, she inevitably arouses affection and admiration. We pay attention to her precisely because she so seldom appears onstage. Miriam makes no effort to stand out, to put herself forward. Consequently, she does not suffer from overexposure. Is this perhaps a strategy to make herself desirable?

We met her for the first time on the banks of the Nile, secretly looking after her baby brother, whom their mother, the despairing Yokheved, was forced to abandon in a little basket. When Miriam reappears, Moses is a man in every sense of the word. He is married and a father, and leader of a people who have, under his leadership, fought their way out of slavery, a people he has just liberated so that they may have their rendezvous with destiny and God. He has just ended his stunning Song at the Sea, in which the children of Israel express their gratitude to the Almighty for saving them. It is *"Ashira lashem,"* a song in the first person singular. At that hour everybody was a poet: "For the horse of Pharaoh went in with his chariots and with his horsemen into the sea. And the Lord brought again the waters of the sea upon them. But the children of Israel walked on dry land in the midst of the sea." When the song ends, the next verse belongs to Miriam: "And Miriam the prophetess, the sister of Aaron, took a timbrel in her hand; and all the women went out after her with timbrels and with dances. . . . And Miriam said to them: sing all of you, sing ye to the Lord for He hath triumphed gloriously, the horse and his rider hath He thrown into the sea."

So much for Miriam. The story continues without her. Amazingly, the Revelation at Sinai, the handing down of the Ten Commandments, the laws about Shabbat and the sanctity of the family, the arduous crossing of the desert, the endless complaints of the wanderers culminating in the creation of the Golden Calf: all of this happens without another word about Miriam, the person responsible for saving her brother's life.

We follow Aaron's activities, Joshua's intelligence report from the land of Canaan, Bezallel's artistic endeavors, but Miriam? Where is she? What is she doing? Was the birth of Israel an event for men only? It is true that the text is no more revealing about Moses' wife, or Aaron's. But Miriam's role is different: she entered the story on a brilliant note. She is a prophetess, but one whose few words have nothing to do with prophecy. Why does the text silence her? At this point in the tale we have almost forgotten her.

Then, suddenly, she resurfaces.

The narrative has lingered over Eldad and Medad, two young men who belonged to the seventy elderly advisers whom Moses, on God's instructions, had gathered around him to conduct the affairs of the nation. All others are nameless. Eldad and Medad formed a group apart. They began to act like prophets. Jealous of Moses' honor, a man (the Midrash identifies him as his son Gershom) informed him of their scandalous behavior and even urged him to lock them up. Moses' answer was "Would that the entire nation were prophets."

The topic is ambition and envy, and the text illustrates this further through a drama involving diet. What to eat, what not to eat. And then, abruptly, the spotlight falls on Miriam: Miriam and Aaron, or Miriam with Aaron, privately lash out at Moses about the Kushit, or Ethiopian, he has taken for his wife. And the siblings add: "Has the Lord spoken only through Moses? Has He not spoken to us as well?"

"And the Lord heard it," says the text. His response is a masterful defense of His emissary: "Moses is the humblest of men upon the face of the earth." Having reprimanded Aaron and punished Miriam, God leaves them. Covered with leprosy, Miriam turns white as snow. Aaron begs Moses, who begs God, to help their sister, not to leave her half dead, humbled, isolated, ravaged, dead-in-life. God is merciful. He orders Miriam away from camp for seven days. The people wait for her.

Here again we cannot help but feel compassion for Miriam. It was not she alone who slandered Moses. Aaron was also there. Why then was she singled out for punishment?

A few chapters later, we come upon one more reference to Miriam. The people stopped for a while in a place called Kadesh. It was there that she died, and it was there that she was buried.

Poor Miriam. No longer did they call her prophetess. Her death is told in half a sentence. And the text goes on to inform us that the people wept for her brothers, not for her. "She was buried there," in the wilderness of Sin. The word "there" is painful. It is too vague. The place had no name? There was no national funeral. No eulogies. No collective mourning. Didn't the people care? Were they preoccupied by other things? Listen: Miriam had just been committed to the earth, says the text, when "there was no water for the congregation; and they gathered themselves together against Moses and Aaron, crying 'Why have you made us come out of Egypt, to bring us into this evil place' " without fruit or water.

There seems no obvious connection between the two episodes. And yet they may be cause and effect. Because the people did not honor their prophetess in death, their own lives were in jeopardy. Neither God nor the children of Israel seem to have cherished her sufficiently during her life, but she does remain in Jewish memory a person we respect and love.

But here we may ask: Suppose the Bible is fair in its treatment of Miriam. Suppose she deserves no better. Suppose she was not on her brothers' spiritual and moral level. To explore this possibility, let us return to Scripture.

At the outset, Miriam had followed her mother to see what would become of her little brother. We know that she acted shrewdly and fearlessly on the baby's behalf, but beyond that we are told nothing. Did she subsequently go for occasional walks near the royal palace to catch a glimpse of him? Did she visit Pharaoh's daughter to inquire about his welfare? Did she try to establish contact with him later, just to remind him of his Jewish origins?

As for her song at the Red Sea, the text is enigmatic. Why is Miriam identified as Aaron's sister, and not Moses'? Might the implication be that she was jealous of her younger brother's position? Was it to demonstrate her own strength that she called the women together? Was that her purpose, to organize the first feminist movement in Jewish history? To say to the men, "Be careful, we also know how to rejoice and compose poetry?"

But what in fact did they sing? The first verse of Moses' song but with a slight variation. Moses sang "I shall sing," in the first person singular. But when he said "I," he spoke for the entire community of Israel. As for Miriam, she used the second person plural, as if issuing a call, an order to her feminine audience: "Sing to the Lord." It was an order. This fairly modern interpretation emphasizes her ambitious side. Envious of Moses and Aaron, she tries to build a political base for herself by appealing to women. She must have said to herself that she too lived through the exile in Egypt, participated in the liberation, heard God's voice—why hasn't she been called upon to play a more significant role in Israel's evolving society? In other words, she sounded like a politician, a power seeker. She no longer wished to live on the margins, in obscurity. Her appeal—"Sing the glory of the Lord!"—would therefore seem a rousing appeal to women to seize power, or at least a share of it.

Which would explain her part in the slander of Moses. The text does not use the plural *"va'yedabru,"* *they* spoke evil of Moses, but *"va'tedaber,"* *she* spoke. It is Miriam who initiated the vilification. Aaron either listened in silence or made his contribution to the exchange afterward. Would he have spoken at all if his sister had said nothing? That is why the punishment fell on her alone.

Would that be why the people did not mourn her death? I don't believe that. May the Jewish student in me rise to her defense? Let us consult Talmudic sources. According to a Midrash, Miriam was a precocious child. Rabbi Shimon bar Nahmani says so: at the age of five, she was already assisting her mother in midwifery. Summoned by Pharaoh to hear his decree that all firstborn Hebrew males be drowned, little Miriam made fun of him by sticking out her tongue, saying: "Just wait! Sooner or later God will take care of you!" Enraged, Pharaoh wanted to have her killed, but her mother persuaded the Egyptian monarch to spare her: "She is a little girl; she doesn't know what she is saying." But of course she did know.

As she knew that the future belonged to Moses. She had predicted it to her father: Moses will be the liberator of the children of Israel. Her father, deeply moved, gave her a kiss on the forehead.

Her purpose in gathering the women together after the crossing of the Red Sea? The Talmud does not hesitate to make a virtue of it: just as Moses sang for the men, so Miriam sang for the women. A prophetess, she did nothing on her own account. If she sang, it was because God inspired her to sing. Only one verse? So what! Since when does a poem's meaning or literary value depend on its length? Besides, is there a more beautiful exalted call to a community to sing together? Her outcry is a pure plea for spirituality, for transcendence! And of course, the verb form *"shiru!"* (sing!) proves that she was addressing women and men both! How can we fail to thank her for striving to unify all the people in a song of thanksgiving, in a celebration of hope?

Interestingly, the commentator "Klei Yakar" says she did not burst into song because she was a prophetess, but rather she became a prophetess *because* she burst into song.

How then are we to make sense of the charge of slander? According to the Talmud, the tale teaches us the dangers of slander, the punishment for it, and the universality of both. More precisely, if Miriam, the sister of Moses and Aaron and unique prophetess in the Pentateuch, was capable of committing that sin, who could claim to be immune to it? Further, if Miriam, so great, so holy, was punished, who could expect to emerge unscathed? The story teaches us that even Miriam had to submit to the fate of all lepers, isolation and humiliation, to be cured.

Let us add that slander—*lashon ha'ra,* an evil tongue spreading spiteful or malicious gossip—is unanimously abhorred in the rabbinical tradition. The wild beast, says the Talmud, kills by biting its prey; the serpent shoots its poison toward the one it is looking at; so there is contact between predator and prey. But slander is worse: something is said in Galilee, and it wounds or kills someone in Rome.

Our greatest sages have written extensively on the evil aspect of slander, which according to Maimonides can shake the universe to its foundations. The celebrated philosopher said that malicious gossip annihilates three persons: he who spreads it, he whom it strikes, and he who hears it. In other words, the gossip-monger, the victim, and the listener. In the Jewish tradition, it is worse to listen to slander, to receive it, than to spread it. Maimonides forbids us to approach or even to be in the company of an individual guilty of slander.

In truth, "evil tongue" is often inadequately interpreted. More than evil speech, it means the tongue of evil. To insult someone, to discredit him, to defame him behind his back, is to serve the powers of evil.

But why should slander be punished by leprosy? To mark the guilty clearly, to show that evil cannot be done with impunity. One may not do evil and pretend to be a friend. Leprosy isolates the evildoer and marks him as a culprit. So this account of slander belongs to the moral history of our people.

Still, this does not explain why Miriam alone was punished. Nor why she was cured, she who never repented, at least not to our knowledge. Certainly, Moses interceded in her favor. But can anyone repent for another? And didn't Aaron, Miriam's accomplice, deserve punishment also? True, he did repent: *"Yes,* we have sinned," he said to his brother. But is that sufficient to appease divine wrath?

Troubled by the injustice inherent in this tale, some Talmudic sages opened a serious and probably stormy debate in an effort to resolve the problem.

Listen to Rabbi Akiba: Often compassionate toward women because of his ever-perfect wife Rachel, he cannot accept that when two people commit the same crime only one is punished. He believes that Aaron was also punished. He also became a leper. If the text does not say so directly, it is in order not to embarrass him.

Now listen to the immediate response of Rabbi Yehuda ben Beteira: "Akiba, Akiba, one day, on judgment day, you will have to explain yourself. Either you are right, in which case you have discovered what the Torah concealed, or you are wrong, in which case you have defamed a *Tzaddik* like Aaron." According to this sage, Aaron was reprimanded but not punished.

Then there is a third hypothesis: that Aaron was punished as Miriam was, but that God cured his leprosy in the next instant.

At any rate, we realize that the Talmud does make an effort to defend Miriam. Indeed, it goes so far as to suggest that the text must be reinterpreted. If Miriam raised the matter of their brother's marriage to a Kushit woman in Aaron's presence, it was to save Moses from himself—that is, to induce him to remarry Zipporah and produce children.

She who was without husband or child, in those days an old maid, and in ours single, enjoyed playing marriage broker. A midrashic legend claims that it was she who insisted that their father, Amram, remarry Yokheved, the mother of his children. The legend adds that Aaron and Miriam danced at their parents' second wedding.

So Miriam the prophetess possessed real powers of persuasion. Everyone seemed to obey her. Only Moses did not listen. Is that why she challenged his august position?

Yet midrashic sources suggest that God looked kindly upon Miriam. As long as she lived, the drought was not severe. After her death it became acute. The fruit trees, according to legend, all withered.

Who took care of Miriam when she fell ill? Who diagnosed her disease? Only the High Priest could do that. Not Moses. Aaron? Being her brother, he had to disqualify himself. So it was God who took up the task of curing Miriam. How remarkable, says the Midrash: it was

God who punished her, God who determined her illness, and God who cured her.

What did the people of Israel do immediately after Miriam was laid to rest? We noted earlier as we read the text: they clamored for water.

The story goes that there was in the desert a miraculous fountain or spring of fresh water that bore the name of Miriam. Counted among the ten things that preceded creation, this fountain, always in motion, accompanied the children of Israel everywhere. It possessed the power to cure the sick as well as to slake thirst.

But if this fountain or spring possessed the power to cure the sick, why didn't Miriam use it to remove her own leprosy? Because the shoemaker walks barefoot? Or because, according to the Talmud, a prisoner cannot free himself?

Incidentally, where is the fountain called Miriam now? Abba Hiya said: Whoever climbs the peak of Mount Carmel and sees a fisherman's net at the bottom of Lake Tiberias, is gazing at Miriam's spring.

STRANGE, Miriam had the ability to help others but not herself. But then the people of Israel have never been affectionate with or faithful to their leaders. Isn't Moses proof of that? His contemporaries caused him so much suffering that one may wonder whether God's decision to bar him from the promised land was not a reward rather than a punishment. Only after his death did the people understand his unique greatness.

It was worse with Joshua: when he died, no one even bothered to come to his funeral. They were too busy, says the Talmud. Busy working in the fields, pruning the vines, or whatever.

The Talmud tells us who buried Miriam: her two brothers. Alone? Probably. The people? All they could think and talk about was water. Scandalous but probably true: with no respect for their two leaders' mourning, they clamored for easy answers, simplistic solutions. The mood became so ugly that Moses and Aaron fled, taking refuge in the special tent that was the home of the spirit of God. To be alone. Alone with the memory of their sister, who had barely left them. Today we would say, to sit shiva.

Then an astonishing thing happened: God chased them away. Those are the words of the midrashic account. God chased them out of His tent. "What are you doing here?" He asked. "Your people are thirsty and you sit weeping for old Miriam?"

Thus we learn that the unhappy prophetess did not die young. At the same time, this version saddens us. Why does God call her old? Is there no courtesy in heaven? And why did God disturb Miriam's brothers' mourning and speak in such an impatient, menacing tone? Is this how we talk to people just back from the cemetery?

But God's voice is law. Despite the respect we must show to the dead, the living take precedence. A funeral procession must yield the right-of-way to a marriage procession. It is more important to celebrate life than to weep for the dead. When it is a matter of sparing men and women the agonies of thirst, mourning even for a prophetess must be interrupted.

What a moving woman Miriam was. Alive, she spent most of her days in the shadow of her brothers. Dead, she counted for less than an anonymous Jew, unhappy and parched.

Perhaps her faith was that of a typical older sister who sacrificed herself for her family. She accepted all misfortunes, provided that her younger brothers were happy. She went as far as to remain single in order to take care of her family.

The slander? This is her principal transgression. But since Moses forgave her, we will too. Why not be chivalrous?

There is another problem: her envy of her younger brother. It was not Moses' marriage to a Kushit woman that bothered her; what set her on edge was his superiority in his dealings with God. Love and envy are irreconcilable. That Miriam tried to bring Aaron over to her side, to make him a kind of co-conspirator against their brother, seems unworthy of her. Rather than taking pride in her younger sibling, one might say that she was perhaps working to undermine his authority.

How can such a flaw in a biblical heroine be explained? An important conclusion must be repeated: unlike those in the sacred history of other religions, our ancestors were not saints. It is because they were human that they touch and affect us in our choices and commitments.

What do I love about Miriam? First of all her name. Perhaps it bears her secret and her destiny. *Mar-yam:* the bitterness of the sea. Or perhaps *meri-yam,* the revolt of the sea, the rebellion at the seashore, against the sea. Remove the *resh* and you have *mayim*— water. Her whole life was lived under the sign of water. We meet her on the banks of the Nile, we find her on the far shore of the Red Sea. We leave her, or she leaves us, as her people are clamoring for water.

Water is like love: we only appreciate it in its absence. To the thirsty it stands for happiness; to the slaked, the satisfied, it represents the banality of everyday life. Water is the liquid of life but also a call by death and to death.

In my eyes Miriam remains the little girl who, in that time of terror and slavery under Pharaoh, follows her mother to the banks of the River Nile; and responds to the sound of her baby brother's cries.

Simple curiosity? No. Compassion, loyalty, self-sacrifice on her part.

In those times she alone knew where Moses was hiding. But she didn't give up hope that one day the prince of Egypt would return to his family and to his people.

Nadab and Abihu:
A Story of Fire and Silence

THE TRANSGRESSION OF two brothers, the punishment from heaven, the silence of a father: this is a unique story of pain and grief. I confess that some of its aspects elude me. Is it about human frailty and the perils of ecstasy?

In the rich Talmudic and mystical literature, attempts—often contradictory—have been made to elucidate it. None seems satisfactory. This episode confused even our greatest ancient and medieval commentators. If death is often unjust, it is more so when its meaning seems hidden or absent.

Two men, still young and promising, destined for great careers, are mysteriously struck down. Why in public? And why by fire?

Let us read the text:

"And Nadab and Abihu, the sons of Aaron, took each of them his pan and put fire therein, and put incense thereon, and offered alien fire before the Lord, which He commanded them not.

"And there went out fire from the Lord, and devoured them. . . ."

So begins the tale. On the face of it, the narrative proceeds by strict biblical logic. A sin was committed, bringing on an exemplary punishment. The style is clear and to the point. The facts, just the facts: deed, motive, outcome. The text tells us who did what to whom and in what circumstances. It also tells us what followed.

We read on. Having learned of the catastrophe which has just struck the house of his brother Aaron, Moses says to him, *"bi'kro-vai ekadeish . . ."*—Thus said the Lord: I will be sanctified in them that come near me, and before all the people I will be glorified. At that moment, this is all that Moses says to his doubtless stunned brother. And Aaron's reaction? *"Va'yidom Aharon,"* and Aaron held his peace. He kept silent. He wrapped himself in silence; he *became* silence. Meanwhile, Moses busied himself with the practical side of the funeral rites, the specific rules of mourning that apply to priests: "Do not uncover your heads. . . . do not rend your clothing. . . . do not go out from the door of the Tabernacle, the *ohel mo'ed*. . . . Let your brethren, the whole house of Israel, bewail the burning which the Lord hath kindled. . . ."

So ends the dry, precise account of the tragedy, giving way to the sequel, a series of discourses bearing on the event. God's words to Aaron, Moses' words to Aaron and his two surviving sons, Aaron's words to Moses. The chapter ends with the two words *"va'yitav be'enav,"* Moses was content, and doubtless God as well.

Well, I am among those who are *not* content.

Need I say that the theme of this story has always fascinated and even obsessed me? Because of Aaron's silence? There is something else. This chapter gives a new dimension to the subject of brothers as they are presented in the Bible. We are always struck by what sets one in opposition to the other, culminating in division, separation, and tragedy. Cain and Abel: one an assassin, the other his victim. Isaac and Ishmael: utter strangers to each other. Jacob and Esau: fierce enemies, always fleeing one another. Joseph and his elder brothers: a ghastly and depressing story of jealousy, envy, treachery. We understand their misery, their suffering, for which they are in a sense responsible. The day when Joseph was sold by his brothers remains, in Jewish history, a black day marked by blood and ashes.

But Nadab and Abihu are different. They are attached to each other, loyal to each other, and nothing comes between them. Not ambition nor beliefs. They aspire to the same religious perfection, to the same spiritual purity, to the same inner conquests. Their fraternal love is exemplary.

All that they undertake, they do together. Together they decide to intensify their religious quest, to serve God with more zeal, more fervor; together, acting as one, they proceed toward the Sanctuary, and . . .

Together they fall, in the same moment that they breathe their last. For what reason?

We shall try to make sense of that a bit later. For now, let's leave them in their sanctuary, a place forbidden to strangers.

Why is this story told and retold on the holiest day of the year, Yom Kippur? To awaken us to repent? That is the purpose of the entire service. Is there another reason for it? If we are called upon to remember this tale of personal tragedy, is it to teach us that there are events that transcend our understanding? God's motives and ours are not necessarily identical.

THAT DAY must have passed in general rejoicing. In an exalting communal elation. It was the first day of the month of Nissan. A holiday. Were they not celebrating the dedication of the Sanctuary in the desert, and the appearance of God's spirit in the Tabernacle? We can picture the scene. People were dancing, singing, affirming their faith in a national future sanctified by God.

A midrashic legend identifies the happiest person of all: Elisheva, daughter of Aminadab and wife of Aaron. She had every reason to be happy. Her husband was the High Priest; her brother-in-law Moses was the uncrowned leader of the nation; her son Eleazar was his father's first assistant; Eleazar's younger brothers, Nadab and Abihu, were much loved and admired for their piety and devotion to God; her grandson Pinhas was *mashvah milhama,* a sort of warrior-priest. And his brother Nakhshon was serving as a tribal chief.

The Sifra comments, *"be'ota sha'a kaftza ha'puranot . . ."* It was then that the catastrophe fell on that first family of Israel, and hence on Israel itself. Two illustrious young priests, the sons of Aaron and Elisheva, suffered death by fire, and the people were torn from their joy and plunged into distress.

The event roused an understandable and lasting interest among commentators. How could the two young sons of the first Jewish family have provoked heaven to such implacable wrath? We shall divide our exploration into four parts. First, we shall try to see just what their transgression consisted of, since there certainly was a transgression, the text says so emphatically. Second, what did the punishment consist of? Third, what can be said in their defense? And fourth, what was the reaction among those close to them?

In the biblical text, the sin is stated succinctly but a bit vaguely: "Nadab and Abihu introduced a strange [or: alien] fire within the Sanctuary, a fire that God had not commanded of them." That was all; but it was enough. A strange fire. An impure fire, one that was profane. This accusation is obscure. "That God had not commanded of them." What does that mean? Are we dealing with one sin here, or two? Is any fire not commanded by God profane by definition? Is whatever God has not commanded forbidden merely because it is strange? Was Nadab and Abihu's sin simply to have done things their own way, when they should have waited for a command from above? To put it another way: in religion, will any initiative, any original idea, any innovative project be disapproved of and condemned on high?

Rashi has not far to seek. A native of Troyes, a wine maker, he finds many explanations not in women but in wine. It is wine's fault. Nadab and Abihu had drunk too much; it's as simple as that. Doubtless they started with one glass, like everyone else, with everyone else, just to say *"l'chaim,"* to take part in the general rejoicing. And they couldn't stop. They sat down to eat, sampling the best dishes, which made them thirsty again. So they entered the Sanctuary inebriated. That was the mistake which then became a transgression. It is prohibited to enter the Sanctuary when not in possession of all your faculties, when your mind is elsewhere.

But if they were drunk, doesn't that mean they were unaware? And that it was an involuntary act on their part to rush toward God, or toward the secret of God, with a strange fire in their hands? Since when is a man condemned to death for an involuntary sin, or offense, or crime?

In the Tractate of Sanhedrin, we find a more serious hypothesis, one that remains pertinent today. It goes back to the immemorial conflict between generations. Nadab and Abihu, it would seem, lacked respect for their elders. In the Tractate of Erouvin it is said, "The sons of Aaron died after daring to teach the Law in the presence of Moses." Worse: ambitious, arrogant, Nadab and Abihu were impatient to see Moses and Aaron gone—dead—so they could succeed them as masters and leaders. "One day, when they were walking in a procession behind Moses and Aaron, with the people following, Nadab and Abihu spoke together, and the first said to the other, "But when, when will these old men finally die?; it is time we assumed the leadership of our generation." At which God remarked, We'll see who buries whom.

We must add that there are differences of opinion in the Midrash about this legend too. Rabbi Youddan states in the name of Rabbi Ivvo: Nadab and Abihu said, really said, those irreverent and offensive words, thus betraying their impatience to succeed their father soon, very soon. But Rabbi Pinhas does not believe it; according to him, they only entertained such thoughts in their minds. Still, whether in thought or in speech, the two brothers do themselves no honor.

It was the late Itzhak Itzhaki, the Israeli historian of biblical geography, who pointed out to me an interesting comment by Cassouto. The latter noted that another man had named his sons Nadab and Abiha (very much like Abihu): this was the wicked king of Israel called Jeroboam son of Nebat, Jeroboam the evil ruler of Israel whom Scripture calls *"hoteh u'mahti et ha'rabim,"* a sinner who drove others to sin. Now what was Jeroboam's problem? Envy. He envied King David. He insisted on being first everywhere. A midrash recounts: One day God grasped him and said to him, Repent, and you and I and David son of Jesse will walk together in the Garden of Eden. Jeroboam asked, Who will go first? David, answered God. In that case, said Jeroboam, I refuse.

Just as Jeroboam wanted to do away with legitimate kings, Nadab and Abihu, it is said, wanted to see their father and their uncle disappear, for they were too famous, too important, too powerful.

Question: We can understand why Nadab was punished; it was he, after all, who allegedly made those unfortunate remarks about Moses and Aaron. But Abihu said nothing; why did he deserve the same punishment as his brother? Answer: because he said nothing. He should have protested. His silence made him an accomplice.

Even the apparently beautiful and moving friendship that united the two brothers is said to have been feigned and flawed. The Midrash reproaches them for it, and calls it one of the causes of their abrupt demise.

Bar Kappara declares in the name of Rabbi Yirmiya son of Eleazar: Here are the four causes that occasioned the death of Aaron's sons: They came too close to the Sanctuary, they bore an untimely sacrifice, they introduced a strange fire, and they did not consult together on the procedure. Put another way, it was by accident that they found themselves in the same place at the same time, by accident that they committed the guilty deeds. In other words, they were together but not united.

Thus at the heart of the legend there lurks a tendency to darken the brothers' names. Too pushy. Too arrogant. Too insolent. Toward God, whom they insulted by approaching drunk, and toward their contemporaries. When you are Aaron's son you must behave with at least minimal decency. When you are young, you should not wish the death of those who are no longer young, and from whom you have received a glorious heritage, with its many burdens and privileges.

Another idea: Nadab and Abihu clung to their single marital state. Refusing to marry, they violated the first biblical commandment, to be fruitful and multiply. But for what reason? To what can we attribute their refusal to marry? To despair over their people's nebulous future? Perhaps to an excess of piety? Is it possible that they chose not to marry because they had decided to consecrate themselves solely to God? If it were that, we would be tempted to understand them and even to respect them. But that was not the true reason. Their refusal to establish families sprang not from their passion for God, but from their pride, from their vanity. Preoccupied with their own destinies, they did not deign to consider others.

Clearly, in their exaggerated opinion of themselves, they did not believe any woman in the world deserved them, thinking, "What woman would be a worthy match? After all, one of our uncles is our sovereign, another is our tribal leader, our father is High Priest and we are his deputies . . ." Thus, a legend insists, through their doing, numerous women in Israel remained old maids. Of course they could have married other men, but they preferred to wait for Nadab and Abihu. Well, the tradition does not forgive these two young men the tears of solitude that so many beautiful and virginal women shed because of them.

Not too attractive, these two sons of the High Priest of the Jewish nation and of Jewish history. Rather objectionable in their need to assert themselves and command attention. Why are they presented in such somber light? To justify their early death? To explain God's sudden wrath?

We should note immediately, however, lest this version seem too convincing, that the general view suggests the opposite, that Nadab and Abihu were "guilty" of wanting to do too well, to serve God with ever more passion, more fervor, more fire.

Every time Scripture mentions the death of Nadab and Abihu, says a midrashic text, it gives the reason. Why? So we may know that this was their only fault, that because of this alone they died that horrendous death. So people of ill will may not say: Who knows what other sins, committed in secret, brought death upon them.

The old French proverb "The better is the enemy of the good" would apply to them. They were not content to be the respected sons of the High Priest, carrying a weighty legacy on their shoulders; they wanted to do things that their father himself would not have dared to do—enter the Sanctuary bearing a fire that God had not commanded.

Even earlier, on Mount Sinai, they had gazed upon the face of the Lord from too close, something which incurs the death penalty. It was because even close up, God seemed to them far off. They knew perfectly well that it was impossible and forbidden to move forward, to approach the Almighty too closely, but the urge was too strong for them. They wanted to abolish any space at all between the Creator and His creatures. *"Amdu le'hossif ahava al ahava,"* comments the Sifra: They believed they could, should, add to their love of God a greater love, more imposing, all-encompassing, in order to melt into His radiance and fulfill themselves in it.

Here is a glowing portrait of all imaginable human and Jewish virtues. In the eyes of the Zohar they are young, just twenty years old. And bubbling with religious activity. A midrash states, "They were handsome." Physically? Morally as well. Thirsting for perfection, they dreamed of nothing else. A midrash asks, Why does the Bible repeat twice the word *va'yamutu,* which means "they are dead"? Is it to indicate that they also died in the world to come? No, answers the midrash. It is to tell us that they died before dying. How? By remaining celibate. In other words, they truly had a part in the world to come, the world of truth.

They have been compared to the four Talmudic masters who dared enter into the Pardes, the orchard of forbidden knowledge. Like Ben Azzai, they perished for gazing where one must not gaze.

The Midrash considers at length the circumstances in which the two men died. We know that they were the victims of fire. Nothing unusual in that. In religious morality everything is consistent. *Mida k'neged mida:* measure for measure. Since they offended heaven by fire, by fire they were punished.

In the Tractate of Sanhedrin the scene is described in close detail: two fine jets of fire blazed out of the Sanctuary and divided into four; two of them penetrated Nadab's nostrils and two Abihu's. Thus their souls were burned away, but not their bodies. The latter remained intact. There were no visible wounds and no visible scars. Death was instantaneous, like a candle snuffed out. Other commentators think otherwise: that the bodies were devoured by flames while the souls remained intact.

Rabbi Akiba leans toward the first theory. The question is one of physical death. But then there would have been two corpses within the Sanctuary. How could these be removed, if entry was forbidden? Two hooks were set into their mouths, and people pulled them out.

Question: why did God choose to punish them on a national holiday? Did He not hesitate to disrupt the festivities surrounding the inauguration of the Tabernacle?

Answer: in fact, Nadab and Abihu were living in a kind of reprieve. Weren't they supposed to have died at Sinai for having "gazed too closely upon the face of God"? Why didn't they die immediately? Because on Sinai, says God, Israel espoused my Torah; that was their celebration; and I was surely not going to mar it with an execution. I would bide my time . . . And the Midrash comments: It is like the king who discovers, on his daughter's wedding day, that the "best man," the couple's good friend, has committed a grave sin deserving capital punishment. To have him executed on the spot would spoil the princess's joy. He preferred to wait for a holiday of his own. In this case, God waited for the day of the Sanctuary's inauguration. It was of course the people who gave themselves over to joy and ecstasy, it was the people who danced and sang, but it was God's holy day that they were celebrating: God had found His place on earth, in history, at the heart of a human community—isn't that a reason to rejoice?

Then came the disaster. Fire was emitted from the Lord and it devoured them, these two sons of Aaron; they died before God. In God?

WHO GAVE THE NEWS to the unfortunate parents? We presume it was Moses, for it was he who spoke to his brother in God's name: *"Bi'krovai ekadeish"*—I will be sanctified in them that come near me, and before all the people I will be glorified. Did he say anything before that? If so, what words did he use? We would very much like to know, in case, God forbid, someone else should find himself in similar circumstances. But the text is meager; it does not reveal what the prophet said to his elder brother to make him understand. It tells us only the argument that Moses passed along in the name of the Lord. It may be that he said nothing else, and that Aaron understood the profound, and profoundly harrowing, significance of *"bi'krovai ekadeish . . . ,"* that sometimes we must be ready to die, we must actually die, to be close to God. And that it is by death and not only by life, that the Name of the Lord is sometimes sanctified. We can imagine the father, stupefied, overwhelmed; doubtless he is wondering if this is not a nightmare—he just saw his two sons near the Sanctuary, he knows their religious fervor, their spiritual capacities, and now they are no longer alive? Is that possible? *"Va'yidom Aharon,"* the text declares. In two awe-filled words it says everything. And Aaron held his peace.

Was he in the grip of grief? Of despair? Aaron's silence lends itself to several interpretations. We shall set forth a few of them. But before that, we may ask: Why does no one speak of his wife? The mother of Nadab and Abihu—who broke the news to *her*? Where was she when her two sons vanished from her world? And how did she live through it? Most unjustly, the biblical text proves too modest, too discreet, about the reactions of Elisheva daughter of Aminadab. Could it be because she chose not to be silent, to express herself in another way?

The Midrash, as usual, imagines what the Bible conceals. Here Elisheva sobs. And laments. That's a natural human response. The High Priest's wife is also a mother. At the sudden death of her two sons she cannot remain stoic. When the heart is torn, it screams in pain; when the grief is too heavy to bear, it breaks.

And according to Rabbi Moshe ben-Nahman, the Ramban or Nahmanides, the father also broke down. Aaron would have been totally inhuman not to have. Some commentators hasten to specify that he wept for his sons' sins; others suggest that he shed tears for his own. He grew calm only when Moses consoled him with the already famous words: *"bi'krovai ekadeish . . ."* The Midrash adds these sentences from the mouth of Moses himself: "Aaron, my brother, I have known for a long time, because God told me, that God wishes to be sanctified by those closest to Him. I thought He was speaking of me, or of you, but I was wrong: your sons were closer to Him." That is when and why Aaron held his peace, a peace not of resignation but of acceptance. His brother's argument reassured him: Nadab and Abihu were not guilty. It was by their love of God, and by God's immeasurable love for them, that they lost their lives, which became offerings. Their death was therefore an act of *kidush Hashem;* in dying they glorified His Name. So much so that, according to Rashi, it was to reward Aaron for his worthy and trusting attitude that God, a few verses later, speaks to him directly, personally.

With all due respect to our tradition, these theories trouble me. Whatever a father's role, whatever his public responsibilities, he cannot and should not, in my opinion, accept calmly, in faith and resignation, the sudden death of his children! If Abraham could protest against the identical punishment inflicted on the just and unjust alike, why shouldn't Aaron echo his protest? How could a father tolerate such a tragedy falling on his immediate family? Is it because he—a peacemaker, a peerless mediator, gentleness and harmony personified—was afraid to quarrel with the Lord? In that case he eludes us altogether. If the need for peace means submission, submission at any price, do we not run the risk of descending into excessive humility and thence into servitude?

Careful! We're running too fast. What is so pleasing about the midrashic literature is that we find in it both the thing and its opposite. One midrash suggests an idea, and immediately another answers, *"ume'idakh gissa,"* on the other hand . . .

True, one legend tells us that the High Priest Aaron chose faith, confidence, and acceptance. But another urges us to imagine otherwise. According to this version, having heard the news, Aaron cried out, uncomprehending, full of pain, "All the children of Israel gazed upon You, Lord, when we crossed the Red Sea, and then they saw You again at Mount Sinai, and none suffered for it; but my sons—was it not You who commanded them to enter the Tabernacle or the

Sanctuary, a place that no one not a priest may penetrate and emerge from alive? And why did they enter? To gaze upon your power and Your glory! And yet they paid for it with their lives!"

I like this explosion of grief on Aaron's part. Here the father is stronger than the High Priest. How can we not feel compassion for his suffering, his distress? What he asks of God, he has a right to ask. Apparently—still according to the midrashic version—God thinks so too. For He tells Moses to console Aaron with the words *"bi'krovai ekadeish . . ."* Better yet: Aaron learns that his sons could have escaped the death penalty. It is Moses himself who reveals it to him in the name of the Lord: whoever enters the Tabernacle or the Sanctuary without permission will become a leper; such is the divine will, such is the Law. Would Aaron have preferred to see his sick sons Nadab and Abihu banished from the camp? Cast out from their people? Unclean? Marked by a divine reprimand? In other words, it was for their own good that their lives were taken. And there Aaron agreed. A leper's life, far from the community, would have been a lingering death for his sons. Better to die on the spot, without suffering. To die a heroic death. That is why *"va'yidom Aharon,"* Aaron held his peace. We detect a spark of knowledge and of gratitude in his silence.

But here too the Talmudic sages do not agree. Rabbi Aha ben Zeira poses a question that must make us tremble if we seek imma-nent and transcendent justice at the same time: "Korah and his peo-ple came quarreling to the Tabernacle and they were burnt up, while the sons of Aaron wished to bring their sacrifice to God but without quarreling, and they too were consumed by fire: is this just?" And fur-ther along, "General Titus, Titus the wicked entered the Holy of Holies with a naked sword in his hand—he slashed the sacred cur-tain, the Parokhet, and profaned the name of God, and he went out in peace, unharmed. . . . But the sons of Aaron went into the Taber-nacle intending to offer their sacrifice to God—and what happened to them? They were brought back burnt to cinders. . . ." Here again the question arises: what is justice? Was Titus, the enemy and destroyer of Jerusalem, worth more than Nadab and Abihu? Was his life, his destiny, more precious than theirs?

Let's return to the narrative. Aaron holds his peace; he is silent. Lost in thought. Forlorn. Unable to act. It is Moses who takes care of the funeral arrangements. He is the leader. He must be prepared to deal with any and all circumstances, and he knows it. He orders Mishael and Elzaphan, the sons of Aaron's uncle Uzziel, to carry the brothers out of the camp. To Aaron and his two surviving sons, Eleazar and Ithamar, he explains how they must conduct themselves.

Then it is God who speaks to Aaron: "Do not drink wine or strong drink, thou, nor thy sons with thee." He also tells him that the whole community will mourn the two brothers dead by fire, and if not—if the community fails in this observance—divine wrath will descend upon it.

And life goes on.

THIS TALE COMPRISING a few short verses is among the saddest and most mysterious in the Bible. It grips us; it takes us by the throat.

Is there a greater sorrow for man or woman than to bury a child? It is against nature. It smacks of a curse. Why is war the worst of all evils? Because it reverses the laws of nature. "Woe to the generation in which parents bury their children," says the Talmud. Doesn't that evoke all wars?

We link this tragedy of Nadab and Abihu to others equally overwhelming, personal and collective, and we read it on Yom Kippur to inspire repentance. Whoever weeps reading of the death of Aaron's two sons, says the Zohar, will not suffer the same fate; he will not see his children die young.

Determined to make sense of this drama of apparent injustice, Rabbi Abba bar Avina says: the death of the just serves as expiation for their contemporaries.

Is there then a useful and fruitful element in the death of the innocent? It is hard to conceive. Isn't Jewish tradition opposed to death? Isn't it an inevitable tragedy, a catastrophe of which God alone knows the secret, a secret that only God can decipher? Has tradition not taught us for generation upon generation that only life is sacred, that death is always impure, and that we must choose life and the living? That asking questions of the dead is a sin?

The fact that the text stresses the reasons for the punishment is in itself meaningful. That happens frequently in Scripture. If we skip several chapters we arrive at the chapter in which we hear God tell Moses why he will not be buried in sacred ground. What God says is terrible, extremely unjust if not cruel: You and Aaron have trespassed against Me; you have not glorified My name, and that is why you will not set foot on the land I have promised your people. Yes, it hurts to read that. Moses our master, our guide, our interpreter, the prophet of prophets . . . He, a sinner? He, a rebel against God? What has he done to deserve those final divine rebukes? How is it that God did not see fit to say a few consoling words to him?

The answer may be simple: Moses knew that he would never reach the land of Canaan, and God, in His pity, wanted to tell him why. To a man worthy of his name and his destiny, nothing is worse than uncertainty. Nothing is more overwhelming than the unknown.

That is the reason the text tells us why the sons of Aaron were punished by death.

But something inside keeps me from making my peace with this tale of two young brothers who, whatever one may say about their impulsive spirits, tried to overcome snares and obstacles to approach the Creator of all beings and all things. And to love Him.

Isaac was also about to die by fire; but God spared him.

Nadab and Abihu were not spared.

Why didn't the God of love spare so many descendants of Moses and Aaron?

To bring them closer to Him, He tore them from our midst.

Why?

Va'yidom Aharon. And Aaron the father held his peace. Like God. For God.

And all that we, his distant disciples, can do is to join our silence to his. Shall we be comforted by it? Are both of the same nature? I do not know.

Esau and Jethro:
Gentiles in the Bible

IN THE BEGINNING, the tale is not about Jews.

God created heaven and earth, the sun and the moon, plants and trees and all the creatures living in the air and in the sea. It is only afterward, on the sixth day, that He created man and woman, for whom the entire universe was destined.

As one French philosopher said: what a pity that the creation of man came so late—when the Creator must have been a bit tired.

In Talmudic literature, the sequence of events possesses its own logic. Our sages believe that because man came after the other creatures, he was meant to be guest of honor, the crown jewel of His creation. Before inviting a guest to come and stay with you, there must be a place—a palace—where he and his children could dwell and prosper simply as human beings and part of the human family. Adam and Eve were the first such distinguished guests.

Were they Jewish? No. They were not. Nor were their children Cain and Abel. Noah wasn't Jewish either. In the biblical text, the story of creation is totally devoid of any Jewish reference. Actually, until Abraham and Sarah appear on the stage, none of the characters is Jewish. Some were good in the eyes of God and of their fellow human beings, others were not. There were among them just men and women who were blessed with longevity, and wicked people who perished at a young age. All were pagans—and yet they occupy a place in creation.

Thus students of Scripture—especially Jewish students—are entitled to question the sources of our religious and national memory. Why are we told these stories? Why does the destiny of primitive pagans concern us? Why didn't the Almighty make things easier for us—and for Himself—and decree right from the start that the first man and the first woman were Jews—as all their descendants would be? Why did history have to wait centuries upon centuries before discovering its first Jews? Was it because God sought to protect His people from vicious anti-Semitic attacks—so we could not be accused in all languages, in all situations, of forever wanting to be the first?

Was it God's attempt to tell his people: Beware of misplaced vanity! You are not the only ones in my world! Others have preceded you and some may even accompany you on the long road toward redemption! But then, God will remind other nations that it was through His people, the people of Abraham, that He has revealed Himself to the world, it is through His people, the people of Moses, that He has given the Law, it is through His people, the people of David and Isaiah, Sarah and Ruth, that His will is to be fulfilled.

And so, the Bible written by Moses—a Jew—speaks also of the lives of men and women who were pagans to the end. Their story too is worth remembering. In other words, they too were part of Jewish history.

Let us examine the case histories of Esau and Jethro, two major figures in Scripture. Both played essential roles in the drama of our people. What has been our tradition's attitude toward them? Once we answer that question, we may discover what Jews felt—and perhaps still do—toward non-Jews in general.

FIRST, it is important to note that these two are not considered strangers in the Bible. They are part of its texture. Without them, the biblical narrative would not be the tale of endless defiance and confrontation between individuals and communities that it is.

Esau belongs to the family of Israel itself. As for Jethro, he is different, but he is never seen as an outsider: how could Moses' father-in-law be an outsider? We owe to him Moses' personal and judicial welfare.

Now I feel I must confess an awkward empathy for Esau, Jacob's older brother. In a way, one feels sorry for him. I see him always alone and lonely, bitter and distressed. Except for his old father, who is blind and helpless, nobody likes him, least of all his mother, Rebecca. Her suspicion of him is mixed with animosity. One imagines her always plotting against him. No wonder he is seldom at home, preferring to wander in the woods. That is his kingdom; there his solitude is less unbearable.

One wonders: why does Rebecca dislike her elder son so much? Even before she gave birth to him, she resented him. Quoting Talmudic sages, Rashi explains: While pregnant with her twins, she felt each one move as she passed different locations. When she was near a House of Study, it was Jacob who stirred; Esau did the same only when she was near a temple of idol worshipers. In other words, they began quarreling even when they were in their mother's womb. Intrigued, Rebecca went to consult Shem, the head of the famous yeshiva bearing his name. His explanation was clear: each of the twins will found a nation, and the two will be unable to live together; one will ascend only when the other descends. The rise of the one will mean the other's decline. That is why Isaac's pious spouse favored her younger son. And God too. Doesn't the text declare that "the oldest will be servant of the youngest"?

Poor Esau. Like his uncle Ishmael, he is not born yet, but he is already maligned and sentenced to an accursed destiny. Whatever he does, whether good or bad, is negatively interpreted. Take the incident of his birthright. Imagine him that day. He is hungry, so hungry, in fact, that he is starving. As for his brother Jacob, he is cooking a stew of lentils: "I am tired," says Esau. "Give me some of your red stuff." "All right," answers Jacob. "At a certain price. And the price is your rights as firstborn." What could Esau do? He accepts.

Now, a good man should willingly share his meal with his brother. Why then is Jacob setting terms, and exorbitant terms at that?

Nevertheless, the Midrash criticizes him, not Jacob. Naturally, Esau eats and drinks to diminish his hunger and thirst. But what does the Midrash say about him? *"Hikhnis imo kat shel pritizim"*—he had brought a group of young hooligans with him to drink with. We may wonder aloud, where in the world does the Midrash find even a trace of evidence that Esau was not alone at that moment? Why are the commentators so hard on him? Not one negative word is uttered about Jacob's business tactics. All criticism is directed at Esau.

Said Rabbi Yohanan: on that day—when he bought a plate of lentils to assuage his hunger—Esau committed five sins: he raped a girl who was already engaged to another man, he killed a man, he denied God's existence, he ridiculed the resurrection of the dead, and he gave up his rights as firstborn.

Really—all in one day? Where did Rabbi Yohanan learn about it? On what factual basis did he bring these charges?

In general, Esau seems to be a target for slander. For instance, while Jacob stayed home studying, Esau loved to go hunting. The word used is *tzayid*, which literally means hunting. So what? Is hunting forbidden in the Bible? But for Talmudic commentators *tzayid* has a different meaning. For them it means that he was deceitful, lying to his father to please him, cynically pretending to be excessively pious . . .

Still, isn't Jacob more shrewd than Esau? Hasn't he cheated him of his firstborn rights? Hasn't he taken advantage of Esau's hunger? Hasn't he trapped him?

Worse: doesn't Jacob usurp Esau's identity when he appears before his blind father so as to receive the blessings that were meant for Esau? Had Esau not been starving, would he have done anything to displease his father?

Actually, it was Esau's mother who was responsible. It was she who staged the entire scene, she who masterminded the plot to deprive Esau of what was rightly his. Jacob merely followed instructions. What to wear and when, what to say and how: manipulated by Rebecca, Jacob deceived both his father and his brother. Was Esau aware of what was happening? Was Isaac? Isaac must have sensed something was wrong, for he questioned Jacob: "How is it that the voice is Jacob's, but the hands are Esau's?" When he finally heard Esau's tragic cry, he was seized with great terror. At that moment, according to Rashi, he saw hell open under him. Commented the ancient Tossafistes: Isaac trembled twice in his life, once during the *akeidah*, when he saw his father, knife in hand, ready to slaughter him, and now. But now his fear was even greater. For he began doubting his own judgment, wondering what sin he could have committed to make him bless the wrong son. What did Isaac think of Jacob then? From his words it is clear that he was profoundly upset with the way he had deceived him.

As for Esau, one understands his despair. He cried out in pain because suddenly he realized the magnitude of his tragedy: he was the innocent victim of a family plot. His brother's lie was stronger than his father's truth. It was too late to change the facts, too late to alter the outcome. And Esau's response? Will he now hate his brother? Rebecca thinks so, Scripture does not. The text speaks of Jacob's fear rather than of Esau's intentions. Still, for midrashic commentators, they are evil.

For instance, after a lengthy separation, the two brothers met, embraced, wept. Esau too. Was it because he was moved to see his younger brother again? It would have been natural. But the Midrash insists that Esau's tears were false; that his friendly behavior was hypocritical. Why then did he weep? Because he had wanted not to kiss his brother but to bite him on the neck. And he couldn't because God had turned Jacob's neck into ivory or marble. Had Esau broken his teeth? In any case, he felt pain; that's why he sobbed. Strangely, it was Rabbi Shimon bar Yohai—the fierce adversary of all heathen culture—who gave Esau the benefit of the doubt, saying that Esau had truly been moved by Jacob's humility. But in general, Esau is always suspected of the worst possible motives.

This complex chapter becomes even more so when we invoke a decision—in the name of the same Rabbi Shimon bar Yohai—that makes Esau Jacob's implacable and eternal enemy. *"Halakha b'yadua, Essav soneh et Ya'akov"*—It is both reasonable to assume and legal to believe that Esau hates Jacob. Rabbi Gershom son of Rabbi Akha declares: "At the end of time, Esau will wear a *tallit* and take his place among the *Tzaddikim*. And it will be God Himself who will throw him out." For, in the eyes of our tradition, Esau is not only Jacob's enemy but the enemy of all that is noble in human beings. Was he inhuman? A great Hasidic master commented: when Esau discovered how cheated he had been by Jacob, he shed two tears. It is because of them that the Jewish people were destined to shed many more throughout their exile.

Was Esau completely innocent? If so, Jacob would be completely guilty. But it is more complicated than that. In claiming Isaac's blessings, Jacob has not really lied, since he had acquired them legally from his older brother. Then why did Isaac favor Esau? Is it that he felt sorry for him, since Jacob was Rebecca's favorite? Did he try to balance the injustice of that favoritism?

Yes, this is a perplexing chapter. No one emerges from it unscathed. Still, Jews are descendants of Jacob, not Esau. Jacob was a liar? Esau was a hunter, thus moved by and to violence. Between words and deeds, history has chosen to celebrate the first.

THAT SAID, Jacob's children were not all saints either. Far from it. What they did to their brother Joseph was evil. So jealous were they of Jacob's love for him, they relentlessly plotted to kill him, and threw him into a pit filled with snakes and scorpions. While he was howling with pain, what did they do? They ate their meal.

Earlier, a tragedy of a different sort occurred. Its victims were Gentiles who converted to Judaism under duress. Remember? For understandable yet regrettable reasons, Shimon and Levi, self-appointed avengers of their sister's honor, massacred all the just circumcised males of Nablus. The crime was so savage that on his deathbed Jacob reprimanded them. Should we now feel sorry for the men of Nablus, their victims? Where were they when their prince raped Dinah? Have they been punished for their crime? Didn't their indifference make them into accomplices? But then, does it mean that Shimon and Levi were just? Did they conduct a proper investigation of the crime? Did they establish the guilt of some and the innocence of others? They decided on their own to mete out collective punishment—that is why Jacob castigated them. The punishment did not fit the crime.

IN TRUTH, collective guilt and punishment do exist in Scripture. They are suffered by enemies—the Egyptian children who perished during the ten plagues—and also by Jews.

But the fate of one particular tribe was much worse: all the Amalekites—men, women, and children—were condemned to death. Why? Because they were the first to attack the Hebrews, who had just left Egypt physically exhausted and spiritually weakened. In their cowardice, the Amalekites assaulted mainly the old and the sick. That's why they are despised in the Bible. They represent not the strangers, not even the heathens, but the enemy on the level of the absolute. Must one have pity on them?

Wait. We are not there yet. We are still in Egypt.

HERE, a passionate defender of human rights could easily take on the case of Egypt's Pharaoh. What do we have against him? That he oppressed the Hebrews? They were not the only ones to suffer under his rule. Egypt was full of tribes reduced to slavery. Were the Hebrews more wretched than the others? Not before Moses' reappearance. It was only when the onetime Egyptian prince-turned-fugitive returned and began mixing in Egypt's internal affairs that Pharaoh's official policy changed. Is it far-fetched to try to understand him? As the supreme leader of a powerful nation, could he allow anyone to destabilize his regime? To God's emissaries Moses and Aaron he says, "Go away! You are disturbing the peace! You are interfering with productivity!" Pharaoh probably thought that if he were to yield now, he would end up yielding everywhere. Soon other tribes would demand the right to live in freedom, and worse, in dignity. And soon power would end up in the hands of the rebels. What would Egypt be without its cheap labor? And so he ordered his taskmasters to be more severe and more brutal than ever.

Pharaoh was such a harsh ruler, so insensitive to the suffering of others, so inflexible in his oppressive policies, that the great Rebbe Menahem-Mendel of Kotzk could not repress his astonishment: "There is a man whose convictions do not weaken. In spite of God's words and of his miracles, he remains defiant."

But when Pharaoh understands the gravity of the situation, he seems ready and willing to submit to God's will. What happens then? *"Va'yehazek Hashem et lev Paro"*—at that moment it is God who hardens Pharaoh's heart. The ensuing suffering is willed by God, not Pharaoh. Then why is Pharaoh punished? How does one justify the collective death of all the firstborn of Egypt? Hasn't Pharaoh done *teshuvah*? Has he not repented? Didn't he tell Moses, during the darkness that had descended on his country, *"lekhu ivdu et Hashem,"* go and serve your God? There again, *"Va'yehazek Hashem et lev Paro,"* God hardened Pharaoh's heart and made him refuse to free the children of Israel. The text omits all doubt: without God's intervention, Pharaoh would have opened the gates, allowing the Jewish slaves to leave as free men and women, and go to meet their God. And countless children would have been saved . . .

Ah, what a gifted and motivated defense attorney could have done before a jury with Pharaoh as defendant . . .

No DOUBT Balaam would have wanted such representation as well. A good case could have been made for him too. Though King Balak hired him to curse the children of Israel, he refused. Even when the king offered him treasures, he maintained his refusal. When finally he left his home and went to the front to observe the Hebrews, the only words that sprang from his lips were blessings. Indeed, they are so beautiful that they have become part of our prayers: *"Ma tovu ohalekha Ya'akov . . ."* How pleasant thy tents are, O Jacob . . . and how good your dwellings, Israel. . . .

And yet he is mistrusted. The title of prophet is denied him. Some sages claim that he was merely a sorcerer. He is generally referred to as the wicked Balaam. In some quarters he is ridiculed for his physical appearance, one-legged and one-eyed. How is one to explain such insensitive behavior toward a handicapped man who, in addition to everything else, refuses to be our enemy?

One sage goes so far as to affirm that Balaam's blessings have turned into maledictions, with the exception of those dealing with education and study. *"Am levadad yishkon,"* for example—"This people will be alone and isolated." Is it good or bad for Israel to live in solitude? Since the answer is ambiguous, why is only the negative interpretation accepted? Even if Balaam's intentions were bad, since when is someone judged by his intentions rather than by his deeds?

These questions have already been raised with regard to the first Pharaoh of the Bible, the one who met Abraham and his wife Sarah.

Listen:

There was a famine in the land, and Abram—as he was still called—went down to a neighboring country to escape it. As he was about to enter Egypt, he said to his wife Sarai: I know what a beautiful woman you are. If the Egyptians see you, and think "she is his wife," they will kill me and let you live. So please say you are my sister. A good and obedient wife, Sarai consented. Thus when Abram entered Egypt, Pharaoh's noblemen praised Sarai's beauty to Pharaoh, and took her to his royal palace.

Consequently, things went well for Abram. He was given sheep, oxen, asses, camels, male and female slaves. But God afflicted Pharaoh and his household. They all fell ill, and he was told why. So Pharaoh summoned Abram and asked him: "What have you done to me? Why did you say she is your sister when in fact she is your wife? Take her and go!"

Abram's answer has not been recorded in the biblical text, though the Midrash uses all its literary powers to persuade the reader that nothing happened to Sarai in Pharaoh's palace. Then why was he punished? Granted, he was drawn to her beauty; but if he hadn't touched her, why was he afflicted? One commentator does insinuate that he *tried* to touch her. Then again, why shouldn't he have, since, in his eyes, she was not married?

The answer? He had no business exploiting the difficult situation of a family of refugees just to satisfy his personal needs and manly vanity. He had before him a defenseless woman stricken with both hunger and fear. Why didn't he send her back to her "brother" with some food for both? He was a ruler without compassion—that is why he was punished.

It is with a sense of joy that one at last discovers in Scripture and its commentaries a Gentile who is treated with affection by almost everybody. His name is Jethro.

On the surface, he seems to be a simple, let us say one-dimensional character who impresses us mainly as a family man. His daughters bring home a foreign visitor and he thinks immediately of his unmarried daughter, Tsipora. They are married and he is kind to his new son-in-law, offering him work as a shepherd. Later, when Moses emerges from Egypt as leader of his people, Jethro raises no objections, doesn't tell Moses to come home to his wife and children. Instead, Jethro brings the family to Moses in the desert. Still Jethro is undaunted by his son-in-law's fame. He goes on to offer him useful advice on how to conduct affairs of state and helps him establish a judiciary system. Invited by Moses to join the new nation, he gently refuses, arguing that his duties toward his own family and tribe oblige him to return to Midian.

Clearly, his behavior is admirable, sincere, and beyond reproach. He is present only when needed. He speaks only when asked. He has no hidden agenda. He never thinks of using his high position and connections for his own benefit. No one could ever accuse him of nepotism or corruption.

Naturally, in midrashic literature the man and the attitude toward him are more complex.

He is generally shown in a positive light. After all, Moses himself treats him with great respect. Remember: Moses kneeled before him when they met in the desert. This is perhaps why many sages feel compelled to exaggerate his virtues. Most of them believe he converted to the Jewish faith. He is called *"ger shel emet"*—a true convert or a convert to truth. Is this to distinguish him from all other converts? Perhaps. Everything is done to emphasize his singularity. For instance, he is placed "under the wings of the Shekhina." And he is supposed to have declared: "I have served many idols, there isn't a god whom I have not worshiped, but none can be compared to the God of Israel." To illustrate his particular values and rare moral gifts, he is said to have been opposed to Esau—and, naturally, Esau is the loser. Isaac's son is treated less favorably than the in-law Jethro.

In fact, in at least two instances, he obtains a better rating than Moses himself.

In the first episode, Jethro and Moses are discussing wedding plans. A Midianite priest, Jethro agrees to let Moses marry Tsipora on one condition: their first son must be consecrated to idolatry. Strange as it may seem, Moses does not object. In other words, here Jethro was more loyal to his pagan faith than Moses was to his Jewish faith. But in the end, nothing of the kind happens. Both Moses' sons were Jewish.

In the second episode, Jethro hears stories of all that happened to the children of Israel in Egypt and afterward. *"Va'yishma Yitro,"* says the text. He only heard but did not see. Still, these rumors made a tremendous impact on him. Hence the importance of hearing in the Jewish tradition. Few other traditions have as many words for listening. Says the Midrash: when the ear hears, the entire body becomes alive. Also: hearing is the last of the five senses to leave a dying person. So, when Jethro heard of all the wonders that the children of Israel experienced, he exclaimed: "Blessed be the Lord for saving you from Pharaoh's bondage." Rabbi Papos commented that it is quite possible that this passage is meant to criticize Moses and the six hundred thousand Jews who left Egypt with him. They were ungrateful, according to this sage. It is as if to say: In spite of all the miracles God had accomplished for your sake, it took Jethro to bless Him and thank Him! Why did you take so long?

Jethro—the inventor of gratitude in Jewish history? Isn't thankfulness a principal element of Jewish morality?

No wonder Jethro has many admirers in Talmudic literature. Still, he does arouse a measure of skepticism in some quarters. Is it a way of balancing our view of the man? In Scripture, no one is perfect—neither perfectly good nor perfectly evil.

Thus some sages question Jethro's true motives in wanting to be so close to Israel. Was it because of the greatness of the Torah God gave to His people? Or because of the defeat the children of Israel had inflicted on their enemies, first the Egyptians and then the Amalekites? In other words, was Jethro motivated by love or by fear? Was it love for Israel or fear of God that made him a trusted ally of Israel? Is it possible that he simply wanted to be on the winning side? *Va'yihad Yitro* may easily be interpreted as "he had goosebumps." Was he too impressed? Too frightened?

Nevertheless, the accepted image of him is good, even glorious. When he rejects Moses' invitation to join the people of Israel in a leadership position, he invokes the perfect reason, which is gladly quoted in the Talmud: "I shall go home and see those who are close to me, and I shall convert all of them to the study of Torah."

Actually, says a midrashic source, Jethro was a friend of the Jews even before meeting Moses, and surely before becoming his father-in-law. He proved this when he served as royal adviser to Pharaoh in

Egypt, together with Balaam and Job. When Pharaoh was faced with having to resolve the Jewish question, Balaam suggested rejecting Moses' request to let his people go. Job remained silent and Jethro alone was on the side of the oppressed. For his cruel position, Balaam died a tragic death. For his neutrality, Job was made to suffer. As for Jethro, Pharaoh sentenced him to death. But he managed to escape. And to enter Jewish history for good.

According to midrashic fantasy, Jethro and Moses had already met when Moses was still a child. One day, the boy Moses seized the royal crown from Pharaoh's head and placed it on his own. Shouting that that was lèse-majesté, priests and astrologists gave it a somber interpretation: clearly, the child aspired to one day replace Pharaoh. Hence they urged Pharaoh to put the boy to death before it was too late. Fortunately, Jethro was present at the debate and suggested a more charitable solution: let two plates be placed before the child, one filled with burning coal and the other with precious jewels. If he seized the jewels, that would mean the priests were right in seeing in the earlier action a signal from the gods. If he touched the burning coal, it would simply mean that, like most children, he was drawn to shiny objects. Moses was about to touch the jewels when Jethro (or the Angel Gabriel) kicked him. At this, Moses picked up a coal instead and put it in his mouth, a gesture that saved his life—even if it made him a lifelong stutterer.

Thus we learn that at times it is by forsaking gold and jewels that one may prosper. But remember: this lesson was given us by Jethro.

Practically, we learn from all that preceded that one must never grant collective innocence nor collective guilt to any community. Every human being deserves to be judged for what he or she stands for. As for Jethro, whether or not he converted, he is worthy of our respect.

And the Amalekites?

Suppose an Amalekite man appeared before a rabbinic court, expressing his desire to be converted? On the level of pure Halakha, the candidate would not leave the court alive. Such is the law: whoever sees an Amalekite must kill him. But in reality, this could not be carried out—nor will it ever be. The possibility of encountering an Amalekite is implausible, and it has been so for innumerable centuries—more precisely, since the time of King Sennacherib, the Assyrian ruler who defeated King Ezekias and deported many men from vanquished nations and the ten tribes from Judah as well. The mixing of ethnic communities has made it forever impossible to identify an Amalekite. So the law may never be implemented.

IN CONCLUSION:

Since in Scripture Esau and Ishmael were human but not wicked, why have they been transfigured in midrashic imagination? And who are we to impute evil intentions to certain Gentiles today? We are not here to judge, only to bear witness. Self-respect is linked to the respect of others. To show disdain to another is to become a victim of one's own arrogance. To humiliate another is to debase oneself.

Said Rabbi Yehoshua ben Levi:

This is how the people of Israel justify before God their special relationship. They tell Him this parable: Sentenced to be sent away by the king from his palace, his wife told him: am I not the only woman that welcomed you under her roof? No, answered the king. It is I who chose you over all other women. No, said his wife. All women rejected you, I alone accepted you. Similarly, the people of Israel told the Lord: Master of the universe, am I not the only nation that has consented to receive thy Law? I pushed them away, answered the Lord. No, said the people of Israel. They did not want you. Why did you go to Mount Sair? Wasn't it to offer the Torah to Esau's descendants? And didn't you go to Mount Paran to offer the Torah to the descendants of Ishmael? You were ready to give it to them, but they were not willing to receive it. We were. We alone. Alone to say *"na'aseh ve'nishma"*—accepting the Law even before You gave it to us. . . .

In other words, the children of Ishmael and those of Esau had every opportunity to become, like their brothers and sisters, full-fledged Jews. If they had accepted, Jewish history and history in general would have been different. Was the choice theirs? All human beings choose what they are. But their past is contained in their present. With whatever I say and do, I may justify or not the faith of our ancestors in their future—for aren't we precisely that? Their future?

Does it justify the strains the oldest and most sacred of our texts nourishes toward such Gentiles? It is difficult, even painful, to come up with a plausible answer to this question, I admit. Naturally, a case could be made showing that Scripture is not much kinder to our Jewish ancestors. Moses' contemporaries could probably sue its adherents for slander. As slaves, they had to be persuaded by divine miracles and human pleading to leave Egypt. At Sinai they were asleep and God had to use thunder and lightning to wake them up and give them the Torah. Then, hardly had they gained their freedom than they rebelled against God and his emissaries. They were never satisfied, rarely grateful. Instead of thanking the God of Israel for having saved them from bondage, they worshiped the Golden Calf. They constantly complained: not enough meat, not enough bread, not enough water—when they had water, it was bitter. What they did to their leader Moses was not only unjust and uncivilized but also, quite frankly, embarrassing. So ugly was their conduct that the Almighty declared them unworthy of the ultimate reward, which was to enter the promised land.

Why are these tales told? First, because they happened. There is no cover-up in the Bible. The verse "Thou shall not hate your brother in your heart" is an injunction against hypocrisy: if you hate your brother, say so! Do not hide it from him. Open hostility is less dangerous than concealed hatred.

But there is another explanation. Beginnings are always violent, as they mean disruption of an existing order. That is why there is so much violence in our biblical tales.

Better to have violence in the beginning rather than later. Ultimately these violent tales preach against violence.

Is it too late to imagine ancient and timeless beginnings as warnings? It is not too late to remember that the tale is not for or about Jews alone, it is a Jewish tale for all of us.

Gideon, a Judge
Who Is Special

Now I invite you to meet an ancient judge unlike any other. Actually, the same has been said about all of them, and rightly so. All have some distinctive features that characterize their personality. But Gideon is still a case apart. The fourth in the line of judges separating the conquest of the land from the establishment of Jewish monarchy, he is special.

I hope you have carefully studied the chapters dealing with Gideon in the Book of Judges. I have read them ten times. With each reading, they offered me more enchantment. Most major topics about the human and Jewish condition can be found here: attitudes toward ambition, power, discipline, unity, solidarity, faith, peace—with one notable exception: love.

Gideon's story also begins badly, on a note of divine despair, and ends well, almost as the human fulfillment of a heavenly promise.

Like those who preceded him and those who followed him, Gideon too is called upon to combat with skill and vigor the traditional enemies of Israel. He too finds obstacles that seem unsurmountable. He too will eventually emerge as the savior of his people—our people. Still, there is something about him that makes him different.

First of all, he is appointed to his prestigious yet difficult national position not by a celestial voice but by an angel. He sees and hears that angel both in his sleep and while he is awake. One would like to get the angel's physical description: is he big, well built, joyous, energetic, sportsmanlike—or, to the contrary, small, frail, melancholy, with an intellectual look on his face? Sorry, but biblical texts are not journalistic reportage. Here what is said is important. The message outweighs the graphics.

Secondly, Gideon is lucky, for it is God Himself who dialogues with him. It is in the text. Gideon argues with God. And God needs to give him unusual signs and must perform various miracles to persuade him to accept a mission that will transform him into a new man.

Unknown heretofore, he now enters legend.

IN THE BOOK OF JUDGES, Gideon's tale begins at the end of the chapter that relates the stunning defeat of the Canaanite general Sisera. Though leading a well-armed, gigantic army, Sisera is brutally killed in his sleep, in the arms of a Jewish heroine, Jael, whose individual heroism inspires Deborah, the illustrious leader and poetess, to sing a song of admiration and gratitude for her courage.

What a marvelous piece of poetry that is! With beautiful lyricism, Deborah describes Israel's victory. Then, near the end, one feels a trace of compassion on her lips—compassion not for the fallen commander of the enemy army but for his anguished mother. Listen: "Through the window she gazed / Sisera's mother peered through the window / Why is her son's chariot late in coming? Why are the hoofbeats of his carriages so late?"

One cannot but like her for her compassion. Doesn't King Solomon warn us against rejoicing over the enemy's downfall? Still, Deborah also remembers the danger of excessive pity in times of war. She goes on imagining Sisera's mother waiting for her dead son: "The wisest of her ladies answer her, and she too, offers herself explanations: Are they not finding and dividing loot? A comely captive, or two comely captives for every man; booty of colored garments for

Sisera, booty of colored embroidery, doubly embroidered garments for the necks of the looters. . . ."

And Deborah concludes her song with these words: "So may all *your* enemies be destroyed, O God. And let those who love Him be like the powerfully rising sun," which, according to most commentators, gains power as it rises at dawn. Is it a blessing at all? Doesn't the sun also go down? "Those who love Him," sings Deborah. *Him*—not those who love *You*?

The chapter ends with a few well-chosen words filled with serenity and hope: *"Va'tishkot ha'aretz arba'im shana."* For forty years the land finally knew the blessings of peace.

At this point, one feels like applauding: thank God for the good news! Israel needs and deserves some respite, some breathing space. So—bravo Jewish history, thank you God of Israel, thank you for allowing your people to live for a while far from the outbursts of hatred and bloodshed, out of reach of enemies determined to oppress them and make them despair.

Forty years of national tranquillity on the borders, is there a greater blessing in the world?

The question sounds good. But it elicits yet another question: is tranquillity always a blessing? It may seem so while it lasts. Like everything else, like love or money, it all depends what one does with it. If it is used for good endeavors and worthy goals, it is commendable. If it is misused, it is not.

Let us read of the next phase of Jewish history. It immediately follows Deborah's song. Listen to the opening line of the next chapter: *"Va'ya'assu B'nei Yisrael et ha'ra be'einei Hashem"*—and the children of Israel did what was evil in the eyes of God.

On the simplistic level, this opening is not unusual in the Book of Judges. Remember, that period does not enjoy a good press, either in biblical or in Talmudic literature. While reading the verse *"Va'yehi bi'yemei shefot ha'shoftim"*—it happened once upon a time during the period when the judges were judging—Talmudic sages wondered: why such repetition? Isn't it the task of judges to judge? The question is pertinent—as is the answer formulated by Rashi: *"Oy lo le'dor she'shofet et shoftav,"* woe to the generation which is passing judgment on its judges. In other words: there are times when everything and everybody is corrupted, for all is evil in the eyes of God.

Such is the case of Gideon's generation. What were its sins and transgressions? The text does not enter into details, as if to say: the verse covers the general situation of moral decline. The entire community went astray. The second half of the same verse sounds as punishment: *"Va'yitneim be'yad Midyan sheva shanim"*—So God delivered the children of Israel into the hands of Midian for seven years.

Remember, in ancient parchments, such as the Torah scroll, there is no punctuation. So we may, as an experiment, do away with the periods separating the verses. Now the new sentence would read as follows: "And the land was peaceful for forty years, and the children of Israel did evil in the eyes of the Lord, and the Lord handed them over to the Midianites." A long sentence? Yes, but it makes sense. It is the eternal relationship between cause and effect, sin and punishment. This idea appears frequently in sacred texts. When the people of Israel move away from the Law, they will regret it. Even when God forgives, He does not forget.

But what is the cause in this case? Israel's sins leading to Midianite domination? Yes, but is there nothing before that? What about the forty peaceful years? Aren't they the primary cause? I repeat the question raised earlier: Is peace always a blessing? Here one gains the impression that there was a general atmosphere of complacency, probably due to excessive self-confidence. Things were going well. People were happy. No outside peril, no inside crisis. No confrontation with an invincible enemy. No unsurmountable challenge. Adults were busy making money, children playing in the garden. Teachers were teaching, adolescents discovered love. All was well on all the fronts. Too well, perhaps. So well that people forgot to whom they owed their happiness. That is how and why they did evil in the eyes of God—they did so perhaps without even realizing what they were doing.

Is this a lesson for generations to come? Faced with outside pressures, we mobilize our energies. We resist. In a world that hates us for being Jewish, we become more motivated, more courageous, more inventive—in other words, more Jewish. On the other hand, in a more tolerant and emancipated society, our front line appears to be less solid. Cracks become visible and numerous. Seduction is now a greater threat than persecution. Has anyone ever established reliable statistics on the number of Jews we have lost to assimilation, as compared to oppression?

And yet I do not believe peace to be dangerous to the Jewish spirit. During King Solomon's reign, Judah was at peace, and spiritually things were not bad at all. During the Golden Age, Jews and Muslims lived at peace with one another; and both of them bequeathed literary, philosophical, and theological masterworks to their respective religions. Oh yes, peace is truly a great blessing—when it is not a mirage.

Let us go back to Gideon. As a judge, is he really different from the others? He is less known than Samson, perhaps less perplexing than Jephthah. Is it that his biography is sketchier than theirs? It includes neither romantic adventures nor unnecessary words leading to the death of an innocent daughter. Of his life one knows only what is revealed in the text. Is he married? Yes, though nothing is known about his wife. Military experience? No idea why he was chosen to lead his people into battle. Any special religious education? His father, Joash ha-Ezri, was an idol worshiper. So were many of his contemporaries. As was Gideon himself? It is not clear. When he first appears on the stage we see him helping his father "threshing wheat at the winepress, to hide it from the Midianites." Then an angel appeared and said to him: "The Lord is with you, O mighty hero!" Now, had the angel appeared before someone else, Gideon would have remained a laborer, just as, if not summoned by God, Jephthah would have remained an outlaw and Samson a womanizer. But all three were chosen. Jephthah because of his leadership qualities and Samson because of his strength. But why was Gideon honored by the angel's visit? Actually, he was not the only one to see or hear the angel. Let us return to the story—and the text.

For seven years, dominated and oppressed by the Midianites, "the children of Israel made the holes, the caves, and the strongholds which are in the mountains. And it came to pass that whenever they would sow, the Midianites, helped by the Amalekites and the people of the East, would overrun them, destroying the produce of the land as far as Gaza, leaving no sustenance for Israel, neither sheep, nor oxen, nor donkeys."

Clearly, Israel's situation was desperate. Militarily weak and most probably demoralized, it inspired all its neighbors to join the aggressive Midianite alliance, invading the territory of the tribe of Menashe, bordering with the Valley of Jezreel, robbing and pillaging public stores and private homes. Their goal? The destruction of Israel's economy and livelihood first, then of its national sovereignty. Though terse, the text indicates the cruelty of the aggressor. No commentary is needed. But there is one. In the Midrash. It mentions the complicity of certain elements that collaborated with the enemy, bringing him to the hiding places where Jews kept their food reserves. Hence the striking expression *"Va'yidal Yisrael me'od"*—Israel was very impoverished. Said Rabbi Itzhak: impoverished in good deeds. Said Rabbi Levi: impoverished in everything.

Then, unable to bear it any longer, *"Va'yizzaku B'nei Yisrael el Hashem"*—the children of Israel cried out to the Lord. And the Midrash, as always full of imagination, offers us an illustration of the event:

This is how the children of Israel spoke to God. "When princes transgress the Law, it is enough for them to bring an offering, and they are forgiven. An anointed one who errs, it is enough for him to bring a sacrifice, and he is forgiven. But we have nothing to offer you, what can we do to be forgiven?" "Let the entire people bring one ox alone, and it will be accepted as sacrifice," answered the Lord. "But we are impoverished," cried out the people. "We do not even possess one ox." "All right," said the Lord. "Give me words of Torah, say some prayer, and that will be sufficient." "We do not know how to pray," said the children of Israel. Then God said to them: "All right, then weep, just weep, that will be sufficient."

They wept—and God received their tears. And he answered their silent prayers. He sent them a prophet. A Talmudic source identifies him as Pinhas son of Eleazar, the fiercest among Moses' disciples and faithful followers. If it was him, he must have been at least two hundred years old. Some sages believe that Pinhas, like the prophet Elijah, roams around history and the world on special assignments, bearing God's words to those in need.

In the text, the prophet addresses himself not to Gideon alone but to the entire community of Israel. His message is harsh, almost pitiless: "Thus said the Lord, God of Israel: I brought you up from Egypt and I removed you from the house of slavery. I rescued you from the hands of the Egyptians and from the land of all your oppressors, I drove them away from you and gave *you* their land. I said to you: I am the Lord, your God, do not fear the gods of the Amorites, in whose land you dwell—but you did *not* heed my voice." That's all he had to communicate on God's behalf. The rest was up to their imagination. As if to say: I have given you all that—and you have let me down. That is why you have been suffering. Then, an angel of God came and sat under the elm tree in a place named Ofra. Who was the angel? *Malakh* in Hebrew means emissary or messenger: was he the prophet who had spoken to the whole community? All we know is that the place under the elm tree belongs to Gideon's father, Joash ha-Ezri. Gideon is threshing wheat while the angel, seated under the tree, speaks to him as to an old acquaintance, greeting him flatteringly with the words "mighty hero." Why was the angel seated?

Let us interrupt the narrative and quote a marvelous midrashic commentary:

It is generally admitted that Gideon is neither a just man nor the son of a just man. Actually, in the Tractate of Rosh Hashanah he is mentioned, together with Jephthah and Samson, as one of the *reikim* or hoodlums of the community. That is why the angel sat down instead of addressing Gideon immediately. He needed time to find in Gideon something special, some kind of virtue, that would make him worthy of his task. Finally, he saw him with Joash ha-Ezri as they were threshing wheat. At one point, Gideon turned to his father and said, "Father, you are old; should the Midianites arrive, you will lack the strength to run away. Better go home, I shall work for you." So, the angel, reassured, turned to Gideon and said, "You have fulfilled the commandment of *kibud av*, of honoring one's father; you deserve to be the savior of the children of Israel."

In the text itself, the image of Gideon is unlike that of Jephthah or Samson, rather attractive. Neither arrogant not too modest. He is a young man who remembers the lessons of Jewish history he must have learned in his childhood—and who dares to question their validity or at least their relevance.

When the angel addresses him with the customary courtesy: *"Hashem imkha gibor ha'hayil,"* which means "May God be with you," or "God *is* with you, man of courage," Gideon doesn't ask him: Who are you, what do you want? He must have heard the prophet and made the connection between his admonishment and the angel's greeting. His answer reflects a bit of nervousness mixed with irritation: "I beg you, Sir, but if God *is* with us, why then have all the woes befallen us? And where *are* all the miracles our fathers always tell us about God freeing us from Egypt? And why has God abandoned us now and handed us over to the Midianites?" In other words, has God given us freedom only to take it back?

Here, lo and behold, it is no longer the angel but God Himself who answers: "Go with this strength of yours and you shall save Israel from the grip of Midian. Behold, I have sent you!"

Gideon should be happy—but he is not. Now he wants more. He wants certainty. He wants more than words, he wants proof that he was not dreaming or hallucinating. And so, like many of his peers among the prophets, he speaks with humility about his own shortcomings: "I beg of you, my Lord, with what shall I save Israel? Behold, my section is the poorest in the tribe of Menashe, and in my father's house I am the youngest!" In other words, how do you want me to undertake my mission without the proper means to fulfill it? Instead of reprimanding his skepticism, God gives him further reassurance: "I shall be with you, and you shall strike all of Midian as if it were a single man!" Now Gideon ought to be satisfied! He is not. What else does he want, our future hero? He says what is in his heart. Now he demands proof that it was really, unmistakably, truly God's voice he has heard. Listen to the way he formulates his wish: "If I have now found favor in your eyes, then please, give me a sign that it is you who is speaking with me!" And, thinking perhaps that God or his angel needs advice on how to do things, he offers it to him: "Please, do not depart from here until I return to you with my offerings." And God acquiesces: Do not worry, "I shall remain here until your return." Gideon returns, prepares his offering, and a flame comes out from the rock and consumes it before his eyes. Then the angel too disappears. At last, with all these signs, Gideon's last possible doubt has vanished; he is now persuaded that it was an angel, and that the angel was an angel of God. At this point, he is overcome with fear: is he going to die even before he can wage one battle for his people? Again God reassures him: "Peace unto you, do not worry, you will not die." In an outburst of gratitude, Gideon honors God by erecting on that very site in Ofrah an altar which he names "Shalom." The text says that this altar can be found there to this day.

Some of you may decide to go immediately to Israel and look for the place. But before you do that, I suggest we stop for a short while and reflect on the passage we have just studied together.

In Talmudic literature, special attention is given to it by a great number of sages. Gideon's encounter with God, or His messenger, presents some difficulties. They simply fail to fully understand God's choice: another man could have been a better candidate, more suitable for such a tremendous task. Not the youngest of a family, with no special virtues or gifts, and surely without political or military experience.

Listen to a Midrash: In those times, when the people of Israel endured extreme pain and distress, God was looking for someone who would plead to Him on their behalf, but so poor were they in good deeds and piety that He found none. Then, all of a sudden, Gideon appeared before His eyes. Gideon appealed to God for his humility, compared to that of Moses himself. One source says it explicitly: *Yeruba'al* (pseudonym for Gideon) *be'doro,* Gideon in his generation, *Ke'Moshe be'doro,* was as important as Moses was for his. Why? Because like Moses, Gideon pleaded for Israel even when Israel was involved in sin. The text itself hints at such interpretation. When God answers Gideon, saying, "Go with *this* strength," one is allowed to wonder: since Gideon hasn't done anything yet, what strength is God referring to? Obviously, He refers to Gideon's strength as displayed in his courageous response to the angel. He did not speak on his own personal behalf but on behalf of the people of Israel, who, contrary to His miracles in the past, have now been abandoned, deserted by God. Admit it, that took audacity. At that very first moment, during that initial encounter, yesterday's laborer became Israel's spokesman to God. That is why, says the Yalkut Shimoni, God, blessed be He, said to Gideon: since you had enough strength to defend the cause of Israel with me, you will become its savior. For when Israel is in danger, to become its defender is both a privilege and a priority. Listen to a Talmudic commentary: when Gideon, at the beginning, refused, or at least showed little enthusiasm, to accept the divine mission to save Israel, he committed seven sins. Still, God Himself forbade anyone to criticize him by taking all those sins on Himself. When Israel is in danger, God expects Gideon to become not its prosecutor but its defender.

Having received the signs, the principal elements of proof of his divine appointment and the promise of success, Gideon was ready. It was in a dream that he received from God—or His messenger—his precise marching orders: to search for and destroy all idols and their altars. And in place of the *ashera* post symbolizing the god Baal which belonged to his father, erect an altar in honor of the God of Israel.

How did he know that the dream was more than a dream? He knew. Fearing the hostile reaction of his father's household and the inhabitants of the city, he and ten of his men waited all day to carry out God's instructions that night. Next morning, the city people awoke and found all their idols and sanctuaries in ruins. One can imagine their anger. In fact, it's in the text. The action moves at a breathtaking pace: "They said to one another: 'Who did this thing?' " They began investigating. Feverishly, they sought for clues. Someone must have witnessed the destruction. "It's Gideon son of Joash who did this thing," was the unanimous opinion. They rushed to Joash and said to him: "Hand over your son to us; he must die, for he demolished the altar of Baal and has cut down the *ashera* post that was near it." Interestingly, they sought to punish Gideon alone but not his accomplices.

In the Midrash a question is raised: Why did Gideon need ten men to help him? Because he was afraid? Afraid in spite of God's assurances to stay with him and protect him? But then, what is the worth of all the compliments showered upon him? One sage at least offers him his support: Gideon needed ten men because, by obeying God's will, he wanted to sanctify His name in public. And for an act of *kidush Hashem,* a minyan of ten men is required. Still, he was the leader of the group. A follow-up question: Who denounced him? Was it one of the ten helpers?

Let us turn our attention to the city in which the story unfolds: Ofrah, as a community, as an urban center, is not a place of which the inhabitants or their distant descendants could be proud today. Frequently attacked, robbed, and humiliated by neighboring Midianite invaders, the citizens seemed to prefer submission to military, political, or even religious resistance. They got used to enmity and danger. Between two invasions, life continued as usual, gray and routine. The Midianite cult of Baal was celebrated, an altar to its glory erected, with the head of the community in person in charge of its daily upkeep.

It is not that the members of the tribe of Menashe broke their covenant with the God of Israel: they continued to have faith in Him and recall His miracles on their behalf. One legend has it that the episode in which Gideon plays the first part has taken place on Passover eve, or the day after, and that is why both the prophet and Gideon evoke the miracles performed by God in Egypt and afterward. People think of God because of the past, and of Baal because of the present: it's more comfortable.

In truth, Ofrah is not a unique case. The Bible and the Books of the Prophets are filled with tales in which God's wrath is poured over His people who are still too attached to idols. If there is one law on which God never compromises, it is the commandment against idolatry.

Except that idolatry takes on a variety of forms. That, for instance, of a Golden Calf, an ox, a tree—or of a human being. The absolute commandment forbidding idolatry, *"Lo yih'yeh be'kha eil zar,"* is strangely formulated. For those of you who know Hebrew it is clear that the verse ought to say *"le'kha,"* to you or for you, not *"be'kha,"* in you. This kind of transgression is more subtle, for it aims at the individual rather than the action. Its name? Vanity. A vain person is an idol worshiper, for he believes that he is superior to others, worthier than others, more intelligent and gifted than all of them: the vain are their own slaves, their own idols.

In Ofrah people are less refined. Their idols are man-made objects. Do they really believe in their divinity as good pagans do? Their sin lies in their complacency in following Midianite customs and practices. Searching for easy solutions, they compromise. They think that it is possible to attain a coexistence between God and idols. If they are outraged by Gideon's deed, it is because he imperiled not their happiness—how could they be happy under foreign domination?—but their stability. Actually, they hope that his father will be as indignant as they are. After all, isn't he also an idol worshiper? Hasn't he erected an altar for Baal on his own grounds?

But they forget that Joash is a father. It is the father, the Jewish father, not the half-assimilated man who confronts the enraged mob. His answer is brilliant, sharp, logical. Listen to the text: "And Joash said to those standing near him: Is it for you to avenge Baal? For you to come to his rescue?" He goes as far as agreeing with their judicial condemnation of the culprit: "Whoever offended him must die while it is still morning. But if Baal is a god, let him punish the man who destroyed his altar."

In other words, it is one or the other. Either Baal is a god, and thus all-powerful, capable of defending his own interest, or he is not a god, and thus powerless. In both cases, your anger is misplaced and your thirst for vengeance misdirected. The best thing for you to do is go home and leave us alone.

Strange as it may sound, that is exactly what happened. It is enough for one man to speak with courage for the mob to quiet down. One voice of reason can prevent catastrophe. Gideon's moral strength allowed that of his father to surface: father and son, united in faith, moved their community to reject bloodshed and idolatry. That day, says the text, Gideon received the surname Yerubaal, the victor over Baal, or the one who planted fear in Baal. That is how he is named in the Book of Samuel.

In general terms, Gideon is no longer the same. What produced the change in his personality? His encounter with God or His messenger? His faith, which he so dramatically recovered? His triumph over Baal and its worshipers? His conviction that it would surely provoke war with Midian? As a matter of fact, it will be a war not only with Midian but its allies as well, headed, as always, by the Amalekites.

Let us reopen the text:

"All of the Midianites, the Amalekites, and the sons of the East gathered together, crossed the Jordan, and camped in the Valley of Jezreel." And without any transition, the text reveals Gideon's new role: "God's spirit clothed Gideon. He blew the shofar, and the family of Avi-ezer was with him. He sent messengers throughout the tribe of Menashe, which also joined his troops. He then dispatched emissaries to the tribes of Asher, Zebulun, and Naftali, and they too became allies and companions-in-arms against the aggressor."

Well, Gideon has outdone himself. Yesterday's wheat thresher has overnight turned into a real statesman, demonstrating true qualities of political leadership and strategic command. Facing a multi-national and multiethnic enemy, he manages to create a multitribal army that remains linked by the same past and faithful to the same

God, all motivated by the same desire to ensure the religious and national sovereignty of their people and its land.

All things considered, the situation seems promising. Israel is united; it has a leader.

However, in lateral sources quoted by the Malbim, this beginning seems less encouraging. A pincer maneuver seems to have backfired, and units of the three armies that came to the rescue of Menashe were destroyed on the battlefield. One source maintains that Gideon's brothers also died there. Hence Gideon's sudden depression.

His customary sickness has awakened: he is overcome by doubts. The new Gideon is unable to get rid of them. At every step they grow in intensity. Before, it was so much easier. He threshed wheat by day and slept well at night. He knew how to protect himself and the wheat from the Midianites: the family's hiding places in the mountains were useful. Now, things have changed. Ever since God noticed him and placed growing responsibilities on his shoulders, he anticipates with anguish each event, every decision: he doubts his own judgment, he doubts himself. In spite of God's earlier kind words and gestures, he, the former laborer, a simple mortal, son of an idol worshiper, is still wondering whether he was worthy of his election; indeed, of his place in Jewish history.

At the very moment when the drama is knotted, before sending his troops for the first time to do battle with a powerful enemy, in his unexpected weakness he again needs to be reassured. For this, he challenges God. Granted, other leaders have done so—with heavenly permission, mind you: in the Jewish tradition, it is permitted to submit certain demands to the King of the universe. God knows both the beginning and the outcome. Man wants to obtain a spark of that knowledge, which is only natural. At times, God agrees. He even agrees to be tested. That too is part of our religious tradition. But in this case, doesn't Gideon go a bit too far? He addresses God as follows: "If you wish to save Israel through my hand, as you said you do, behold: I am spreading out a fleece of wool on the threshing floor. If there will be dew only on the fleece, and the entire ground will be dry, then I will know that you will help Israel through my hand, as you said you would."

This time again, God is willing to please him. "Gideon arose next morning and squeezed the fleece. He pressed dew from the fleece, a full bowl of water." Is Gideon happy now? No more self-doubts? He has received dramatic evidence of God's favorable attitude toward him, he must at last be at peace with himself.

Well, he is not. Like a child who plays games showing that he never runs out of new requests, Gideon dares to go further: "Do not be angry with me, I will speak only this last time. I will test you again but this time through the fleece of wool: let there be dryness on the fleece alone and let there be dew on the entire ground around it." Again, God was not angry at all. He did what Gideon wanted him to do: "On that night there was dryness on the fleece alone, and there was dew on the entire ground around it."

What can the reader say about such a double victory, God's followed by Gideon's? Patience, please. The war hasn't even begun yet. And Gideon's anxiety hasn't finished.

In the light of these events, Gideon has all the reasons in the world to feel proud. Proud of having united his people, proud of being the commander in chief of an immense army, proud of having collected so many promises, so many assurances from God. From now on, everything will be all right. Forward march, till victory. Our general well deserves a cup of champagne, kosher, naturally.

Not so fast, please.

Now it is God's turn to spring some surprises. Just as Gideon and his troops camp at Ein Kharod, facing the Midianites in the valley, God tells him that in His view the army is somewhat too big. Budgetary reasons? No. With God, all arguments are theological. With all these warriors, Israel is bound to win the battle, but what will public opinion say? That they won the war—they, not God. Therefore? Therefore a reduction in human participation is required. To allow Gideon to save face in front of his officers and men, God offers him clever practical advice on how not to embarrass soldiers who want to

go home but are worried over criticism: "Tell the people that whoever is afraid and trembles, let him turn back and depart at dawn
from Mount Gilead." Cowards in Gideon's army? No. Family men
eager to return to their families, that's all. Still, surely no one would
heed Gideon's call, or at least only a few would leave their comrades
to fight battles without them. You are mistaken. Twenty-two thousand men withdraw, only ten thousand remain. Not bad, as armies
go. A few divisions, regiments, brigades, composed exclusively of
elite fighters: all volunteers, the best, the purest, the most motivated,
the idealists. They will know how to fight valiantly, and win.

Well? Will the war finally begin? At the risk of upsetting lovers of
war stories, I feel compelled to warn against unnecessary haste. In
the eyes of God, who is after all the supreme commander of all
armed forces, Gideon still has too many troops. He is going to lose
many of them—not to the enemy but to God, who says that He
alone will decide who will be let go and who will stay. He asks
Gideon to take the remaining troops to the river. A new test is waiting for them there:

"Everyone who laps the water with his tongue as a dog laps, stand
him apart, as you will also separate everyone who kneels on his knees
to drink. And it happened that the number of those who lapped were
three hundred men, and all the rest knelt on their knees and drank
from their cupped hands. God then said to Gideon: through the three
hundred men who lap shall I save you and I shall deliver Midian into
your hands—and let all the others return to their homes."

Poor Gideon, who, with the overwhelming majority of his troops
gone, all of a sudden emerged as commander of a small group of
three hundred men. And it is with them that he is called upon to fight
an international military alliance! And he is supposed to come out
victorious! For this once, one understands his doubts. Except that
now they are less founded, since God has unequivocally, without
reservation, pledged to him that with these three hundred men he
will be victorious.

Of course, you may ask: what is this bizarre story about drinking water all about? Some men lap the water, and get an A, whereas others, the majority, kneel and drink from their cupped hands, and get an F? Where is logic in all that?

Let us open the Midrash. There everything is simple. Those who kneel to drink water have always knelt before idols, so they could not fight courageously against other idol worshipers. But, you may argue, since when is water an idol? Water is not an idol. Still, when one is bent over water, what does one see? One's own image. It is that image, says the Midrash, that they began to worship. Haven't we concluded a while ago that narcissism is a form of idolatry?

Now—having reached the very end of our capacity for both curiosity and patience, aren't we entitled to witness at least one battle, be it only to see how a few hundred young Jews defeated huge enemy armies? Sorry, we must wait for nightfall. For the dream of the oncoming night. Without dreams nothing is possible.

That night Gideon has a dream. What, a dream? Gideon sleeps? He will shortly act out the destiny of his people—and manages to fall asleep? Oh yes, he has strong nerves. All military chiefs have iron nerves. Having given the final OK for the D-Day invasion of France, the Allied supreme commander, General Eisenhower, went to bed and slept. But then, didn't Jacob—*lehavdil*—do the same the night before his fateful encounter with his brother Esau? Didn't he, in a dream, see a gigantic ladder whose tip touched the sky?

In his sleep Gideon hears God ordering him to go down to the enemy camp, which is practically already his. Had the dream stopped there, it would have been all right. But it continues with God adding the following advice: "But if you are afraid, take with you Foura, your young aide, and go there together. You will listen to what is being said in that camp. You will come back encouraged."

God was right. Gideon, the great hero, is afraid. He does what God has told him to do. The two men clandestinely penetrate the Midianite camp, which is filled with innumerable soldiers from all the nationalities in the region. Normally, before a spectacle of such power, Gideon would lose courage. But suddenly he hears two Midianites chatting about current events. One tells the other of a dream he recently had: a noise had arrived in the camp and made his tent crash. To which the other answers: it is the sword of Gideon son of Joash that is responsible for that; God has already decided to hand over the Midianite camp to him. Call it God's psychological warfare—but it is enough for Gideon. He realizes that the enemy army is demoralized. He quickly returns to his small group of soldiers and orders the attack.

For amateur strategists I suggest they read in the Book of Judges the passage describing the nocturnal offensive, with its many spectacular aspects. Gideon proves to be a brilliant commander with extraordinary imaginative powers. He uses horns, torches, and loud yelling to terrorize, shock, and paralyze the enemy. He knows how to benefit from the element of surprise by spreading confusion in the enemy ranks—the Midianites expected an army of thousands, not a small brigade of hundreds. The mobility of Gideon's officers, the psychological tricks, the secret transfer of some units from Ein Kharod to the Hill of More, the mobilization of other Jewish tribes, the swift decisions whom to send where, with what arms, to do what at what time, the order to conceal the flames of the torches, the pursuit of fleeing enemy troops in total disorder, the decapitation of their chieftains: you read the running story of these battles as if it were excellent reportage by professional war correspondents. Everything is in it. The intelligence of the commander in chief Gideon, the discipline of his men as they pursue the vanquished enemy soldiers: one would think that Gideon had never done anything else in his entire life.

Was it his idea to launch this exemplary preventive war? Was it God's? Now it's over. On the battlefields, the weapons fall silent. Israel's victory is total.

End of story? No. For Gideon, the wheat thresher who overnight became the triumphant savior of his people, it is far from being finished. The Midianite army is defeated but not annihilated.

Add to this a new episode. All of a sudden, almost with no transition, the text reveals a quarrel between Gideon and the tribe of Ephraim. Let us study the context: with the Midianites on the run,

Gideon asks the people of Ephraim, dwelling near the Jordan River, to intercept them and finish them off. The mission is magnificently accomplished. Two Canaanite princes are captured and beheaded by warriors from the tribe of Ephraim, who present their heads to Gideon. You would expect now to witness a scene of embracing and rejoicing among brothers. Again, you are mistaken. Let us read together.

"The men of Ephraim said to Gideon: what is this thing that you have done to us, not summoning us when you went out to fight Midian?" And they argued with him *behozka*, vehemently or violently.

What! Saved from death or slavery, Jews have nothing better to do than to quarrel? Oh yes, that happened then, and that happens these days too. It's part of human nature and social structure: we are together when facing danger, we move away from one another when the danger is over.

But things quiet down—thanks to Gideon. He flatters them, saying, "What have I now done compared with you?" And he uses a poetic metaphor: "Are not the gleanings of Ephraim better than the vintage of Avi-ezer? Into your hands God gave the Midianite leaders, Oreb and Ze'eb, and what have I done compared with you?"

Though these words could have been interpreted differently— emphasizing God's divine intervention rather than the courage of the neighbor's or cousin's warriors—they impressed Ephraim. The incident was quickly closed.

But there will be others.

While pursuing the Midianites, Gideon and his three hundred men (none of them fell in battle) crossed the Jordan and went through the city of Sukkot. To its inhabitants he said, Give us some loaves of bread, for we are exhausted and still hunting down the two kings of Midian, Zevakh and Tzalmuna. Incredibly, the leaders of Sukkot refused not only to feed them but also to believe them. They said, Are the kings already in your hands? Why should we give you bread? Losing his cool, Gideon predicted their punishment: "When God delivers the two kings into my hands, I shall thresh your flesh with desert thorns and briers." Gideon got the same reception in

Penuel. The same skepticism, the same lack of gratitude, the same insolence.

The real end of the war was now close by. Gideon and his men captured the Midianite army and brought its two kings to Sukkot. Meeting an adolescent in the street, Gideon asked him for a list of the city's dignitaries. The adolescent wrote down—which is proof that already then, everybody could read and write—seventy names. Gathered at a solemn session, Gideon addressed them not without sarcasm: "You wished to see the two Midianite kings before feeding my men. Here they are." Gideon kept his word. All seventy were punished. As were the leaders of Penuel, whose tower he demolished: they used to be proud of it; they no longer were proud of anything. Some inhabitants resisted with weapons; they were killed.

Having settled his accounts locally, Gideon turned his attention to the two royal captives. He questioned them: Who were the men you executed in Tavor? "They were princes like you," they replied. "They were my brothers," said Gideon, "sons of my mother. I swear before God who is eternal that had you spared them, I would not sentence you to death."

Question: was it only now that he discovered the death of his brothers, or was it a trick to see if the prisoners would have the courage to tell the truth? Opinions are varied. Anyway, for obvious reasons, the kings had to pay with their lives. What follows in the text is a surprise: "Gideon said to his oldest son, Yeter: Stand up, kill them." What! He had children? They weren't mentioned before! Where were they? What kind of father was he? Still young, Yeter did not draw his sword. He was afraid, says the text. Afraid of whom? Of what? Did the father insist? All we know is that both prisoners told Gideon that, as a matter of protocol or pride, they preferred to be beheaded by him. That was their last wish and Gideon granted it.

This time the war is *really* over. The people of Israel, recognizing what they owe Gideon, urge him to become their king, with the promise that his son and his son's son would inherit the crown. Gideon refuses: "Neither I nor my son nor his son will be your king: God alone is our king." Nevertheless he asks one favor: let the jewels taken from the enemy be his. He does not want them for himself. He makes them into an *efod,* a special vestment for the High Priest, which he hangs in his home in Ofrah. Doubtless he wishes that the people forever remember their debt to God. But the opposite occurred: people came to see the *efod* as if it were an idol. Comments Resh Lakish in the Talmud: three men lived a happy long life: Abraham, David, and Gideon. The first two deserved it, the third, Gideon, did not, for in producing the *efod* he turned the people of God away from God.

WE ARE ABOUT to reach the denouement of this disturbing story of a man who, even when he meant well, never succeeded in doing things without being criticized.

Granted, thanks to him, the country knew forty years of prosperity and peace. Gideon could go home and live a normal life with his family. We are told that he had many wives and seventy sons.

Listen:

After Gideon passed away, the children of Israel prostituted themselves again by adopting the cult of Baal, replacing their faith in God. They forgot the Eternal One, who saved them from all their enemies. And they showed themselves ungrateful toward Gideon, who worked and fought so hard for their well-being.

Like Joshua, he died alone and abandoned by the people whose defender he had been, first against God, later against the enemy. How are we to comprehend such a lack of gratitude on the part of a people who believe in it more than others? One sage comments: it is by behaving unkindly toward the House of Gideon that the people forgot God.

It is not for nothing that, as we have stated earlier, the generations of the judges are described with such harshness in Talmudic literature. Was it because of their penchant for idolatry? Their desire to forget where they came from was worse.

Gideon never forgot. I love him. Because he was not afraid to doubt certainties.

Samson:
The Weakness of a Hero

O<small>N THE SURFACE</small>, this tale may sound like a suspense story. A man is torn between his obligation toward God and his love for a woman. His heart is a battlefield. Polarized by two forces, which side will win?

Once there was a man endowed with such physical strength that no army could defeat him. The Greeks would have made him a god equal or superior to Hercules. Rome would have crowned him emperor.

In Jewish history and legend his name evokes the fantastic. He is Samson, or Shimshon, the heroic warrior who prevails over nature and its laws, over men and their aspirations to grandeur and conquest. He laughed at his enemies, whom he effortlessly vanquished. Nothing frightened him. The most savage beasts feared him. With one hand he was capable of reducing an entire mountain to dust. With both he gathered three hundred foxes and fastened torches to them to bring fire to enemy fields. His only weakness? Women. He who could stand up to mighty adversaries, yielded quickly to their charm and their beauty.

And yet he was a Nazir, a Nazirite, an ascetic man consecrated to

God, one of God's chosen. A man whom God needed to avenge His honor and save His people.

How can this be? How can a human being be made of such contradictory tendencies? On the one hand, the text describes his astonishing record as a judge in Israel; on the other, we frequently find him with attractive females who, moreover, are not even Jewish.

Samson, or the ambiguity of sacred heroism. Sometimes a conqueror, often a victim. Samson, or the man who eternally falls in love. Though he is strong against the mighty, he yields to what people once called "the weaker sex." Samson, powerless to master his roving eyes, unable to control his instincts. Samson young, Samson old. Samson and Delilah. The prisoner. Samson, courageous to the bitter end, dragging his haughty torturers and executioners down to share his own death.

The character amazes and overwhelms us by the challenges he constantly sets himself. From one episode to the next, we admire him, we love him, we pity him. And in the end we do not understand him: must he be so blind before losing his sight? Isn't he aware of the mysterious links between Eros and Thanatos, between love and death? And then, his parents, good Jewish parents, has he forgotten about them? Can't he guess, can't he imagine the grief he inflicts on his poor mother by his romantic adventures with pagans and their daughters, and especially with the *femme fatale,* Delilah? Oh yes, Samson entertains us, worries us, enchants us by the mere fact of his existence. It is reassuring to know that when the people of Israel are in danger, one man alone is able to defend them. But why alone? Doesn't he have companions, allies, friends? Why doesn't he raise an army? Why doesn't he organize a resistance movement? Isn't he a chief, a commander? Doesn't he believe in his people's will to fight for their own independence? Freud's biblical curiosity should have been directed at Samson, not Moses. Is it possible that Samson often accomplished his physical feats mostly to impress a beautiful lady?

When we study ancient Jewish history, we are exploring its impact on modern times. Samson worked, fought, loved, and died in Gaza—and Gaza is more topical than ever. Will the hatred toward Israel ever subside? Will peace prevail? What is required to stop violence as a method to attain national goals? Certain social conditions have changed since the age of Samson, but not human nature.

The tale of Samson, a story of blood and sensuality, charged with the romantic and the patriotic, has intrigued great thinkers, painters, and composers, from Milton and Voltaire to Handel and Saint-Saëns. But the most striking literary treatment was by Vladimir Jabotinsky. If Milton addressed himself to Samson because he too became blind, Jabotinsky made him the protagonist of his novel because he personified Jewish physical resistance to the military power of a foreign occupier. His advice to the Jewish people? Arm yourselves, and learn to laugh. But in the text, the character also deals with ethos in Jewish experience.

A few words about the image and concept of the hero in Jewish thought. Oddly, no fighter, no victor has been granted that title. *"Shimshon ha'gibor,"* Samson the hero? No trace of it in the Book of Judges, not even in midrashic sources. Physical force never impressed our sages, who defined heroism otherwise. *Ethics of Our Fathers* states: "Who is a hero? It is he who resists his instincts." In other words, heroism involves man's conquest of himself. To *renounce* something that one desires, to overcome passion, is heroic. Physical force is disdained in Talmudic circles. When Resh Lakish began studying Torah, he lost his physical powers. "The Torah weakens those who study it," believe our masters. Why do we say, at the end of the reading of one of the Five Books of Moses, *"hazak ve'nit'hazek,"* be strong and strengthened? Because having read the entire book, one becomes weak.

But Samson doesn't appear to have spent time in study. Is that why he was unbeatable for so long?

Let us read the text:

"And the children of Israel did evil again in the sight of the Lord; and the Lord delivered them into the hands of the Philistines for forty years."

Thus opens chapter 13 of the Book of Judges. The story is a series of connected, institutional episodes which illustrate divine justice as it moves between severity and compassion. Because the children of Israel sinned against God, He handed them over to the enemy. As a result, the Jews underwent so much suffering and humiliation that Samson was dispatched to save them. Nothing happens by chance. There are no coincidences in Jewish history.

The early chapters narrate the sacred more than the profane exploits of our hero. To stress that this is a real human being and not just a figment of the imagination, the text supplies abundant detail. We are told all that he does and all that he endures from his birth to his death.

At the beginning, divine Providence and intervention dominate the tale. A mystical atmosphere reigns from the first verses.

"And there was a man of Zorah, of the Danite family, whose name was Manoah."

As happens often in biblical accounts, his wife—unnamed—was "barren and bore not." Why the repetition in this factual report? The text is clearing the way for an angel who will express himself in the same manner. Speaking to the woman, he says: "You are barren, and have no children. But you shall conceive, and bear a son." Does he hope to convince her by repetition? Does he expect her to be incredulous, like Sarah before her? He continues: "Now therefore beware, I pray thee, And drink not wine nor strong drink, and eat not unclean thing, for lo, you shall conceive, and bear a son; and no razor shall touch his head: for the child shall be a Nazirite unto God from the womb. And he shall begin to deliver Israel out of the hands of the Philistines."

What does Manoah's wife do? She drops everything and rushes to tell her husband the thrilling news: "A man of God came to me, and his countenance was like the countenance of an angel of God, very terrible. But I asked him not whence he was, neither he told me his name. But he said to me, Behold, you shall conceive and bear a son. And now drink no wine nor strong drink, neither eat any unclean thing, for your child shall be a Nazirite to God from the womb to the day of his death."

We may admire her discretion! A stranger came to announce the most important piece of news of her life, and she never even asked who he was. More: she never really took a good look at him. The proof: she offers her husband no physical description of the face, except that he has the countenance of an angel of God. How did she know what an angel looked like? Perhaps her overheated imagination ran away with her. She was doubtless so moved by the news that in passing it along to her husband she embellished it a little. The angel had said, "The child shall be a Nazirite from the womb." But to her husband the woman quoted the angel as adding "to the day of his death." Is this to show that, God forbid, women are always reliable? That they are excitable and apt to exaggerate?

In general, her report to her husband of her conversation with the angel is incomplete. She does not mention what he had told her about her being barren, nor his injunction regarding her son's hair. She does not even relate his promise that her son would save the people of Israel.

Her husband Manoah's reaction? He prays: "Let the man of God whom You sent come again to us, and teach us what we shall do unto the child that shall be born."

But hadn't he heard what his wife said? Hadn't she told him precisely and clearly what *they* were obliged to do? Had he so little confidence in her memory?

Nevertheless, the angel returns. Faithful to his habits, he appears before the woman, not the husband. Now too she is alone in the fields. As before, she rushes to tell her husband, who hurries back with her. Breathless and full of trepidation, he asks: "Are you the man who spoke unto the woman?" "Yes," says the angel. "Tell us what to do with the child," Manoah says. The angel repeats his instructions yet a third time. But something is wrong: Manoah had asked the angel what *they* should do with the child, and the angel answers what *the mother* must or must not do . . .

Afterward, like Jacob before him, Manoah asks, "But what is your name?" And the angel replies: "Why do you ask my name? It is Peli," meaning "marvelous" or "miraculous." Upon hearing this, Manoah and his wife bring an offering to God. As for the angel, probably unwilling to expose himself to further questioning, he rises to heaven in the flames of the altar. Here a double transformation takes place. Up to now it is the woman who is excited, not her husband. But now their roles are reversed. In the throes of fear, Manoah cries out: "We shall surely die, because we have seen God." His wife takes it more calmly: "If the Lord wished to kill us, we would not have lived through all these events."

Listen:

"And the woman gave birth to a son, and called him Samson. And the child grew, and the Lord blessed him. And the spirit of the Lord began to move him at times in the camp of Dan between Zorah and Eshtaol."

So everything is all right. The parents are happy, God is pleased with his young Nazirite. The people are oppressed and hungry? Well, they're used to that.

Suddenly, the unthinkable occurs. One day, Samson, the young ascetic adolescent consecrated to God, leaves his parents' house and ventures into Philistine territory, to Timnath. As tourist or scout? Did he somehow learn that destiny had set up a trap for him there? We know only that he falls in love with a woman. What! He, the man who must renounce earthly pleasures, enamored of a woman, and a pagan to boot? A good son despite all this, he asks his parents' consent to marry her. We can imagine his parents' distress. They say to him, Couldn't you find a wife among the daughters of your own people? Perhaps they added, Why must you cause us such anguish? What will the neighbors say? Aren't you too young? And what will you live on? But Samson is stubborn: she is the only woman he loves. The Nazirite is human; his senses are alive, his desire burning.

Is this the first woman he has ever noticed? Is she his first love? If so, we understand. First love *is* special. We discover or invent all sorts of qualities and virtues and find them in the beloved. Is she beautiful?

Yes, the most beautiful girl in the world. Also the most graceful. To his parents he says, She pleases me well. From that point on, things happen quickly. What he desires he will possess. The girl says yes. Nothing can come between him and the object of his desire. A young lion attacks him? He tears it to pieces. He says not a word to his parents. Afterward, he is moved to look at the carcass of *his* young lion. A swarm of bees has gathered within it. He scoops out the honey, of which there is plenty, and offers some to his parents without telling them that he had taken it out of the carcass of the lion.

The wedding takes place. It is grandiose. Thirty young men of Timnath take part in the festivities, which last seven days. Samson tells them a riddle: "Out of the eater came forth meat, and out of the strong came sweetness." The winner is offered "thirty sheets and thirty changes of garments." No one is clever enough to suggest a solution. So they enlist the complicity of a double agent—the young bride. She should make him tell, isn't she their fellow citizen, their sister? She lets herself be persuaded, and so does Samson. How can he resist the tears and the charms of his young wife? He confides in her and she passes the answer along to the others. Immediately Samson realizes what has happened. Furious, he goes down to Ashkelon, kills thirty men, strips them, and flings their garments to the winners.

The marriage is over. Finished. To rub salt in the wound, Samson learns that his wife has married a Philistine friend. She didn't wait long to betray him.

Despite all his heroics, Samson is not the star of a B-movie: he loves women, but they don't return his love. Will he never learn? He has no luck with them. He thinks he's making conquests, but he is the victim. In the end it is a woman, Delilah, who will bring about his downfall.

We cannot deny the duality of the character as he is presented in the biblical text. He has remained a Nazirite—that is, he must not shave or cut his hair, nor drink wine—but he carouses with his friends. He is a fighter and as such unbeatable, but his physical strength derives always from the spirit of God. He is a Jew, but more often than not we see him in Philistine territory. He is consecrated to God, but in thought and deed he goes about chasing pagan females.

Is this the kind of behavior we expect from a political leader, from a judge appointed to arbitrate the differences of his tribe and the conflicts of his people? Does he even know the Law? He seems more an athlete, an acrobat, a kind of gladiator, than a moral guide.

The text calls him inspired: "the spirit of the Lord came unto him" is an expression we frequently find in the story. On the other hand, can we say that he is inspiring? If so, what does he inspire? Fear of heaven and love of God? We don't see him attending synagogue. Generosity to his neighbor? If that motivates him, the text is rather discreet about it. The commandment of honoring one's parents? The respect one owes them? Love of Israel? He is busier with another kind of love . . .

Samson a role model? Samson an example to the young?

THE TRUTH IS that in this whole picaresque narrative few characters are above suspicion. We hardly need mention Samson's women: they all cheat, they all play with him the better to sell him to his adversaries. His friends? They incite his wife to turn away from him. His former best friend seizes the first opportunity to run off with his bride. His in-laws slam the door in his face. The angel? All right, we never question angels. Besides, this one never answers, at least not to the point. Samson's parents? A just man and a just woman, surely. Otherwise they would not have been blessed with a Nazirite son like Samson. But how did they rear their only child? Didn't they spoil him a bit too much? Did they ever criticize him or punish him for a lapse of speech or conduct? And why did they let him spend so much time away from home? Why did they fail to make him realize that a nice Jewish boy's place is not among Philistines? Obviously he had many, too many Philistine friends. Weren't thirty local companions, all Philistines, invited to his wedding? And his parents said nothing? Why did they let him marry a pagan woman? Why did they become accomplices by helping him with the hand of his chosen bride? Why did Manoah's wife not behave like a good Jewish mother who, in that situation, would scream, tear her hair out, cry to heaven and earth for mercy?

As for Samson, how can we explain his apparent indifference to the possible anguish of his parents? Did he love them enough, did he even consider them? Didn't he realize that in marrying a Philistine girl—not only pagan, but the daughter of the oppressors—he ran the risk of breaking their heart? Did he feel no compassion for them? How did he think they felt as they attended his wedding surrounded by Philistines? In the end he confided his secrets to his wife, but not to his father and mother. Did he trust a Philistine woman more than his own flesh and blood?

Regarding his qualities as a political and military leader, the truth is, they are hard to identify. A leader must be able to mobilize his community and motivate its soldiers. But he did everything by himself. All alone he inflicted punishment and reprisal upon the enemy. He was always, as in the earliest days, a solitary warrior who rose up against the enemy. Worse: incidents in which he figured usually centered on him as an individual, as a ridiculed, infatuated, rejected husband, and not on the people of Israel. Is that why they never rallied behind him, to support him in battle?

Still, I cannot shake off the suspicion that during his rule *the people* were lacking in courage and dignity. We do not leave the commander to fight alone. We do not abandon him in prison. Worse: who delivered him to the enemy? The leaders of the tribe of Judah. The text says so. Granted, he belonged to the tribe of Dan on his father's side, and to Judah only on his mother's, but wasn't he a Jew, a proud Jew? He always insisted on his Jewishness. How could Jewish leaders do that to him, especially when they knew the fate awaiting him at the hands of a ferocious enemy thirsting for revenge? And where were the leaders of Dan? Why didn't they intervene? Then again, if the people were weak, was it not their chieftain's fault?

And yet . . .

As usual, the Midrash sees matters in a different light. There everything is both more subtle and amplified. And shaded.

In the opinion of some commentators, Manoah and his wife were worthy of visits from an angel, so close were they to perfection. The verse "There was once a man named Manoah" is interpreted thus: "a man" signifies a unique man, unique in his generation, that is, better, purer, more pious, more devout, more just. His wife also? Naturally. Otherwise a just man like him wouldn't have married her.

Others emphasize their humane aspect. Instead of explaining their barrenness by divine will, the couple blamed each other. Manoah said, It is because of you that we are childless. And she said, It is *your* fault, it is you who are sterile. The angel's role was to restore domestic harmony.

Why did the wife distort the angel's promise by adding that the son would be a life-long Nazirite? Because she really thought so. Not being a prophet, she could not foresee Samson's spiritual decline. Besides, what mother could imagine such a thing about her cherished only son?

As for Samson himself, the makers of Talmudic legends rely on the expression *ki to'ena hi* to explain his blinding passion for his first Philistine spouse. "It was God's will." More simply: ultimately heaven is responsible. For everything. For his seeking a quarrel with the Philistines, for his provoking them to provoke him, for giving him a pretext to fling himself upon them and strike them with the full force of his rage. His parents could not know, says the text. They could not surmise that their son's behavior was part of a grand strategy devised by God Himself.

Here we touch on a strange topic called *"Mitzva ha'ba'a mitokh avera"*—a good deed resulting from transgression, a concept that has been distorted and abused by false Messiahs, the Sabateans and their followers, the Frankists.

Is it possible that a violation of the Law could produce something beneficial if not holy?

Some Talmudic sages answer in the affirmative. They offer as an example Lot's daughters, who made their father drunk and bore his sons, which was of course sinful. But they had meant well. Thinking that the world had come to an end at Sodom, they wanted to save the human species. Commented Rabbi Nahman bar Yitzhak: a transgression with pure intentions surpasses an intentional good deed. Luckily this attitude is overruled in our tradition.

Who then, in the story we examine here, is guilty, and who is innocent? Certain sages do not hesitate to take a position: of the Jewish protagonists few are guilty. The parents are surely beyond reproach. Their son's marriage to a Philistine girl? She was *not* really a Philistine. Surprised? Yes, these wonderful commentators assure us: she had converted long before, probably clandestinely. Samson, no matter how infatuated, would never have caused his parents pain. It's quite simple: if he married a girl, she must have been Jewish.

As for his numerous extramarital affairs culminating in bloodshed, this is seen as a shrewd tactical ploy, a ruse, a manipulation. In his blessing upon his children, Jacob compared the tribe of Dan to a serpent. Like the serpent, say some commentators, Samson did not kill for pleasure but in self-defense. Like the serpent, Samson adapted himself to his social and ethnic surroundings, the better to surprise his prey. In other words, Samson was a superb secret agent, an underground fighter. Fearing collective reprisals against his people, Samson *acted* the libertine, the Don Juan. He was careful to make the Philistines think that if he burned their fields and struck down their young men, it was not out of patriotism but for more intimate reasons.

BRAVO, SAMSON. By fooling his enemies, he has managed to rehabilitate himself. Explaining the secret of the name "Shimshon" (*ki shemesh u'magen Hashem elokim,* God is the sun and shield), Rabbi Yohanan declares, "Even as God protected the world, so Samson protected the people of Israel." In the Tractate of Rosh Hashanah, he appears presiding over a court intellectually and morally equal to that of the High Priest Aaron.

Better yet: in the midrashic literature of the Palestinian Amoraim, after Bar-Kochba's heroic and tragic revolt, some sages see further, much further, and see in Samson the Messiah himself.

It is Rabbi Hamma bar Hanina who states it with disconcerting assurance. He bases his reasoning on Jacob's prophecy before his death, in Genesis 49:16: "Dan shall judge his people, as one of the tribes of Israel. Dan shall be a serpent by the way, one that bites the horse's heels, so that his rider shall fall backward." (They even say that after a vision of Samson's fearful death, Jacob lamented, saying he did not think that he, the hero, was going to die.) It was then that Jacob cried out, *"li'yeshuatekha kiviti Hashem"*—O Lord, your help is my hope. For Rabbi Hamma bar Hanina the message is clear: since Samson son of Manoah belongs to the tribe of Dan, Jacob is referring to *him*. For twenty years he will serve as judge in Israel, judge *of* Israel. And since, on his mother's side, he belongs to the tribe of Judah, it is clear that he will be the Messiah of the line of David— David who will also descend, much later of course, from these two tribes.

The Sifre is even more specific. Quoting a biblical verse in which "the Lord showed *Moses* all the land of Gilead, unto Dan," the commentator says, "God pointed out to him the future Savior of Israel. . . . And who was it? Samson son of Manoah."

Samson the savior, the Messiah of Israel? Is it thus that our ancestors, our people's teachers, guides, and visionaries, imagined the Messiah of David's line?

Why? Only to confer a transcendent meaning on a being who operated in *real* situations? To link his legend with that of Bar-Kochba, whose image, as presented to us, is also far from the profoundly spiritual aspirations of our people? Possibly. I've never reproached anyone for an excess of imagination—unless that person called himself an historian.

But in my opinion, what we have here is a confusion of names. Those who saw a future savior in Samson believed in two Redeemers and were probably referring to a Messiah of the seed of Joseph, not David.

A tragic Messiah, a savior abandoned, beaten, tortured, a Messiah defeated and killed in battle, that is the fate of the Mashi'ah ben Joseph, the Messiah son of Joseph. The fate of a hero who does *not* triumph over destiny. A hero who has slipped up somewhere, who, for reasons that he himself could not fathom, allowed himself to be destroyed by dark forces.

Finally, it is not the Philistine armies that defeated Samson. It is first and foremost the Jewish leaders of Judah who, threatened by the Philistines, delivered him up to them. On that count his fate was more tragic than the Messiah son of Joseph, who fell in armed combat against the enemy.

WE HAVE ARRIVED at the end of Samson's adventurous life and at the climax of his turbulent story. At this point, all trials, conquests, and disappointments are behind him. In prison, in chains, what does he think about, what memories stir his hopes, or illuminate them? The episode of the three hundred foxes, living torches, unleashed upon the enemy's fields, must give him pleasure. And the story of the jawbone of an ass? Ah, how he surprised the Philistines, freeing himself suddenly from the strong ropes that bound him and, taking up the jawbone, killed one thousand men. Afterward he was dehydrated, feverish. Fearing death, he called on the Lord: "Thou hast given this great deliverance into the hand of thy servant: and now shall I die for thirst?" God performed a miracle: He cleaved a hollow place in the jawbone, and water sprang forth. Why did Samson not thank heaven? Did he regret this omission? One commentator says this was the turning point of his life. He forgot his obligation to give thanks. Ingratitude is the first sign of indifference. A man who does not know how to say thank you—something in his psyche is already impoverished.

In the cell for those condemned to death, does he think back to his first wife, burned to death in a fire set by the Philistines? Or to the harlot he visited in Gaza? His enemies surrounded the house, preparing to kill him in the morning. Who tipped them off? The harlot? No matter. At midnight, "he took the doors and the gate of the city, and the two posts, and went away with them, bar and all, and put them upon his shoulders, and carried them up to the top of a hill that is before Hebron." Ah, the look on their faces when those armed men saw that!

Then at a place called Nahal-Sorek there was Delilah—the most striking and captivating of all women. He saw her and loved her. It was as simple as that. Listen to the Midrash:

"It is with his eyes alone, without touching her, that he conquered her." For the first time the text uses the verb "to love": *va'ye'ehav.* He had scarcely seen her when he fell madly in love with her. Love at first sight. If he had known more about etymology, he might have sensed danger by her name alone. Delilah derives from *dal,* impoverishment, diminution. Even if that had not been her name, says the Midrash, it should have been, because it was she who impoverished Samson's heart, mind, and soul.

The seductress, the enchantress made no effort to resist the Philistines' demands upon her. She knew just how to pull his secret from him . . . He tried to stall, to invent stories. Finally, he told her about his hair. As a Nazirite, it was a symbol of his strength. One midrash claims that she used Lysistrata's method, and said to him, If you won't tell me the truth about yourself, you can't have me.

To be fair to our hero's manhood, we add another midrashic commentary: the whole time he was in prison, the men of Gaza came to offer him *their* women, so that they might bear his children. Irony of ironies: he had actively chased women, and now they were brought to him. That's what it is to be vanquished and imprisoned: you let things happen. It is not the hunger or the sleeplessness or the cold or the thirst or the solitude: it is becoming an object in the hands of others—an object of cruelty or of love, it does not matter, and you do not have to be inside a prison to be imprisoned.

But Samson *is* in prison. Caged, he becomes a wild beast trained to entertain, to perform. The worst of his humiliations? While he once inspired fear, he now inspires laughter. He has become a spectacle, a pastime. This is unquestionably the most tragic part of the whole tale. It is here that the enemy's cruelty finds its most brutal expression. Now we understand why, much later, Agag, king of the Amalekites, like King Saul, probably preferred death to captivity.

In their cowardice, the Philistines carry their cruelty even further: they gouge out Samson's eyes. Is it possible that those eyes worried them? That they endowed them with a power as mysterious as that inherent in Samson's hair?

In truth, what he saw, he took. Samson lived by his gaze: where he glanced, he ruled. Measure for measure, says tradition. The punishment is linked to the sin. Avshalom sinned with his long, beautiful hair, so he died hanging by his hair. By his eyes Samson committed his sins, according to one midrash; his eyes were punished. From now on his imagination will be the worst of his tormentors. Whom or what does he think about? The wrongs he committed? Their irreparable nature? His parents, long dead? His people, who are doing nothing to liberate him, who have never shown any compassion toward him, much less solidarity with him? God and His messenger? Is Samson angry at the angel who predicted that he would be a Nazirite?

As for his special status as a Nazirite, how does he view it? Does he realize that the whole concept of asceticism turns on *shmirat ha'lashon*, the obligation to be prudent in speech? Just say "I am a Nazir" and you are. Just say "my son will be a Nazir" and he will be. So beware . . .

Weeks and perhaps months have passed since Samson's capture. His hair has begun to grow out, but not enough to restore his original strength.

An adolescent boy leads him to the place of execution. Once more he is in Gaza, a city which has always meant, and perhaps will always mean, trouble for Israel.

Who is the boy? I would give much to know his name. I picture him as sweet and gentle, the text itself suggests this. Samson leans on his fragile shoulders. The boy speaks to him. And guides him. One last time Samson wants to feel free, to act like a man, master of his own movements. And thanks to his unique young friend, he will be.

The immense temple of Dagon, with its gigantic columns, is

crowded with revelers. The whole population of Gaza is there, on the balconies, to enjoy the spectacle. Below, forgetting the part played by Delilah, the Philistine princes thank their god for delivering their formidable enemy into their hands. "Let him entertain us," they cry. The prisoner complies. The text does not tell us how, but it is easy to imagine. Doubtless they make him dance like a bear, lurch like a clown. Delighted and proud, they all applaud.

To the young friend holding him by the hand Samson says, "Let me feel the pillars, that I may lean upon them." To save the boy's life Samson asks him to go, to leave him alone. The prisoner is going to avenge himself, and he knows how. He also knows why. And most of all, for whom. This time the honor of Israel is at stake, the honor of the God of Israel.

As long as his enemies tortured Samson, he said nothing. But now they were attacking God. They were mocking and ridiculing the God of Israel, who gave His Name to the people of Israel. To the prisoner this has become intolerable. It is a matter of *kidush Hashem*, of sanctifying the holy Name. Samson wraps his arms about the pillars to his right and left. And he murmurs a prayer: "O Lord God, I pray thee, remember me, and strengthen me, I pray thee, only this once, O God, that I may be at once avenged of the Philistines for my two eyes . . . Help me make them pay for at least one of my blinded eyes." The midrashic version set down by Rav is more explicit: "Remember, Lord," says Samson, "that during the twenty years when I was judge and commander in Israel I never asked anyone to carry my walking-stick from one place to another." In other words, he never asked anything of anyone. Has Samson become a humble hero? A man alone. Turning his possible failing into virtue, he insists that all he had to do, he did himself. This is the true prince, the true leader: he feels no need to diminish others to prove his own superiority. In Jewish tradition, true victory neither requires nor implies the defeat of the enemy. He who humiliates, humiliates himself.

And God grants Samson's prayer. *"Tamut nafshi im Plishtim,"* cries the condemned man. Let me die with the Philistines. Let my end be theirs as well. He causes the columns to sway and tremble. And in a deafening roar, the building collapses. And, says the text, "the dead which he slew at his death were more than they which he slew in his life."

Then, and only then, his brothers and the members of his tribe came down from their camps and took care of the funeral arrangements. It seems that Samson was finally loved. They all accompanied him to his last resting place. Between Zorah and Eshtaol, he was laid to rest in the tomb of his father Manoah.

The tale ends with a brief reminder: *"V'ehu shafat et Yisrael esrim shana"*—and he was a judge to his people for twenty years. Why the *vav h'akhibur*? Why the *"and"* he judged?

A commentary of the Midrash: this verse applies not to the past but to the future; even after Samson's death, he inspired fear and awe in his people's enemies. He went on defending his people for another twenty years.

Yes, that too is part of Jewish history and memory. One generation is sometimes protected by another.

Question: Since everybody died, how do we know what he said?

We mentioned the young boy who led him into the temple. I said how deeply moved I was by that adolescent who was Samson's last friend and whose life he wanted to spare by sending him away. Well, I believe it was that boy who told the story. Samson's voice was powerful enough to be heard outside. Samson entrusted him with his memory.

Some of us remember older men and women who did what they could "over there" to save younger comrades, saying to them: you are young, you may live, tell our tale . . .

Saul and His Lost Kingdom

T HIS IS THE story of a journey—a journey to the end of fear, to the end of night, filled with melancholy, solitude, and anguish.

It is a heartbreaking story, one that deals with all the elements, all the themes that constitute the fabric of tragedy in life and literature: prophecy and madness, hope and betrayal, jealousy and acceptance, military adventures and secular ambitions, poetry and thirst for power; it even deals with the occult.

There is drama in it. And suspense. And action. On many levels, for many reasons. It is a story filled with passion, but lacking compassion; its characters, in constant conflict, are unable to cut themselves away from misfortune—a misfortune that is hunting them down and that, in a way, they are pursuing with an intensity that ultimately cannot but crush them.

The isolation of a king—the first and last of a dynasty. The fall of a kingdom, the birth of another. The deterioration of a dream, of a friendship too. One leaves this tale overwhelmed by grief.

T HREE MEN WALK quietly in the night: the king and his body-guards, silent shadows moving breathlessly so as not to make a sound. The enemy, powerful and bent on vengeance, has established camp nearby, at Shunam. To reach Ein-Dor, a tiny village in the foothills of Harei-Ephraim, they must follow a narrow path bordering the Philistine encampment. The smallest carelessness, the simplest error, could be fatal.

This is why King Saul has chosen to discard his royal attire. Should he be captured by the Philistines, he would be taken for an anonymous, unimportant Jewish wanderer.

After several hours, the three men reach their destination. Huddled in darkness, Ein-Dor is asleep. Blind houses; the village is motionless; lifeless.

Still, the three visitors manage to find their way around. Perhaps the king's companions are familiar with the place. One of them knows the person the king wishes to meet: the local sorceress. One of the last to remain alive; for the king has massacred most of them. And she agrees to receive the unknown visitor, listen to his plea, and help him, only because one of his companions is known to her. One midrash claims that she was the mother of his principal lieutenant, Abner. Well, what does he want from her? To put him in touch with a dead man. That's all? Nothing could be simpler. She wants to know: What man? The king, still incognito, tells her: Shmuel—Samuel. She does her work and sure enough here is Samuel back from the other side, back from the world of the dead. Only now, because of him, does the witch recognize the king. She is frightened, but he reassures her: nothing will happen to her; she is safe. But he, the king, is far from being reassured. How could he be?

Samuel, the prophet, speaks to Saul in anger: "Why did you disturb my peace?"

"I need you," says the unhappy king. "I need help. I am going to war tomorrow without knowing whether God is with me or against me. I am afraid. Help me; you can, you alone can. Tell me God's will—only you can do that since God refuses to speak to me or even notice my presence. It's as though I don't exist for Him. You, the prophet and defender of God's first king, you must come to my aid."

But Samuel, from beyond death, refuses, and continues angrily:

"You want my help? Now? First you deny God's word, ridicule God's command—and now you wish to be helped? No, you are lost. And it is time you realized it. Your enemies will defeat you in battle; you will perish and worse: your kingdom will perish with you, Another man will follow you, succeed you as king of Israel—and his house will not be destroyed, ever."

And the prophet withdraws, leaving King Saul shattered by despair, unable to speak, to cry, to move, to protest, to howl, to throw his pain, his anguish, into the face of history, into the night which, outside, grows more and more menacing. He wants to return to his headquarters, to his home, but he feels weak. So much so that the witch feels sorry for him and offers him a meal. Eat, she says. It will do you good. Indifferent, proud, he rejects her pity. We now leave the occult and the scene becomes real, realistic, almost grotesque: his two companions join the sorceress in insisting that he eat. And he gives in. And Saul, once upon a time a mighty and glorious king, partakes there of his last meal. Then he leaves.

He returns to his camp, where his sons, his lieutenants, his soldiers, are waiting for him. He walks slowly, slower than before, lost in thought; he lives his last night fully aware of it. Tomorrow, for his ultimate battle, he will not be able to count on anyone. For him and his allies, it will all be finished tomorrow. He knows it, and he goes toward death alone. The king, anointed by God, is alone like God—and silent like him.

AT THIS POINT of the narrative, perhaps we ought to stop briefly to catch our breath and also to examine the meaning of this strange episode: how are we to understand Saul's nocturnal visit at Ein-Dor? Did he want to see Samuel again in order to come closer to God once more? Didn't he know that the way to God does not lead through the violation of his laws forbidding contact with the dead? Didn't he understand that by soliciting the help of the witch he but increased the distance separating him from his only source of salvation? Did he really think that Samuel, prophet and priest, messenger of God, would address him in a language other than that of anger? Or was he that desperate? And if so, since when? And whose fault was it? That of men who had abandoned him or that of God who had rejected him? If God was the reason, if God was the answer, why didn't he turn to him directly, without intermediaries? Could it be that he came to Samuel fully aware of the futility of his move? Could it be that he knew that it was for nothing—that nothing could or would change after their meeting? Is it possible that he came to Ein-Dor in order to be defeated once more? To be humiliated again? To attract Samuel's anger and the old witch's pity? To illustrate his downfall and accelerate its pace? And bring to a climax the process of self-destruction?

These are but a few of the disturbing questions we are confronted with when we explore the life and career of King Saul. There are more, many more. Some will necessarily remain unanswered. But even so, the very questions will help us get a better understanding of an extraordinary character—extraordinary because of the problems he raises and the events he recalls; he is both pathetic and mysterious, both disquieting and beautiful, and human, profoundly human even, if not especially, in his shortcomings.

We are immediately conquered by him. Majestic and simple at the same time, he inspires sympathy and commands respect. After his coronation, he does not settle in a luxurious palace, nor does he look for praise and glory. He works like everyone else, behaves like everyone else, and uses his position to strengthen the security of his country. Having accepted Samuel's constitution, he installs a state council with ministers and officers, and transforms every village into a fortress, every citizen into a fighter.

When Nahash, king of the Ammonites, launches an attack from across the Jordan against the tribes in Gilead, Saul calls for collective action. He orders a yoke of oxen to be cut into pieces and sent to the neighboring regions with a warning: whosoever would not follow Samuel and Saul, this would be done to his oxen. And everybody understood. And everybody followed.

Israel's political history begins with him. During his rule, Israel becomes a power to be reckoned with.

But then—why was he pushed into degradation? Why did his kingdom end with him? Why was he condemned to live with a past, but denied a future? Because he offended Samuel's sensibilities? Because he wished to spare the life of Agag, king of the Amalekites? Or because he visited the old witch at Ein-Dor? Or simply because God changed his mind and suddenly preferred David? Here was a man, good and faithful, whom God made leave the house of his father. Saul had never dreamed of becoming king, had never aspired to rule over anyone—he had been chosen by God for a task that he did not seek. Why then was he slandered, judged, punished? Did God draw him closer only to strike him better?

No wonder that he has captured the fancy of the great among poets, painters, composers. Rembrandt and Holbein, Byron and Rilke, Lamartine, Handel, D. H. Lawrence and André Gide, all were inspired by the tragic nobility, the romantic gravity of his singular yet exemplary destiny. More than any king that followed, Saul intrigued creative spirits. More even than David, whose impact was greater both historically and metaphysically, Saul attracts anyone who approaches Judaism from an aesthetic or ethical viewpoint. David and his conquests make us proud; but it is Saul and his failures that intrigue us. More complex than David, more tormented, more tortured, Saul pulls you along to mountain heights and then drops you into the abyss. Few ever experienced as many metamorphoses, as many dramas, as many breakdowns, as he did; few destinies ever followed as fast a rhythm, or had as many ups and downs in rapid succession. Few men knew such glory and few lost it for reasons as absurd.

Saul: a flame caught in the tempest. Saul: a triumph of melancholy. His is a story of solitude. A beautiful adventure that turned sour. An *acte manqué*. A story of misplaced pity. Let us try to lift the veil covering his face and his illness.

We intend to draw a protrait of Saul using various texts from midrashic literature. Stories will be as interesting to us as history—we shall look at legends as much as at facts, if not more so, for legends, in a sense, are as instructive as facts: they are what enriches and stimulates memory.

The narrative opens with a rather banal episode about mules who have gone astray somewhere in the fields—or in the text—just like that, by accident, without telling us why. Their owner, a man of the tribe of Benjamin, sends his son Saul to recover them. Without success. Instead, Saul meets Samuel, who tells him, with no preparation or introduction, that he will be king. And so—he did not give up a kingdom for a horse, but mules for a kingdom.

Suddenly, Saul changes: he becomes another person. The text says so with great emphasis: *"Ve'nih'ye le'ish aher."* He falls under the influence of Samuel, he turns into an emissary of God, a man above men; a man with a secret. He is marked by destiny, becomes part of the chosen class. From that moment he no longer expresses himself as before, in terms of daily work and sustenance. He forgets his mules, his mind is elsewhere, his soul is in a turmoil. He joins a group of wandering prophets and adopts their bizarre behavior. He sings and dances and shouts like them; he takes part in their services with ecstasy. His former friends are astonished and wonder aloud: What? *Hagam Sha'ul ba'nevi'im?* Saul—a prophet? It seems incredible to them, impossible. His uncle questions him: all this is very nice, very entertaining, but what about the mules—where are the mules? And Saul must leave the lofty level of spiritual discoveries and come down to earthly affairs. And speak about . . . mules. Don't worry, he says, they have been found. And that is all he says. He does not reveal the great change that has occurred in him, a change that instantly turned the poor shepherd into a ruler. He keeps his secret to himself. Not even his prophet-friends are informed.

The fact that his joining the prophets provoked such surprise means that he did not fit the part; he neither looked nor behaved like a prophet. He was neither particularly pious, nor learned, nor observant, nor wise, nor ascetic.

Actually, we do have his description. The Bible tells us that he was young, handsome, good-hearted, and tall; head and shoulders above all other men in Israel. He was virtuous and shy—as are many giants who find their physical strength somewhat cumbersome. What else? He was a good son. He listened to his father and obeyed his orders

without questions: for three days he looked for the lost mules—
because his father had asked him to do so. His visit to Samuel was his
father's idea; Saul himself would not have taken the initiative—so
deep was his respect for his father. And when the prophet mentioned
something about royalty, he answered modestly that he did not
deserve such an honor—and anyway that his father was waiting for
him . . . and for the mules.

The Midrash describes him more poetically, more imaginatively—
and less realistically. He is pure. And "innocent like a one-year-old
baby." Extremely devoted to his people, infinitely loyal to God. Brave,
always ready for battle in the name of Israel and the God of Israel. An
excellent Jew and a valiant soldier, he observes the religious precepts
even while in military service. Strange, but the Midrash seems to prefer him to David: David, says the Midrash, had many wives; Saul only
one. David marched behind his troops, while Saul led them into battle. David loved to take, Saul liked to give. After defeating Amalek,
Saul divided the loot and gave one sheep to each of his two hundred
thousand soldiers. Actually, his generosity ought to surprise no one,
according to the Midrash; it was a family trait; he inherited it from his
grandfather Aviel, who was a *Tzaddik,* a just man, who enjoyed giving dowries to poor girls to help them get married. He also took it
upon himself to light the streets of his town so that, in the evening,
people could find their way to the Houses of Study. With such ancestors, how could Saul go wrong? No wonder that the Midrash calls
him *Behir Hashem*—God's chosen.

Was he really God's chosen? Yes and no. Samuel, and beyond him
God, did not want Saul to be king for the simple reason that they
wanted no king at all. God and God alone is the king of Israel. And
Israel must serve Him and Him alone. Him—and not mortal, capricious, vain, arrogant, and cruel kings. Samuel says so openly, explicitly. Let us read the text: "And the elders of Israel asked Samuel to
appoint for us a king to govern us like all the nations." Samuel, the
supreme judge, outspoken, perceptive, tried to dissuade them, warning them: the king will exploit you, he will use your men as soldiers,
your women as servants . . . But his arguments made no impression

on his listeners; they held on to their idea, they wanted a king; they wanted to be like other nations. So it was *faute de mieux,* for lack of a better solution, that Samuel—acting for God—granted their wish and chose Saul. Significantly, Saul was neither a judge nor priest nor prophet, as though to stress the point that since there must be a king, he should come from the people and remain attached to the people.

Thus here is the new Saul; he no longer belongs to his family alone, nor to his tribe alone, but to the entire people of Israel. Designated and anointed secretly by Samuel, he will be elected, crowned— or confirmed in his election—by all the tribes meeting in plenary session at Mitzpa.

It is worth noting that at first Saul tried to hide. Was it a game? Instead of summoning him by his name, Samuel made all the men of all the tribes march by; and as they filed past Samuel, he looked at them in silence. Finally, people realized that one man was missing. Eventually, Saul was found among the baggage. He is the one, said Samuel, he is your king. And the people shouted: Long live the king! And "Samuel told the people the manner of the kingdom and wrote it in a book." This was the first constitutional document in history stipulating the obligations, the duties, as well as the privileges of a king with regard to his subjects. Then Samuel sent everybody home. Saul too, though he was king, was sent home. King against his will, he returned to his routine. And the text does not hesitate to admit that, right away, there were among Saul's new subjects those who whispered their discontent—which was a sign of weakness. Samuel heard them too and said nothing—which was a sign of something else, a sign of conflict, one of many.

The king's first open conflict was with Samuel. And, in a way, it could be defined as an impersonal conflict between spiritual and secular authorities; on the one hand the prophet, on the other the ruler. The prophet wished to interfere in the nation's political and social affairs and, naturally, the king opposed him. Saul thought he would be sovereign, but always behind him stood the towering figure of Samuel. The king did nothing without consulting his prophet, who served as his principal adviser and as his conscience. This should have bothered him, but it did not. For Saul needed Samuel. Whenever the prophet was away, the king felt lost. Was he that insecure? The fact was, he wanted nothing more than to share his powers with the prophet. Just imagine: he went so far as to disturb Samuel's eternal peace to obtain his advice and help. He could not function without him—and that was what troubled and annoyed him.

His complex, ambiguous feelings toward Samuel were made even more complicated by other elements that had entered their relationship. Saul knew that he owed Samuel a great deal, if not everything. Did he resent Samuel for reminding him of his debt? Then too, Saul knew perfectly well that Samuel was against monarchy. A matter of principle? Surely. Still, Saul could have subconsciously entertained some doubts in this respect. How could he be sure that Samuel's opposition was not of a personal nature? We must not forget that the emergence of royalty was linked to the extinction of the institution of judges. Samuel was the last. And actually, why was he? What had happened to his two sons Joel and Aviya? People had shown them little respect; they did not resemble their father. They lacked his moral authority. Though they served as local judges, they were said to have yielded to corruption. Instead of going to the people, as their father did, they let people—the wrong people—come to them. That was why they could not succeed their father, and that was why Samuel had to allow Saul to take over center stage. So the judge could have felt bitterness toward the king—or, at least, the king could think that he did. Hence Saul's ambivalent feelings toward Samuel throughout his entire life.

But then, that was true also of his relationship with the other people around him. His favorite poet and musician, David. His daughter, Michal. His son, Jonathan. And even . . . God.

To understand this strange—though oddly appealing—character, let us turn to his background and examine the setting and context of his dramatic career.

We are in the middle of the tenth century before the common era. Besieged, oppressed by its neighbors, the people of Israel suffer from internal divisions along tribal lines. Everyone fights for his own ground, for his own aims, and is indifferent to the fate of the others. As for the enemy, he is powerful and ruthless—and everywhere. His armies are numerous: the Edomites, the Moabites, the Arameans, the Ammonites, the Amalekites. The beaten, humiliated people of Israel no longer possess the necessary iron for the fabrication of swords—the Philistines have taken it all. As they have taken the *aron ha'brit,* the sanctuary holding Judaism's most sacred writings. Disarmed, Israel. Vanquished, God's people, the people that are supposed to bear witness to God's glory and eternity. Fear is everywhere. And resignation. Then one day, King Nahash of Ammon tells the inhabitants of Yavesh-Gilead that if they capitulate, they will be allowed to remain alive, but only with one eye. To ridicule and frighten them even more, he tells them: go and run, run seven days in any direction and try to find refuge with any people; we shall catch you and we shall see you on your knees.

In their despair, the inhabitants of Yavesh-Gilead send an appeal to Saul. Would he come to their rescue? He accepts the challenge, organizes a retaliatory action, and saves the honor of Israel, thus justifying the hopes history has placed in him. Saul: the military leader, the commander and protector of his nation, the defender of its name. Saul: the judge, the teacher, the king—a mixture of Samson, Samuel, and David. He is the first to impose the principle of national unity and national defense to his dispersed people; the first to view events in their historical perspective. The first to invoke solidarity as a patriotic duty: whenever a part, a fragment of the nation is assaulted, the whole must react. Under his reign, the people of Israel became one not only spiritually, but physically as well.

Chosen to wage war, Saul can no longer find peace; until his last day he fought the enemies of his people—there were always enough left to provoke him. Hardly had the southern front quieted down than the one in the north flared up. Neither Israel nor her enemies ever won a definitive victory. As a result, there was constant uncertainty everywhere; a sense of insecurity that was felt collectively and individually. The king himself was affected by it. He grew moody, suspicious, temperamental, even in his private life. Just as he suspected his enemies on the borders, he suspected plots in his immediate entourage. Poor king, he had, after all, no royal tradition or inherited experience to fall back on; he did not know how royalty should behave. Poor king, he needed a mentor to teach him what to do, what to say, when and where. One day, when he wanted to assert his independence, he decided not to wait for Samuel, but to start sacrificial ceremonies without him. Samuel, of course, flew into a rage, and predicted his punishment right then and there: the House of Saul was bound to crumble. Saul understood that he would never be able to free himself from his private and official tutor. And this realization must have hurt as much as the prediction about the future of his kingdom.

He became melancholy, sad, withdrawn, subject to fits of anger and depression. From time to time he followed strange impulses. For instance, he massacred all the priests of Nov and all those allegedly endowed with occult powers—in other words, all those who escaped his royal discipline, all those who reminded him of his own limitation.

Then, to make things worse, a new hero appeared in his life and in the life of his people: David—a man as brave as he, as handsome as he, and also chosen by God to reign over his nation—the same nation. Saul loves him and hates him—for the same reasons; for his intelligence, his courage, his poetic sense, his musical abilities, his loyalty. He is what he, Saul, had been—and more so; he is what he, Saul, would like to be.

As soon as David arrives on stage, he steals the show. Goliath defies Saul, but it is David who responds to the challenge and defeats him. The singing voice is David's, and it alone is able to disperse the darkness in Saul. Just as Samuel dispels his doubts, David disarms his sadness. And again, as with Samuel, Saul needs David's presence. Surely, at one point, he had to start resenting it; he had to realize how dependent he was on David. As with Samuel, Saul becomes aware of how insecure he is in this relationship as well. The king is king, but he is not sovereign.

His resentment of David is even deeper than that of Samuel. The prophet is severe—and unhappy though the king may be, he understands why. But David is kind, always kind, and gracious, and helpful—and Saul cannot understand why David is so attached to him, so devoted. What can he want, what is he after? He must have a reason, a motive . . . Saul simply cannot believe that David's attachment to him is genuine, disinterested. To play it safe, the king tries to have him marry his oldest daughter. David declines the offer, as though to stress that he expects no reward for his services—and this confuses Saul even more. Finally, Saul makes another attempt and offers him his youngest daughter, Michal, in marriage. Was she prettier than her sister? Or was David in a more conciliatory mood? Or did he think that it wasn't polite to offend a king—and a father— twice? Whatever his reason, he agrees to marry Michal.

Now it would seem natural for David to serve his father-in-law. And Saul, normally, should no longer find it disconcerting. But he does. He remains suspicious. He feels that David stays around him too much, and not enough with his wife, Michal. When David is not with him, he wonders: Where is he? What is he doing? With whom is he plotting? He becomes increasingly convinced that David is seeking to push him aside and seize power. And so he goes on to persecute him, torment him, punish him, to help *himself* overcome his inner need to be with David, to listen to David's melodious voice. Were it not for his children, he would kill David to set himself free, to break the spell. Michal and her brother Jonathan are David's informers and protectors. Whenever danger looms, they warn him, and he leaves. As a result, Saul's anger is boundless: the whole world is against him—his own children included.

And here, why not admit it, in spite of or because of his complexity, Saul seems to us profoundly pathetic: one cannot but empathize with his fate. His sadness is not a delusion. It is real—rooted in reality. And we understand his anger. Just remember: it was he who militarily, psychologically, prepared his nation for battle and victory—yet it is David who is carried in triumph. Worse: David is praised at Saul's expense—the young warrior is compared to the old king, and naturally David comes out ahead. What did the man in the street say? That Saul killed the enemy by the thousands, but that David did it by the tens of thousands! Why such gratuitous analogies from an ungrateful nation? Why could the people not applaud David without hurting the old king? Why did Samuel, in his position as prophet and God's spokesman, go as far as to anoint David in secret, behind the king's back? No wonder that Saul was enraged, and that he felt the normal urge to get rid of the young usurper. What could he have thought but that David had intentionally, deliberately, deceitfully come close to him, allegedly to help him and entertain him, when in reality he wanted to steal his crown and his kingdom! Having reached those conclusions, how else could the king act? Should he have shrugged his shoulders and accepted his fate with equanimity? Impossible! The more he thought of David, the more he felt he was unmasking his shrewdness, his opportunism. Not only did David prove to be a masterful manipulator and politician, he also managed to alienate the affection of all the people dearest to him: first Samuel, then Michal and Jonathan! How can one not feel sympathy for Saul, the most tragic and lonely of our kings? How can one not take his side? Having come this far in one's investigation, one inevitably feels closer to him than to David.

Especially since David's behavior during the last phase of Saul's reign strikes us as singularly unethical. Saul's suspicions and personal animosity put aside, where *was* David when Saul readied himself and his army to face the enemy in their final confrontation? Where he should not have been—on the enemy's side. In an enemy fortress—Tziklag—where he had pledged to remain neutral. Just imagine: Here were Jewish soldiers going to war to defend their homes and their honor, and David did not join them! Jews might be killed by the hundreds—was David going to stand aside and watch? The nation was in danger, Israel could suffer shame and defeat—and David was to remain an onlooker! But then, if this was the situation, who was there left for Saul to rely upon? Granted, David had fled to Tziklag to escape Saul's vengeful wrath. But this was an emergency! Why didn't he return to lead his troops! Was he afraid? This was when Saul needed him more than ever, when he would have received him with honors! So why did David stay at Tziklag? Was it weakness? But then, if a hero like David weakened, how could Saul count on the resolve of his officers and their men? Small wonder then that, several hours before the attack, Saul needed to talk to someone . . . albeit a witch! Betrayed by his allies, abandoned by his friends, rejected by God— where else could he have turned?

God was against him, and Saul knew it. Hadn't Samuel said so over and over again? The final break had come during the unfortunate episode with the Amalekite king Agag. Saul had disobeyed Samuel: he had refused to execute his royal adversary; he had given in to his feelings, to his compassion. Yet he was his own victim. Was that a reason to condemn him irrevocably? Yes, said Samuel. Because Saul was too kind, too charitable, because he was unwilling to behead a human being, be it his enemy, he was doomed to lose his kingdom. Between the voice of heaven and that of his heart, he chose to listen to his heart. But then, in our eyes his sin couldn't but make him more attractive. If nobility be a sin, how can one dislike the sinner?

His humanity is emphasized and treated with deep understanding in midrashic literature. Saul, we are told, refused to kill not only Agag, but also the civilians among the Amalekites—and the animals that belonged to them. Contrary to Samuel's strict orders, he argued as follows: does not the Torah prohibit the slaughter of an animal and her young on the same day? How then, he argued, could I kill parents and children together? And, he went on to say, "Even if men have sinned, wherein lies the guilt of animals? Even if the adults have committed crimes, what have the children done?"

How can one not praise him for these questions? One wonders whether he expected an answer. Well, he did get one, but not from Samuel—Samuel must have found it difficult to refute such arguments. The answer came directly from a *Bat kol,* a heavenly voice, which admonished him: "Do not overdo things—do not be more just than necessary." Meaning: an excess of charity may be sinful. Nonetheless, he refused. He refused to kill.

That was his mistake, says the Midrash. For Haman would be Agag's descendant—so that Saul is responsible for Haman's planned massacre of Jews later. Or, as Resh Lakish put it: "Whoever chooses to show pity to a cruel person, will in the end be cruel to men capable of compassion." It is all a question of timing: misplaced pity is potentially no less dangerous than unnecessary cruelty. And that is why Saul deserved to be punished.

Still, we are moved by his humaneness. Between a king who is too cruel and a king who is not cruel enough, I clearly prefer the latter. Saul, after all, never sought to occupy a position where he would have to kill. God compelled him to accept it—without ever telling him that royalty, or authority, also involves the shedding of blood. Couldn't he turn to God and say: Tell me, Master of the universe, why did you lift me so high if you meant to push me down later? Why did you choose to make me king, only to repudiate me later, and for what reason? For not being able to kill a human being, just like that, face to face? You knew, you knew from the beginning that David would be king, and that his line would last forever, not mine. Then why did you need me? Why did you make a fool, an executioner of me? Why did you make me play a part on someone else's stage— David's—without telling me that it was only a part, a game?

King against his will, hero or antihero against his will, Saul went to see the witch not in order to find Samuel and God, but to inform them of his break with them: the play was over.

IT WAS. The final act is sheer drama. Left alone, alone with his sons and soldiers, alone with his desperate truth, he goes into battle knowing that all is lost. His sons are slain. His soldiers—beaten. As for himself, he begs his arms-bearer to kill him. And, absurdity of absurdity, the servant refuses to obey because the plea came from a king; it is forbidden to lift a finger toward someone anointed by God. Thus, his royalty works against him to the very end: had he been a simple officer, his servant would have obeyed. But Saul is not a simple man. And so he falls on his sword and dies.

Even then, David somehow manages to steal the scene from him by suddenly appearing in the text to deliver the eulogy for both the king and Jonathan, his best friend: "The beauty of Israel is slain upon thy high places; oh, how are the mighty fallen. . . . Saul and Jonathan were lovely and pleasant in their lives, and in their death they were not divided: they were swifter than eagles, stronger than lions. . . . Oh, how are the mighty fallen."

This lamentation is poignant, majestic, and lyrical. But in the Midrash David is reprimanded by God: "What? Saul has fallen and you feel like singing?"

No. Of the two, David has the less appealing part. We weep for Saul and stay away from David. And we disagree with tradition's choice.

But in the name of fairness, let us examine the situation from another viewpoint; let us look at David more closely. Let us see the relationship through his eyes.

Granted, in his youth he does seem rather . . . pushy; pretentious. Nobody asked him—he volunteers to challenge a giant warrior; he is at the right place at the right moment, in the right role. Goliath must be defeated? David will do it. Israel needs a hero? David. The king needs an analyst? David. Sure of himself, decisive. But then, what should he have done? Nothing? Should he have let Israel bow before Goliath and allowed the king to sink into despair? Since there exist no absolutes in life, every choice necessarily means compromise. David chose to ignore appearances; only results count. Only the people and its destiny are important. He went everywhere—volunteered for every mission—because he was needed; he alone, he alone could do what he did. And when a nation's life is at stake, how can one think of appearances and interpretations?

Moreover, David's behavior toward Saul was in fact above reproach. He was respectful, obliging, as well as loyal and admiring. He never sought to harm him; quite the contrary, he only wanted to help. He did not wish to succeed the old king, but on the contrary keep him healthy and in power. All he wanted was to serve him, to comfort him—to cheer him up. As soon as the king needed him, he was there—even when it meant exposing himself to peril or death. Why? It's simple: because he loved his king. He really loved him, as only a poor shepherd boy could love the sovereign who rescued him from anonymity and poverty and befriended him. David loved Saul with all his heart; he gave him his time and his energy; he fought for him and his name. And if at first he refused to marry the king's eldest daughter, it was precisely to prove to him how pure his feelings were; how untainted, disinterested, and selfless his love was for the king.

Saul has fits of unjustified violence: David says nothing. Saul persecutes him; he is silent. Saul makes him into his personal scapegoat; David still says nothing. Saul wants him dead—and David still continues to serve him, to worship him. Expelled from the royal quarters, exiled, hunted everywhere, David does not respond in kind. He never seems to have expressed hatred for Saul, or even anger. On three occasions he manages to get inside Saul's tent, on three occasions he has the opportunity to kill him—and his companions urge him to do so: kill the sick old man, they say, kill him, or his jealousy, his spite, his hate will destroy you. But he doesn't do it—he isn't even tempted. David somehow understands that they are both victims. Saul is God's victim, David is Saul's. And it is because of the depth of his understanding that David is given the privilege of conferring upon his kingdom an eternal dimension.

Of course, David is no saint. And Scripture admits it. His adventure with Bat-Sheva leaves a stain on his name, a blemish on his life. His military operations are praised, but only half-heartedly; he fought too many battles, shed too much blood. Thus the Temple in his city will be built not by him but by his son, who symbolizes peace.

Yet the essential difference between the two kings emerges clearly: Saul signified internal tension and conflict, while David represents their resolution: it was David, not Saul, who ultimately unified the people.

Furthermore, Saul lacked self-assurance, which is necessary to obtain and retain power. He was forever making decisions and regretting them. True, in the Midrash, his motivation for letting Agag's cattle live is idealistic, but not so in Scripture, which claims that he merely wanted to appease his soldiers by giving them the enemy loot. Yet when Samuel questioned him about it, Saul did not dare admit the truth. Listen to the text: When the prophet met the king, the king told him that he did fulfill God's command to kill the Amalekites and all that belonged to them. Really? said Samuel, then what is the meaning of this bleating of sheep in my ears, and the lowing of oxen which I hear? And Saul answered: It was the people who spared the best of the sheep and oxen to sacrifice to God. And the prophet retorted sharply: What does God want? Oxen? Or to be obeyed?

No—Saul did not respond like a king. He did not have the courage of his convictions. He did not accept responsibility for his acts. David did.

Another difference: Saul was jealous, David was not. But what was Saul jealous of? David's popularity and fame. People praised David more than him—and that Saul couldn't bear. And what was the praise all about? Killing. People said: Saul killed thousands, but David slayed tens of thousands. But then wasn't Saul a humanitarian? Wasn't he against capital punishment, against killing? He should have been pleased to be known as one who only kills thousands.

Also: in spite of his humanitarian language, he had martial tendencies. David's symbol was the harp, Saul's was the spear. He always seemed to have one in his hands. After promising immunity to the surrendering Gibeonites, he broke that promise and massacred them—which no king must do, which no man must do.

He was indecisive, unable to handle things by himself. Why did he allow Samuel to serve as intermediary with God? David needed none. Man, as a general rule, can and must address God directly— and this is even more true of kings chosen by God. Saul doubted too much and David not enough. Thus Saul would have been an excellent philosopher. But David was a better king.

And lastly: David punished his enemies on the outside, while Saul was forever haunted by his internal opponents. David fought invaders, Saul his own subjects. If Saul could have eliminated David, he would have done so gladly. David could have killed Saul—but did not. That is why David, and not Saul, was allowed to found Israel's everlasting line of kings, which will begin again with redemption.

True, Saul suffered. But suffering is no excuse. He was wrong in making others suffer. David too suffered, but he used his suffering to create songs and generate joy.

In conclusion, having come to agree with history's judgment favoring David, we must add that, in spite of all objective considerations, in spite of all reasons of state, Saul—yes, Saul—continues to move us. There is human strength as well as weakness in his wounded soul. At times he appears even more majestic than his successor. A painting by Rembrandt shows him half-hidden by a curtain, weeping silently, while listening to David's singing accompanied by his harp. He was sad, this first king of Israel. And his sadness has survived him.

If only he had decapitated Agag . . . That was the real beginning of his fall. Why did he refuse? Was it pity for a fallen king on whom God had vented his wrath? That, we could have understood. But again the text prevents us from going too far afield. It has its own explanation. Saul chose not to kill Agag, but instead to chain him, torment him, publicly humiliate him and keep him alive as an eternal prisoner, as a reminder of his eternal defeat. And here, we must admit, death itself would seem more humane, more charitable. Agag himself preferred it. Listen to the text: Samuel ordered him brought before him, "and Agag came unto him in chains. And Agag said: surely the bitterness of death is at hand. And Samuel said: as thy sword has made women childless, so shall thy mother be childless among women. And Samuel beheaded Agag before the Lord in Gilgal." Agag went to his death acquiescently. For him, death was a liberation. From his chains.

Misunderstood himself, Saul was incapable of understanding others. He understood nobody. He should have been more aware of Samuel's suffering at having to transmit God's word and God's will without being able to change them. He should have tried to understand David's conflict, David who was compelled to replace him, though he loved him. Nor did Saul empathize with his own children, who, out of love for him, tried to stop him from committing the irrevocable. Saul was alone and never managed to go beyond his solitude.

He was alone when he died—and suddenly, in our legend, he is forgiven and even rehabilitated. Look at Saul, said God to his angels. He knows that he is going to die, yet he faces death with his eyes open, and better yet: he is taking his sons with him. Why? So as not to die alone? One always does, anyway. Saul, a strange king: in his compassion, he spared the life of an enemy ruler—but his compassion did not extend to a Jewish king, the first in history, the unhappiest as well.

Saul killed Saul. And his gesture does not surprise us. Suicide means a wish to be at the same time executioner and victim—mortal creature and Angel of Death. It is a gesture which combines giving and receiving. In life and in death, Saul remains unique. His tragedy was caused by himself. He was his own enemy—and we all remain his friends.

Samuel and the Quest for Mercy

H<small>IS STORY BEGINS</small> in prayer and ends in rage.

How is one to comprehend his stubbornness, his inflexibility? How is one to understand his harshness toward Saul, his anointed leader? And his brutality, his cruelty toward the king of the wicked Amalekites, Agag, how can it be explained? Since when does a prophet of God act in the role of executioner?

Admit it: in the cast of biblical characters, Samuel is among the most perplexing ones. How is he to be defined? Is he the altruistic leader who thinks only of God and His people, and never of his own social position? Or is he an egocentric, jealous of his prerogatives?

One day he seems to want to please, only to regret it the next. Destined to shake up history itself, why does he find it so dificult to be a father? Capable of grandeur and of tenderness, why is he also so unforgiving? As the last of the judges and the first of the prophets, is he meant to be an example of God's rigor or of His charity? If God's goodness is limitless, mustn't man's be too? Often there seems little room for kindness in Samuel's heart.

Why?

Though he is already dead, Samuel continues to persecute his favorite victim, Saul, the first illustrious king of our people, as is illustrated by the episode at Ein-Dor.

It is impossible for a student of biblical literature not to feel shock: how could a prophet of the God of Israel treat another human being so heartlessly, especially when that person is in such distress? Even if his nocturnal visitor were not a king, even if he had not waged heroic battles on behalf of his people, even if he had not brought honor and security to the land of Israel, how could God's messenger inflict such pain on Saul in his darkest hour?

We mention Saul again because it is not possible to evoke Samuel without linking him to Saul, whose adult life and destiny he shaped and dominated. There is between them a profound and mysterious bond that is not to be found in Samuel's relationship with the other king anointed by him, David. With David, his behavior is relaxed and peaceful. There is never a conflict or misunderstanding. Not so with Saul. With him, the relationship is tense, feverish, forever fraught with risk and peril, alternating between ecstasy and despair. No one, not even David, has brought such pain to our people's first king. It is as if Samuel had entered Saul's life specifically to punish him and make him doubt himself and his mission.

And yet . . .

LET US GO back to the beginning. The First Book of Samuel shows us a good Jewish family that leads a serene life but also has its problems. Elkana son of Jeroham, from Ephrat, has two wives: Penina and Hannah. The problem? He hates the first and loves the second. What makes it worse, he has children from Penina but not from Hannah. A pious man, Elkana goes regularly to visit "the house of God" in Shilo, the Jewish religious capital, and bring offerings to heaven. He returns with presents for Penina and her children—but those he gives Hannah are doubly precious. For great is his love for her, particularly because she is unhappy. The text speaks a lot about her pain. She cries, she cannot stop crying. Naturally, her husband tries to console her, at times naively. His argument goes like this: "Why do you cry? Just because you have no children? Why do you need children when you have me—am I not worth more than ten children?" She keeps on sobbing, so much so that she loses her appetite. She stops eating altogether.

Perhaps it was also Penina's fault. Could she have been gentler, kinder to her poor rival? But in fact she was nasty. That's what the Midrash says. To illustrate Hannah's virtues, it emphasizes Penina's shortcomings. For instance, in the morning, when she was washing her children, she would ask Hannah: "Why are you still in bed when you should be preparing your little ones for school?" Or "It is chilly outside. Are they warmly dressed?" As if she didn't know that Hannah was childless. Such meanness was too much for Hannah. She returned to Shilo, wept a bit more, and addressed her prayer to the Lord: "If you remember your maidservant, if I am given a son, I shall consecrate him to You—never will a razor touch his hair." In other words, even before he was born, she made him into a Nazir.

Interestingly, our Talmudic sages do not question her right to commit a nonexistent son to God's service. Instead, they invent arguments for her. They make her say: "O Lord, God of hosts, you have created so many human beings, is it that difficult for you to give me one son?" And in case God doesn't understand, she tells him a parable: "A beggar appears at the entrance to the royal palace where the king is entertaining his guests. Give me a piece of bread, he asks one servant, then another, but all turn him away. So—he pushes his way inside and approaches the king himself: Majesty, he says, you have treated so many guests to so many courses. All I want from you is a piece of bread." Thus Hannah, seeing so many Jewish pilgrims from all over the country gathered in Shilo, exclaimed: "You have so many children here, O Lord—and I don't even have one!" And God took pity on her.

A variation on the same theme: pleading with God, Hannah says, "Everything you created in a woman has a purpose: eyes to see, ears to hear, the nose to smell, the mouth to speak, hands to work, feet to walk. You also created in her the breast to feed her offspring—look at mine, O Lord: why did you give me a breast since it has no one to feed?" Faced with the power of such logic, God couldn't help but accept her plea.

In the biblical text, the story is told in more realistic terms. On that day Hannah was in Shilo, silently repeating her prayers to heaven. Eli the priest noticed her, thinking she must be drunk, for no sound left her lips. "Stop drinking," he warned her. "I drank neither wine nor beer," she replied. "All I did was pour out my heart to God." The priest gave her his blessing. That night Elkana made her pregnant.

Nine months later—six, according to one Midrash—Samuel was born, bringing great happiness to his parents. Thus Hannah let her husband go alone on the annual pilgrimage to Shilo; she stayed home with her little boy. When she finally did travel to Shilo, she brought Samuel with her. She introduced her son to Eli the priest and reminded him of their previous meeting, saying, "This is the boy I prayed for." The verse is, in many ways, both difficult and significant: *"Va'yiten Hashem li et sh'eilati asher sha'alti me'imo"*—He responded to my question or to my quest—*"ve'gam anokhi hishiltihu la'shem kol ha'yamim asher haya hu sha'ul la'shem"*—and I loaned him to the Lord for all the time the Lord needed him. Remember the phrase which is supposed to explain the name Hannah gave her son: it contains four references to the verb *sha'al*—shin, aleph, lamed: to ask, to loan, to borrow. Later, these words may help us explain certain difficulties in Samuel's behavior.

For the moment, in the text, Hannah is happy. In her happiness she composes a prayer which remains among the most poignant and beautiful of our liturgy (1 Samuel 2):

> My heart exults in the Lord,
> my strength is exalted in the Lord.
> My mouth speaks against my enemies
> for your rescue is my joy.
> There is none holy like the Lord,
> there is no God without you,

there is no rock outside you.
Broken is the bow of the mighty,
strong are the weak. . . .
It is the Lord who causes death
and creates life.
It is God who gives riches or poverty,
it is He who lifts up
and brings down.
From the dust he raises the poor
and the needy from the ash heap.

Well, well. Hannah, who used to recite her prayers in whispers, is now expressing herself like a poet, better yet, like a prophet. She speaks—no, she sings—and her song penetrates all those who, throughout the centuries, have felt the need to articulate their pain or their gratitude.

She is happy and yet she separates herself from her beloved child. Faithful to her pledge, she leaves him with Eli the priest, entrusting him with his education. Was she aware of the bad reputation Eli's school—or "House of God"—had in the Bible? His two sons were known to be corrupt, as were other priests there. Still, Hannah had faith in her son. But according to a Midrash, she almost lost him. He was too precocious. In spite of his tender age, he managed to solve a difficult Halakhic problem. And this he did in the presence of Eli the priest, who, visibly embarrassed, reprimanded him: didn't the little boy know that whoever teaches in the presence of his teacher is committing a transgression which theoretically deserves capital punishment? Luckily Hannah was still there. And of course she used her greatest weapon: her tears. Eli tried to comfort her: "Do not worry, I shall pray for you and God will give you another son, he'll be better than this one." But Hannah cried out: "It is this one I wanted." And Samuel was saved. He is loved by his mother and also by Scripture. Shielded by God, he is simply perfect in everything he does. Above criticism. A just man, he inspires admiration, respect, and awe.

Elkana and his cherished wife were at peace at last. The heavens were smiling upon them. They had more children: three sons and two daughters. A midrashic legend adds an astonishing detail to the picture: each time Hannah had a son, Penina lost two of hers. When only two were left, Hannah interceded on their behalf—and they were spared.

As for Samuel, he grew up well. Eventually he became Eli's chief assistant—he rather than the priest's two sons, who abused their family status for personal gain.

By now, Eli had become old and sad. God had stopped talking to him. The text says: *"U'dvar Hashem haya yakar ba'yamim ha'heim; ein hazzon nifratz"*—and God's word became rare in those times; as was man's vision.

A touching episode describes the end of his reign and the beginning of his young successor's. Eli was bedridden most of the time; his eyesight was getting poorer and poorer. The impression the reader gets is that the priest was no longer functioning. One day, Samuel heard a voice calling him; he responded: *"Hineini,"* here I am. At first, he thought it was Eli who needed him: "Did you call me, Master?" "No," answers the old priest. "I did not call you. Go back to sleep." Samuel went back to bed, only to hear the voice for the second time. Again, he ran to the old priest: "Here I am, you called me." "I have not called you, my son. Go back to sleep." Then God called him for the third time, and again Samuel ran to the old teacher's bedside: "You called me, so I am here." Now Eli understood whose voice Samuel had heard. "Go back to sleep," he told him. "And if you hear the voice again, just say: speak to me, O Lord, your servant hears you." Samuel went back to his bed and heard God's voice again. Naturally, he followed Eli's instructions, repeating his exact words. But when God spoke, what He said must have terrified young Samuel. What he heard was a blunt condemnation of Eli the priest: "I shall punish his house for ever. . . . I shall do so because of the crime his sons have committed, and which he did not prevent. . . . This crime will be expiated neither by offerings nor by sacrifices."

A disturbing passage. First of all, Samuel heard God's voice three times and did not recognize it! Second, Scripture doesn't really mention the specific nature of "crimes." Eli's sons, Pinhas and Hofni, must have been guilty of more serious transgressions than approriating a certain meat that did not belong to them. A Midrash suggests that they, and certain other young priests, may have indulged in, let us say, some illicit sexual activities. Was this enough to move God to such everlasting anger? (His rigor is so extreme that one cannot but feel sorry for Eli. Actually, he is one of the innocent victims of the story: he had done nothing wrong. His only mistake was in not repressing his sons' "perversity." The sons were *"b'nei bli'al,"* says the text: they were lawless individuals; *"lo yadu et Hashem,"* they failed to recognize God's name and power. Comments the Midrash: "they pretended that the heavens were empty." So now we understand why they had to be punished. But why the father? Are there no limits to paternal responsibility? Eli's sons were not minors. They were already grown. Why then did the father have to suffer because of their sins? Wasn't he punished enough simply by being their father? And if God wanted to say something about him, why didn't He speak to him personally instead of confiding in his young pupil?

Eli must have sensed that something was wrong because as soon as Samuel was back, he questioned him: What did God say to him? Samuel tried to hide the truth from the old priest. But when his benefactor insisted on hearing the full truth, without any embellishment, Samuel repeated God's words. *"Va'yigdal Shmuel,"* says the text: and Samuel grew or Samuel became great. And God was with him. And the entire people of Israel—from Dan to Beersheba—learned that Samuel was faithful to the prophet or that he himself was a prophet. As for Eli the priest, one can imagine what the old father must have felt at that moment, but all he said was: "May God do what pleases Him."

Well, God was not pleased. Neither with Eli nor with his demoralized people. So demoralized was Israel that, after a fleeting victory over Philistine aggressors, it lost thirty thousand men in battle. The Ark of the covenant was captured by the enemy. Eli's sons were killed. Hearing the news of their deaths, Eli—at the age of ninety-eight—fell from his chair and died of a broken neck. He had served for forty years as judge in Israel.

Thus Samuel's formative years came to an end. Now he was his people's only spiritual leader.

Until now his path was clear, without obstacles. A perfect disciple, forever loyal to his master, Samuel showed Eli respect and devotion. Was he a good son? He must have been, for there is no mention in Scripture or in the Midrash of his parents' complaining about him. As leader, he knew how to mobilize the energies of his people, who, under his supreme command, inflicted on the Philistines a defeat of such magnitude that, during his entire lifetime, until his death, they did not dare attack the Jewish nation again. His popularity is essentially unmatched among religious leaders.

He married, had two sons—Joel and Aviya—and was unanimously respected as judge. The Midrash emphasizes both his wealth and his integrity: he was frequently on the road but traveled always at his own expense. Unfortunately, what happened to his mentor Eli happened to him too: his two sons, also judges, went astray. Money-hungry, they allowed themselves to be bought, thus betraying the Law ruling over the nation and its citizens. As a result, the elders of Israel felt compelled to appear before Samuel, saying: "Since you are old and your sons do not resemble you, give us a king to govern over us so we shall be like other nations."

And here, for the first time, we discover something negative in Samuel's character: he is displeased by the request of the elders. Frustrated, he addresses a prayer to God, who reassures him: "Do not take all this to heart. . . . They are not against you but against me. They are fed up with me, not you. Whatever they have done to me since I rescued them from Egyptian bondage, they are now doing to you." In other words, "Are you better than me? Why should you be luckier than me?" And God gives him a sound piece of advice: "Listen to them. . . . But tell them what is in store for them . . . what having a king will mean to the nation." And so Samuel recites before the leaders the law governing royalty in Israel (1 Samuel 8:11):

The king will take your sons and appoint them to his chariots and to be his horsemen, and to run before his chariots. And he will appoint for himself commanders of hundreds and commanders of fifties, and some to plow his ground and to reap his harvest. And to work on his weapons to make war. He will take your daughters to be perfumers and cooks and bakers. He will take the best of your vineyards and olive orchards and give them to his servants. . . . And on that day you will cry out because of your king but the Lord will not answer you.

Did God give Samuel all these details so that they would be repeated in public? Samuel does everything he can to warn and frighten the Jews, but his voice has lost some of its power. The Jews want a king and say so. They even say why. They want to be like other nations. They are tired of being a special people, a people apart, chosen by God and by history for who knows what obscure missions. They want to be neither superior nor inferior to other nations. Is that too much to ask? Pressed by the elders and counseled by God, Samuel gives in. And that is how Saul is crowned.

Let us stop for a moment. The prophet and judge-turned-king-maker has obeyed with a great deal of reluctance. In fact, he is angry. But why? On what grounds does he oppose a monarchy whose roots can be found in Scripture? The Torah stipulates that the king must be Jewish, the brother of his subjects, that's all. But Samuel is against royalty altogether. Is it because he believes that God and God alone is Israel's king? That God and God alone is to be obeyed—He and not mortal kings, whose vanity and capricious behavior make them unavoidably suspicious and potentially corrupt? Is Samuel, in this respect, more demanding than the Bible?

Some of his critics believe that his resistance to the whole idea of royalty is personal, motivated by jealousy. Had the elders simply asked for a king, he might have accepted. But in the process of making the request, they slandered his sons. They were corrupt? It's one thing for him to know it, and another for them to declare that they know it too. Furthermore, they explicitly requested a king "to judge them." But wasn't he, Samuel, still their judge? They need a leader? Didn't he lead them into battle, didn't he gain military victories for their nation? He was old—so what? In other words, he was, according to his critics, like the politician who doesn't know when to leave the stage. He clings to power instead of leaving it with grace. Is it out of spite that he crowns an unknown youngster who spends his time looking for lost mules and ends up as ruler of a kingdom? Could it be that Saul's anointing was actually a vindictive act whose purpose was to show the silliness, the absurdity of popular interference in national policy?

But these critics forget that Samuel only follows divine instructions. It is God who tells him to implement the idea of royalty. It is God who sets the stage and tells how to go about finding the candidate. Samuel is looking for Saul and is found by him.

The two form a strange pair. The opposite of Samuel, young Saul is everything but charismatic. From the outset, he moves us by his naïveté, his innocence. He displays no trace of ambition, deceit, or envy. His father sends him to look for donkeys. So he goes, and after three days, the good and obedient son that he is, he feels bad: his father may be worried over his prolonged absence. People advise him to go and seek the help of a man called "The Seer." Little does he know that their encounter will be a turning point in his life as well as in the life of his nation. When the prophet tells Saul of his new status and career, he is incredulous: "I belong," says he, "to the smallest tribe of Israel; to one of its youngest families: why then do you speak to me like this?" In other words, leave me alone with your bizarre fairy tales about Jewish royalty. He accepts the crown only when he becomes *"ish aher,"* another man.

A king against his will, Saul wanted to go on living as a simple citizen. Samuel was still the true leader of Israel. And Saul paid him the homage due his rank. When he waged his first war against the Ammonites, he did so also in Samuel's name. Was the prophet satisfied? He should have been. But, since Saul's appearance on the stage, the prophet seemed constantly troubled, frustrated, even bitter.

An example: after the victory over the Ammonites, Saul and the entire population rejoiced at a huge gathering at Gilgal. And Samuel? Didn't he feel gratified that his candidate had done so well? Apparently not. And yet he was there, he even made a speech. What he said is indicative of his mood: "I heard your demand," he began. "You wanted a king? Here he is. As for myself, I am old . . ." In other words: he accepted the consequences of a situation which he did not like but could not control. What he said made sense. But suddenly he changed course. Like Moses (to whom he is often compared), he indulged in a plea *pro domo:* "Since my youth I have been in your midst. So tell me, in the presence of the Lord and his anointed emissary, whether I have taken an ox from someone or a donkey from someone else. And whether I have ever stolen anything from anyone or been bought by anyone. Tell me and I will answer you. . . ."

What happened to our beloved prophet? what was he talking about? Who ever accused him of stealing? Who ever leveled any accusation at all against him? Guilty of corruption of justice, he, the incorruptible? His sons—yes, that's a different matter. But then why should he have to justify himself before his people, and at a festive and solemn gathering to boot? And why did he ask for an immediate response, a clean bill of health? Did he feel rejected and thus insecure to the point of needing support from public opinion?

At this moment we discover an anomaly in the midrashic treatment of a biblical character. Generally, the Bible glorifies its heroes, whereas the Midrash, in its iconoclastic mood, humanizes them by uncovering their weaknesses. In the case of Samuel, it is the opposite. Scripture accentuates his failings while the Midrash emphasizes his virtues. Sorry: in the biblical sources themselves the attitude toward him is twofold. Infinitely generous toward the young Samuel, less so toward the old. As an adolescent, he is close to perfection: *"Ve'ha'na'ar Shmuel,"* and the adolescent Samuel, *"holekh va'gadel,"* constantly grows, *"va'tov,"* and he is good, *"gam im Hashem ve'gam im anashim,"* he is good with God as well as with people. Few men in Jewish history have received such praise. It is only when Samuel is older, when he has acquired high position, when he has influence, when he is involved in a variety of ways with the life of the people, that as a character he becomes problematic. Hence the need in midrashic literature to balance the portrait by exaggerating in the opposite direction.

What isn't said about him? Born circumcised, he is among the eight princes and founders of humankind. He was twelve when he was endowed with prophetic powers. The Palestinian Talmud calls him *"rabban shel nevi'im,"* a master of prophets. Wealthy, he never profited financially from his position. Though thirsty, he never drank from a public well. When traveling to sit in judgment, he rode on his own donkey. His misfortune was his two sons: they aged him prematurely. It was because of their unworthy behavior that he died at fifty-two. His relations with Saul were not happy either. Did he ever have moments of happiness?

We can understand his objective problems as a father. But we have difficulties in comprehending his relationship with Saul. At a certain point a painful tension developed between them. Even after their separation, Samuel had affection for his young protégé. He "mourned"—the term is in the text—over his downfall. He felt disappointed that God had changed his mind and replaced Saul with David on the throne. But then, why did he have outbursts of anger toward Saul? They preceded the episode with Agag.

A major incident occurred when Saul organized a victory celebration after a major defeat of the Philistines. Everybody was there except Samuel. Saul and the people waited for him one day, another day, seven days. Finally, Saul began the ceremony without him. It was almost concluded when Samuel appeared. In a rage. Was it entirely his fault? Not Saul's? Why did the new king begin a popular event without Samuel? Granted, the prophet was late, so what? Didn't Saul owe him his career? Couldn't he have been more patient?

But let us turn the question around: Why was Samuel late? Why did he make his king and his people wait for such a long time? If he had an unexpected obligation to meet, a call from God for instance, why didn't he dispatch a messenger to inform the king of the emergency? Whatever the reasons on either side, Samuel's reaction to Saul's alleged haste does seem a bit unreasonable.

It is anger—an explosion of burning anger—that the prophet offers Saul when the king comes to greet him: *"Meh assita?"* What have you done? And why have you done it? Saul tries to explain: "The enemy was nearby, the people were beginning to lose heart, and you were late. I had no choice, I had to begin without you." The prophet refuses to accept the king's apology: "You did the wrong thing. . . . Thus your reign will not last. . . . God has already chosen someone else to rule over His people."

Such a lack of comprehension on the part of a prophet seems unfair. Poor Saul: what happened to him was unjust. God had chosen his successor even before he committed his sin, if it was a sin at all. And what if in fact he had been trapped by both God and Samuel with the sole purpose of provoking his downfall? After all, the date for the celebration had been set by Samuel himself. Saul was on time, so were the people. Samuel alone was late. Why then didn't he grant the young, inexperienced king a special dispensation for extenuating circumstances? It is sad to admit but Samuel seems to have waited for the king's error. Even if Saul had not acted with such haste—or rather with such punctuality—Samuel would have announced to him the end of his reign. Why such a lack of compassion on his part toward a man like Saul who, more than often, was ready and willing to share power with him and, in fact, did nothing without consulting him? From that moment on, nothing could bring them together. Everything separated them. Samuel treated Saul not as an adversary but as an enemy. Is it possible that, in the beginning, he drew him closer to himself so as to better hate him afterward? Was it his hate that he threw from his grave to the despairing king in the home of the witch at Ein-Dor?

To explore these texts is to face a choice between the prophet's extreme harshness and the king's apparent humaneness, between God and his victim, between loyalty toward Samuel and affection for Saul. It is impossible to choose one without distancing oneself from the other.

As mentioned earlier, their final clash occurred after Israel's stunning victory over the Amalekites. Israel sighed with relief. Another tragedy had been averted. Vanished, the threat of death and humiliation. Everybody ought to be exuberant and celebrate the military triumph of brave Jewish warriors over their hereditary enemy. But victory, instead of creating national unity, occasionally tears it apart.

Poor Saul. God was against him, and he knew it. (Samuel never stopped hammering it into his mind.) Eventually, the king grew melancholy, moody, isolated. Suspecting the whole world of plotting against him, he ordered the slaying of the priests of Nov, and the witches. David's arrival on the scene didn't help matters. The young shepherd with his golden voice became a national hero. At what point was Saul aware of David's clandestine coronation? The last period of his reign is depressing: he let himself fall deeper and deeper into the abyss. And all this because, earlier in his life, he had not waited for Samuel at a popular ceremony! On that day he understood that he would never free himself from his mentor's hold on him.

What occurred later, after his victory over the Amalekites, after his refusal to execute their king, Agag, was a confirmation of what he had felt then, at Gilgal. Why had he disobeyed the prophet's order? He simply couldn't bring himself to kill his prisoner. A victim of his own compassion, Saul had to endure Samuel's wrath and God's. Because he was too kind, too charitable, incapable of beheading a human being, be it his enemy whose eyes were fixed on his, he was condemned to lose his kingdom. Between the voice of God and that of his heart, he chose to listen to the latter.

Too sentimental, Saul? Maybe. Between excessive humaneness and boundless harshness, I prefer the first. Finally, it was the prophet who, with one swing of the sword, beheaded Agag, saying: "Just as your sword has made many mothers childless, this one will make yours childless." Is he commended for his gesture? The lack of unanimity in the Midrash is meaningful. One sage believes that Samuel tortured Agag before putting him to death. Another maintains that he castrated him. Before dying, Agag questioned Samuel: "Is this how a prince is executed in your land?" Hence a third theory: actually, Saul was not as innocent as he appears. Nor was he as kind. If he refused to kill Agag it was because he sought to humiliate him—and that is why he needed him alive. And that's why Agag preferred death. So? Down with Saul and long live his adversary Samuel?

BEFORE BRINGING this exploration to a conclusion, perhaps we ought to come back to a theme that has been haunting its various phases from the beginning: the animosity that Samuel nourished toward Saul. Interestingly, it transcends both personal and theological considerations. In fact it preceded them. How is one to explain it? Why should a messenger of God be resentful of a man also chosen by God, if for other missions? After many months of reflection and research, I think I stumbled upon a theory. It is linked to the problems of language.

Earlier, we learned why Hannah called her son Samuel or Shmuel: because *"va'yiten Hashem li et sh'eilati asher sha'alti me'imo"*—God had fulfilled my wish—*"ve'gam anokhi"*—and I too—*"hishiltihu la'shem"*—I loaned him to God. Attention was drawn to the almost obsessive repetition of the word *sha'al*, which occurs, variously used, four times in one sentence. That word is clearly on her mind, preventing her from thinking of anything else. But then the question arises, if she thinks so much of *sha'al* why doesn't she call her son Shaul? She chooses to call him Shmuel, which means something else, it means the Name of God. Is this why the prophet carries a deep anger toward Saul? Not for receiving some of his tasks—such as waging war—but also, and above all, for usurping his name?

As for us, readers and students of biblical tales, it is incumbent upon us to accept the idea that both the king and the prophet have their place in our collective memory. Of the two, who is more human? Samuel, who communicates God's will in history, or Saul, who is mainly concerned with the present? For Samuel, the question is simple: God wants all Amalekites to be killed—all of them, with no exception. For Saul, a man of violence and blood who has seen his soldiers kill and be killed, death is not an abstraction. Of course,

Agag is an Amalekite, but he is also a human being. Is Saul against collective guilt and punishment? No. He had ordered the execution of false priests, sorcerers, and witches. So why has he singled out Agag for mercy? Was it perhaps a sudden impulse on his part to allow Samuel the prophet to act as Saul the king? Or was it a way for him to challenge the Almighty, as if to say: Master of the universe, you want me to kill this man—tell *me* so, speak to me personally, not through another person, and it will be done.

But God never spoke to Saul. He spoke to Samuel, who heard a voice and did not realize that it was God's.

Is this one of the lessons we draw from this tale? That it is possible that God speaks to us—and we don't know it?

To paraphrase Rabbi Pinhas of Koretz, questions remain questions— but we must continue.

Isaiah, a Prince of Prophets

"THIS IS THE vision of Isaiah, son of Amotz, in the days of Uzziah, Jotham, Ahaz and Ezekias, all kings of Judah. Hear, O heavens, and give ear, O earth, I have nourished and raised children, and they have rebelled against me."

Thus begins the painful, feverish, and angry message that Isaiah—a terrible, exalted, and strange prophet—was instructed to deliver to his people in the name of the Lord.

We are immediately struck by the sense of frustration implicit in these words, which read like an indictment. No divine emissary has gone so far in his rebukes and charges as this disillusioned, bitter man. Nothing is omitted. On Isaiah's lips Jerusalem evokes a kind of Sodom and Gomorrah. Indeed, the prophet himself draws the analogy. Listen to him: "The ox knows his owner, and the ass his master's crib. But Israel does not know, my people does not consider." And further: "Woe unto this sinful nation, this people laden with iniquity, a seed of evildoers, children that are corrupters. They have forsaken the Lord, they have provoked the Holy One of Israel unto anger, they have gone away backward. . . ."

What drove this eloquent Jewish spiritual guide to blacken the name of his people? Is it not a prophet's task to defend Israel? Sometimes, in Talmudic literature, Isaiah is compared to Moses: both called heaven and earth to witness. But whenever God seemed too severe, too impatient with the children of Israel, Moses hastened to place himself between them and their celestial Judge. He even threatened God with resignation, if His compassion were delayed. Yes, out of his infinite love for his unfortunate and stiff-necked people, Moses allowed himself to address God almost as His courtroom adversary. Why did Isaiah never do the same? Because in a pinch, as it were, God could do without an Isaiah but not a Moses?

Other questions arise from this book throbbing with beauty and permeated with as much sorrow as hope. Some bear on Isaiah's identity, others on the texts attributed to him. Isaiah is so shrouded in enigma that over the centuries eminent scholars, Jews and non-Jews alike, versed in scientific criticism of the Bible, have suggested various theories about the identity (or identities) of the author. Accordingly, the vocabulary, tone, and structure of certain early chapters, as well as their content, differ greatly from later passages. Thus, they conclude that the book's two parts were written by different men. To which more orthodox thinkers might reply, as Isaiah is only repeating God's words, why not admit that God was perfectly capable of changing style between chapter 1 and chapter 40?

Another question. We know how the prophet died—in a cruel and tragic manner. We also know why: he had uttered a few impudent, unjust, and unkind words. But since when is a prophet responsible for what he says? Isn't he supposed to be transmitting God's words?

Shall we begin again?

"This vision of Isaiah son of Amotz. . . ." This purely biographical opening line provokes a question we intend to explore later: since Isaiah died during the reign of Manasseh, why is this king's name omitted from the text?

Let us study this more closely. What does the first word, *hazon*, mean? Usually it is translated as "vision." But what sort of vision, a waking or hallucinatory one? Perhaps a dream?

Three terms are generally used to designate a prophetic message:

massa, or verbal communication, *dvar,* or divine word, and *hazon.* According to some Talmudic scholars, only Moses heard God while fully awake. The other prophets received his words in a dream or a trance. In Isaiah's case the term *hazon* hints that he "saw" the message. What did he see? The words? The reality they conjured? The deplorable state of the nation? Surely this injunction implies a somewhat literal account of moral decadence in the culture of Judah. But later on the vision shifts, evoking celestial imagery not unlike Ezekiel's. So it is a true vision the text will convey to the reader, a vision so disturbing and concrete that the prophet will suffer its consequences: he will be punished.

A PROPHET'S NAME is often linked to God. Zechariah, or "God remembers" (or "remembering God"). Ovadia, or "servant of God." Yeshayahu or Isaiah: "God has come or will come to his aid."

His father Amotz was King Amatzia's brother. So the prophet is of the royal family. Is that why he is called "Prince of prophets"? There is another reason. His style is unlike any other: lofty, authoritarian, compelling, majestic. Like all prophets charged with a mission by God Himself, he knows that he may say anything. Before him, mighty rulers are humbled. But now we are focusing on the prince as he addresses ordinary men and women in their own language, to tell them how evil, destructive, and self-destructive he finds their ways. And when he speaks to people, again it is from above that he informs them of the displeasure they provoke among the celestial spheres. Rabbi Levi's response in the Talmud? Isaiah could allow himself such bluntness because he was the king's nephew. And he quoted a proverb from King Solomon: "The rich man is wise in his own conceit." In other words, the rich man is known by his arrogance.

Like Moses, Isaiah begins his discourse appealing to heaven and earth to serve as witnesses. But there is a difference in their opening statements. Moses first invokes the earth, and then the heavens; with Isaiah, it is the reverse. Why this disparity? The answer is simple. Moses was standing *above* his people when he spoke of their faults and duties; so he looked at the ground below first. But Isaiah stood *among* the people when he was conveying the divine word; so he looked up at the sky. Still, both accused their contemporaries of every imaginable sin. Of course, Moses was not only a prophet but also a political and military leader of tribes on their way to a land not yet conquered and a freedom not yet achieved, while Isaiah was constantly obliged to confront one king or another ruling over the daily life of a nation already established. Their names? Uzziah, Jotham, Ahaz, and Ezekias . . .

Who were they? We know Ezekias best of all, because of his troubled relationship with Isaiah. But who was Isaiah? We shall open his biographical file, but in the name of honesty if not of truth, it is now incumbent upon me to glance at my own.

The exegetical method applied to the Book of Isaiah I learned from a master who influenced my attitudes toward learning. His name was Harav Shushani, and his pedagogical powers cannot be exaggerated. He figures in many of my tales and memories.

His legend was shrouded in a dense and fascinating mystery. No one knew where he came from or where he disappeared for days or weeks at at time. He was fluent in many languages and cultures. The Babylonian and Palestinian Talmud as well as Greek and Roman philosophers, Ugaritic and Akkadian texts, Homer and Shakespeare, Erasmus and Einstein: he spoke with passion about nuclear physics, Aztec history, and any other subject in the encyclopedia.

It was with Shushani that I studied in France after the war. The first chapter took us several months. The first verse . . . over a week.

But do not worry. I propose to move along a bit faster.

BORN PROBABLY IN Jerusalem during the eighth century before the common era, Isaiah seems to have been head of a school of prophets, or perhaps just an ordinary school. In any event, he was an influential citizen. His public activities covered the period from 740 to 700. The text tells us clearly, in a breathtaking flashback: "In the year that King Uzziah died I also saw the Lord sitting upon a throne, high and lifted up, and his train filled the temple. Above it stood the seraphim: each one had six wings, with two he covered his face, and with two he covered his feet, and with two he did fly. . . ." Isaiah experienced that vision in the year of King Uzziah's death, in 740 before the common era. From then on he was involved at the highest level in the major social and political events of the period. In his prophecies, we often see him admonishing sovereigns or their ministers amid an anxious, curious—and heedless—population. He was married. He had three sons and a daughter.

In those days there were still two Jewish kingdoms, Israel and Judah. Both were threatened by the rise of two great powers, Assyria and Babylon. Pekah, the usurper king of Israel, together with King Rezin of Damascus, revolted against Assyria and tried to persuade King Ahaz of Judah to join the alliance. Isaiah advised Ahaz against this. The rebellion could only damage his country. As a result, the rebels invaded Judah. To ward off this peril, Ahaz sent emissaries to ask King Tiglath-pileser for help. The king obliged. Judah thus became dependent on Assyria. But upon Ahaz's death, his son Ezekias followed Isaiah's line and remained neutral. This time, however, it was Egypt that attempted to draw Judah into an armed alliance against Assyria. When Ezekias vacillated, Isaiah "walked about barefoot or stark naked for three years" to illustrate the fate awaiting the Egyptians and their allies, after their defeat: they will be poor and shamed. In the end, Ezekias yielded to military pressure and revolted against Assyria. The result was predictable. The new Assyrian ruler, Sennacherib, invaded Judah and besieged Jerusalem. At this, everybody, including the king, lost heart, except Isaiah. Now he who had been against war exhorted the people to stand fast. He assured them that the capital city would be saved, and it was. A miracle occurred, sowing death in the ranks of the enemy armies. The prophet had not been wrong. Would the people of Judah finally take his warnings seriously? Unfortunately, prophets are only listened to afterward, when it is too late. This time too he was right.

In reading Isaiah we understand why prophecy died with the

destruction of the Temple. Before that, living in relative peace, the Jewish people were psychologically capable of coping with the terrible lessons the prophets taught them; afterward, they were not. Of course, it was the prophet's mission, in the early stages, to disturb people, frighten them, make them aware of their transgressions and the inevitable punishments.

Perhaps in this context we can understand the reluctance of many prophets to assume their missions. Moses had replied to God: "Why me? Take my brother instead. He is a better speaker." Jeremiah found another excuse: "I am only a child." Isaiah displays a different attitude. Let us look at the text: Having seen God on His throne, and having heard the angels cry *kadosh, kadosh, kadosh,* and the voice that shook the doorposts in their foundations, Isaiah "said Woe is me, for I am undone; for I am a man of unclean lips, and I dwell in the midst of a people of unclean lips, for mine eyes have seen the King, the Lord of hosts.

"Then flew one of the seraphim unto me, having in his hand a live coal, which he had taken with the tongs from the altar.

"And he laid it upon my mouth, and said, Lo, this hath touched thy lips; and thine iniquity is taken away, and thy sin purged.

"Also I heard the voice of the Lord, saying Whom shall I send, and who will go for us? Then said I, Here am I, send me."

This time it is quite clear: unlike his colleagues, Isaiah volunteered. And he senses the nature of his assignment: to reveal to the Jews of Judah the shamefulness of their behavior, to inspire them to get a grip on themselves, to repent. He knows that God will ask him to say harsh things to the people, and he is ready. He does not even have to ask.

Listen to the Midrash: "That day the Lord lamented to Himself: But who then can I send? Who will take up the task I lay upon him? I sent Micah, and they beat him; I sent Zechariah, and they killed him; I sent Jeremiah, and they threw him into a pit. . . . And Isaiah hastened to answer, Here I am, send me, I am ready."

Is it possible that he wished to be a martyr, that he took pleasure in the prospect of suffering? Or was he determined to advance his career as prosecutor, enjoying a task which allowed him to chastise the people of Israel?

In the Talmud our sages are pleased with him; they withhold no praise. In all things he seems to have surpassed others. He was born circumcised and lived a hundred and twenty years. Other prophets speak only of their own people, whereas Isaiah, in his vision, addresses the whole of humanity. "Whom have you consoled?" he is asked. "Only our generation?" "No," he replies. "I console all generations." None of My children loved them so much as Isaiah, says God. Furthermore, according to the sages, none of the prophets understood what they were prophesying; they spoke the words in a kind of altered state, except for Moses and Isaiah. Listen to this midrashic declaration: "All the apocalyptic prophecies that Jeremiah foresaw for Israel, Isaiah had thwarted them off long before. . . . And more: all that Ezekiel saw, Isaiah saw." But while Ezekiel is compared to a villager thrilled at the sight of the king, Isaiah is like a city dweller: he sees the king more often and is thus less impressed.

Since the midrashic literature does not speak of more than one Isaiah, how can we reconcile the accusing if not vengeful tone of the first part and the consoling voice of the second? He who punishes through love ends by consoling through love. He who predicts persecutions and oppression cannot fail to promise deliverance and redemption. No one is as harrowing as Isaiah when he rebukes, nor as comforting when he consoles, announcing the end of suffering and the dawn of happier days. We can even go further and say, it is precisely because Isaiah was so pessimistic that he was ultimately given such a generous, encouraging, and reassuring role.

And yet he cannot help but wonder if God is not manipulating him a bit too much. But isn't that true of all prophets?

WHAT IS THE essence of prophecy? What is its function? Unlike the oracles of antiquity, the biblical prophet is not content merely to predict the future. For him, it is the ethical element that prevails. It's simple: to sin is to invite punishment. He knows it, and he wants others to know it. In other words, it is not hard to guess what the future holds for us; all we have to do is to examine our present behavior. Let an individual or a group repent, and hope is permitted and even inevitable. Without repentance, we are doomed.

In Scripture there is the problem of true and false prophets. How can they be identified? The former are disturbing, the latter soothing. And also, the former reinforce and celebrate the Law, the latter bend it or oppose it. In addition, only the true prophets possess the gift of foresight; false prophets do not. This last trait becomes evident only when proof is needed to establish who is who. Only time will deliver the verdict.

The true power of the prophet derives from his moral conviction. And from his courage and persistence in expressing it. He does not represent any political group, nor is he the representative of any social class. Typically, he is alone. Alone against kings, governments, the well-to-do, the notables, alone even against the entire nation. Anyone at any time may strike at him or humiliate him, and some have done just that. Nevertheless, nothing—neither seduction nor threat—can sway him. He never flatters, never aims to please; he is an enemy to all complacency; he is the bearer of truth and ethical concerns; and nothing and no one can make him say what he doesn't want to say, or silence him. Should he fall silent, his silence itself bears witness.

What did the prophet try to teach his generation and ours? That submission to God alone is acceptable. That man need fear no threat in expressing himself freely. Self-censorship is still censorship. A slave who wishes to remain a slave is submitting to punishment. As members of the human family, slaves are free, but they are not free to renounce their freedom. That's the Law.

Still, although he is God's messenger, the prophet must be careful in speaking to his people. He must not go too far in his admonitions. Exaggeration is forbidden and risky. To exaggerate truth is to distort it. It is thus incumbent upon the prophet to reject excess.

But what can the prophet do when it is God who tells him to be excessive? Isn't it God Himself who dictates to His spokesman and emissary the ideas to formulate and the words to use? How then can He hold the prophet responsible?

Suddenly we detect in the commentaries a note of hesitation if not suspicion toward our glorified prophet. They reproach him, for example, for not going in person to see King Ezekias and instead letting himself be represented by "assistants."

Let us see this incident in its historical context. Because it was dangerously divided, Judah was going through a difficult period. A certain influential figure, Ravsheka, tried to seize the throne. Having failed, he went over to the invader Sennacherib, who sent him back to his country at the head of a powerful army, to prevail upon Jerusalem to submit to Assyria. "Do not resist," said Ravsheka, the Jewish "collaborator" with the Assyrians. "Your battle is lost in advance. Heaven itself will not come to your aid."

A royal delegation, composed of Elyakim ben Hilkiyahu, Shebna the scribe, and Yo'ah ben Assaf the secretary, went to meet Ravsheka on the city wall. Interestingly, their instructions were to listen, not to reply. But when King Ezekias received their report, he rent his garments and went to the Temple in sackcloth. Was he afraid of national defeat? He was depressed, bewildered: how could a Jew, especially a Jew with a high position in society, join the enemy? He dispatched emissaries to the prophet Isaiah to ask his advice. Isaiah answered through his own envoys that the king had no reason to fear: the country was in no peril. As mentioned earlier, Isaiah's vision was accurate. The invader withdrew his troops and the kingdom of Judah was saved. Everything was all right? No, everything was all wrong. Instead of thanking the prophet for his encouragement, the Talmudic sages were annoyed with him for sending representatives to meet with the king; he should have gone himself. Wasn't that the same reproach that was addressed to the king? He too might have taken the trouble. Unfortunately, both men were stubborn in their ill-timed pride. The king said, let Isaiah come to me; after all, didn't the prophet Elijah go to King Ahab? Isaiah said, let the king come to me; didn't Jehoram the son of Ahab go to the prophet Elijah?

The people are divided, the country is in peril, the enemy is just beyond the city walls, and these men of rank and eminence have nothing better to do than to play games of protocol? If Ezekias were a wicked, arrogant tyrant, then perhaps we would understand his actions. But he is not. On the contrary, the text always presents him in a favorable light as a pious, God-fearing Jew. When things go wrong, what does he do? He prays. He implores heaven. He trusts in divine benevolence more than his armed forces. He is a most unpretentious king.

During the war against Sennacherib, Ezekias pleads with the Almighty: "I cannot pursue the enemy or even defend myself against him; be charitable, and You strike him down while I sleep." But is he not humble enough to leave his palace and go to the prophet during this serious national crisis? It is strange, but tradition does not condemn either of these figures. Instead, it brings God in to mediate. God arranges things so that the king falls ill. Now, He tells his prophet that he cannot refuse to pay a sick call on him. The Law obliges him to do so. And so it is done.

The scene that follows is astonishing: "In those days Ezekias was sick unto death. And Isaiah the prophet, son of Amotz, came unto him and said unto him, Thus said the Lord, set your house in order for you shall die and not live.

"Then Ezekias turned his face toward the wall, and prayed unto the Lord, and said, Remember now, O Lord, I beseech Thee, how I have walked before Thee in truth and with a perfect heart, and have done that which is good in Thy sight. And Ezekias wept."

It is not clear how long Isaiah remained at the sick king's bedside after that. But when God assigned him his next mission, He used the term *halokh ve'amarta*, Go and tell Ezekias, meaning go back and tell him that I, God of his ancestor David, have heard his prayer, "and I have added fifteen years to his life." How did Isaiah answer? The text does not tell us. Did he accomplish his new mission? No doubt. But once more the text makes no mention of it. The Midrash makes a point of this.

For various reasons—still matters of protocol?—the sages suggest tension, if not conflict, between the king and the prophet. Why does Isaiah feel it necessary to repeat his ominous announcement "you shall die and not live"? According to one midrashic source, it is to inform the king that he will die in this world and will not live in the other. Why this harshness? Says Kohelet-Raba: "Having heard the prophet's verdict, King Ezekias said to Isaiah: 'Isaiah, it is the custom when we visit the sick to say to them, Heaven will take pity on you; if it is a doctor, he will say, you may eat this or that, you may drink this but not that; and even if he sees the sick man is suffering from an incurable disease, he does not tell him brutally, "you are going to die," but tries to cheer him up—whereas you come marching in and announce coldly that I am going to die. Well, I will not heed your words or your prophecy. I am turning to prayer.' "

A variation on the same theme: After their brief exchange, the king asked the prophet why he deserved to die prematurely. "Because you fathered no children," said the prophet. The king explained that he knew that his sons would have been wicked; it was wiser not to have any. At this, Isaiah became angry: "Who gave you permission to meddle in God's mysteries? You had only to do your duty, to marry and beget children, and leave it to God to do what He thinks proper." "In that case," said the king, "give me your daughter and I will marry her" (thus we learn that Isaiah had a daughter). "Too late," said the prophet. The decree had already been signed. It was then that the ailing king turned to prayer, quoting his ancestor David, who said, Even when the knife is at your throat, you must not lose hope in divine intervention.

As it turned out, King Ezekias lived for another fifteen years. And Isaiah was not happy. Was this a blow to his self-esteem? A refusal to accept celestial appeals and reversals? Is it even conceivable that he was ignorant of the value of repentance, he who never ceased reminding the people of its weight? Is it possible that he judged King Ezekias completely irredeemable?

Whatever the answer, Isaiah began a discussion with God about his hurt pride: First you tell me to announce his imminent death, and now You change your mind? What will he take me for? Besides, this is a man of rank, he will not believe my new message, I will have lost all my credibility with him. Then the Lord, blessed be He, reassured him: Do not worry about it. The king is a humble man, he will believe you. At any rate, the future is not yet known, anything is still possible . . .

In reading and rereading this legend, we remain confused. The dialogue is painful and profoundly human; it casts a favorable light on the king but not on the prophet. In truth, the king was right. Isaiah could have been more delicate, shown greater sensitivity and compassion toward a man he had known for a long time, often as an ally.

Was Isaiah too harsh? Inflexible? Cold? Is this why he will die a tragic death? Because of his strange attitude toward the king? Not at all. It is because of his extreme severity toward the people of Israel.

According to legend, King Ezekias eventually married the prophet's daughter. One of their sons was Manasseh. This son, crowned king while still a boy (twelve years old), began to persecute the prophet, whom he accused of heresy, no less. On what pretext? To take revenge for the troubles the prophet had brought to his father?

From the Talmud, again: in the Tractate of Yevamot we read that Shimon ben Azzai found, in a genealogical scroll in Jerusalem, a passage saying that Manasseh killed Isaiah. Rava commented that he accused him, judged him, and had him executed. In other words, everything unfolded according to the Law. There was a proper trial. The defendant appeared before a tribunal and heard himself indicted for three violations of Jewish tradition. Manasseh himself served as prosecutor. Listen:

(1) Your master Moses was warned by God: "No man shall see me and live," and you claim to have "seen" God seated on His throne on high. And you still live.

(2) Your teacher Moses said, "Who is like unto our God, Who

answers all who call upon Him." Thus God is everywhere. But you say, "Seek God there where He may be found; pray to Him when He is High," that is, we do not find Him everywhere.

(3) Your master Moses said, "I will fulfill the number of thy days," that is, that each man will live only the years allotted to him, but you say, "I will add fifteen years to your life."

Clearly, these were serious charges going to the heart of the Jewish religious tradition rooted in the Law of Moses and Israel.

The tribunal asked the defendant if he wished to speak. He did not. To one witness he seems to have said, "The truth is, I could have explained everything but Manasseh would not have listened." In other words, as a last favor to the Jewish sovereign, better say nothing than let his murder be unjustified. Isaiah preferred to fall back on miracles. He pronounced a holy name and an immense cedar opened before him. Isaiah took refuge within it. Undaunted, Manasseh had a saw brought and began to cut through the tree. But when the saw reached the prophet's mouth he died—for it was by his mouth that he had sinned when he stated that he lived "among a people whose lips are unclean."

In fact, we recall that Isaiah was already punished for this by an angel who burned his lips. But here the biblical text and the midrashic commentaries differ. In Scripture, the burn brings him expiation and forgiveness. In the Midrash, the sequence is more sorrowful. After Isaiah's outcry about "unclean lips," God rebukes him: "Hear, Isaiah! You claim that your lips are unclean, and I have no quarrel with that; after all, that is your concern. But you said that those of the people of Israel are equally unclean, and there you overstep the bounds!"

Thus Manasseh's accusations were of no real importance. Isaiah had to settle his difficulties with Moses and God alone. Isaiah's tragic fate was a result only of his unfair defamation of Israel.

And here we touch upon a theme which has lost none of its immediacy since that time. When the people of Israel's honor and security are in question, just how far can one go? Who tells us when to speak and when to be silent? When to praise and when to criticize? For a Diaspora Jew, the problem takes on a redoubled intensity: has he or she the right to interfere in the internal affairs of the Jewish state, of which he shares the joys but not always the distress? Can we in good conscience declare ourselves for or against this or that Israeli policy, when we are not on the spot to enjoy Israel's blessings or suffer its afflictions?

Some say: yes, the Jews have that right. And they point to the prophets as examples. Except that all prophets save Ezekiel lived *in* Israel. Do we have the right to say what Israelis say about their leaders and their attitudes?

Furthermore, even prophets were reprimanded for being too judgmental of their people. Moses himself was punished. Unfairly? Yes. God commanded His messengers to criticize, to judge, to condemn; when they did it, He lost His temper.

In the case of Isaiah, God had recourse to an ungodly man for the expression of His mood and His will. For Manasseh—let's say it bluntly—is ungodly. Talmudic legends confirm the premonitions of his father Ezekias. The latter, finally married, took a walk with his two sons, Rav-shakeh and Manasseh, still little boys. A good father, he carried one son on each shoulder. And he heard them chatting: "This skull is so bald, you could fry a fish on it," one said. And the other answered: "You could use it as an altar for sacrificing to the idols." Enraged, Ezekias shook himself. The two boys fell off his shoulders. Rav-shakeh died, Manasseh did not.

Manasseh's name itself derives from the verb *nasha,* which means "he has forgotten." Yes, Manasseh has forgotten his faith, his duty to God, and his obligations toward his people. He is said to have destroyed the altar, encouraged idolatry, profaned the Temple, raped his own sister, committed murder. He is among the very few who will be forever barred from the life to come. And it is this man who preaches Jewish morality to the Jewish prophet? It is this man who defends the honor of Moses? Is that why Isaiah refused to defend himself? Because it was beneath his dignity to debate a traitor to God and his Law?

LET US RETURN to the question raised at the start: the first verse of the book mentions four kings, all Isaiah's contemporaries. But there were five. Why is Manasseh missing from the list? Because he was evil? Since when is censorship practiced in our prophetic literature? Jewish history knows other kings no less impious, and their misdeeds have been recorded. Why should we not learn of the exhortations that Isaiah doubtless directed at this insolent and rebellious ruler?

That question is not discussed in the commentaries. Was it excessive modesty? Shyness? Embarrassment? It seems to me that we must look for the reason in the prophet's character. A proud man, he imposes discipline and knows how to discipline himself. Though he did not always agree with Ezekias, the latter was a valuable, even an honorable interlocutor. Manasseh was not. Yet Manasseh, this grandson who turned out badly, was *his* responsibility. Wasn't it Isaiah who all but forced Ezekias to marry? He even gave him his own daughter as a wife. Manasseh was their son. But now the young king disappointed Isaiah profoundly as a ruler and as a Jew. Is it possible that when the prophet realized his grandson's sinful behavior, he decided to put an end to his prophetic career? In other words, if Manasseh's name is not included in the first list, is it because Isaiah had ceased to be a prophet during his grandson's reign?

IN CONCLUSION, I think again of my old teacher Harav Shushani in Paris. Without realizing it, we are following his teachings now. Look: we have not gone much beyond the first verse.

Perhaps that is the essence of the prophetic tragic condition. Eternally caught between God and the king, God and his creatures, duty and compassion, he must inevitably be torn apart. That is why most prophets tried to evade their mission. They know that it is an impossible one. His emissaries cannot win. God is not only the King of

Kings but also the father of Israel. To speak evil of His people will displease Him in the end. Only Isaiah volunteered for the task. Was he prepared to choose God over Israel? He knew that he could expect no reward. And yet his love of God was stronger.

Now we understand why, in Talmudic literature, it is the same Isaiah who accomplished a dazzling metamorphosis in the second part of the book bearing his name. There he is the eloquent consoler, unequaled as a bearer of promise. Who can read the chapter "Be comforted, my people" (chapter 40), without being swept by an irresistible emotion? I read it in 1979 in Moscow, and I shall never forget what I felt then. Gathered around the Bima, hundreds and hundreds of Russian Jews, young and old, repeated each word silently, moving their lips as if to better savor and remember.

In Jerusalem, God said in Isaiah's voice: "For Zion's sake I will not hold my peace, and for Jerusalem's sake will not rest." And also, "I have set watchmen upon the walls, O Jerusalem, which shall never hold their peace day nor night." Also, "And I will rejoice in Jerusalem, and find joy in my people; and the voice of weeping shall be no more heard in her, nor the voice of crying. . . . And they shall build houses, and inhabit them; and they shall plant vineyards, and eat the fruit of them. . . . And it shall come to pass that before they call, shall answer. . . . And the wolf and the lamb shall feed together side by side, and live in harmony."

What a glorious vision of a world at peace! When we speak of hope for humanity, it is always Isaiah's which we evoke.

Isaiah, the most sorrowful and the most confident of prophets: like other prophets chosen by God to serve as spokesman and witness, he was also His victim.

Hoshea: The Strangest of All Prophets

O N THAT DAY, as always, the prophet rises early to go to the Temple in Jerusalem and briefly pray for its welfare. The priests are still fulfilling their duties, sacrifices are being offered to the Lord. It is only after the Sanctuary's destruction that they will be replaced by prayers.

The Temple is still intact and the people of Judah are not on their knees. Life is more or less normal. The country is sovereign. In fact, there are two countries and both are independent. Are they content? Are they happy? If living in sin does not preclude happiness, the inhabitants of Judah and Israel have no particular reason to complain. Their military is strong, their economy prosperous. In spite of the tense geopolitical situation of the region, forever plagued by strifes between neighboring great powers, the danger to the Jewish states is not from without but from within. Their structures are not stable. The kingdom of Judah has been governed by Jotham since his father Uzziah was afflicted with leprosy. As for the kingdom of Israel, it experiences much turbulence. Since Jeroboam II's death, the throne has changed hands several times.

Meanwhile, in distant Greece, Homer is completing his *Iliad*.

There culture will be, and to some extent already is, shaped by philosophers and oracles. In Judah and Samaria, words are spoken by prophets.

Does Hoshea know what his future might be? Does the prophet know that he will become a prophet? That God has chosen him for a mission whose nature is still concealed from him? If so, he must wonder what he will be called upon to say, or more precisely, what form his message will take and to whom it will be addressed. Actually, this preoccupation surely applies to all prophets: both emissary and spokesman for God, the prophet is often surprised. He never knows beforehand the words he will be ordered to utter. Will he be expected to appease the people or make them tremble?

Still, the prophet we are about to meet has not yet been given the task of prophecy. He is still a simple person. And when God chooses to speak to him, ordering him to do certain things in His name, his astonishment will match our own.

Let us read the text, shall we? It opens with the customary introduction: "The word of the Lord that came unto Hoshea, son of Be'eri, in the days of Uzziah, Jotham, Ahaz and Ezekias, kings of Judah, and in the days of Jeroboam, son of Joash, king of Israel."

Then comes the appeal, or the mission, which is rather disturbing, to say the least: "And the Lord said to Hoshea, go, take unto thee a wife of whoredom and children of whoredom. . . ."

What! Could this be the glorious and inspired beginning of a beautiful but unenviable prophetic career? What kind of prophet is this man who, instead of praying, studying, and fasting (meditating and working on himself, in the depths of his heart and soul), is heading toward a woman known mainly for her promiscuity? And what about God's role in this bizarre story? Why does He dispatch Jonah to Nineveh to save its inhabitants from sin and punishment, and send Hoshea to enjoy the pleasures of the company of a woman whose social reputation is notably unvirtuous?

(Well, there we are: the text offers us an episode unparalleled in the dramatic history of Jewish prophecy. A prophet and a prostitute united by the same sentence, in the same design deprived of the slightest trace of sacredness.) As we would say in the yeshiva, *"mai ka mashma lan?"* What in the world could it all mean?

Fortunately, generations of sages and their disciples were equally intrigued by our subject and his destiny.

HOSHEA son of Be'eri hears the voice of God ordering him to go and get himself a prostitute for a wife. What is his reaction? What does he feel? What does he do? Does he try to argue or even to ask God to repeat the order: "O Lord, God of Abraham, Isaac, and Jacob, could I have heard you correctly? Please tell me again, but slowly . . ."

If so, the text does not mention it. In fact, it says very little about procedure. Between cause and effect, the distance is astonishingly short. God knows what He is doing. His logic is not necessarily ours. His word is sufficient. It is irrevocable. What follows is logically unavoidable. The divine order is "Go get yourself a prostitute," and the prophet simply obeys. We know what God's thought is but not the prophet's. What is going on in his head, in his heart? Is he perturbed by the unprecedented nature of his assignment? What is his reaction to it?

But wait a second, where does one find a prostitute . . . when one is a prophet? Where would he get an address? Just imagine him knocking at the door of a local rabbi or policeman: Sir . . . could you help me? . . . Is it possible, on the other hand, that having heard the divine order, he *knows* how to fulfill it? It is the order alone that matters. The voice. It now vibrates in him and he will never be separated from it. God's voice will now become part of his very being.

Still . . . how can he be sure that the voice is God's, and not his own? Or Satan's? How does one distinguish the source, the identity, and the truth of a celestial voice? There, a possible answer may exist: if the voice brings you back to yourself, it is not God's. It is God's only if and when it brings you closer to your fellow human beings.

Hoshea should be able to discern the prophetic voice. After all, his father Be'eri was a prophet too. This is ascertained by a Talmudic source for which we should be grateful, since, in matters of biography, that of Hoshea is rather sketchy at best; in fact, it is extremely poor. We know little about him as a person, and even less about his father. On what basis does the Talmud find it proper to identify Be'eri's vocation? On this premise: whenever the text mentions the name of a prophet together with that of his father, it means that both were prophets. The Talmud goes further by adding a surprising detail: only two prophetic verses are attributed to Be'eri. And since, in those good times, it was impossible to compose an entire book with only two sentences, they were included in the Book of Isaiah.

Another biographical detail: we know where Hoshea lived. His residence? Jerusalem. There too, we learn it not from the text but from its midrashic commentary. And we deduct that by omission. When the text does not indicate the precise location of a prophet's quarters, it means he lived in Jerusalem.

Good. Thanks for the information. But does this mean there were prostitutes in the holy city of David? And that it was possible, socially acceptable, for a nice young man of a respectable family to marry one of them without creating an uproar?

Let us talk a bit more about prophecy and prophets in general.

When you study ancient history you read about Athens and its philosophers, Egypt and its pyramids, Babylon and its astronomers, Rome and its senators, and . . . Jerusalem and its prophets.

Now we face a question that has accompanied us throughout our entire pilgrimage to the kingdom of Judah of those days: What is a prophet? A preacher? A visionary capable of predicting the future? One who carries God's words to His creatures? Who intercedes in heaven on behalf of his people? How does God speak to him? In a dream? Through symbols? Is the prophet possessed by God's spirit only at certain moments, while remaining "normal" the rest of the time?

A fascinating character on more than one level, the prophet (or the prophetess: prophecy was not exclusively a male occupation) is a profoundly human person, aware of his or her weaknesses and short-comings. Few sought the appointment. To be God's emissary is nei-ther enviable nor pleasant. Eternally caught between polarized forces, he never knows a moment's peace. Involved in the thorniest matters of state and society, fearing no one and demanding nothing for himself, he is inevitably persecuted either by heaven or by the people. He is never satisfied, rewarded, at peace with himself and his social environment. He constantly risks imprisonment, humilia-tion, and death. Disarmed, he is defenseless. In choosing him, God chooses for him. "A prophet who rejects his prophetic vocation is theoretically guilty and punishable by spiritual death." That is the Law.

Hence the prophet is often tragically isolated and ontologically solitary. Is he different from the people around him? The message comes from God, but it is the prophet who delivers it. The words he uses, the images he conjures are theirs too. But they resonate differ-ently when they come from him. On his lips, everyday words acquire an unforgettable tonality, a lasting intensity.

We already raised questions regarding Hoshea's special mission. In philosophy, all questions are valid, but in matters of faith they had better be preceded by answers. When a question brings me closer to God, God is the answer. When the question moves me away from God, God becomes the question. But isn't God present in both situa-tions? God is forever *in* things, never outside.

BACK TO HOSHEA.

From the outset, the text offers an important element of informa-tion by placing the story in its time frame. Let us reread the open-ing lines: "The word of the Lord that came unto Hoshea, son of Be'eri, in the days of Uzziah, Jotham, Ahaz and Ezekias, kings of Judah, and in the days of Jeroboam, son of Joash, king of Israel."

So now we know the period, around 750 before the common era, and that may help us comprehend somewhat more about both the events and the characters in the story.

Let us look at the four kings of Judah mentioned in the story. Uzziah, crowned at sixteen, reigned for fifty-two years. His son Jotham reigned for sixteen years, as did Jotham's son Ahaz. Ahaz's son Ezekias, who succeeded him, reigned for twenty-nine years. As for Jeroboam, king of Israel, he reigned for forty-one years in Samaria.

So many kings in the life of our prophet. But how old was he when he became a prophet? And how long did he live? A Talmudic source says: ninety. No wonder he was called "the old man." Rabbi Abraham Ibn Ezra says he was younger. It is possible that Hoshea prophesied during the last year of Uzziah and the first of Ezekias, and covered the kings in between. What is certain is that his mission lasted during the entire reign of Jeroboam.

But what exactly was his mission? Listen to the second part of the verse, which I omitted earlier. I did so intentionally. Let us read the verse in its entirety: "When the Lord first spoke through Hoshea, the Lord said to him: Go, take yourself a wife of harlotry and have children of harlotry [and here comes the punch line], for the land commits great harlotry by forsaking the Lord." On the surface this could mean: Go and do what so many, too many others are doing. In other words, let the prophet demean himself in public, to serve as an illustration of the people's own degradation.

Let us stay there for a moment. Hoshea addresses himself mainly to the tribe of Ephraim, which, to him, personifies the northern kingdom of Israel at the time of Jeroboam and his immediate successors. Thus it may be useful to learn more about its state of affairs. Materially, things are good. Militarily secure, the country is in a period of dazzling prosperity. Spiritually, the picture is less enviable. Soon after he ascends to the throne, King Zechariah, son of Jeroboam, is slain by Shalum, who, in turn, is murdered by Menahem. In the ten years following Jeroboam's death, five kings seize power, three of them through violence and bloodshed. Plots and counterplots constitute the fabric of political life. As far as religion is concerned, the situation seems catastrophic. Animal idols made of wood or stone have again become popular. Idolatry is contagious. The God of Israel? Forgotten. His Law repudiated, His holy covenant betrayed.

Generally speaking, with the rare exceptions of Kings David and Solomon, a Jewish monarchy is not something to boast about. It is enough to read what the prophets say about it to measure the magnitude of its moral decline. Isaiah, Jeremiah, Habakuk, Amos, and Micha: their pain, anger, and desperate outbursts help us understand why, in the beginning, God would have preferred His people not to be a monarchy. But the people stubbornly insisted upon having their kings and so becoming like all the others. And like the others they became. It is in this light that we can perhaps understand why God made Hoshea marry a harlot. As if to say: look at yourself, people of Israel . . .

Hoshea's task then, is, to put the situation into words. He shouts, he alerts, he protests, he warns, he threatens. Listen:

> O Ephraim [the northern kingdom]
> You have played the harlot,
> Israel is defiled.

Hoshea speaks of God's anguish and sorrow, of God's disappointment:

> It was I who taught Ephraim to walk,
> I took them up in my arms;
> But they did not know that I healed them.
> I led them with cords
> Of compassion
> With the bands of love.
> I became to them
> As the one who eases the yoke on their jaws,
> I bent down to them and fed them gently. . . .

What emanates from these complaints? Don't look for an answer. You found it already. It is a painful feeling that lovers and friends know all too well: disappointment. When things go wrong, when one partner feels wounded, betrayed, and bewildered. Still in love, he or she cannot understand: why does the other behave this way? What have I done to deserve such a behavior?

Now, we might perhaps understand this drama, since it unfolds on a higher theological level. It reflects the decadence in the relations between a unique couple: God and his people. More than his peers, Hoshea seems better qualified to speak of the special bonds connecting the God of Israel and the history of Israel. It is the story of a marriage. It took place at Sinai and the Torah was and remains the marriage contract. Thus through Hoshea speaks the voice of an unhappy husband—God—who feels abandoned by his beloved, the people of Israel. It is as if God had said: I chose you, I loved you, I protected you, I saved you, remember? And you, what have you done to sustain the purity of our love? You are searching for other possibilities, other outlets, other sources of joy, and in so doing you have betrayed both of us. You have cheapened, trivialized, and blemished our love and our happiness, you have made yourself unworthy of our beginnings.

In his pain, God addresses himself to the people themselves, in the second person, *you*, but also in the third person, *they*:

> She (Israel) did not know
> That it was I who gave her
> The grain,
> The wine and the oil.
> It was I who gave her
> The silver
> And the gold
> Which they then used for the idol Baal.

And further:

> It was I who knew you in the wilderness,
> In the land of drought.

> Yet, when they were well fed,
> And their heart was uplifted,
> They forgot me.

And also:

> What am I to do with you, Ephraim,
> And with you, Judah?
> Your love is like a cloud in the morning,
> It is the dew that so quickly evaporates . . .

Other prophets are harsh, demanding, and rigorous; their appeals are wrenching. They too denounce the people's promiscuity, complacency, and forgetfulness as they turn their back on their Creator. But Hoshea's role is different. To them God is father, judge, and king. To Hoshea he is husband. A humiliated husband, deceived and betrayed by his spouse, his adulterous wife.

That is why Hoshea is ordered to "take" a prostitute for a wife. To show the people that they have prostituted themselves by espousing alien gods. As if He is telling the prophet: "You do in your private life what *they* have done to me in public. I am wedded to a people of prostitutes!"

But is this explanation satisfactory? Isn't Hoshea, by virtue of being a prophet, different from other men, supposed to be better than any of them? Furthermore, doesn't he worry that they might reject his pleas? And what if they reacted with arrogance: who are you to preach morality to us when you yourself sought out the sweet company of harlots?!

On this last point, let us emphasize that as a prophet Hoshea is not obliged to defer to the people. As with all prophets, God alone is his Master and Judge; only God can make him alter his tone or remain silent. Between popularity and faith, his choice is made. God may hold it against him . . . but more about that later.

For the moment, I must admit that in spite of its theological implication, the story of the harlot, on its purely personal level, remains puzzling to me, as it does to certain Talmudic and post-Talmudic commentators. Faced with its inherent enigma, they try to solve it.

The simplest and easiest way, as mentioned earlier, would be to declare that, quite logically, Hoshea had to follow God's will. When God orders, no one has the right to say no or even to ask for explanations. God does not have to explain.

Fortunately, certain great minds, mainly from medieval times, choose to go further, and deeper, in their inquiries. For Maimonides, Ibn Ezra, and the Radak, for example, the whole story is either a vision or a dream. Maimonides, as always, expresses himself with great clarity: "God would never do anything that would present his prophets as drunkards or imbeciles. . . . No, this episode is part of a prophetic vision." Rabbi Abraham Ibn Ezra concurs: "May God, blessed be He, save us from believing that He really ordered His emissary to take a harlot as a wife and to have children with her. . . . All this took place in a dream only." In other words, the entire story is nothing but poetic fantasy; literary fiction.

In real life, as God's emissary, servant of his will and servant of his Law, Hoshea could not transgress that Law. Doesn't the Torah explicitly state that a prophet who pretends to have the right to change the Law is by definition a false prophet? Aren't we ordered to observe the biblical laws of purity? In other words, there was no such wedding between a prophet and a prostitute—it took place only in someone's imagination. Or was it perhaps a "lapsus," a slip of the tongue? Was Hoshea a victim of his own eloquence? Rashi's hypothesis is not too far from such a view. He also does not believe that we deal with a real event. The whole thing was a parable, an allegory. The prophet merely chose to tell it as if he had himself lived it to make its impact stronger.

Now this ought to satisfy even the fiercest skeptics in our midst. Still, some difficulties do remain. And Don Itzhak Abrabanel, one of my favorite commentators, is aware of them. They derive from the fact that the text before us speaks of the episode as fact. God tells Hoshea: "Go, take a prostitute for a wife." And Hoshea does exactly that. He does take a harlot. We even know her name, which tells us

something about her: Gomer, daughter of Debalim. Rav, an important Amora, a teacher of the first generation, Shmuel's friend and
adversary, comments on the name *bat divlayim* as follows: a girl of
whom everybody had something bad, something derogatory to say.
On the name Gomer, he offers a play on words: *"Gomer she'hakol gom-
rim ba."* Gomer means conclusion, end, attainment. In other words,
either they all ended up with her, or came to an end with her; or all
who had an encounter with her went to the limit. And Rashi does not
hesitate to be more explicit: *"Bi'atam ve'ta'avat libam"*—she was a
woman with whom men, full of desire, could accomplish the act
without obstacle. Well, Shmuel's commentary centered on Debalim
or Divla'im: she was sweet like a fig. Rabbi Yohanan believes that
"Debalim" comes from *Debala,* meaning everybody could trash her.
A later rabbinic commentator was kinder: "Everybody looked at her,
so great was her beauty." Oh yes, Gomer, daughter of Debalim, did
exist. Her avowed profession? Prostitute. It's as simple as that. It's in
the text. However, some commentators do not give up trying to
defend the prophet and, indirectly, his spouse too. To limit the damage, they make use of the expression *eshet zenunim,* which, in their
view, does not mean "harlot" but "woman capable of harlotry," or a
woman *of* harlotry, whatever that means. In other words, when
Hoshea married her, she was not yet a prostitute. And thus the narrative quietly continues. There was a wedding. Afterward? Listen:
"Gomer conceived and gave him a son. And the Eternal One told
him: call your son Jezreel, for soon I will punish the House of Jehu for
the blood shed in Jezreel. I shall put an end to the House of Israel. On
that day, I shall break the arc of Israel in the Valley of Jezreel."

Thus the prophet became husband and father. And God, who
mingled in Hoshea's private life by playing the matchmaker, goes so
far as to suggest a name for Hoshea's firstborn son.

But the story does not end here. Let us read: "Gomer conceived
again and gave birth to a girl. And God said to Hoshea: give her
the name Lo-Ruchama [the one for whom there is no pity], for I shall
no longer have pity for the House of Israel; it will no longer be
forgiven."

Hoshea considers his own life irrevocably linked to the life of Israel. His third child, a second son, is named by God "Lo-Ami"—this people is not mine, its god is not Me. Here one fails to understand: why are the prophet's children punished? Why are they humiliated and made to bear such shameful names? Are they children of prostitution? And if they are, is it their fault? And God in all this? "Upon her children I shall have no pity," He says. No pity? Why?

Few prophetic sayings are as severe, as harsh. God's predictions and warnings, born of bitterness, seem to be designed solely to elicit fear and cause pain.

> Plead with your mother, plead
> For she is not my wife,
> And I am not her husband,
> That she put away her harlotry from her face
> And her adultery from her breasts,
> Lest I strip her naked and make her as in the day she was born,
> And make her like a wilderness,
> And set her a parched land,
> And slay her with thirst.

And later, He continues lashing out at the people:

> So I shall be to them like a lion,
> Like a leopard I will lurk beside the way.
> I will fall upon them like a bear robbed of her cubs,
> I will tear open their breast and will devour them like a lion
> As a wild beast I would rend them . . .

Listen further:

> I will destroy you, O Israel . . .
> The children will fall by the sword,
> The little one dashed in pieces,
> The pregnant women ripped open. . . .

How could Hoshea, a prophet who is human, more human than others, live with such dreadful premonitions, with such images fraught with horror and death? How could he carry such visions of cruelty and death? How could he live with a woman who evokes and illustrates such sin and punishment? With the birth of every successive child, the family's misfortune grows more cruel. Then why have more children? Why maintain the appearance of family life? Hoshea ends up by repudiating Gomer, daughter of Debalim. And God, again, interferes in his private affairs.

Let us listen to Hoshea:

And God speaks to me and says: Go once more and love a woman who is beloved by another and is an adulteress; love her as the Lord loves the people of Israel, though they turn to other gods and love cakes of raisins. So I bought her for fifteen shekels of silver and a homer and lethech of barley. And I said to her: You must stay and remain mine for many days; you shall no more play the harlot or belong to another man—so I will be to you.

Question: who is this woman? Is she the first wife or a new one? Also: God tells him to love her, whereas earlier he told him to "take her." Hasn't God given Hoshea a much more difficult task? What is easier, to seize a woman or to love her?

The consensus among commentators is that in both situations the woman is the same. And therein lies the key to the tale. It can be expressed in one word: *teshuvah*. Repentance is possible. And it is endowed with a healing and redeeming quality. At the end, husband and wife are reconciled—as are God and Israel. In Jewish history, no breakup is eternal. As a consequence of *teshuvah*, God the husband will love Israel the wife with greater passion. It is no accident that that particular chapter of Hoshea—*shuva Yisrael*, Repent, Israel—is read in the synagogues on the Shabbat between Rosh Hashanah and Yom Kippur.

"Shuva Yisrael," says the Lord. "Return O Israel, return to the Lord your God,

> For you have stumbled because of your iniquity.
> Take with you words
> And return to the Lord.
> Say to Him: take away all iniquity,
> Accept that which is good,
> Our lips will replace the offering of bullocks.
> Assyria shall not save us,
> We will not ride upon horses,
> We will say no more "our God" to the work of our handsmen,
> In Thee alone the orphan finds mercy.

Suddenly all is well. The last chapter reads like a happy ending. All is forgiven, Israel will blossom. "Who is wise, and he shall understand these things?" wonders the prophet. "For the ways of the Lord are right, and the righteous shall walk in them, but the sinners shall stumble in them."

The same story may have contradictory effects. It can strengthen the faith of the believer just as it may diminish it in the nonbeliever. Does this apply to the strange and disturbing tale of Hoshea and his even stranger relationship with the adulterous Gomer, daughter of Debalim?

In the text, the tale of the prophet Hoshea finds its denouement, but not so in midrashic literature nor in popular fantasy. Thus in the volume *sefer ha'dorot*—the *Book of Generations*—one may read the following passage on Hoshea's death: "The ancient sages of Saloniki believe that the prophet, still in Babylon, asked for his coffin to be put on the back of a camel, which would find its way to the place where he would be buried. The camel arrived at the cemetery of Safed. There, the local Jews found in a satchel his letter with specific instructions. And so he was buried there with fitting honors."

In the Midrash Hoshea's destiny is less glorious. There one encounters toward him a kind of distancing which ought not to surprise us. One feels a certain resentment over his harsh, horror-filled premonitions of Israel's future. Granted, he only said what God told him to say. But it is easier to be angry at God's messenger than at God. We know that in some cases God Himself turns against His emissary. When Noah, after the Flood, asks God why He hasn't shown compassion toward the children, God admonishes him: "What? Now you are talking?" Noah should have spoken up earlier—before the tragedy. Moses did it. When, at the time of the Golden Calf, God tells his favorite prophet, "Your people have sinned," Moses answers: "*My* people, not Yours?"

(As far as Hoshea is concerned, we read in the Tractate on Passover a disturbing passage in which God tells the prophet: "It is because of you that I inflicted on my people three punishments!")

Hoshea, in the biblical text, is infinitely obedient. Perhaps a bit too obedient? Is this why, in midrashic sources, he became a symbol of reconciliation and peace?

Whenever the Talmud wishes to emphasize the importance of peace, almost at any cost, it quotes from Hoshea: *"Habor atzabim Ephraim, hanah lo,"* which means, "Joined by idols, leave or let him alone."

This is how Rashi interprets the verse: "Ephraim is so attached to idolatry that he is unable to detach himself from it. Therefore, dear prophet, stop reprimanding him. It's pointless." Usually, Rashi's commentaries are rooted in Talmudic sources. And when faced with two interpretations, he chooses the one favorable to Israel. Not now. Actually, he could have chosen the one attributed to Rabbi Eleazar Hakapar, a sage of the fifth generation after the destruction of the Second Temple who taught at the Academy of Lod. Rabbi Eleazar transforms the meaning of the verse, making it positive. Playing on the term *habor,* which means adhesion, cohesion, and unification, he says: When the people of Israel are united, God leaves them in peace—even if they remain attached to idolatry.

Fortunately, Rashi uses the same idea for his understanding of another verse from Hoshea: "Their heart is divided, now shall they be found faulty: He shall break down their altars, He shall spoil their images." Comments Rashi: "Great is the value of peace, for even when the children of Israel adore idols but live in peace among themselves, Satan is powerless to denounce them. For in the time of Hoshea, God said: *Hanah lakhem*, leave them alone.

Hoshea, the tormented prophet of doom, is now a messenger of peace—and hope. But a hope born of frustration, incomprehension, and distress.

Listen now to a midrashic tale in which the reader is surprised to feel sorry for our angry prophet. It is offered to us in the Tractate of Pesakhim (on Passover), in which Hoshea's behavior is described and discussed—and finally even explained.

When the Holy One, blessed be He, told the prophet Hoshea, "Your children have sinned," he should have answered, like Moses before him: "*My* children, not Yours? Aren't they the descendants of Your beloved Abraham, Isaac, and Jacob? Have mercy on them. They are worthy of Your compassion!" But he did not respond that way. Instead, says the Midrash, he displayed a greater detachment, saying: "Master of the universe, the entire world is Yours. You are free to do whatever You want. You are displeased with Your people, go ahead, take another in its place!" Then, shocked by His emissary's words, God wondered: "What shall I do with this *zaken?*" which means old man or sage. He prepared an elaborated script which we can read together. God thought to himself: "I shall tell him: 'Go, take a woman of prostitution for a wife who will give you children of prostitution.' And he will obey. Later, I shall order him to send her away. If he is capable of doing it, I shall do so too: I shall send away Israel" (In other words, I will choose another people).

So Hoshea, obedient as always, went to see Gomer, daughter of Debalim, a woman of bad reputation, and married her. She gave him two sons and a daughter, and it is quite possible that they led a normal life until the Holy One, blessed be He, told the prophet: "Didn't you learn anything from your teacher, Moses? Don't you think you should follow his example? From the moment I spoke to him, he separated from his wife—yet you remain with yours." In other words, what are you waiting for? Leave her at once! Hoshea's answer? "Master of the universe, I cannot do that! I have children, she is their mother. I cannot divorce or repudiate her!"

That was the moment God was waiting for. He said: "You whose wife is a prostitute, you who don't even know whether your children are truly yours, you cannot leave her and them, and you dare to tell me to separate myself from my children, the descendants of Abraham, Isaac, and Jacob, all tried and chosen by me? Have you forgotten that the people of Israel are one of my masterworks—the Torah, the heavens and the earth, and the Temple of Jerusalem are the three others—for whom the world was created? And you have the audacity to tell me to change my people for another?" Realizing the seriousness of his sin, Hoshea burst out in tears and begged the Lord's forgiveness and mercy. But the Holy One, blessed be He, went on reprimanding him: "Rather than plead for yourself, why not plead for Israel?" That is how Hoshea, the prophet of anger, became the defender of his people.

And now we see him as a trusted ally and benefactor. His weaknesses? The prophet is a divine messenger but a human being, nevertheless. He can make mistakes, but they are always rectified. And forgiven. Thus, his visions of catastrophes may have materialized in our time, but surely not in his. On the contrary, his words became carriers of promise and of exultant blessings: "And the children of Israel will be as numerous as the sand at the sea." Or: "Lo Ruhama," No Pity, became "Ruhama," Compassion Will Vanquish Cruelty. "Lo-Ami," Not My People, became "Ami," Yes, My People. There was no divorce between the God of Israel and the people of Israel.

It is in Hoshea that we read the beautiful benediction one recites every morning when wearing the phylacteries or *tefillin:* "*Ve'erastikh li le'olam* . . . And I shall betroth thee forever; yes, I shall betroth thee unto me in righteousness, and in judgment, and in grace, and in compassion. I shall betroth thee in faith, and you know the Lord."

It is God who makes that vow.

All we are called upon to do is to echo His words and allow them to penetrate our very being and to make them part of our own.

IN THE TALMUD

Rabbi Tarfon's Humility

In the Tractate of Kiddushin, which deals with the legal aspects of marriage, we come across an intriguing yet moving tale about the great sage Rabbi Tarfon, known for his learning and modesty as well as for his profound, consuming respect for his mother.

We are told that whenever she wanted to get into bed, he would kneel so that she could put her feet on his back. Naturally, he would do the same when she wished to get out of bed as well.

In case you are wondering about the source of this story, the answer is provided in the text: it was he himself, Rabbi Tarfon, who told it. In fact, the text even relates the circumstances of his telling it.

One day he came to the *beit ha'midrash,* the House of Study, where a lively discussion was going on about the biblical commandment which orders us to honor our parents. Apparently, Rabbi Tarfon joined the conversation by stressing his own scrupulous observance of that commandment. But the sages were not impressed. "Oh," they said, "you did not do even half of what the commandment expects you to do." And they added a strange question: "Has your mother ever thrown her purse into the sea without your making her feel ashamed?" In other words: has your mother ever been in a capricious mood in your presence, without being made to feel foolish?

If Rabbi Tarfon replied, there is no record of it in Talmudic literature. From what we know of his character, we may surmise, however, that he swallowed his colleagues' curious reaction in silence.

Still, this episode raises questions one cannot ignore.

One: is it conceivable that the renowned and respected Rabbi Tarfon, a teacher and close friend of the greatest scholars of the time, boasted of something he had done, namely fulfilling one of the Ten Commandments given by the Almighty God at Sinai? Since when may one take pride in obeying God's will?

Two: how is one to explain the patronizing attitude of his peers in the House of Study? Where is the connection between his words and theirs? Between his infinite respect for his mother and their seemingly supercilious question about her purse? Where is the logic in all this?

And three: why does the Talmud tell us this tale? Just to demonstrate that, in its dialogues, one may say anything to anyone? Is it used perhaps to defend rigorous interpretation of the Law? Or to warn us against it?

If humility is Rabbi Tarfon's trademark, it is not his alone. It is, one might say, what all sages have in common. Naturally, they all share an irresistible thirst for truth and piety, but this can blossom only in an atmosphere of humility. Let a single trace of pride be added to the quest, and it will lead to self-delusion and hypocrisy. It is about the vain person that God says: "He and I cannot dwell under the same roof." Where vanity appears, the spirit of God, the Shekhina, recedes, leaving frustration and distortion in its wake.

Still, humility is not specifically mentioned in the 613 commandments in the Torah. Nowhere is it written that men and women must be humble. The reason for its absence may be that all commandments are to be fulfilled consciously. One must think of what one does—and why. That is why certain good deeds and prayers must be preceded by appropriate words expressing intent. When you recite the blessing over wine and bread, you think of its meaning. You are aware of the moment, marked by your desire to find grace in the eyes of God. Moreover, you try to deepen your awareness and your commitment by pushing yourself to think higher and come closer to the source of all beginnings.

Of course, when humility becomes externalized, when someone says, "Look how modest I am," it inevitably becomes false. People may compete in every other area of human endeavor, but not in humility. True humility lies in the subconscious.

(An anecdote: A rabbi in a shtetl comes to the synagogue on Yom Kippur eve to do penance. He falls to his knees, beats his breast and pleads with God to forgive him his sins: "Have pity on my soul, O Master of the universe! Who am I? A weak and vulnerable creature! I am worthless, I am a nobody . . ." One of the synagogue's dignitaries hears him and decides that what is good for the rabbi is good for him. He too falls to his knees, asks for forgiveness, and cries out: "Forgive my occasional misconduct, O Lord! Who am I? A nobody, a nobody . . ." As he is about to leave, he hears the poor beadle of the congregation, repeating the same litany: "I am nobody, I am nothing . . ." Disdainful, the dignitary shrugs his shoulders and says: "Look at him—look who calls himself a nobody.")

Let us take Moses as an example of true humility. What does the text say about him quoting God? *"Ve'ha'ish Moshe anav mi'kol adam . . ."*—And the man Moses was the most humble of men in the world . . .

This verse follows the passage in which Miriam and Aaron say some unkind things about their famous brother. They resent his special status with its many privileges: Who does he think he is? Hasn't he married a black woman? God speaks to him, so what? Hasn't God spoken to them as well? It is then that God declares Moses to be the most humble man on earth. But . . . what is the connection? Is God trying to make up for having punished his envoy so often? Does Moses' humility have anything to do with his siblings' hostile criticism?

I believe it does. I believe that Moses was there, nearby, when his brother and sister gossiped about him. He heard them. His possible reaction? He may have thought to himself: they may be right, I may be unworthy. Therein lies his humility. Therefore, he is not angry at them: how could he be if they told the truth? God is angry at Aaron, at Miriam—not at Moses. God is especially angry at Aaron and Miriam because of Moses' inner doubts. That is why God pays tribute to his unusual humility.

Indeed, Moshe Rabbeinu, our teacher and master, was and is humble. And since we all are his pupils, it is incumbent upon us to follow his example. Our sages urge man to be *"hatzneh lekhet,"* *"shfal ruah,"* and *"anavim,"* meaning modest and humble. But not timid. In the *Ethics of Our Fathers* we are told to fight timidity: A timid person cannot learn anything.

We just quoted from the *Ethics of Our Fathers* a saying to the effect that excessive timidity can become an obstacle to learning. If I am bashful, I may not dare to ask questions or object to answers. The Hebrew word for timidity is *bayshanut,* which derives from *busha,* shame. That does not mean that a bashful person should feel ashamed—it means perhaps that it is a shame for a person to be bashful. Timidity is different from humility. The two are not necessarily compatible. One can be humble without being bashful at all.

Let us look at Rabbi Tarfon. Was he humble? Yes. Was he timid? No. You want proof? Listen to a Talmudic tale:

When Rabbi Eliezer fell ill, four old men—that is how sages are described in the Talmud—came to visit him: Rabbi Tarfon, Rabbi Yehoshua, Rabbi Eleazar ben Azaryah, and Rabbi Akiba. Rabbi Tarfon spoke first: "You are better than a drop of rain; for a drop of rain is beneficial in this earthly world alone, whereas you, your teaching is beneficial in both this world and the world to come."

Another story: When Rabbi Yishmael lost his children, four old men came to comfort him: Rabbi Tarfon, Rabbi Yose the Galilean, Rabbi Eleazar ben Azaryah, and Rabbi Akiba. Rabbi Tarfon was once again the first to speak, this time with words of consolation.

And a third legend: While studying in his native town, Loud (Lydda), Rabbi Tarfon and other teachers tried to answer a simple but urgent question: What is better for man: study or action? Once again Rabbi Tarfon's answer was heard first: action, which seems very revealing.

What strikes us in all three cases is Rabbi Tarfon's assertiveness. Why is he so impatient? He is always the first to take the floor, the first to state his position in debates. Where then is his humility? Did he see himself as a leader or spokesman, he who was never elected to the presidency of any academy? Did he consider himself more erudite than Rabbi Akiba, more able in Halakha than Rabbi Eleazar ben Azaryah, more eloquent than Rabbi Yose the Galilean? True, he was probably older than most of them, but was that a valid reason to put himself forward on every occasion?

Perhaps it is time to open his file. Rich with legal opinions and biblical interpretations, it is unfortunately poor in biographical data.

We know nothing about his father but quite a lot about his relationship to his mother. He had an uncle called Shimshon. Did he have brothers or sisters? We don't know.

His name, Tarfon, derives from the Greek word *tryphon*. In those days, it was not uncommon for parents to give their sons Greek or Roman names, like Alexander, Sumakhus, Antigonus, Hyrcanos, or Marion. Parenthetically, it may be of interest to note that certain Jewish names from the Bible are not found in the Talmud. There is no Rabbi Abraham or Rabbi Moshe or Rabbi Aharon. Is it that Jewish parents of that time were too much in awe to use the names of the first believer, the first lawmaker, and the first High Priest in Jewish history?

Born approximately twenty years before the destruction of the Temple, Rabbi Tarfon died about fifty years after. Dates in the Talmud often lack precision. What is certain is that he was alive and well while the Temple was at the center of Jewish life in Palestine. Equally certain is that he witnessed its destruction. And yet he rarely, if at all, spoke of it. One cannot help but be intrigued by his silence. Why didn't he refer to the ransacking of Jerusalem, the profanation of the Sanctuary, the children dying in the street? Was it simply a matter of discretion or shyness? Did he feel unable or unworthy to speak of a catastrophe of such magnitude? The same applies to his personal tragedies. He says nothing about the death of his wife and, later, of his children. Is it that he had *too much* to say?

That he lived in the shadow of pain and tragedy is clear from descriptions of certain events of his life.

After the death of his wife, he married her sister and asked her to take care of his children. Some of them must have died young, but there is no indication of the circumstances. One of his daughters must have been married, since there is a strange legend about a grandson of Rabbi Tarfon. Listen:

Rabbi Yehuda the patriarch or president, the esteemed editor of the Mishna, arrived in Rabbi Tarfon's native town. He met with his local disciples and asked them whether a son of Rabbi Tarfon lived there, adding that Rabbi Tarfon, whom he called *Tzaddik*, had brought much harm to his children. Harm? Well, let's open brackets: Rabbi Tarfon used to swear "on the life of his children" to prove that his opinion was correct; his peers didn't appreciate that, hence the criticism by Rabbi Yehuda ha-Nassi, who wanted to know if at least one son had survived the curse. No, his informers told him. Rabbi Tarfon's sons had died; but a son of his daughter lives here. The informers went on to tell him that all the prostitutes who made two coins per customer gave him the second—and according to another version, twice the second—for *his* services. Rabbi Yehuda asked to see him and made him an astonishing offer: "Repent," he said, "and I will give you my daughter for a wife." One version tells us that Rabbi Tarfon's grandson accepted the proposal; he married Rabbi Yehuda's daughter, then divorced her. The second version claims he refused to marry her in the first place, for he didn't want people to think that a woman caused him to repent. Both versions, however, agree that he *did* repent.

Fatherless, just as his children were motherless, Rabbi Tarfon showed great compassion to all orphans. To bring up an orphan, he would say, is to constantly fulfill the commandment of giving charity.

We already know how attached he was to his mother, whom he revered more than any other person around him. One Shabbat he saw one of her sandals fall off as she took a walk outside. Since the law of Shabbat observance forbade him to pick it up, he bent down and spread his hands out under her feet so that she could walk on them until she reached home, and after that, until she climbed into her bed. Later, when he became ill and great masters came to pay him a sick call, his mother said to them, "Please pray for my son Tarfon. Pray for him, for he treats me with extreme care and honor." When asked to elaborate, she told of the incident with the sandal. Here again, the sages were not impressed. To his mother they said: "Had he done that a thousand times, he still wouldn't have fulfilled half the biblical commandment about honoring one's parents."

Well, I fail to understand Rabbi Tarfon's distinguished colleagues. What motivated them to diminish him, to put him down, and in the presence of his mother at a time when he was ill? Was it to show their impartiality toward a man who was not only learned but also wealthy?

For Rabbi Tarfon *was* wealthy. In fact, he was known—also—for his considerable wealth.

One day, the sages sought to define the essential attributes of a rich man. One said: rich is he whose riches make him happy. Another said: rich is he who is satisfied with what he has. But Rabbi Tarfon offered a definition more worthy of Wall Street than of any Talmudic academy. Said he: rich is he who possesses a hundred fields, a hundred vineyards, and a hundred employees working in them.

Another example: There was a debate in the academy over the quality of oil to be used for Shabbat lamps. Everyone but Rabbi Tarfon said that any oil will do, as long as it gives light. Rabbi Tarfon insisted on the best quality available. But what about those poor Jewish families that had to be satisfied with oil of a lesser quality?

Does this apparent insensitivity to the less fortunate explain why, at times, some sages seem to resent him? In those days, wealthy scholars were few. Many made their living as cobblers, masons, or physicians. Where then did Rabbi Tarfon make his fortune? Probably he inherited it. And since he was not particularly generous, he must have aroused envy and discontent.

More than one source emphasizes his avarice, his greed. One text mentions unpleasant rumors spread about him. For instance, it is said that as a priest, he received *teruma*—a kind of charity reserved for the priestly caste—each day, even after the destruction of the Temple. Was it due to the pressure of public opinion that he announced his decision to distribute among the poor all the special payments he received from parents who had to redeem their firstborn sons? The story goes that Rabbi Akiba felt compelled to use a subterfuge, to get some of his money to the needy. Listen:

One day, Rabbi Akiba offered Rabbi Tarfon a business proposition— or, according to another version, it was Rabbi Tarfon who asked Rabbi Akiba to help *him*. The deal involved purchasing some property, which sounded like a good investment. So Rabbi Tarfon gave his friend four thousand gold coins with which to conclude the transaction. After a while, Rabbi Tarfon asked his new agent: where is my property? Come, Rabbi Akiba answered. Come with me. He took him to a *beit midrash* where pupils studied Psalms, especially a verse about great wealth being distributed among the poor. "This is your property," said Rabbi Akiba, pointing to the pupils. Was Rabbi Tarfon a good loser? He kissed his friend on his forehead and said: "Rabbi, *alufi*—my teacher in wisdom and my master in good manners, accept my homage." And right there he gave him more money to give away as charity.

The Talmud, which relates this episode, does not conceal its astonishment: "If this is so, then why do people reproach Rabbi Tarfon for his lack of generosity? Doesn't he give enough?" The answer: "He gives a lot, but not enough for a man of his means."

Apparently, as we shall see, he did have his favorite charities . . .

One day, while Rabbi Tarfon and his disciples were engaged in study, he noticed a bride passing by. Was she alone? Did she look distressed? Without hesitating, he asked his wife and his daughters to take her inside, wash and perfume her, dress her in beautiful clothes, give her precious jewels, and dance before her, as is the law according to the School of Hillel, and bring her to her husband.

In general, he felt compassion for victims of society and despair. Once, the young son of a certain Guranus ran away from school and, fearing his father's anger, threw himself into a well and died. The case was brought before Rabbi Tarfon: what was one to do with his body? The strict law is harsh for suicides. Not only does it forbid burial within the consecrated grounds of the cemetery proper, but the family is not allowed to mourn. Here, Rabbi Tarfon showed his kindness: the victim was young, he said, so young, he was at that moment not in his right mind, and so he was entitled to the rituals due someone who died of natural causes.

Like Rabbi Akiba, on occasion, he too knew how to use his cleverness to help others overcome sadness. Listen to what he did during a period of famine: he married—fictitiously, of course—three hundred women. As the wives of a priest, they were entitled to receive their share of special charity.

And this: A fierce humanitarian, Rabbi Tarfon opposed capital punishment. Like Rabbi Akiba, he said that if he were a member of the Sanhedrin, no man would ever be executed. This drew bitter commentary from the academy President, Rabban Shimon ben Gamliel: "With this kind of moderation, one but encourages bloodshed."

MANY OF HIS legal opinions are related to priestly duties and privileges. He himself was a priest not only on his father's side but also on his mother's.

With his friendly adversary Rabbi Akiba, he debated one day the law requiring priests performing services in the Temple to be without any physical blemish. Rabbi Tarfon's position was more lenient than Rabbi Akiba's. "I remember," he said, "seeing my lame uncle blow the shofar in the Temple's courtyard." Unconvinced, Rabbi Akiba explained that it must have been during an assembly, not a sacrificial ritual. There is a difference. When sacrifice is involved, the slightest physical imperfection is enough to keep the priest away. At that point, Rabbi Tarfon exclaimed: "I was there, I saw and heard everything, and you were not even present. All you have is your power of interpretation; and yet you know more than I. Akiba, Akiba, to leave you is to leave life itself."

This is true humility. How many scholars are willing to defer to the ideas of their adversary in the heat of debate? Rabbi Tarfon easily admitted the validity of his opponent's views. Actually, his positions rarely gained acceptance in the academy, though he did not seem offended or angered by this. And yet his spiritual and intellectual qualities are duly recognized.

Rabbi Tarfon once stated that in matters of man-woman relations one cannot be too careful or too strict. "One must not even stay alone with one's mother-in-law." The rigidity of the statement made one student of Rabbi Tarfon smile in disbelief. The student was punished soon after for succumbing to desire and committing a sin with *his* mother-in-law.

Another time, an adversarial student asked Rabbi Tarfon a question knowing he would be unable to answer it. An angry Rabbi Akiba reprimanded the student: "I can see how happy you are to have embarrassed our teacher; I would not be surprised to learn that your time is now limited." That exchange took place around Passover. When the holiday of Shavuot arrived, seven weeks later, the student was no longer among the living. Note that it was Rabbi Akiba, not Rabbi Tarfon, who predicted his punishment. And I must emphasize: predicted, not caused. Nor willed. Haven't both proclaimed their strong opposition to death sentences? Rabbi Akiba knew that to hurt a sage is to offend the honor of Torah. When sages protected one another, it was the Torah they sought to shield. In spite of the arguments and counterarguments in the academies of those days, there was finally a marvelous solidarity among the scholars. They were united by an irresistible passion for learning.

Rabbi Tarfon's allegiance to Torah was absolute. In Talmudic literature he is called "the father" and also "the teacher of all the people of Israel." Both titles point to his profound love for his people. Its welfare mattered to him. Was he, like his friend and disciple Rabbi Akiba ben Yoseph, on the side of the young, glorious, and tragic general Bar-Kochba, who, sixty-odd years after the fall of Jerusalem, led an insurrection against Rome? His position is not known.

What is known is that he was against Rome. Like most sages?

Probably more than most. In the Tractate of Gittin—involving all divorce-related issues—we find his decision stating that "even if and when the laws of Gentile courts are similar to those of Jewish ones, one must not have recourse to them in matters of litigation." He was especially harsh toward the New Christians, whose books he wanted burned, even though they contained the name of God. Did he have contact with them? Some sources suggest that he engaged in theological disputations with these people. Though from the image he projects, this does not sound credible. He was not exactly what we would call today an ecumenicist.

Still, some believe he took part in a long dialogue with a Christian apologist of the second century called Justin Martyr. Born in Nablus, where he was known for his missionary activities, Justin wrote a book called *Dialogue with Trypho*. In it the author and a Jew discuss Greek philosophers, God, and the conflicts separating Jews and Christians. Justin tries to convince the Jew, who in turn, tries to prevail upon the Christian to repent and return to their common faith, the faith of Israel. Both fail.

This Jew Trypho is a man I like, but I am not alone in thinking that he is not our Rabbi Tarfon, who, rather than argue with outsiders, preferred to interact with the Torah and its commentators.

Rabbi Yehuda ha-Nassi compares Rabbi Tarfon to a pile of walnuts or pebbles: if one is removed, all shift around. When a disciple came to him for an explanation of a rabbinic decision or saying, the erudite master would immediately quote from Scripture and Mishna and Midrash, using examples from Halakha and Aggada. A simple question was enough to lead him to touch on every aspect of Jewish learning. And the young visitor would leave with his mind tremendously stimulated.

The praise for Rabbi Tarfon's pedagogy is well deserved. Today one would call it Socratic. He began by raising questions and asking his pupils to deepen and broaden them before formulating their own. Often he would ask their permission to raise a question. He would say *"eshal,"* may I ask? At times, he would freely admit that he did not know the answer.

How can one who loves questions more than answers not love Rabbi Tarfon, at least, for that?

But since it is generally accepted that he was truly humble, why was he so often *the first* to voice opinions in the presence of his illustrious colleagues? Wouldn't it have been more appropriate, and surely more humble, for him to defer to the others, to listen to them?

LET US GO back, shall we, to our analysis of humility as a central concept in the Talmudic and rabbinic universe.

Ordinarily, we are taught that it is incumbent upon man to be humble in the presence of God. How can he or she not be? Facing the King of Kings, the Judge of all the living, the Almighty Creator of all that exists and will exist, how could one not feel small and insignificant, more useless than a pebble and weaker than a leaf trembling before a storm?

Facing the Eternal God who is one and whose name is one—in whom all beings, all words, all memories are united—how could a human being who is, by definition, mortal and defenseless, not feel the weight of his or her own weakness? In other words, for most of us, humility before God seems so natural that we wonder why our sages insist on its importance.

But they, in their wisdom, teach us the meaning of humility in another context as well—the humility of men and women in their relationship to one another. To be humble before God is easy; to be humble before another person is not. Isn't it in man's nature to feel closest to himself? Hence the Talmud's insistence on warning us against self-indulgence and, above all, self-adoration, which is compared to idolatry.

Who today is audacious or blind enough to claim that, because of ethnic or religious reasons, he or she is better or worthier than another? Who is arrogant enough to claim to possess the only key to all the gates of heaven?

True humility is judging oneself with severity and judging others with understanding.

For a humble person, even the most obstinate sinner deserves respect, for we do not know the essential truth about someone else. Therefore I am unable to put myself in his or her place. Truth, in its totality, is known to God alone. And He desires to be humble in going down to the level of his creatures—and joining his people in exile. From this we learn that though it is not included in the list of the biblical commandments, humility is implicit in them, for it is written *"ve'halakhta bi'drakhav,"* or *"imitatio dei"*: man must follow in God's ways. Just as He is humble, we must be. And more so.

Another realm of humility exists in our relationship to the Torah. In its presence one can yield neither to pride nor to vanity. The commandment against idolatry, "Thou shalt have no other gods," refers to pride, according to Rabbi Shimon bar Yohai: you yourself must not be a god. The self, the "I," is not only hateful, if I may quote Pascal, it is also sacrilegious. God alone may say "I." Whoever glorifies his or her own self will end up in opposition to himself and to God. How can man say "I am," asks the Midrash, when he may be gone tomorrow? "Woe to vanity," says a Talmudic sage, "woe to vanity that pushes its servants to the grave."

Vanity is dangerous, states the Talmud, listen to its consequences: if the vain man is a sage, his wisdom will be taken from him; if he is a prophet, he will lose his prophetic powers. Countless masters, teachers, and moralists have, throughout the centuries, warned against the sin of pride: "What is its fruit?" asked Rabbi Shlomo Ibn Gabirol. He answers: "The fruit of pride is hatred." Said Rabbi Bahya Ibn Pekouda: "Which is the worst of all sins? Vanity." Listen to a strange legend: God said to the wicked king Jeroboam son of Nebat, who symbolizes all that is evil in the history of Jewish royalty: "Repent and I, you, and the son of David will walk together in paradise." "Who will walk first?" asked the king. "The son of David," said God. Therefore Jeroboam refused. The moral of the story: the wicked king was doomed by his own vanity.

Similarly, many Talmudic aphorisms praise humility as one of God's virtues: Hasn't He abandoned high mountain peaks to give the Torah at Sinai, which is the lowest? Hadn't He neglected tall trees to speak to Moses from a bush? In other words, it is through humility that Torah is preserved. "Even if you are perfect in all things," says the Talmud, "if you lack humility, you have nothing." And the Midrash declares: "These are the seven rewards given to the humble man or woman: they will have their share in the world to come, their teaching will be remembered, the Shekhina will rest on them, they will be spared all punishment, nothing evil will happen to them, the whole world will feel sorry for them, and, best of all, the humble man will not have to live with a wicked woman." Also in the Talmud: "Even if the whole world tells you that you are a *Tzaddik,* a just man, say to yourself that you are wicked, a *Rasha.*" In other words, the true *Tzaddik* is he who thinks that he is not. The Midrash recalls a useful piece of advice Rabbi Akiba gave Shimon ben Azzai: "Remove yourself from the seat that is meant to be yours in the academy; go back a few rows until people start telling you to go closer and higher—and even then, do not go; for it is better when people tell you to go up to a higher seat than when they shout for you to go back."

But even humility requires prudence.

Listen to an anecdote: a vacancy occurred in the rabbinate of a large congregation, and its leadership came to plead with a renowned scholar to accept the prestigious post. But the master refused, saying: "I am not the man you need. I lack knowledge and experience. I am not learned enough, nor am I pious enough." Brokenhearted, deeply taken by his humility, the leadership turned to another candidate. This one had heard about the conversation with the first scholar and saw how impressed the leaders were with his modesty. So he spoke in the same manner: "I am not the spiritual leader you need . . . I lack so many things . . ." At that point, a friend of his who was present whispered: "Stop—It's bad for you to continue in this vein. *You,* they'll believe."

Of course, the trouble with the second candidate was that his humility was false.

Speaking of humility, the great Hasidic master Rebbe Bunam of

Pshiske said: "Every person should have a piece of paper in each of his two pockets. On one piece, he should write down the Talmudic saying 'The whole world was created for my sake alone'; but the other should carry the biblical verse 'I am but dust and ashes.' " What is important is not to confuse the pockets.

That the Torah demands humility from those who study it is illustrated by the secret it harbors. This secret cannot be pierced, for it deepens as one comes closer to its gate. Let's call it the secret of the secret. Whoever pretends to know it still has a lot to learn. Inexhaustible are the treasures of Torah.

Thus, the question arises: How can one learn without being demanding? And how can one be demanding and not offend the Torah? Where does one get the audacity to question a sacred text which bears the seal of God? Isn't this showing disrespect? The Amoraim of later generations never refuted decisions of earlier Tannaim. If they didn't, how can we? Isn't an attempt to master the content and style of Torah arrogant? The Saducees thought so, but the majority of rabbinic scholars did not. For them and for us, it is important to know that though the Law was given by the Almighty, its interpretation belongs to us.

This explains the duality, better yet, the plurality of opinions we meet in the Talmudic tradition. *"Eileh ve'eileh divrei elokim hayim,"* states a heavenly voice: both schools, that of Shammai and that of Hillel, express God's living words. And yet they agreed on only eighteen issues. If that is the case, why should we follow the Hillelites? The Talmud explains: because they were humble and respectful toward their adversaries, whose opinions they always quoted first.

Rabbi Tarfon's way was a bit different: he too was polite and courteous, although he was overruled. He never kept a grudge against anyone. When he once disagreed with the majority and lost, and went on acting against its ruling, he paid for it in silence.

A story: the disciples of Shammai and those of Hillel had an argument, as always, but this time it was about the practical implementation of the commandment related to the credo the Shema, which according to Scripture one must recite "sitting at home, or walking on the road, lying in bed in the evening and getting up in the morning. . . ." For the disciples of Shammai it was simple: one must actually recite the Shema while sitting at home, while walking on the road, and so on. The disciples of Hillel were more flexible. What was important for them was to recite the prayer. As always, the Hillel students won the argument. But once Rabbi Tarfon wanted to test Shammai's method. He recited the Shema while lying down at night—probably not at home—and was attacked by robbers. Some sages said: that was a punishment for going against the majority. But Rabbi Tarfon did not complain.

Another time, he did complain. One night he happened to be in his own garden when a guard, thinking he was an intruder, beat him up. In fact, the beating was so brutal that Rabbi Tarfon began shouting: "Go tell my people that Tarfon is being murdered." That saved him. Later, he felt remorse for having used his rabbinic position, and thus his connection with Torah, to save himself. Actually, says one version, he could have bribed the guard to stop. But we know of his special attachment to money—just as we know how humble he was when learning or teaching Torah. Here we must return to the question that has plagued us for some time: if he was so humble, why did he always speak up first?

At the risk of surprising you, I will suggest that it was *because* he was humble that he spoke first. According to the academic custom of that time, it was always the youngest, the least influential, the least erudite who spoke first—so as not to be influenced by the greater scholars' opinions. Thus, if Rabbi Tarfon spoke first, it was because he believed that he was the least learned person. In that case, who was the humblest man at the academy? Rabbi Tarfon.

I owe you one more explanation. It concerns Rabbi Tarfon's boasting in the *beit ha'midrash* and his colleagues' reference to his mother's purse. Actually, my feeling is that he was *not* boasting. He was just trying to show that the pure *mitzvah* of honoring one's mother is unlimited, because much depends on the mother: it is up to her to say when enough is enough. But his colleagues disagreed, maintaining that extremes are never healthy.

Before we conclude, allow me to add one more biographical item. There are texts that place him in the category of the "ten martyrs of the faith," tortured and murdered for having studied and taught Torah and having observed its commandments. Somehow it does not seem probable—although the circumstances of his death remain surrounded with mystery. He who used to be present when his teachers or colleagues passed away, when his hour came, it seems that he was alone. Perhaps I am unfair. Perhaps they did come. If so nothing about it has been recorded. One thing is clear: had he died as a martyr, there would have been witnesses.

I love Rabbi Tarfon. I love him, although I do not always understand him. I fail to understand why the defeat of Judah, the tragedy of the destruction of Jerusalem and its Temple, play almost no role in his teaching. Was he trying to tell us that silence too can be a response to extreme suffering? And that some secrets, protected by silence, must remain inviolate?

A story: in order to strengthen his thesis concerning a law dealing with the priestly service in the Temple, Rabbi Tarfon relates that he was with his uncle Shimshon one Yom Kippur in the Temple, when he managed to hear the High Priest just as he utterred the ineffable name. Composed of twelve letters, that name was known to the High Priest alone and to some of his discreet and reliable assistants, who would have been called upon to serve had anything happened to him. If an unworthy person heard the ineffable name by accident, he miraculously forgot it in an instant.

Thus, thanks to Rabbi Tarfon, we realize that forgetfulness is always possible. In other words, to know the secret is not enough; one must learn how to safeguard it. That is not easy? So what! Who says it is easy to carry the Torah, although truly it is she who carries us? When we conclude one of the five books of Scripture, we raise our voice and say to the man who was honored with the last reading: "*Hazak*, be strong"—why? Because study of Torah demands such an effort that it weakens us. Thus we need encouragement. And strength.

Let us end with two of Rabbi Tarfon's beautiful and profound aphorisms.

He said: The day is short (meaning: life is short), and there is so much to do, but the workers are so lazy . . .

He also said: *Lo alekha ha'melakha ligmor,* no one is asking you to complete the task, but you must begin it.

So we are beginning and beginning, again and again . . .

Rabbi Yehoshua ben Levi

L EGEND HAS IT that one day Rabbi Yehoshua ben Levi met the prophet Elijah at the entrance to the cave where the celebrated Rabbi Shimon bar Yohai and his son Rabbi Eleazar had been hiding from the Romans for thirteen years. Seizing the opportunity, the old sage put a question to the prophet—and when the old sage asked questions, they were never simple. "When will the Messiah come?" he demanded. "Go ask him yourself," said the prophet. "But—where will I find him?" "At the gates of Rome," answered Elijah. (Some sources say: at Caesarea or Antioch.) "But—how will I recognize him?" asked the old sage. Again there are two versions of the prophet's answer. According to the first, he offered the sage a guide. According to the second, he gave him specific instructions: "The Messiah can be found among the sickest of the beggars at the entrance to the city." "But how will I identify him?" asked Rabbi Yehoshua ben Levi. "Oh, that will be easy," answered the prophet. "Watch the beggars: all of them remove their bandages and then tie them all at once. He removes and ties his bandage one at a time, thinking that he might, at any moment, be summoned to deliver his people and must not be delayed."

The old sage hurried to Rome, identified the Messiah among the beggars, and ran to greet him: "Peace unto thee, my master and teacher." "Peace unto thee, son of Levi," replied the Messiah. "When will the master come?" inquired Rabbi Yehoshua ben Levi. "Today," answered the Messiah.

So the old sage returned home. Again he met the prophet, who wanted to know, "How did it go? Have you seen him?" "Yes," answered the sage. "What did he say?" "He greeted me." "How did he greet you?" "He said: Peace unto you, son of Levi." "Good," said the prophet. "This means that both of you are assured a place in the world to come. What else did he say?" "He lied to me." "How did he lie to you?" "He said he would come today, but he did not." "Oh, you didn't understand him," said the prophet. "When he said today, *ha'yom,* he was referring to the biblical verse *'ha'yom im be'koli tish-me'un'*—'today, if you listen to me and obey me.' "

An enchanting tale but also a disquieting one. Each of its characters presents problems. Why is it important for us to know where the sage and the prophet had their meeting? What is the connection between a simple answer to a greeting and a person's share in the world to come? And why did Elijah dispatch Rabbi Yehoshua ben Levi so far away? Isn't he supposed to know all answers to all questions? Then why didn't he answer this one? Isn't he—he too—called upon to play an essential part in the ultimate redemption? Also, why did the Messiah play games with the sage? How could he not have been moved by his earnestness? I also fail to understand Rabbi Yehoshua ben Levi. How could he so readily accuse the Messiah of lying? He who had so vigorously fought against slander—and who had so consistently praised the virtue of humility—why did he not opt to study further or to ask Elijah to explain to him the Messiah's strange answer, instead of dismissing it outright as falsehood? The Messiah a liar? How could a Jew—let alone a pious and learned Jew—utter such blasphemous words?

Said Rabbi Yehoshua ben Levi: "Every day a heavenly voice is heard at Mount Horeb, proclaiming: 'Woe to humankind for abandoning the Torah.' For a Jew to neglect study means to forget his or her origins. To turn away from what our teachers taught us is to betray them—and ourselves as well." Said Rabbi Yehoshua ben Levi: "Even what a good disciple will say before his master about Scripture, Mishna, Tosefta, and legends, Moses has already heard at Sinai." Moses? All of us, through Moses and thanks to Moses.

A STRIKING, colorful personality: no one could meet him and remain unaffected. Imagination, piety, respect for scholars, love of God and of Israel: all these virtues, and many more, can be found in Rabbi Yehoshua ben Levi. He was a dynamic teacher, a generous friend. Unlike the great president Rabbi Yehuda, he ordained all his disciples— at times without Rabbi Yehuda's consent. His commentaries are often breathtakingly beautiful, his interpretation of biblical verses astonishingly audacious. No wonder he inspired so many legends about his gifts and powers. He saw what was hidden from others. He visited forbidden sites. He not only fought with angels, he vanquished them.

Was he a mystic? Not much is known about his life. Extremely articulate, vocal, open-minded . . . always in motion. A homiletic genius, a preacher, a storyteller. Nothing in the sources indicates that he was dominated by or even attracted to mysticism. Some Talmudic commentators claim that his father was the scholar Levi ben Sissi.

About this special teacher, Levi ben Sissi, a brief story: Though he was head of his own school, both in Babylonia and Palestine, he was never ordained by his teacher Rabbi Yehuda ha-Nassi. Nevertheless, Rabbi Yehuda showed him deep affection. He honored him by inviting him to recite benedictions at his son's wedding feast. Later, when people from Simonaia asked Rabbi Yehuda to recommend a rabbi who would serve not only as teacher and preacher, but as scribe and tutor for small children, he suggested only one name: Levi ben Sissi.

When the new rabbi arrived, he was received warmly by the community. They erected a high platform for him and began asking him questions on the Law or Halakha. When he was unable to answer, they thought: he is not good in Halakha, but surely he must be excellent in stories or Aggada. They asked him questions on Aggada. Again, he could not answer. What about Scripture and the prophets?

They inquired about a verse in the Book of Daniel. Sorry, Levi ben Sissi was incapable of answering *any* question.

You can imagine the dismay of the leaders of the congregation. They hurried back to Rabbi Yehuda ha-Nassi: "Is he really the best you can recommend?" "I swear to you," answered Rabbi Yehuda, "that his erudition equals mine." He then summoned his disciple and asked him the very same questions the people of Simonaia had asked—and this time Levi ben Sissi answered them all. "What happened to you there?" asked Rabbi Yehuda. "They put me on a stage," said the scholar. "The homage they paid me was too high. It was too much for me. I forgot everything I knew." Was he really our Rabbi Yehoshua's father? Maybe. Several commentators say he was just another Jew—another Levite—named Levi.

Born in the southern city of Lod, Rabbi Yehoshua lived in the first half of the third century of our common era and was a distinguished Palestinian Amora of the transition period between the Tannaim and the Amoraim. By the time Lod became impoverished—so much so that people there wept, for they had no means to change their clothes for Shabbat and the holidays—he was already an old man. Eventually, he moved to Tiberias, where he stayed until his death.

At some point, he must have met Rabbi Yehuda the Prince, for he insisted on following some of his customs. His teachers were Eleazar Ha'kappar and Bar Kappara, but he was also known to quote decisions and sayings by Antigonus and Oshaya. Though he enjoyed a strong reputation as a man of Halakha, his real fame stemmed from his inventiveness in Aggada. There he surpassed many of his peers with his wit and wisdom. It is said that he penetrated the most secret of spheres, reporting on the battles Moses had to fight when he ascended into heaven to receive the Law, and on life in paradise or hell. No wonder that he was the prophet Elijah's favorite conversation partner.

What do we know of his private life? He married once or twice. One of his wives was the daughter of a scholar named Rabbi Yossi bar Peters. They had at least one son—Rav Yosef—possibly two, and several grandchildren whom he himself introduced to Scripture. During his long life, he taught in Lydda but also visited other academies, mainly the one in Tsiporis. Possibly because of his family connection with the Jewish leadership—his son had married the daughter of Rabbi Yehuda Nesiah—he threw himself into communal affairs. At times he would join delegations to raise funds among Diaspora Jews or to plead for his community before the Roman authorities. He once went to Caesarea together with Rabbi Hanina on such a mission. When the Roman proconsul saw them, he rose. When asked by his aides why he had stood up before Jews, the proconsul answered, "They looked to me like angels." But angels are not necessarily good students. Neither are dignitaries. "Because of my communal activities and public service," said Rabbi Yehoshua ben Levi, "once I forgot almost everything I knew." He was too busy as a rabbi—too busy to study.

He must have been quite wealthy, for when Reb Hiya came to visit his academy, on a simple weekday, he was served a twenty-four-course meal. An astonished Reb Hiya asked Reb Yehoshua's disciples, "If you eat like this during the week, what do you do on Shabbat?" They replied, "On Shabbat, the number of courses is doubled." Later, when Rabbi Yehoshua ben Levi visited Reb Hiya, we are told that Reb Hiya gave his students several gold coins to buy large amounts of food for his honored guest.

Did Rabbi Yehoshua ben Levi really serve forty-eight-course meals on Shabbat? There are two possibilities. Either he really did—in which case he loved to go to excess in matters of hospitality; or he did not—in which case he just loved to exaggerate. Whatever the answer, it would certainly fit with his extreme nature. Listen to his sayings: "Whoever says Amen during Kaddish may be certain that *all* evil decrees against him in heaven have been revoked." "To slander a fellow human being is like violating *all* the commandments of the Torah." "He who slanders a scholar is *sure* to be sent to hell." He had even more unusual things to say about the importance of study: "You have a headache? Study Torah. Your throat aches? Study Torah. Your bones hurt? Study Torah. Heartburn? Study Torah. Your entire body hurts? Study Torah." Also: "Whoever teaches his son or grandson Torah, it is as if he received it himself at Sinai."

Even more daring are those of his sayings relating to the Almighty. For instance, he knows what God did when His children were slaughtered. Listen: "When the enemy approached the Temple to destroy it, the Temple was defended by six hundred thousand angels, ready to protect it. But then they noticed that the Shekhina itself was indifferent to the plight of the Jewish people; and so they left."

A Midrash:

The Holy One, blessed be He, summoned the ministering angels and said to them: "If a human king mourns a son, what is the customary thing for him to do?" They replied, "He hangs sackcloth over his door." He said to them, "I will do likewise." Again he asked, "What does a human king do when mourning?" They replied, "He extinguishes the lamps." "I will do likewise," he said. "What else does a human king do?" They replied, "He overturns his couch." He said to them, "I will do likewise. What else does a human king do?" They replied, "He rends his purple robes." He replied, "I will do likewise. What else does a human king do?" "He sits in silence." He said to them, "I will do likewise."

Here, too, one feels Rabbi Yehoshua ben Levi's compassion for the Jewish people. Like Moses, he always takes their side. The Golden Calf? It had to happen, said he. Why? So that God could illustrate the meaning of repentance. "When the Jewish people suffers," said Rabbi Yehoshua ben Levi, "God too suffers. And all the people in the world suffer." And he went on to say: "If the nations of the world only knew that when the Jews commit transgressions, they too must endure punishment, they would assign two policemen to every Jew to prevent him from sinning." On another occasion he said: "If the nations of the world only knew how important the Sanctuary is to them too, they would do everything in their power to save it from destruction."

But the Temple was destroyed. And the Sanctuary was profaned.

And Rabbi Yehoshua ben Levi kept on remembering our national catastrophe. Instead of fasting one day—the ninth day of Av—he fasted the next day too. For him, the fires were still burning. What is astonishing is not that he fasted two days instead of one, but that he did not fast *more* than two days. And also that not more of his contemporaries followed his example. After all, let us not forget: if they could no longer see Jerusalem in all its splendor, they could still see its ruins. By that time the decree forbidding Jews to enter Jerusalem except on Tisha b'Av had already been abrogated by Septimus Severus, then—twenty years later—by Emperor Caracalla. There *were* Jews in Jerusalem, there *was* Jewish life in Jerusalem. But how could Jews dwell in God's destroyed city without endlessly weeping over their loss? How could Jews anywhere go on with their lives without remembering their tragedy? How could teachers teach and students study, and merchants sell and customers buy, with so many tragic memories surrounding them?

Strange—intellectual life flourished in the land of Israel. That was not true in the rest of the Roman Empire, nor in the rest of the world. Most of the important events that occurred during the first half of the third century were political or military. Except for Diophantus, who, in Alexandria, proudly produced the world's first book on algebra, no great cultural achievement can be traced back to that era. It was a time when emperors followed one another in violent death. Caracalla killed his co-ruler Geta and was succeeded by Heliogabalus, who was succeeded by Alexander Severus. He, in turn, was murdered by Maximinus, who was assassinated by his troops and succeeded by Gordian I, Gordian II, Balbinus, Pupienus, and Gordian III. Christians were persecuted, their martyrs became saints.

Meanwhile, in the land of Israel cultural life continued to blossom. The number of academies grew rapidly—as did the number of students and teachers. There were so many students who wished to become rabbis that the *nassi*—the president—decided that all ordinations would require his approval. Why was this necessary? Because in the beginning every teacher had had the right to ordain, and had used it. Then the president visited a village and found a student who, though ignorant in matters of Halakha, acted as rabbi. Was there dissension on this point between the president and Rabbi Yehoshua ben Levi, who was determined to keep his rights and privileges? Some of the commentators believe there was. Still, the president and Rabbi Yehoshua ben Levi were related and their relationship was known to be excellent. There was no indication that they ever quarreled. But then Rabbi Yehoshua ben Levi never quarreled with anyone. Except, of course, over points of the Law—though the discussions never degenerated into conflicts. Disputes, he said, can make a generation sinful. Peace was one of his favorite themes. In general, he was kind and compassionate, even toward sinners. He himself declared that he never used his authority to ban anyone for any of the twenty-four transgressions that normally warrant excommunication. He once felt he had to place a curse on a Saducee or a "Min"— probably a member of the new Christian sect—whom he had judged offensive. He knew exactly when and where to utter his curse so that it would be the most effective. But when the moment came, he—conveniently—fell asleep.

It is simple: Rabbi Yehoshua ben Levi was unable to curse another human being. *"Ve'rahamav al kol ma'asav,"* he said. Just as God is merciful with all His creatures, we must be compassionate toward all people.

But let us not make him into a saint. There are no saints in Judaism. Only just men and women. The difference? Saints are supposed to be perfect, and no human being is perfect. Just persons aspire to be just. Still, they inevitably make mistakes. In other words, they are people who, like everyone else, occasionally live at odds with themselves.

Rabbi Yehoshua ben Levi loved all people, but Jews more so. He was angry with Israel's enemies. He once sighed upon seeing beautiful fruit trees: "O trees, trees," he said. "To whom are you offering your exquisite fruit? To the pagans who caused such suffering to our people?" On another occasion he said: "The Almighty stands on Mount Moriah and sees not only the ruins of the Temple but also those who were responsible for them. He relegates them to the fiery bottom of the abyss that is hell."

As a teacher, Rabbi Yehoshua ben Levi's strength lay in his extraordinary curiosity. His favorite expression was "Why?" "Why is Israel compared to an olive? Because, like olives, Israel grows in all seasons." "Why does God promise redemption with a paradoxical statement, *'be'ito ahishena'*—I shall hasten redemption in due time"? Isn't it either-or? "If He hastens the event, then it will be before its time. If it occurs in its time, it will not have been precipitated!" Rabbi Yehoshua explains: *"Zakha*—if Israel is worthy, *ahishena*, then I will hasten redemption; *lo zakha*—if Israel will remain unworthy of redemption, it will still come, but in its own time." Unable to resist a poetic image, he adds: "If Israel is worthy, the Redeemer will appear riding in fiery, golden clouds; if Israel is unworthy, he will arrive riding on a donkey."

It is also he who asked: Why were the *Anshei Knesset Hagdola*—the members of the great commonwealth—so special? Because they have restored the divine crown to its rightful place. Moses had proclaimed: *"Ha'keil ha'gadol ha'gibor ve'ha'nora"*—God is great, mighty, and awesome. Then came Jeremiah, who said: "Pagans are dancing in His Sanctuary—where is His awesomeness?" So he stopped using the word "awesome." Then came Daniel, who said: "Pagans have enslaved His children—where is His might?" So he stopped using the word "mighty." But the *Anshei Knesset Hagdola* gave deeper meaning to those words: His might lies in His ability to contain His anger at the wicked; as for His awesomeness, it is ever present. Were it not for the fear of heaven, the nations of the world would have long ago devoured the Jewish people.

In his approach to the interpretation of the Law, he combined simplicity and depth, moderation and commitment. He even enjoyed making puns. His appeal to listeners crossed all social boundaries. His tales were captivating, his aphorisms were endowed with such common sense that they could not fail to leave an imprint.

He was utterly repelled by vulgarity. One need never utter an obscene word, he said. Look at Scripture: even when it must confront something unholy, the description is understated. Not surprisingly, ancient Hebrew was called the sacred tongue, because it contained no obscene words.

In general, he was careful with words. *Mila besela*, he said: if a word is worth one coin, silence is worth two.

Speaking of money, he knew its value well: it can even purify bastards. He also said, "Whoever is bitten by a snake, will thereafter be afraid of a string."

What was important for him was respect in human relations. Who is a miscreant? he asked. It is someone who offends his fellow student in the presence of their teacher. If he so often emphasizes his distaste for slander in all its forms, it is because slander violates human rights from a distance.

On the basis of what we know of him, he must have been universally respected, popular in all circles, at peace with the world and himself. Actually, I don't believe he was at peace with the world. I don't believe that he had no opponents, no enemies. I don't believe he was liked or even respected by everybody. Nor do I believe he was always at peace with himself.

Oh yes—he was a good father, a marvelous grandfather, an inspiring teacher. Still, there was something in his life that was not right. Otherwise, he would not have been so preoccupied with dreams. Few Talmudic masters have been as concerned with dreams as he was.

What if you dream of a river? Or grapes? What if you see a shofar in your dream? Or a dog? Or a bird? Or a lion? A well? He had answers for all these questions. Was he the Sigmund Freud of the third century? Hardly. He dealt not with psychoanalysis but with prayer. He had biblical verses as references for all the dreams. Recite the verses and everything would be all right.

But he also had powers—mystical powers. Could he have been a mystic after all? He performed miracles—that we know. When a severe drought struck his city, he prayed, and the heavens opened. Rabbi Hanina's intercession for rain had not succeeded in Tsiporis. Rabbi Yehoshua ben Levi was luckier.

As for his visions, listen:

When Moses ascended into heaven, he found God weaving crowns or ornaments around the letters in the Torah. Said God: Moses, do people in your place not greet one another? Moses answered: No, a servant would not dare to greet his master. To which God replied: You could have—at least—wished me success with my work.

Another story by Rabbi Yehoshua ben Levi on the same subject:

When Moses ascended into heaven, the angels felt provoked. They turned to God and asked: "What is a mortal doing in our midst?" "He came to receive the Torah," answered God. "What?" they exclaimed. "You have preserved a treasure for 974 generations since creation, and now you want to hand it over to a man of flesh and blood?" God demanded Moses to answer them. "I am scared," said Moses. "With one word, they could destroy me." "Hold on to my throne and give them your answer," said God. "Master of the universe, what is written in the Torah you have chosen to give me?" "It is written: I am thy God who has delivered you from Egypt." "Tell me, angels, said Moses. Did you go down to Egypt? Were you enslaved by Pharaoh? What need do you have of the Torah?" Since the angels did not answer, Moses continued: "What else does the Torah say? It says 'Do not worship other gods.' Do you dwell among people who worship idols? The Torah also commands us to rest the seventh day: do you need to rest, do you work at all? Honor thy father and mother, says the Torah. Do you have parents?" Apparently, logic sometimes works, even in heaven. The hostile angels became Moses' best friends.

But one of them, a former angel named Satan, was not happy. He appeared before God and inquired: "Where is the Torah?" "Down below, on earth," said God. So Satan visited the earth: "Where is the Torah?" he asked. In vain. Satan tried his luck with the sea. The sea pleaded ignorance. The abyss? Same answer. Death? Still the same answer. "Master of the universe," cried Satan. "I searched everywhere and failed to find the Torah. Where is it?" "Go ask the son of Amram," said God. So Satan went to see Moses: "Where is the Torah that God has given you?" Moses answered: "Who am I that God should give *me* the Torah?" At that point, God intervened, calling Moses a liar. "I was telling the truth," said Moses. "How could I imagine myself worthy of receiving your most precious treasure?" God was pleased by his answer: "Because you are so humble, the Torah will be called by your name."

Rabbi Yehoshua ben Levi's son, Rav Yosef, also had mystical experiences. One day he fainted and died. Somehow he was brought back to life. "What did you see up there?" his father asked him. "I discovered there a world in which everything is upside down: those who are strong and mighty on this earth, are weak and powerless up there." "What about us?" wondered the father. "We remain the same both here and up there." In other words: don't worry, father, your virtue is transcendent.

How could the prophet Elijah resist such a man?

Theirs was a beautiful but stormy friendship—with ups and downs, crises and adventures, separations and reconciliations. Elijah was as close to Rabbi Yehoshua as anyone. They would meet on Mount Carmel, or on the road, or near the entrance to Rabbi Shimon bar Yohai's cave, and they would discuss endless questions related to study.

Of course, Rabbi Yehoshua was not the only one who had a relationship with the prophet. Other *Tzaddikim* enjoyed similar privileges. They also benefited from what is called *"gilui Eliyahu"*—Elijah revealed himself to them. But they saw him once or twice, always for specific reasons, usually to solve an immediate problem, whereas Rabbi Yehoshua saw him many times, just to chat. Furthermore, whereas other sages needed their soul to ascend to heaven so as to meet the prophet, Rabbi Yehoshua brought the prophet to him, all the way down to earth. Whatever the sage wanted, Elijah granted him. Listen to how the prophet found a way to satisfy him: There was a ship caught in a storm with a young boy aboard. Elijah said to him: "If you promise to do what I ask you, I will save the ship. I want you to go to Lod where Rabbi Yehoshua ben Levi resides. Take him outside the city, to the big cave there." "But he is a great man and I am nobody," said the young boy. "He will not follow me." "He is a humble man," said Elijah. "He will follow you." Of course, the ship was saved and the boy managed to get the sage and bring him to the cave as requested by the prophet. Once inside, the boy showed him a stone which suddenly shone with such intensity that its light reached the horizon. Commented the Talmud: See how humble Rabbi Yehoshua was. A young boy asked him to accompany him for three miles, and he, the sage, didn't even ask why.

Still, Rabbi Yehoshua did have some difficult moments. Once a man was devoured by a lion three miles from the sage's residence. When Elijah heard about this, he became angry: Rabbi Yehoshua should have protected the victim. The rabbi asked how he could have known, since the prophet had not warned him of the impending tragedy. Never mind logic, said the prophet. A just man must help his fellow man, even without knowing.

On another occasion, a mysterious man named Ula ben Kushav— probably a member of an anti-Roman underground group—came to Rabbi Yehoshua for shelter: the Roman police were after him. Naturally, Rabbi Yehoshua took him into his house. Roman soldiers then surrounded Lod and threatened to destroy the city if the fugitive was not handed over. Rabbi Yehoshua ben Levi could have decided on his own. But he preferred to allow the fugitive to reach his own decision. He told him that the Law was against him. For it says that if an enemy lays siege to a community and threatens to destroy it unless any one member is given up, the community's sacred duty is to resist the threat. Better for everyone to die than to betray a human being— any human being. However, if the enemy names the individual in question, the community may cooperate in his apprehension. So Ula ben Kushav was handed over to the Roman soldiers. And on that day Elijah did not appear before Rabbi Yehoshua. Nor the next day. Nor the next week. Rabbi Yehoshua waited and waited. In vain. Feeling abandoned and in despair, he embarked on a ritual of penance and fasting, until finally Elijah returned. "Why did you make me wait so long?" asked Rabbi Yehoshua. Elijah's answer was short and chilling: "I do not deal with informers." "But what I did was in strict conformity with the Law, wasn't it?" cried Rabbi Yehoshua. "True," answered Elijah. "But as a Hasid, a pious man, you should have gone further than the Law. Granted, the man had to be handed over—but why did it have to be by you?"

Still, the two remained friends. So much so that, in the end, they were united by legend even in the way they cheated death. Like Elijah, Rabbi Yehoshua allegedly entered heaven alive. Why? Because of his love for the sick. We are told that he alone was willing to treat patients whose mortal diseases were contagious. Because he had defied death, death was ultimately powerless against him.

Many descriptions of this amazing episode exist in Talmudic, midrashic, and post-midrashic literature. It generally goes like this. When Rabbi Yehoshua ben Levi's final hour had arrived, God dispatched the Angel of Death. "Go and do his will"—in other words, go and take his life. When Rabbi Yehoshua saw the Angel of Death he said, "I would like to see my place in heaven." The Angel consented. "Wait," said Rabbi Yehoshua. "Your sword frightens me. Let me keep it for the journey." Again, the Angel agreed. He then took the sage to a place, high above, from which he could see paradise. At that point, Rabbi Yehoshua jumped inside. The Angel caught him by the edge of his garment, urging him to return. "I swear that I am not going to leave this place," said Rabbi Yehoshua. The Angel appealed to God, who took Rabbi Yehoshua's side. "At least give me back my sword," the Angel pleaded. "No," said Rabbi Yehoshua, who, at that moment, wanted to save all people from death. But God intervened again—this time on the side of the Angel. A heavenly voice was heard: "Give him back the sword. Mankind needs it." Inspired by this story, Longfellow wrote a poem called "The Spanish Jew's Tale: The Legend of Rabbi Ben Levi."

According to another version, the Angel brought an official complaint to Rabban Gamliel, urging him to order the illegal refugee to return home, so that he could take care of him. Rabban Gamliel ruled in favor of Rabbi Yehoshua and even asked him for information on what was going on there. He was especially curious to learn whether there were Jews in hell. Rabbi Yehoshua wrote a full report and gave it to the Angel of Death. What a fall! From angel he had become a simple mailman.

"I have measured hell," Rabbi Yehoshua wrote. "It is one hundred miles long and fifty miles wide. Angels of fire serve as guards. They devour whoever is near them. Hell comprises seven chambers. After all the sinners are chastised and burned, they come back to life in their previous form, only to be punished again. This happens during each day and three times each night." Interestingly, in his new role as reporter, Rabbi Yehoshua tells us whom he saw in hell. Famous names . . .

He also describes paradise with its two gates, each guarded by six hundred thousand angels. There are eighty thousand trees in every corner. At the center stands the Tree of Life. Its fruits have five hundred thousand tastes. A *Tzaddik* arrives, he is led to a golden canopy from which four rivers flow, one of honey, one of oil, one of milk, and one of wine. Paradise, too, is composed of seven chambers. The first is reserved for Rabbi Akiba and other martyrs of the faith. The seventh—for those who failed to humiliate those who humiliated them.

Still another text tells us that when Rabbi Yehoshua received permanent residency in paradise, his old friend Elijah was there to welcome him. *"Panu derekh le'bar Levi,"* exclaimed Elijah. "Make way for the son of Levi." Thus he led him to the place where Rabbi Shimon bar Yohai sat on a throne made of thirteen golden tables. "Are you the son of Levi?" asked Rabbi Shimon bar Yohai. "Yes," said Rabbi Yehoshua. "Was there a rainbow in the sky in your lifetime?" "Yes," said Rabbi Yehoshua. "In that case," said Rabbi Shimon bar Yohai, "you are not the son of Levi." Commented the Talmud: Actually, there was no rainbow in Rabbi Yehoshua's lifetime, but he was too timid to say so.

What makes the absence of the rainbow so important? And what moved Rabbi Shimon bar Yohai to deny the newcomer's identity? The first question has been answered in the Talmud. Because the rainbow is a sign of divine protection over the community, its presence is not needed when a *Tzaddik* is around: it is he who protects his community. Thus we understand Rabbi Shimon bar Yohai's question and even his disappointment: in his eyes, Rabbi Yehoshua would not be a true *Tzaddik* if his people needed the rainbow for protection. What we fail to understand is his answer, "You are not the son of Levi." Who else could he be?

This was not the first moment of tension between the two. A Midrash tells us that Elijah and Rabbi Yehoshua were arguing a legal point. "Let us ask Rabbi Shimon bar Yohai," said Elijah. But Rabbi Shimon bar Yohai refused to see Rabbi Yehoshua—or rather, to be seen by him. Why? Again, because a rainbow had appeared in the sky in his lifetime.

From the beginning of our encounter with Rabbi Yehoshua ben Levi, we have felt the mysterious shadow of Rabbi Shimon bar Yohai hovering above us. Why did Elijah and Rabbi Yehoshua frequently meet at the entrance to his cave? What drew them there? The mystical connection? But didn't we conclude—perhaps prematurely—that Rabbi Yehoshua was mainly involved with *nigla,* the revealed tradition, as opposed to *Torat ha'nistar,* the study of mysticism?

What if we were wrong? And what if our hero had been attracted to it—but dared not admit it in public? His dreams, his visions of Moses in heaven, his meetings with the Angel of Death, his adventures with Elijah, his miracle-making, his use of fantasy—do these not constitute a portrait of a mystical quest?

Upon rereading the existing texts related to him, I discovered a new dimension to his personality: he never went to the end of a quest. A great Halakhist—most of his decisions prevailed—he was not satisfied with Halakha alone. Though an exponent of Aggada, he distrusted it and opposed its being written down. Speaking of one particular legend, which he must have attributed to extraneous influences, he said: "Whoever wrote it will have no share in the world to come; whoever reads it will be punished; whoever hears it will receive no reward." Whatever did not belong to the rational aspect of Judaism was not for him. When someone outside the faith cured his son of some disease with an occult formula, he said: "Better die than live by such practices." But since neither Halakha nor Aggada fully satisfied him, why shouldn't he have explored the irrational, fourth dimension, the mystical one? He was reluctant to penetrate its dazzling universe. He was attracted to the cave where the Zohar was supposed to have been written, but he did not go inside. He stayed at the entrance. Is this why Rabbi Shimon bar Yohai was angry with him? "You are not the son of Levi," he told him. Meaning: the true son of Levi is more daring. In other words, too much humility may become an obstacle to knowledge: exaggerated timidity will prevent you from learning. You are attracted to mystery? Then penetrate it. You will not comprehend mystery by studying its surface. Open its gates and plunge into its depths.

Thus we see Rabbi Yehoshua ben Levi in a very human light. Elijah befriended him? The Angel of Death obeyed him? Still, he had his share of failures. Most notably, he did not manage to deprive death of its power. Why didn't he disobey the heavenly voice ordering him to return the sword to its owner? But then, what did the heavenly voice actually tell him? That people need the Angel of Death. Does this mean that they need to die? That for life to go on, some must stop living?

Indeed, Rabbi Yehoshua ben Levi's major problem was death. That is why he needed Elijah. Consciously or not, he wanted to learn from the prophet how to bypass death. How to enter heaven alive, as Elijah had done. That is also why he wished to meet the Messiah. Because the Messiah is meant to vanquish death—forever.

But death is still around. And its sword is being used in too many places.

I NOW SEE Rabbi Yehoshua ben Levi as a sensitive man drawn to melancholy. Alive, he feared death. In paradise, he could not forget those he had left behind.

He once quoted Rabbi Pinhas ben Ya'ir: "Why are the prayers of the children of Israel sometimes not received in heaven? Because they have forgotten the ineffable name."

Is that *all* they have forgotten? One name?

Abbaye and Rava:
The Greatness of Dialogue

T HIS IS HOW, after the death of its great leader Rav Yosef, the illustrious sage Abbaye became president of the celebrated Babylonian academy of Pumbedita.

Four masters met on that day to discuss the destiny of their orphaned school: Abbaye, Rava, Rav Zeira, and Rabba bar Matna. They all agreed that a new president would have to be elected. But in what manner? Rabba bar Matna had a suggestion: *"Kol she'yomar davar ve'lo yashivu alav, ye'asseh rosh"*—whoever speaks without his words being refuted, shall accede to the high office. His suggestion was adopted, and they all spoke. But all were disputed—except Abbaye. He alone delivered his lecture in silence. When he was through, Rabba bar Matna noticed that *"gava rosho shel Abbaye"*— Abbaye was taller than they, greater than they, perhaps worthier. And Rabba bar Matna exclaimed, *"Nachmani, petah ve'emor"*—Nachmani, speak. Speak and you shall be listened to as never before; as teacher and no longer as disciple or colleague.

And thus began Abbaye's reign.

This little story is impressive and revealing. It shows us something about the process of electing a leader. Clearly, it was up to the electors (namely the great disciples or elite) to determine the choice. In other words, the approach was not entirely democratic, but elections rarely are, since candidates are presented to the voters, rather than selected by them.

Still, essential information about the elections is withheld. We know that the candidates took part in a great debate, but was it public or private, and what was it about? Who said what on which subject? We don't know. Was it in the domain of Aggada or Halakha? We don't know. Perhaps the Talmud deemed this of minor importance. Topical discourses or campaign promises, who remembers them, anyway? Candidates may say anything, as we well know. Unfortunately, the Talmud did not record any of the speeches. In this case, good speakers had a better chance than poor ones. We would like to have had a transcript of Abbaye's address. All we must be satisfied with is the result: Rabba bar Matna's concession speech on behalf of himself and his two defeated colleagues, recognizing the superiority of Abbaye, whom he curiously addresses as Nachmani.

Later, we shall see that, according to some sources, Abbaye's name *was* Nachmani. But in the Talmud it remained Abbaye. Why then this unconscious or even conscious confusion by Rabba bar Matna? Certain commentators do not hesitate to impute to him some ulterior motives: he called him Nachmani, they say, *lignai*—to irritate him; to remind him of his uncle and teacher, Rabba bar Nachmani, as if to say, you owe your election to your relatives.

Rabba bar Matna may also have wanted to warn him not to take himself too seriously: though a master, he remains Rabba bar Nachmani's pupil. The expression *gava rosho*—he grew taller—would then render a tone of disapproval rather than praise. Even if he did not intend to hurt Abbaye, it is clear that he himself was hurt. And we understand why: he too desired the position. Rabba bar Matna must have been angry with himself all the more since it was he who had established the rules of the contest.

Yes, Abbaye became president, while Rabbi bar Matna withdrew into the shadows: no law is associated with his name. At Abbaye's death, his successor would be Rava, whose influence, especially in matters of Halakha, would surpass his own. Abbaye's real rival was Rava, not Rabba bar Matna.

ABBAYE AND RAVA: two names inseparable from one another and both inseparable from the Talmud. As illustrious as Shammai and Hillel, as popular as Rav and Shmuel, they evoke, for generations of Jewish students and dreamers, the color, the tone, the intensity, and the beauty of the Talmudic universe.

To study Abbaye and Rava has become synonymous with the study of Talmud. When Bialik, in his sweet and melancholy poem "Hamatmid," wanted to paint a picture of a young Talmudic student, consecrating his life to study, he situates him in the crossfire between Abbaye and Rava: two names with ancient resonance. Abbaye and Rava: two branches of an ancient tree, comforting the wanderer in the desert and offering him water and serenity.

In dark, oppressive hours of exile, we invoked their names and drew from them the courage and determination to go on. We sang them, we repeated them with fervor; we chanted them with passion. *Amar Abbaye*—and Abbaye said; *amar Rava*—and Rava replied. It was as though, beyond perils and obstacles, their voices could reach us still, through other situations, other enigmas, other burning times.

Abbaye and Rava: carried away by their uninterrupted debate, you suddenly ceased to hear the sound of the enemy. The pogromchiks sharpened their swords—but you were unaware of their presence. You were aware of the Talmud alone—you were enveloped by its fervor. The killers killed, the profaners profaned, but as long as our two faraway masters debated on the various interpretations of God's Law, as handed down by Moses and remembered in the Mishna, as long as they strove orally to rebuild the Temple of Jerusalem in Jerusalem, then away from Jerusalem, the old men and their pupils in the ghettos would refuse to abdicate.

We shall try to meet these two characters, whose attitudes and quarrels affect our own to this day. We shall try to analyze their complex relationship. Unlike Hillel and Shammai, who had no personal contact, Abbaye and Rava were close friends—inseparable friends. One imagines them together, always together, locked in debates concerning a thousand-and-one problems of Jewish life and Jewish attitudes toward life. Were they really as close as legend wants us to believe? They were so different. One is better known, more accessible, more rooted in fact than the other. This is Rava: the former unhappy candidate. The one who loses. How did he "take the election results"? And again—why was Abbaye the winner? Why he, and not Rabba bar Matna, who apparently was their organizational leader and expert, since it was he who proposed the rules? Why not Rav Zeira, so respected in the Talmud? Why not Rava himself, whose prestige was so high and enduring? Only because Abbaye belonged to an important family? Or because he could prevent or discourage opposition? In legal matters, in Halakha, it is Rava who usually has the last word. *Abbaye ve' Rava,* we are told, *Halakha ke'Rava:* when they are in conflict, the law is according to Rava, except for six precise questions known as *ya'el kagam.*

In all other instances, Rava's decision is law for the entire people of Israel. But then, if Rava is so erudite, so clear-sighted, why wasn't he chosen to succeed their teacher? We shall try to see why. We shall go to Pumbedita and join the students of its prestigious academy. We shall visit the palace of the exilarch, and find a last measure of Jewish royalty, Jewish sovereignty.

A story. When they were still young, Abbaye and Rava were together with Abbaye's uncle, Rabba bar Nachmani. They had just concluded their meal and were about to say grace. "Grace to whom?" asked the old teacher. "God," the two boys replied in unison. "Man can say grace to God alone." "And God?" asked Rabba bar Nachmani. "Where is God?" Startled, the two boys kept silent. "Well?" said the old sage. "Which one of you will tell me where God is to be found?" Now they had to answer. So Rava, without saying a word, lifted his finger toward the ceiling: there. As for Abbaye, wishing to outdo his friend, he ran outside and pointed to the sky: there. And the old master, who loved them both, smiled proudly, affectionately, and said, "you shall both be rabbis and teachers in Israel."

Another story. After Abbaye died, his widow Choma came to see the new president, Rava, and asked him to determine her pension. In doing so he didn't mind being generous and ordered that such-and-such a sum of money be given to her for food, lodging, clothing, and so forth. Was she satisfied? No. "You have forgotten an important item," she said. "Wine. I like wine; who will pay for it?" Rava was startled. "I knew Abbaye," he said. "I knew him well; I can testify to the fact that he did not drink wine." "True," said Choma. "He did not; I did." And she continued: "I swear on your head that he gave me wine to drink from a cup that was as long as my arm." While speaking she abruptly pulled up her sleeve and showed her arm. And suddenly, says legend, a great light shone in Rava's study!

And—a prayer. At the conclusion of services, Rava was accustomed to speak to God in these terms: "Master of the universe, before I was born, I was nothing; and now, though alive, I am still nothing. I am dust now—and dust I shall be. I stand before you as a vase filled with shame. Please prevent me from committing any more sins. Please help me dissipate those that I have already committed; and please make them disappear not in suffering but in compassion—your own."

From these three texts emerge the spiritual portraits of our two masters, who were friends since childhood. The enthusiasm of Abbaye, the moderation of Rava. The exhibitionism of the first, the modesty of the latter. But before we examine the two masters further, let us have a look at their surroundings: what was the situation of the Jewish people then? What was the world situation?

We are in the middle of the fourth century, which is a time of profound political, ideological, and religious upheaval. Empires are on the move, mankind is in effervescence. Events follow one another at a quick pace. Between 235 and 285 of our common era, no fewer than twenty-six Roman emperors seized the throne—and only one died a natural death! Then as now, most palace revolutions were conducted by the military. To satisfy them, the rulers granted them honors, medals, and money! The money was taken from the people in those times: from the Jewish people. Before dying, Septimus Severus told his sons: "Be of one mind. Enrich the soldiers. Think of nothing else." To a Jewish delegation that came to plead for tax relief, one emperor declared: "If I could, I would tax you for the air you are breathing."

Rome was living its last hours, its glory was vanishing—and Jews were victims of its spite and vengeance. The rising star was that of the Christians. Their small persecuted sect, whose leader died of solitude, in solitude, was now invading entire kingdoms. The Romans killed one Jew in Judea, and now his disciples had begun to Judaize— or Christianize—Rome. But these Christians, once in power, used it not to stop persecutions, but to redirect them against their Jewish brethren who wanted to remain Jewish. Cruel laws were passed. Listen to the one enacted by Constantine the Great, October 18, 315: "We wish to make it known to the Jews and their elders and their patriarchs that if, after the enactment of this law, any one of them dares to attack another who has fled their dangerous sect and attached himself to the worship of God—Christianity—he must be speedily given to the flames and burnt with all his accomplices." And on March 7, 321, he proclaimed: "All judges and common people of the city and workers in all crafts are to rest on the holy Sunday. . . ."

In other words, theological precepts were being enforced by imperial government. On August 13, 339, Constantine proclaimed: "Marriages between Jews and Christian women of the imperial weaving factories are to be dissolved. This prohibition of intermarriage is to be preserved lest the Jews induce Christian women to share their shameful lives—in which case the Jewish husbands are to be punished with death."

Only one ruler, Julian the Apostate, was concerned with the welfare of the Jews. He wanted to rebuild the Temple in Jerusalem. Contributions began to flow in for that purpose. He wanted, for reasons of his own, to bring back Jewish nationalism and use it for Rome. Would he have restored Jerusalem? We do not know; we will never know: eighteen months later he was defeated and killed by the Persians.

And Jewish sympathies were with the Persians. The reasons are clear. The old regime was bad, and getting worse and worse, for the Jews.

Treated as outcasts by Rome and Byzantium alike, the Jews were prohibited from living normally, proudly, freely. They were not allowed to build new synagogues or houses of worship, to teach Torah, to dream of a future. This hatred of Jews and Judaism increased year by year. It became a contagious malediction. One century later, Theodosius I would say that to be Jewish was "to have an incurable disease which must be eradicated."

Meanwhile, elsewhere, Judaism lived and flourished in Babylon, under Persian domination. Jews had lived there for centuries—more precisely, since the destruction of the First Temple, when victorious Nebuchadnezzar deported King Zidkiyahu and his young heroes. Seventy years later, Ezra and Nehemiah returned to Jerusalem, to rebuild the Temple, but were followed by only a small minority; most Jews chose to stay behind, in exile. Their situation never stopped improving. Wealthy, secure, influential, they even benefited from a kind of spiritual and semilegal autonomy. Certain cities, such as Nehardea, were entirely Jewish. No wonder that in Roman-Persian conflicts, the Jews supported the Persians. They gave money for the war effort; they received military personnel into their homes—and at times lived to regret it. Soldiers are soldiers. They interpreted hospitality in their own manner, often raping the host's wife or daughter. All ended up as problems for our Talmudic masters.

The head of the Jewish community in Babylon was the *resh-galuta*, the exilarch, a sort of president of Jews in the Diaspora. He served as an intermediary between Persian authorities and Jews. Bound to implement Persian policy, he did rule as sovereign, but only internally. As long as he collected taxes for Persia and helped it wage wars against external enemies, he had nothing to fear from his superiors.

The exilarch lived in a luxurious palace. Protected by bodyguards and provided with his own police to assist his government machinery, he was a kind of prime minister or president of a state-within-a-state. His powers were limited in religious matters alone. There, he had to cope with rabbis whose authority superseded his own. Thus there were frequent frictions between the *resh-galuta* and certain *roshei-yeshivot*, presidents of important academies. And in these disputes, the *roshei-yeshivot* tended to be the victors.

For rabbis, teaching in Sura, Pumbedita, and Nehardea conferred an authority more enduring than anything offered by the secular world, and they imposed their will. To appease them, the exilarch gave them certain privileges. For instance, sages and their disciples did not stand in line at the marketplace, either to sell or to buy, for their time was considered precious. They did not pay taxes. Scholarship was still appreciated, learning extolled. The nobility of Torah was superior to all else.

In Pumbedita, the prestigious center for higher learning, the Amoraim continued the tradition of their predecessors, the Tannaim; they explored and enriched the oral tradition as it was handed down to them long ago, at Sinai.

Who were they? In the beginning, they served as interpreters who explained, or simply repeated, the teachings of the Tannaim in Palestinian academies. Later, they themselves became teachers, with their schools, their disciples, their systems, and their pedagogy. Their number was close to two thousand.

Among the most illustrious Amoraim were the two masters whose fascinating portraits we are now viewing.

LET US BEGIN with Abbaye, of whom we know a great deal. We know when he was born, where he studied, and under whom. We know his moods, his habits, his philosophy of life—and yet there are things about him that remain obscure, unknown.

We know that he lived from 278 to 338; and that he belonged to a noble line of priests—he was a descendant of Eli ha-kohen. We know that his father, Kheilil, died before his birth, and that his mother died while giving birth to him; we know that his famous uncle, Rabba bar Nachmani, took him into his home, brought him up, and sent him to study with Rav Yehuda, then with Rav Yosef, who later, having lost his memory, often turned to him for a reminder of his rulings and arguments.

But we don't know his real name. Some sources maintain that Abbaye was only a nickname. What, then, happened to his real name? And to his title Rav? A *rosh-yeshiva* without a rabbinic degree: is it conceivable? Why the mystery?

We are told how he walked in public places with Rav Pappa at his right and Rav Huna at his left. We are told how he behaved as a child, and later as master of his generation. Everything about his personality has been made available, except his name, which has been treated as something totally private. Why?

We know that he was poor, extremely poor. To pay for his studies and sustenance, he worked at night watering trees and flowers. Later, he became a farmer and vintner. Well-to-do but not rich, he did not change his lifestyle: whatever he possessed he shared.

His respect for his fellow man was legendary. He would notice an old man, take his arm, and help him cross the street. At the marketplace, he would greet anyone first—be he or she friend or stranger.

He married at least twice. But we know nothing about his first wife, who bore his children. Of them we don't know much more.

But we do know his second wife. Her name was Choma, daughter of Issi, Rav Yehuda's granddaughter; she was known for her beauty. Abbaye loved her and loved to spoil her. As we saw earlier he gave her wine, while he himself abstained from alcohol. He had a son, Reb Bibi—but whose son was he? Choma's or her predecessor's? In truth, we don't know—just as we are kept in the dark about the brevity of his second marriage: was it interrupted by his death, or by their divorce? All we know is that Abbaye and Choma did not stay together long.

We are informed also of Abbaye's health; he was often sick. In his family people died young. This explains his obsession with death and matters related to death, the futility of the human adventure, the vanity of earthly possessions; from his sayings it's clear that Abbaye was aware of his own frailty. Too many illnesses befell him, too much anguish oppressed him. Often he quoted his nurse, his adopted mother, and his mother-in-law, who taught him all kinds of medical remedies against pain. His body did not leave him in peace.

Yes. We do have enough pigments to paint his portrait, yet the model escapes us. The Talmud is full of Abbaye—the expression *amar Abbaye,* and Abbaye said, occurs in its pages 1,177 times. But we don't know with certainty who his father was, who his mother was, where he was born, where he died, or under what circumstances. Too personal? Perhaps. The Talmud may have chosen to emphasize the public figure exclusively. We know how he looked, how he talked, how he behaved in public, but only in public.

We are told that he was cheerful—even mischievous. He loved to spread joy around him. So much so that Rabba admonished him one day: "Isn't it written, *'vegilu bire'ada'*—one must tremble before the Lord?" "I do," replied Abbaye. Still, he wanted people around him to be happy. To entertain his teacher, Rabba bar Nachmani, he juggled eight eggs in the air and caught them all.

RAV ADA BAR ABA did not behave well toward Rav Dimi of Nehardea. Is this why he died before his time? Some sages believed so. Said Abbaye: No, he died because of me: he humiliated me in front of my students; he sent them to study under Rava . . .

Said Abbaye: At first I studied at home and prayed at the synagogue. Then I heard someone quote Oula that since the destruction of the Temple the Almighty dwells within the four measures of Halakha. Since then I study in the synagogue.

Abbaye: All children of Israel are princes.

Abbaye: The Messiah will come on the saddest day of the year— Tisha b'Av, the ninth of Av. The greatest sadness will turn into the greatest joy.

Abbaye: There are always thirty-six just men in the world worthy of receiving the Shekhina.

Once he saw a man offer to accompany a woman on the road. Suspicious, he followed them so as to separate them, just in case the man had some impure ideas. Then he saw them bid farewell to one another. Regretting having suspected them for no reason, he said: "I don't think I would have the strength to resist committing a sin." An old man reassured him: whoever is greater than his friend, his evil spirit is also greater.

A legend: A woman died, leaving an infant behind. Miraculously, the father's breasts filled with milk, and he could nurse his child. Said Rav Yosef: This must be a great man. No, said Abbaye, he must be bad for having caused the laws of nature to be changed.

Each time one of his students finished a Talmudic treatise, he would organize a reception to celebrate the event, and invited everyone to participate. Abbaye, the sad, unhappy man, the victim of his health and of his destiny, did the utmost to create joy in other people. Is this why he was elected president of Pumbedita?

ABBAYE'S ALLY and ultimate rival, Rava, resembled him in nothing. Yet through his inner life and his faith in words and eternity, Rava's destiny extends Abbaye's.

Rava may be characterized by the following episode. Still young, Rava was studying with his friend, Rami bar Hema, under the great master Rav Hisda. Rav Hisda taught his pupils with his daughter sitting on his knees. Occasionally he would play with her, probably because the mother was away. One day, he asked his daughter: "Which of these boys would you like to marry?" And the little girl, without the slightest hesitation, said "Both." Rami blushed and said nothing, whereas Rava found his bearings right away. "It's all right with me," he said, "but I want to be the second." And whom did the girl ultimately marry? First Rami bar Hama. Then, after his death, she became the wife of Rava.

Rava's marriage is told in detail—and everything else as well. Rava, unlike Abbaye, is the visible man; easily described, understood, and dealt with. His name itself is revealing: "Rava" is an abbreviation of "Rav Abba." He is a Rav attached to his father, who was also a Rav of the third generation of the Amoraim, Rav Yosef bar Hama.

Rava was born at Mekhoza, where he had a happy and serene childhood, studying with Rav Nahman, Rav Hisda, Rav Yosef, and Rabba. A rich landowner, he lacked nothing and could devote his life to study. Nothing but study mattered. Study was more important than prayer. To a sage who spent too much time in prayer, he remarked, "Poor man, he neglects eternity for temporal life." His love for study was illustrated by his aphorism "Whoever studies Torah ascends higher than the High Priest who enters the Sanctuary." He also proclaimed that the study of Torah protects man from all ailments, suffering, and persecution.

Love of Torah, passion for Torah, filled his life and made him into a grand master of Torah. With his rigorous analytical method he attracted the best students. It was said that whoever came to hear him at Mekhoza could never go elsewhere. Why Mekhoza? Rava was born there, and, after Abbaye's election in Pumbedita, he returned to establish his own academy. Was he jealous of Abbaye? No. He voted for him; the vote was unanimous. Still, he felt the need to teach, and remained at Mekhoza for fourteen years.

The two rival schools, with their hundreds of students, competed for the best ones. Abbaye's strength lay in his *Harifut,* the sharpness of his mind, whereas Rava's was in his *bekiut,* his erudition. It was a friendly war between perception and knowledge, imagery and synthesis, content and form. To convey his perspective, Rava said: "One grain of pungent pepper is better than a basketful of pumpkins." And one of his disciples, Rav Ada bar Abba, with typical condescension, said to a friend from Pumbedita: "Instead of gnawing bones in the school of Abbaye, why don't you come and eat fat meat in the school of Rava?" This remark may be taken both literally and figuratively. Yes, Abbaye's teaching lacked practicality; it was too theoretical, too abstract, too rhetorical, while Rava's teaching aimed at being concrete and accessible. Rava knew what to do and when and where; that was his secret; he knew how to handle himself in all situations and what to draw from all sources—and not to rely only on the supernatural.

In Pumbedita, students were clever; they could make an elephant pass through the eye of a needle—whereas in Mekhoza, they were clever enough not to try! An example: we know that at the Temple of Jerusalem, during Passover, people went inside with their sacrifices, each awaiting his turn. When the first hall—the Ezra—was full, the doors had to be closed. By whom? Abbaye and Rava, as always, had different opinions. Abbaye said "by themselves," while Rava said "by the people." What's the difference? There is a difference, says the Talmud. The difference is whether one had to rely on miracles. And Rava said no.

Rava believed in logic. His entire life unfolded according to a rational pattern, never deviating from its course. In his case, not only his public life but also his private life is known. He was married only once; he loved his wife and she loved him: as a widow, she waited for him ten years. They had two sons. If Abbaye's wife was famous for her beauty, Rava's was known for her intelligence, erudition, and temper!

Legend has it that when Abbaye's widow came to see Rava regarding her pension, Rava issued his ruling and went home right away. His wife looked at him and quickly understood that something unusual had happened. "Who came to see you at the tribunal?" she asked. "Abbaye's widow," he said. That was all he said. Upon hearing this, his wife ran outside into the street with a stick in her hand, and chased the other woman out of Mekhoza, shouting, "You have killed three husbands, isn't that enough for you? Do you want to kill mine too?"

From this anecdote, we learn that the attractive Khoma somehow knew how to survive husbands, and also that the sweet daughter of Rav Hisda was not so sweet when it came to protecting her home!

But then, she was right in being careful—and in keeping her eyes open. As a brilliant speaker, Rava attracted crowds on Shabbat afternoons when he lectured on Aggada. There must have been many women in the audience. And yet his wife worried without need. He loved her and her alone. His quality of *yirat shamayim,* his fear of heaven, was all-encompassing.

That explains his harsh judgment of Job: was he guilty or not for complaining against God? Naturally, Abbaye and Rava disagreed. Abbaye said no, Rava said yes. Why should Job be condemned? asked Abbaye. After all, he didn't say anything. True, answered Rava. He didn't say anything. But in his heart . . .

Clearly, Rava had not only admirers in Mekhoza; he also had—like everyone else—critics who were envious, jealous of his position and fame.

Furthermore, he was too frank, too demanding, too severe—and too audacious. He criticized the wealthy for pursuing pleasures, and their wives for their idleness. He reprimanded those who claimed to respect Torah, but showed disrespect for its students. Above all, he was extremely severe with anyone he suspected of hypocrisy. He recognized human nature—and the illusoriness of social triumphs and success. Once he commented, rather sadly: "When I became judge, I was loved by those I set free and hated by those I convicted. But lately I noticed that today's convicts are set free tomorrow, and I understood: when I am loved, I am loved by everybody, and when I am hated, I am hated by everybody."

As judge, teacher, interpreter of the law, and academy president, he made enemies—which was normal. In some quarters he was criticized for maintaining inappropriate ties with the *resh-galuta* and the Persian authorities. Like Shmuel, another great Amora before him, he believed that *"dina de'malkhuta dina"*—the law of the land applies to all citizens, Jews too. He asserted that Jews, too, must pay income tax, and do nothing to disturb the peace.

The Persian emperor, Shapur II, managed to control the exilarch Mar Ukva, who managed to make Rava pro-Persian. Why not? Shapur II respected Jewish scholars and, on occasion, consulted them in matters of Jewish law. As for Rava himself, he was the favorite sage of the queen mother, Ifra Hormuz, who protected him and his protégés from occasional persecutions by the government. When Rava condemned a man to whiplashing for committing adultery, and that man died, it was the queen mother who protected Rava from the emperor's wrath.

In this respect, the Talmud does not conceal a certain hostility toward him from a number of scholars and common people. He was too law-abiding, too passive. He advised Jews to go out of their way not to provoke the Persian authorities; he even permitted them to lie, to pretend to be Persian if necessary.

But Rava never did anything for his own aggrandizement. All he wanted was to help the community of Israel. His relations with the Persian powers were predicated on that basis alone. He was especially concerned with the welfare of scholars. He ridiculed those who stood before the Torah, but not before students of Torah. Rava understood their importance for the community and its future: a people could survive without government functionaries, but not without teachers.

Of himself, Rava would say: "These are the three things I asked from heaven: the wisdom of Rav Huna, the wealth of Rav Hisda, and the modesty of Rabba bar Huna. Well, I received the first two, but not the third—not the modesty." Unlike so many others now, he didn't boast about his modesty. Quite the contrary!

Incidentally, had he yielded to temptation, had he fallen victim to vanity, other sages would have come to his aid and would have reminded him of man's limitations.

One day he decided to give a public lecture on Kabbala. But suddenly an old man stood up against him, and the lecture was not delivered.

Often, he would begin his lectures with a funny story, to catch the audience's attention. At times he would admit his previous mistakes in public: yesterday I was wrong about . . . It happened, therefore, that he would say one thing in the morning and another in the evening. He was so strict with himself that on Yom Kippur he would fast two days rather than one.

When Rava was sick the first day, he would not tell anyone about it. On the second day, he would tell his assistant, "Let it be known that I am ill. Let my friends pray for me, and let my enemies rejoice!"

His father—Rav Yosef bar Hamma—was the wealthy and learned rabbi of Mechoza. But his teacher was Rav Nahman, as was Rav Hisda.

Rava's father had servants who belonged to people who owed him money. He made them work for him. Rava asked him why. A Halakhic debate ensued, and finally the father gave in.

Rav Yosef was also his teacher; he was blind. Rava respected him so much that he would leave him walking backward, his feet bleeding.

Small items:

Rava showed interest in the material and spiritual welfare of his students.

He urged disciples to respect their wives—and so become rich.

It was he who decreed that we must get drunk on Purim.

It was also he who articulated the law protecting defendants against self-incrimination: *"Adam karov le'atzmo,"* man is close to himself, he cannot and must not become his own persecutor.

Legend describes his last moments: Rava was sick and his brother, Rav Seorim, saw him decline. Said Rava: "Please, tell the Angel of Death not to torment me." "Tell him yourself!" said his brother. "It would be of no use," said Rava. "I already belong to him." "All right," said Rav Seorim. "I will tell him, but you must promise me that you'll come back and tell me whether you have suffered." When Rava appeared in his brother's dream, he said, "It was like a pinprick."

At his funeral, as at Abbaye's, the crowd was so dense that the two banks of the River Hidekel seemed to have fused into one. And the treetops touched.

Sadly, neither man had a logical successor. Both schools—Pumbedita and Mekhoza—were forced to close; their disciples were left to themselves. Abbaye and Rava were the last giants of the Talmudic kingdom.

INTERESTINGLY, the problem which separates one from the other is the same which binds one to the other; one without the other would not have been the teacher, the scholar, the person he was. Abbaye needed Rava to be Abbaye, just as Rava needed Abbaye to be Rava. Had they been identical, they would have been poor twins, not friends. It was through their ongoing conflict that each man emerged more genuine and generous.

Thanks to their disputes, the editing of the Talmud reached its apogee. All the sages participated—those from Palestine and those from Babylon. Sources were compared, analyzed, studied, clarified, checked . . . Sometimes a question that had been raised during the first generation of scholars was examined by the second and resolved by the third. Enchanted, you breathlessly read of its course, its progression: the adventure of words, ideas, principles is matched by none—for it transcends time itself. In some instances, it took a century for the cycle to close. And yet the discussion among scholars of different ages is rendered as if they were contemporaries. And wherever you turn, you find the imprint of Abbaye and Rava. There is beauty and friendship in their endless, contentious relationship; they are both our masters.

As disciples, they were equals. As teachers, they remained equals. When Abbaye was elected president of Pumbedita, he did not become Rava's master, since Rava went to establish his school in Mekhoza. Perhaps that was the reason for Rava's move: not to change the nature of their relationship. In their disputes, personal elements never played a role. To the end they remained friends. In fact, friendship was so essential to their lives that Rava said: "Give me either friends or death." What is life without friends—and friendship? And yet, in their private lives, they were different. For instance, both went to have their dreams interpreted. Abbaye would pay for the services rendered, Rava would not. So the interpreter—or analyst—predicted catastrophes to befall Rava, including the death of his wife. For this, Rava never forgave him!

Legally, Rava is always right, except for six questions where Abbaye's decision is law. They deal with subconscious renunciation, divorce, marriage, and false testimony. In other words, six cases involving human relations on the highest level. Abbaye maintains that a false witness is, retroactively, not to be trusted. Also: a person who eats impure meat, not because he is hungry, but because he wants to hurt someone, is not to be called as witness before a court of law. All men are witnesses—we all bear testimony for one another; he who fails, he who lies, he who betrays a fellow man betrays the very idea, the very concept of truth—the very idea of testimony. There Abbaye is right.

And Rava? Naturally he said the opposite! So what? Though Abbaye's and Rava's thoughts were not systematically opposed to one another, they hardly had any system. They completed one another—and together they achieved greatness by conceptualizing Talmudic issues. There Abbaye's questions were sublime, while Rava's defined his legacy. The *harif* interrogated, the *baki* replied. Perhaps that was the reason why Abbaye was chosen as president of Pumbedita: when his turn came to speak, he knew how to express himself and not allow his colleagues to question his position—for one does not question a question, unless with another question. And in matters of questions, he surpassed them all.

In retrospect, of course, there may have been another reason. Rava collaborated with the occupying power, Abbaye did not. Also, Rava was too wealthy, which made it difficult to feel what poor, hungry people felt—whereas Abbaye was always hungry. Moreover, Abbaye had endured sadness and knew how to overcome it. Ill, he feared death, yet managed to praise the holiness of life to others. Confronted with despair, he communicated hope to a community that needed his example.

But the Talmud is their common work; it bears both the fiery seal of Abbaye's questions and the severe imprint of Rava's decisions. Together, they worked on the collective memory that, throughout generations of exile, would assure the survival of our people.

When Rava's hour was near, the heavenly academy was in the

middle of a debate on a subject of Halakha. Some expressed one opinion, others clung to another. Unable to reach a decision, they decided to wait for the arrival of Rava—the master of Halakha. This was the supreme compliment: his decision was law both here and above, in heaven.

Legend fails to mention that Rava was expected not only by the celestial academy, but also by his friend Abbaye, who even there surely continued to oppose him as he did here, below.

That was their destiny. That was the lesson inherent in it: to prove that friendship must not be destroyed by ideological disputes; indeed, friendship must be enhanced by them.

Together, Abbaye and Rava remain immortal, as does their debate on the meaning of life and whatever belongs to it. Abbaye and Rava: two masters, two outlooks, two attitudes—all linked into one. Abbaye and Rava: two faces of the Jewish condition, which they protect rather than tear apart.

Converts in the Talmud

MANY BEAUTIFUL and moving stories can be found in our religious tradition about converts—their kindness and devotion, their selfless love for their new community. But there are others that are rather bizarre.

Listen:

Once upon a time, around the period of the destruction of Jerusalem and its holy Temple, there lived a famous but strange man of whom not much has been recorded. We know only that his name was Onkelos son of Kalonikos, and that he had, with great skill and passion, translated the Bible into Aramaic.

Sorry: there is something else. We also know that he was the nephew of the Roman emperor Titus, the bloodthirsty conqueror of Palestine. And then we know that Onkelos converted to the Jewish faith.

Listen to a story reported in the Tractate of Gittin (on divorce):

Onkelos, whose father Kalonikos married Titus's sister, wished to espouse the faith of the Jews. So he brought his uncle back from his grave and asked him: "Which people enjoy the highest respect in the other world?"

"The people of Israel," said Titus.

"Should I belong to it?" asked Onkelos.

"Jews are subjected to too many laws," answered Titus, so as to discourage him. "You will never manage to obey all of them. My advice? Persecute them instead and you will rise to become a great leader, for it is written (in Lamentations) that whoever oppresses Israel acquires the status of leadership."

Onkelos let him speak and then asked: "What is your punishment up there?"

"It is the one I invented for myself," answered Titus. What was the punishment? The answer can be found in the same Tractate. It tells us that Titus had ordered his body to be cremated and his ashes cast over the seven seas so as to prevent the God of the Jews from bringing him before the celestial tribunal. "That's exactly what is happening to me now," said Titus. "That's how I am being punished. Day after day my body is being incinerated and its ashes thrown into the seven seas."

Dissatisfied with Titus's answer, Onkelos summoned the wicked prophet Balaam from his grave and asked him the question he had asked his uncle: "Which nation is the most respected in the other world?"

"Israel," said Balaam.

"Should I belong to it?"

"No," said Balaam, quoting a biblical verse: "Do not look for Israel's peace and prosperity." In other words, why suffer like Jews, with Jews?

Having received two negative opinions, Onkelos sought a third— and so he brought Jesus back from the grave and asked him the same question: "Which is the most respected of nations in the other world?"

"Israel," said Jesus.

"Should I become Jewish?" Onkelos asked.

"Adhere to what in the Jews is good but not to what is not. For whoever touches the Jews may hurt the apple of his eye."

In the end, Onkelos converted.

Well—there is in this tale something incomprehensible. First of all, Titus's behavior. Just imagine: the supreme enemy of the Jewish people, and whom is he quoting? Jeremiah! How is one to understand Onkelos's strange investigations? What motivated him? Profit? Success? Did he wish to obtain a good position in heaven? Was there nothing spiritual in his quest? And then, was Titus, of all people, the right person to address to get objective information about Jews? And also: why did he practice something which is forbidden by the faith to which he aspired—namely talking with the dead? How could he become Jewish if he began by violating the Law of Torah? Doesn't he know that sorcery is punishable by death?

The topic of conversion links us to the present. Today it is of general interest, not limited to Jews alone. What is the Jewish attitude toward it? Since the Jewish religion traditionally refrains from proselytizing, it discourages conversion. Others do not. Islam's recent successes have concerned Christians, just as some Southern Baptist ambitions have amused some of us. Here we will explore the possible changes Judaism has undergone on this subject since biblical and Talmudic times.

One of the reasons I admire Onkelos the proselyte is his glorious translation of the Bible. We read it as part of our weekly ritual. But I also love him for his deep religious commitment, which made him break with his illustrious family and lose his vast fortune. Still, on many levels, he is somewhat perplexing. And if all the tales about him are not confusing us enough, consider this: the Talmud itself attributes parts of his story to another convert, also a translator, whose name was Aquilas. Some legends are actually attributed to both.

If that is still not enough, listen to a story from the Tractate of Avoda Zora, which deals with issues concerning idolatry. This story too is about Onkelos, but here his father's name is not Kalonikos but Kalonimos. Onkelos is in Palestine, already converted, and his uncle the emperor is still alive. Must these contradictions be reconciled? The Talmud is not afraid of contradictions—in fact, it is not afraid of

anything. There is no religious literature whose texts are so audacious, even iconoclastic, whether by negating hard facts or arguing
with the Almighty Himself.

In this legend, the Talmud imagines the Roman emperor furious
with his nephew, Onkelos, who gave up luxury and security at home
and went to share the misery and the dangers of Jews far away.
He dispatches a company of soldiers to Palestine to get hold of the
young convert and bring him back to Rome. Onkelos greets them in
a friendly manner and recites poetry to them. So impressed are they
that they convert to his new faith.

Stubborn, the emperor sends another company of soldiers to
Palestine and this time orders them not to speak to his nephew. But
he forgets to warn them not to listen to what he says once they have
captured him. These are the words of the prisoner: "It is the custom
for any servant to carry the torch for his superior, and the superior
for *his* superior, and so on until we get to the supreme leader. But can
you tell me for whom does *he, the leader of leaders,* carry the torch?"
"For nobody," reply the soldiers. "How could he? There is no one
above him, no one superior to him!" "You see," says Onkelos, "in our
tradition it is different. We believe that the Lord, blessed be He, himself carries the torch for his people of Israel, as it is written in the
Torah: 'And the Lord walked before them to guide them in a pillar of
cloud during the day, and in a pillar of fire during the night.' " Naturally, the new soldiers also convert.

Beside himself, the emperor sends a third military unit to bring
back his nephew, instructing them above all to avoid any conversation with him! But they too could not avoid listening to Onkelos's
words. When passing a door with a mezuzah, he places his hand on it
and wonders aloud: "Do you know what this is?" "Tell us," say the
soldiers. "In your tradition it is customary everywhere for the king to
stay inside his palace, while his guards protect him from the outside.
In our tradition, it is different: the Lord, blessed be He, is outside, at
the door, and protects those who serve Him and are inside, as it is
written (in Psalms) 'The Lord will protect you when you leave and
when you return, now and always.' " Again, all the armed soldiers

and their officers convert. At this point, the emperor must have worried about losing his entire army. We know of no other soldiers sent to Palestine in pursuit of Onkelos.

The story is charming even if it does not sound plausible. Talmudic sages are known for their tendency to exaggerate in order to illustrate an idea, an attitude, a legal opinion. Example: one sage declares his conviction that at the end of his life Titus—or Nero—the brutal enemy, the ferocious assassin, became . . . a Jew.

Without going that far, the story of Onkelos gets even more complicated. Another convert, Aquilas, also a nephew of the emperor, also asks *his* uncle for advice before converting to the Jewish faith. Only this time the emperor is not Titus but Hadrian.

Their dialogue begins like a routine business discussion on Wall Street, much as one might hear among bankers. Appearing before the emperor, Aquilas explains the reason for his visit: "I wish to go into business," says he. "Before I start I must seek out the opinion of experts. That's why I came to you, my dear uncle. How does one succeed in this field?" And the emperor replies: "When you see a trade that has fallen in esteem, cling to it, for it will go up again." In other words, buy low, sell high. Aquilas thanks him and leaves the imperial palace.

Next we find him in Palestine, where he studies at the yeshiva with such enthusiasm that Rabbi Eleazar and Rabbi Yehoshua take an interest in him. He does not look well. "Perhaps because he studies too hard," say the two sages. He asks them questions of interpretation and Halakha, and they respond. Will he be their pupil? Eventually, he returns to see his uncle. The emperor too notices how pale he looks: "What has happened to you? Have you lost money? Have your business deals gone sour? Has anyone hurt you, has anyone done you harm?" "No," says Aquilas. "Nobody has wronged me." "Then why do you look so pale?" Aquilas tells him the truth: "I have studied Torah. Better yet, I asked to be circumcised." Hadrian is overcome by rage: "Who told you to do that?" The emperor is ready to punish on the spot the evil adviser who thus corrupted his beloved nephew. "Yes, who told you to do that?" Aquilas quietly replies: "But you did. It was your advice I followed." "When have I given you such advice?" roars the emperor. "When I told you," says Aquilas, "about my desire to go into business, didn't you counsel me to choose the trade people scorned most, for it would surely rise again? Well, with your words in my ear I began going around studying people and nations, and found that no one is as humiliated, as denigrated as the Jewish people. So I understood that one day they will be respected again, exalted again."

One can easily imagine Hadrian's wrath. He was after all the wickedest of all emperors, the pagan tyrant who sought to exterminate the spirit, culture, and religious faith of Jews by sentencing their teachers, disciples, and practitioners to death. And of course he could blame only himself for his nephew's decision!

Interestingly, whereas Titus seems to have broken all relations with Onkelos, Hadrian apparently continued to receive his nephew in the palace, to entertain him, to discuss with him various aspects of the Jewish religion. And, at the same time, Aquilas studied with Rabbi Eleazar and Rabbi Yehoshua.

These two converts, Onkelos and Aquilas, occupy a place of honor in Talmudic literature and in the Jewish tradition. Just as Onkelos translated the Torah into Aramaic, Aquilas translated the Prophets into Greek.

But in truth, are they beloved because they were gifted linguists or because they were . . . converts?

THE BIBLE constantly urges the believer to reserve special affection, special love for the proselyte. The commandment *"ve'ahavta et ha'ger,"* and you shall love the *"ger,"* the friendly stranger, appears dozens of times in Scripture. Here the term *ger* does not yet apply to converts. It refers simply to one who is not Jewish but who lives near us, with us, sharing our bread and our pain, our joy and our solitude. In other words, the law does not deal with religious allegiance but with social and geographical notions. *Ger* derives from the verb *lagur—megurim* means residence. The *ger* may freely practice his own religion in our midst; he will not be revered less for that, so long as we continuously feel his or her presence. Isn't this the most moving aspect of tolerance? We want the stranger to remain who he or she is, true to themselves and their own tradition, rather than what we are. We can benefit from each other's experience only if that experience is authentic.

Granted, there were proselytizers in our midst. Abraham and Sarah were the first. Hence they are the spiritual father and mother of all converts—past and future. But while they did try to convert others, it was only to monotheism, not to Judaism.

In Scripture, whenever the word *ger* occurs, it always refers to Gentiles, never to converts. In biblical times, when Gentiles did leave their faith for ours, they were not called "converts" but "Jews." Take the beautiful, heartbreaking example of Ruth. Was there any woman filled with more grace, or endowed with a deeper sense of devotion and identification? Even today, it is her words that the candidate for conversion repeats: *"Ameikh ami* . . . Your people is mine . . . Your God is my God . . . *ba'asher telkhi, eileikh,* Wherever you go, I go, wherever you dwell, I shall dwell, wherever you die I die . . ."

In the Talmud, the concept of *ger* undergoes a metamorphosis. Now the *ger* is by definition a *ger tzedek*—a just stranger, or a stranger inspired by justice, who joined our people to be bound to its destiny. And so, in the Talmud, the commandment *"ve'ahavta,"* ordering us to love the *ger,* the stranger who ceased to be a stranger, is understood in purely religious and judicial terms. Of course, we speak here of converts to, not from, the Jewish faith.

The Jewish religion does not recognize the possibility of leaving for another faith. A Jew will forever remain Jewish. In medieval times, many Jews were forced to convert. Some remained Marranos. Others chose death over apostasy. But what about those Jews who voluntarily espoused the Christian or Muslim faith? Theirs is another story. Some claim they are still Jewish. Are they? Can they be both Christian and Jewish at the same time? Traditional Jews answer no. And yet there are those who continue to "feel" Jewish. And there are others who become enemies of Jews. They are the true renegades. In biblical language, the term that designates them is *zar:* the Jew who uses his knowledge of Jewish laws and customs as a weapon against the Jewish people. Having exempted themselves from the community, they are banished from the community. When, in the Middle Ages, learned rabbis were forced by kings to publicly defend their beliefs, they frequently confronted renegades. Rabbi Yehiel of Paris and the Ramban in Barcelona had to take part in disputations with converted Jews, who remembered what they had learned as Jews. These renegades brought agony and shame to our people.

But just as the renegade is to be kept at a distance, the convert to Judaism is to be loved, shielded, shown great affection. We are bound together in solidarity and gratitude. The convert is existentially and even empirically attached to Abraham and Sarah, our common ancestors, and to Ruth, whose loyalty is rewarded with the promise of the Messiah as her descendant. On Passover, at the Seder, along with all of us, the convert recites the story of Exodus. To the four questions of *"ma nishtana"*—why is this night different from others?— he or she too answers: *"Avadim hayinu le'Pharo be'Mitzraim"*—this night is different, everything in our life is different, because we had been Pharaoh's slaves in Egypt . . ." Really? The man or woman who yesterday was a child of Christian or Muslim or Buddhist parents has a personal connection with Jewish slaves in ancient Egypt? Yes. The moment a convert enters our covenant, he or she shares not only our future but also our past. Thus converts must feel not only that, like us, they fled Egypt, but also that, together with all Jews, they stood at Sinai and received from God Himself the Law that still governs Jewish existence everywhere. But is that technically, rationally possible? How could they have been at Sinai, without having been physically or genetically in Egypt? To this logical question, the Talmud offers a logical answer: by chance.

Yes—on that morning in the month of Sivvan, the ancestors of the converts had found themselves, by sheer luck, together with the entire people of Israel, at Sinai, silently listening to God's voice addressing each and every one individually, using the first person singular: *"Anokhi Hashem elokekha,"* I am the Lord, thy Lord who brought you out of Egypt. When the convert prays, he or she says: *"Barukh ata Hashem elokeinu ve'elokei avoteinu,"* Blessed be Thou our God, the God of our ancestors, the God of Abraham, the God of Isaac, the God of Jacob. How can he say "God of our ancestors?" Since when have the patriarchs and the matriarchs been part of his or her lineage? In this case, retroactive legislation is in place. While it is usually assumed that God Himself cannot alter a man's past, in the case of converts, He can. In accepting the Jewish Law, the convert receives Jewish history too. It is as if he has been given a new memory that replaces his own. No one is permitted to remind the convert of his or her past. It simply ceases to play a role or to exist. The act of conversion transforms the convert into a newborn infant—a new kind of infant with no link to his biological parents. Thus, in theory, but in theory only, we may imagine a situation in which a woman convert is allowed to marry her son who is also a convert—after all, why shouldn't two babies decide to get married?

Clearly, the Talmudic sages have done everything in their power to prevent the convert to Judaism from feeling excluded or marginalized by the Jewish community. The convert must never feel inferior to other Jews.

All the moral obligations and religious duties assigned to the Jew at birth apply to the convert as well. Does the *ger* enjoy additional privileges? Yes, he does. In the Bible, love for the *ger* is almost an obsession. The *ger* is frequently found in the warm company of the Levite, who ranks just below the priest. One must be charitable to the *ger* as to the Levite. One must extend more assistance to her than to the average person. One must make a special effort, an extra effort to understand the special problems facing the *ger*. Indeed, the status of the *ger* is so exalted, the laws favoring the *ger* are so compassionate, that, according to the Midrash, Moses asked God why converts deserve such favoritism. God advanced a reasonable argument: the convert's purity of heart. God said to Moses, "Do you remember what I had to do to persuade the people of Israel to accept my Law? I had to free them from bondage, feed them in the desert, protect them from their enemies, impress them with continuous miracles, one more astonishing than the other. But the convert requested none of this. I didn't choose him, he chose me; I didn't even call him, and yet he came." In other words, the convert is someone special because his or her Jewishness is a matter not of birth but of choice.

And yet we must not allow our fantasy to run too fast. Reality must be confronted and dealt with. The privileges accorded to the proselyte are accompanied by restrictions. For instance, a convert cannot be crowned king. Nor can he assume the role of prophet. That's not all. A convert cannot be appointed to the judiciary. Why can't he serve as judge? Because a defendant must be tried by "his brethren." Do we therefore infer that a convert is not our brother? He is—and his son may very well be appointed to the court, but he himself must be patient, and accept the law even if he fails to understand it. Just as he will not understand the next law, which prohibits him from becoming a priest. Here the Talmud offers us an explanation which may not please him: a convert cannot become a priest, not because he is not of the priestly tribe, but because the Shekhina, God's presence as it were, does not dwell in him. Other explanations are less charitable. Why such sudden intolerance? Is it to show us that special privileges are not to be taken for granted? Or is it that some converts have aroused suspicion somewhere?

In the Talmud, prospective converts are of three distinct categories. First, there are those who wish to convert out of fear—yes, fear of Jewish political power or of Jewish social influence. For instance, in the Book of Esther, we find Persian citizens who converted to Judaism after Queen Esther and her uncle, Prime Minister Mordecai, emerged victorious over Haman, the enemy of the Jews. They were afraid of what Jewish survivors might do to them. So they converted.

Then there are the candidates for conversion who are motivated by greed, who wish to be more successful socially, financially, or politically. These come when Jews live in conditions of security, prosperity, and peace, as during the reigns of David and Solomon. Rabbi Itzhak Alfasi (known as the RIF) explains that when the land of Judah knew periods of prosperity, those who wanted to become Jewish were the wrong people, who came for the wrong reasons. They were not accepted.

Lastly, there are the true converts—those who have no hidden agenda but act out of sincerity. They adhere to Judaism because they believe in its truth.

Must a candidate for conversion submit to tough questioning to detect his or her true motive? The candidate is asked whether he knows, whether he *really* knows Jewish history, which is filled with stories of persecutions, oppressions, and suffering. He is told of the relentless efforts of old and new enemies to undermine Jewish survival. The candidate learns the history of Jewish martyrdom in ancient and medieval times. And he is asked again and again: given what Jews had to endure, why does he wish to become one? Why reject a life of material and spiritual comfort and choose an uncertain future? Furthermore, if a candidate immediately declares, "I am ready and willing to obey all the commandments of the Torah except one," he or she is rejected. In other words, a rabbinic tribunal uses all the logical arguments at its disposal to discourage the candidate from going ahead with his or her plan to live a different life, in a different culture.

The question may be raised: Why does the Jewish tradition make things so difficult for a person wishing to espouse it? Is it that we are—or ought to be—frightened by newcomers? Are we concerned perhaps that the convert will not succeed, in the long run, in freeing himself from past habits and customs? Is that why, for so many centuries, the Jewish people refrained from practicing forced conversion? There were several exceptions: one occurred around the year 135 of the common era, during the reign of John Hyrcanus I: it was he who sought to force Edomites to convert to Judaism. Some thirty or forty years later, King Yannai ordered the massacre of defeated Moabites who refused to accept the Jewish faith. And, our teachers commented, we lived to regret it.

In general, the official line was to discourage conversion. Consequently, in some quarters, deplorable post-conversion practices were recorded. Certain Talmudic expressions regarding converts were not too charitable. Rabbi Khelbo, for instance, stated that *"kashim gerim le'Yisrael ke'sapahat"*—Proselytes are as bad or as harmful to Israel as the plague. I confess, each time I come across these words, I must make an effort to conquer my indignation. How could a master, a sage in Israel make such generalizations? How could he condemn an entire category of good men and women? Let's assume that he had personally encountered insincere and unworthy converts, why condemn all the others to public humiliation?

In truth, other harsh expressions about people and things can be found in the vast Talmudic literature. Consider this: "The best of medical doctors are destined to hell." A consoling interpretation: the best will go where they are needed most? No, perhaps this is not very convincing. In fact, this saying is part of a series of verbal exaggerations.

But we must not forget that it is not the Talmud that makes such statements, it is someone *in* the Talmud. Thus they carry no force of law.

The same is true of Rabbi Khelbo's opinion of converts. We must take it seriously, since he does—as does Rashi. What does Rashi say? Surprisingly, Rashi—our old teacher, guide, and friend—accepts Rabbi Khelbo's theory. And he explains: the converts *are* indeed dangerous. Why? Because they cannot obey the *mitzvot* as naturally as born Jews do. What? Could Rashi also be generalizing? I am not alone in experiencing astonishment. My astonishment is shared by the famous Rabbi Abraham the proselyte, a great tossafist of the twelfth century. But he interprets Rabbi Khelbo's judgment quite differently. Converts are dangerous, says he, for opposite reasons: they are better than ordinary Jews, their practice of *mitzvot* is more authentic—so much so that God says to the born Jews: "Look at yourselves and look at the converts. You have been Jews longer than the proselytes, and yet you are surpassed by them." That is why Rabbi Khelbo resented converts.

Still, the majority favors the convert. Said the great Palestinian Amora Rabbi Yohanan: "Why was Abraham punished by having his descendants exiled to Egypt? Because, in at least one case, he did not allow some people to join the community of God. Once, when he took in some war refugees, he handed them back to the king of Sodom instead of bringing them under the wings of the Shekhina." The moral of the story? When a candidate for conversion comes to you, let your left hand push him away, but your right hand must draw him closer. In other words: even when trying to discourage the convert, don't overdo it.

The Talmud itself shows no lack of converts. Granted, only seven names of descendants of sages have been recorded, but the city of Mekhoza was full of them. We know that from an incident that occurred there. When Reb Zeira came to speak on the complex and painful issue of illegitimate children, he made a disparaging comment about converts. Apparently, many in the audience, converts themselves, threw stones at him.

Among the great teachers, we find Shmaya and Avtalyon, whose protégés were Shammai and Hillel. Their ancestors were pagans who converted to Judaism. Legend has it that they were descendants of the wicked Assyrian king Sennacherib.

Rabbi Akiba son of Joseph was also a descendant of converts, as were Rabbi Yehuda ben Gerim and Rabbi Meir. Said Rabbi Akiba: let a convert fulfill one *mitzvah,* only one, and he will have his part in paradise. He had a student, Binyamin of Egypt, also a convert, for whom he showed particular affection; he called him "my son." Rabbi Yohanan ben Torta, an interlocutor of Rabbi Akiba, was himself a proselyte.

A story:

A poor Jew sold his cow to a pagan, who, after a week or so, brought her back to him. Why? Because she refused to work on the seventh day. In desperation, the Jew whispered in her ear: "Cow, cow, don't you know the law? When you were mine, you had to observe the Sabbath; but you don't have to any more, since you belong to him!" The cow must have been very intuitive, for from then on she worked on the Shabbat. Astonished, the pagan implored the seller to explain to him the miraculous transformation. After hearing the answer, he exclaimed: "If this cow, which has neither intelligence nor language, is able to acknowledge her Creator, how can I, who understand and speak, ignore mine?" He converted to Judaism. His name, Yohanan ben Torata, means Yohanan, son of the cow.

Other dramatic cases have been recorded in midrashic literature. For instance, the case of Queen Helene, who is evoked with affection and gratitude. Having studied Torah, she adopted its laws. During fourteen or twenty-one years, she lived ascetically. Her sukkah, in Lydda, was the largest and the tallest. She gave a golden lamp to the Temple. Her son, King Monbaz, had a mezuzah put on his cane, which never left his hands.

Another legend describes Emperor Nero, who, at the end of his life, allegedly converted to Judaism. Listen:

> While his invincible soldiers besieged Jerusalem, Nero realized one day that no matter where he shot an arrow, it fell on the Jewish capital. Perplexed, he questioned a Jewish boy who crossed his path on the biblical verse he had studied that day in school. The child quoted the prophet Ezekiel: "I shall trust Edom"—which means Rome—"to avenge my honor and inflict punishment on Israel." But Nero, refusing to serve as God's cruel instrument, exclaimed, "The Lord intends to destroy His house and wash His hands in me?" He ran away, converted to Judaism—and Rabbi Meir was his descendant.

We must admit: Talmudic sages did have imagination. Nero questioning a Jewish child about his Torah studies, the emperor of Rome abdicating his throne and converting . . . All this makes us smile. But the legend does contain a moral meaning: for a Jew, racism is never an option. Purity of blood has never been a Jewish concept. It is not blood or color of skin that make the human being the man he is, created in the image of God. Man is judged by himself, he is defined by his convictions and his actions, not by his origins. The heir of a killer is not a killer. The descendants of Haman himself established a yeshiva in Bnei Brak, according to a midrash. And, as we heard, a descendant of Nero became known as a master of Torah in Judea.

The fact is that in spite of the tradition of discouraging conversion, there were, throughout the centuries, men and women who opted for the Jewish faith, especially in the Diaspora. In the Tractate of Pesakhim, dealing with matters related to Passover, a sage goes as far as claiming that God exiled His people with the aim of attracting converts. There were proselytes in Babylonia, Egypt, and Europe. In the Hellenistic period, Jews served in the armies of Alexander the Great, they settled in Alexandria and married there; their wives became Jewish. Josephus Flavius notes in his memoirs that there is no Greek or barbarian city where inhabitants do not observe the Sabbath, light candles for holidays and practice *tzedakah* or charity. Philo maintains that many nations imitated Jewish laws.

What was it in the Jewish religion that attracted converts? The special relationship that exists between Jews and God? That may have been true in antiquity. But what about later, in the Middle Ages? Rabbi Itzhak Alfasi, whom we already quoted, writes: "When Jews lived in peace, they opposed conversions; but these days, when Jews endure suffering and humiliation, converts are welcomed with open arms, with no proper investigation." Were converts attracted by Jewish suffering? Was it the promise of an eschatological change, of redemption, perhaps? Was it the desire to belong to a small people, so vulnerable but thirsting for meaning, so infatuated with God? And to share their consuming passion for memory and live within the confines of their solitude?

What is conversion in reality? A rupture of being? A breakdown of existing structures? An escape toward the unknown? A reorientation of the will? A metamorphosis of the soul? A transfusion of memory? A mysterious urge to self-destruct so as to begin again? What is the role of environment, education, and peer pressure in such a decision?

Certain converts spoke of having discovered truth. Others felt closer to God. Still others, in medieval times, sought to acquire suffering, and became martyrs who, inside their extreme suffering, discerned a pure truth which resembled happiness. But martyrs are not converts, although some converts became martyrs. A martyr is someone who refuses to deny his or her faith, his community, his links to the past. But the convert is someone who has already rejected all that was essential to his previous existence.

Judaism does not recognize conversion to another religion. A Jew who is born Jewish will remain a Jew until death. Other religions also accepted converts to but not from their faith. In the Middle Ages, the Church punished conversion to Judaism with death.

In certain provinces, when Jews were accused of seducing Christians into conversion, harsh collective punishments followed. To protect their communities, great rabbinic authorities, like Rabbi Gershon ben Yaakov of the thirteenth century, implored their congregants not to discuss theology with Christians, so as to avoid the appearance of trying to influence them.

Nevertheless, there were Christians, renowned Christians, who converted. Ovadia the proselyte came with the Crusaders to Jerusalem and converted in 1102. King Louis I's Bishop Aleman Bodo, a priest named Wecelenius, Rabbi Abraham in Augsburg, Joseph Saralvo in Italy, Catherine Zaleshovska in Cracow in 1539, Count Valentin Potocki, Lord George Gordon in England . . .

In conclusion, conversion must be voluntary. And individual. It must never be done under coercion—not even as a result of proselytizing. A Christian need not become Jewish to be respected by Jews. The same applies to the Muslim. I insist on this because a regrettable speech was recently heard in the United States. Some Southern Baptists announced their intention to convert all Jews in America. Well— that is some ambitious project!

Do they think they are living in the Dark Ages? Or that God remained there, a prisoner of their fanaticism? Do they have no other worries? No more social problems to resolve? No homeless people to befriend, no sick children to console, no victims of AIDS or Alzheimer's to comfort? Are there no more wars in the world? Is there no more bloodshed? No more hunger? Is conversion of American Jews their absolute priority? And what happens if we say no?

Would they use force? Should we dialogue with them? Dialogue implies mutual respect. But then their decision shows total lack of respect toward an ancient people who maintain a three-thousand-year-old tradition. If they persist in trying to convert all American Jews, well—let them start with me.

As far as the Jewish attitude to converts is concerned, let us open the Talmud again and go back to Shammai and his old adversary Hillel. Whereas Shammai was rigorous with candidates for conversion, Hillel showed them understanding and tenderness. Remember the pagan who heard Jewish children repeating the tales of the High Priest's magnificence and glory? He became so envious of him that he decided to convert so as to become High Priest himself. When he told this to Shammai and Hillel, Shammai turned his back on the man, whereas Hillel began studying with him the biblical laws regarding priestly privileges and duties. At one point, they arrived at the passage forbidding the stranger to come near the sacred Tabernacle—a transgression warranting the death sentence. The pagan was seized with panic: "This law, to whom does it apply?" "To everybody who is not a priest," Hillel answered. "Even to King David." Then the pagan understood that the Jewish religion does not discriminate in essential matters. And he converted.

Who doesn't remember the other pagan who wanted Shammai and Hillel to teach him the entire Torah quickly, immediately, while he stood on one foot? Shammai chased him away, whereas Hillel gave him the advice that everybody is familiar with: "What you don't want others to do to you, don't do to others." What! That's the entire Torah? Few among us know or want to know that it was meant only as an enticement, a beginning—the sentence being incomplete. The other half reads: *"U'meidah,"* on the other hand, *"zil g'mor,"* go and study. And the pagan converted.

But—you don't have to be a convert to plunge into study . . .

Talmudic Sketches

TALMUD MEANS STUDY. To study Talmud is to study values and principles inherent in study, the illuminated horizons pushed back by study. It also means to study the art of studying. And study implies memory. One studies in order to remember. Without memory, study is futile. *Elythia,* in Greek, means truth. And what is truth? Things one cannot forget.

Some masters are more vivid than others, more imaginative too. Here and there we may meet one who is mentioned once or twice in the Mishna, in the context of a vague Halakhic issue or an odd anecdote related to it. That does not mean they were less important; all were significant. The Talmud is a mosaic; all of its components are essential to its fabric.

The Bible commands us to study Torah day and night. That applies to Talmud as well. Study is seen as a remedy for evil, just as prayer is a remedy for misfortune. With prayer we may move God to intervene in human affairs, but not in scholarly debates. There the scholar's word is mightier than heaven's. In matters of Halakha, does the prophet's opinion have no impact? The master's judgment alone carries weight.

A masterwork unequaled in Jewish memory, the two and a half

million words of the Talmud cover all aspects of human endeavor: literature and jurisprudence, medicine and geometry, geography and medicine, parables and fables, problems relating to the individual in society, questions concerning attitudes toward the stranger, meditations on the meaning of life, psychological analyses and cultural conflicts: "Turn the pages," says one sage, "turn them well, for everything is in them."

For me, Talmud is something else as well. It is an unforgettable song, the song of my childhood.

AN IMAGE: an old tutor, Zeide the Melamed, and his pupils, in a small poorly lit room. Sitting around a rectangular table, we follow him beyond oceans and mountains to Babylonia, to the Galilee, and even to Jerusalem. And there we listen to the stormy debates between the disciples of Shammai, eternally angry, and those of Hillel, known for his kindness, and to the dramatic clashes between Rabbi Eleazar and Rabbi Yehoshua; we surround Rabbi Akiba ben Yosef and Rabbi Hanina ben Tradyon in agony . . . With my friends, we study—no, we sing—the laws concerning the prohibitions of Shabbat. One must not light candles; it's work and one must not work on the Sabbath. One must not put candles out either, but (there is always a *but* in Talmudic texts) may I put out the candle because I am afraid of the enemy, or of bandits? Or because I watch over a sick person who is unable to fall asleep? Then, the prohibition is lifted. Everything is permitted to save lives.

I can still hear the old Melamed, I can still see the old teacher, I see his finger on the page, I hear his sing-song: "Look, children! Our enemies are wrong. The Torah has not been given to us to make our lives unbearable, just the opposite . . ."

WHAT IS TRUE of Torah is more so of the Talmud, which, written in Aramaic, is its multifaceted commentary. To understand the Jews' attachment to the Talmud, one ought to read Rabbi Yekhiel of Paris's heartbreaking litany, which he composed while witnessing the public burning of the Talmud. The man who gave the order, King Louis IX, is, strangely, still referred to as Saint Louis.

When exile becomes harsher, too harsh, it is in the Talmud that the Jew finds consolation and hope. Outside, in the marketplaces of eastern Europe, the excited killers, thirsty for Jewish blood, sharpened their knives, while a few steps away, in narrow houses of prayer and study, masters and their disciples tried to answer the "urgent" question of how the High Priest was dressed on Yom Kippur. In reflecting on the beauty of the past, the Jew felt stronger as he awaited the perils of the future. Study helped him transform time into defiance. By transcending the present, one inhabited a realm in which words and signs were endowed with unusual meaning. A banal incident stands out as special on a Talmudic page. Routine attains a level of sacredness. Nothing is considered trivial in the Talmud.

To deal with so many issues on such a large scope, a great number of scholars were needed: three hundred Tannaim, two thousand Amoraim. Together they represent a gigantic ensemble offering a symphonic work of incomparable beauty and depth. One discovers in its inner landscape the splendor and nostalgia of vanished kingdoms, the profound sadness of enlightened scholars and their exalted students: the Talmud is a vast, turbulent, and yet appeasing ocean that suggests the infinite qualities of life and love of life, as well as the vast mystery of death and the instant preceding death.

And now, let us enter the Talmudic Gallery and visit a master named Shimon. Not Rabbi Shimon but Shimon ha-Tzaddik. The Just. That's all. A living transition, a human link between two eras, he was the last survivor of the Great Assembly and the first sage of the rabbinic period. He remains the only master in the vast corpus of the Talmud to be called Tzaddik. And yet . . . What remains of his teaching? One saying: "These are the three things that sustain the world: study of Torah, service in the Temple, and charity." Admit it: as spiritual or intellectual legacy, this does not amount to much. Still, one feels respect and veneration for him in the Talmud. Is it perhaps because he was both the last and the first? Because two generations could relate to him and seek his guidance?

Quite a lot is known about his personality. He was admired for his piety as well as his leadership qualities. His pedagogical approach was directed not only at his two sons Shimmi and Honio but their entire generation. He was said to have possessed supernatural powers, which he sometimes used.

During his forty-year tenure as High Priest, the first since the return from Babylonian exile, he witnessed miraculous events. For instance: on Yom Kippur it was the High Priest's duty to bring two goats as offerings, one carrying Israel's prayers to God and the other to bear the burden of Israel's sins and serve as scapegoat. But which one should be sent into the wilderness? Usually the decision was left to fate or chance. But under Shimon ha-Tzaddik it was always the goat on his right that was the lucky one. After his death, it was the opposite.

Something else: as long as Shimon the Just was officiating, the thread that was attached to the scapegoat would become white, thus proving that God had forgiven Israel's sins. After his death, this phenomenon would occur only from time to time.

Once he heard a celestial voice in the Sanctuary saying: "The enemy's effort has already collapsed." That day the commander in chief of the assaulting forces lost his life.

His role in military battles was decisive. Listen:

Shimon ha-Tzaddik was a contemporary of Alexander the Great, to whom he remains linked in legend. This is how they were supposed to have met. Shimon the Just came to him to intercede on behalf of Jerusalem. Such intercession was needed because the Kuttiim—Israel's ancestral rivals, the Samaritans—had extracted from Alexander permission to destroy the Temple of the Jewish capital. When Shimon heard this, he donned his official robes and, accompanied by dignitaries of his community, carrying torches, marched throughout the night to meet the emperor. Alexander saw the Jewish convoy from afar and asked the Kuttiim, "Who are they?" "Jewish rebels" was their answer.

Soon after sunrise, the two groups stood face-to-face. When Alexander's gaze fell on Shimon, he left his golden carriage and kneeled before the Jewish High Priest, exclaiming, "Blessed be the God of Shimon the Just." Astounded, the Kuttiim asked, "How can a conquerer like you humble himself before a Jew?" And Alexander replied, "During all my military victories, it was *his face* that appeared before my eyes." Naturally, the Temple of Jerusalem was spared, while that of the Kuttiim, on Mount Grizzin, was destroyed.

Another legend, this one more disturbing: Shimon the Just, having foreseen the hour of his death, informed his close friends, who wanted him to explain how he knew. His answer? "Usually, on the Day of Atonement, I see an old man dressed in white who accompanies me to the Sanctuary; and we always leave together. This year he was dressed in black. And he stayed behind." Shimon the Just died seven days later.

His sons' role in Talmudic literature was less glorious. Envious, jealous, they dishonored their father's legacy. One of them fled to Alexandria, where he officiated as High Priest in the ritual offerings at the local temple, in competition with Jerusalem's.

Are we, because of the sons, meant to love the father less? Let us remember that the Talmud does not believe in flattery or cover-ups. Obsessed with the truth, its commitment to truth is absolute. We learn in its pages that not only were certain children less than dignified, their celebrated fathers were also flawed. Of course, that does not prevent us from admiring Moses or from loving David. Our ancestors were great in spite of their weaknesses; their greatness lies in their humanity, even in their vulnerability. And we love them nevertheless.

But then we love all the sages in the Talmud, even those who lose; sometimes we love them *because* they have lost. But what *have* they lost? An argument? A vote? Shammai lost almost every debate with Hillel. Do we love him less as a result? What would Hillel have been without Shammai? Or Reb Yohanan without Resh Lakish? Or Rabbi Yehoshua without Rabbi Eleazar?

Indeed, the whole Talmud is reflected in every one of its fragments. Start anywhere, at any page, and you will be drawn into a universe filled with fervent sages and their often colorful disciples, whom you will want to know better. Start with one and you will come to love his friend, even his opponent.

NATURALLY, it is impossible to get acquainted with all of them—not even with the most influential ones among them: how are we to judge their impact? All are irreplaceable. Each one's lessons remain an essential part of the Talmud.

Take Shimon ben Shatakh, who, as president of the Sanhedrin, shared power with Rabbi Yehuda ben Tabbai. He was King Yannai's brother-in-law and never stopped arguing with him, to the point that at times, fearing the king's anger, he would hide in the mountains or flee the country.

A story: King Yannai loved military victories, territorial conquests, and the relative glory of absolute power. Having conquered sixty villages, he invited all the sages to celebrate the event. They were served the best food and wine at tables made of pure gold; the mood was exuberant. But among the guests was a man named Eleazar ben Poira, a shrewd manipulator who used his skills to incite people—especially those in power—against the Pharisees, whom he hated with cold passion. "Look at these sages," he told the king. They are against you, but they are afraid to show it." "What do you want me to do?" the king asked. "Try them," said Eleazar ben Poira. "Put the High Priest's emblem on your forehead. And we will see what they will say."

The Jewish people were divided between Saducees and Pharisees. The Saducees demanded a strict literal interpretation of biblical texts, thus rejecting the oral tradition in which the Pharisees very much believed.

There was tension between King Yannai and the scholarly community. The sages resented his decision to do something his predecessors (with the exception of his brother Aristobulos) had not done for five centuries, since the destruction of the Temple by the Babylonians: he proclaimed himself king of Judea. That wasn't all. Yannai appointed himself High Priest, and the sages didn't appreciate that either. That is why Eleazar ben Poira told him: "Put the High Priest's emblem on your forehead; let's see if they'll accept your priestly authority."

King Yannai did so. He appeared in public with the High Priest's emblem. Naturally, the sages were shocked. Probably even scared. Then an old scholar, a certain Yehuda ben Gedidya, spoke up: "King Yannai," he said. "Is the royal crown not enough for you? Leave the priestly crown to the children of Aaron."

The camps—that of the king and that of the sages—separated in anger. Still, Eleazar ben Poira—of whom nothing else is known—was not satisfied: he poured more oil on the fire. With feigned indignation he said, "King Yannai, an average man must keep his calm even when he is offended; he has no choice. But you are no ordinary man: you are king and High Priest: how can *you* remain silent?" "What do you want me to do?" answered the king. "Destroy them," said Eleazar ben Poira. "You want me to destroy them? But they are learned men; what will happen to their learning? They are students and teachers of Torah. What will happen to Torah?" "The Torah," answered the instigator, "is here; she is lying in a corner; anyone can pick her up and make use of her." Persuaded by his self-appointed adviser, the king gave orders to execute all the sages. Says the Talmud: from that day on the world was desolate until the day Shimon ben Shatakh appeared and restored the grandeur of Torah.

No wonder Yannai is not particularly loved in Talmudic memory. He wasn't an appealing character. Driven to hurt those whose knowledge surpassed his own, he persecuted scholars. The luckier ones escaped and went into hiding or left the country. Shimon ben Shatakh's teacher, Rabbi Yehoshua ben Perakhia, was among them. He fled to Alexandria, accompanied by a close disciple, a young man from Galilee who later acquired a world reputation. I am referring to Yehoshua or Jesus of Nazareth.

They remained in Alexandria for some time until Shimon ben Shatakh appealed to his sister, Queen Shlomit, who successfully interceded with her husband. King Yannai gave in. And it was Shimon ben Shatakh who informed the fugitives that they had been amnestied. His letter is worth quoting: "This message," he wrote, "is from the holy Jerusalem to her sister Alexandria to tell her: my husband (Rabbi Yehoshua ben Perakhia) is in your house and I am alone in mine. How long am I to bear such solitude?" On the way back, master and disciple stayed at an inn, in Jerusalem: "What a beautiful inn," Rabbi Yehoshua remarked metaphorically. "Yes," answered the disciple. "She is beautiful, but her eyes are tired." The master resented the disciple's criticism of God's city and sent him away on the spot.

Another version suggests a more concrete approach: the master praised the inn, whereas the disciple criticized the lady innkeeper. That is why Rabbi Yehoshua ben Perakhia exploded in anger: "What?" he said. "You suspect me of looking at the beauty of women?" Incidentally, in other circumstances, Rabbi Yehoshua is criticized in the Talmud for not having held on to his disciple with one hand, while pushing him away with the other. Still, his homecoming was warmly received by his contemporaries. Did the people like him because of his learning or his courageous resistance to Yannai?

Other stories illustrate Yannai's hatred for the sages, and particularly for his brother-in-law, who influenced his sister's judgment.

One day, the sage was visited by three hundred Nazarenes who, in order to be freed from their vows, had to bring three lambs each as offerings in the Temple. The problem was that they were poor and could not afford the price. How could one help them? Shimon ben Shatakh found a legal procedure to grant *half* of them a dispensation. But what of the remaining 150, which meant 450 lambs? He had an idea: he didn't tell the king the truth, he told him that three hundred Nazarenes still needed to purchase offerings. "We shall share the cost," he told him. "You give me 450 lambs and I will take care of the rest." Betrayed by an informer, Shimon ben Shatakh was again forced to run away. It was only when a delegation of foreign dignitaries inquired about him that Yannai brought the fugitive back.

Shimon ben Shatakh was known for his absolute honesty. One

day he borrowed a donkey from an Ishmaelite. To their great joy, his disciples discovered a precious jewel attached to the animal's neck. They showed it to Shimon ben Shatakh, who said, "I borrowed a donkey, not a jewel." The jewel was immediately returned to its owner, who exclaimed, "Blessed be the God of Shimon ben Shatakh."

And yet, as a leader, he could be pitiless. As president of the Sanhedrin, he was once informed that eighty witches were hiding in a cave near Ashkelon. He waited for a rainy day and gathered eighty vigorous young men. Each man was given a new jar containing a clean gown. He instructed them to carry the jars on their heads, and "when you hear my first whistle, put on your gowns; when you hear my second whistle, enter the cave; when you hear my third whistle, let each of you take a witch and lift her up as high as possible." (Contrary to popular fiction writers, witches cannot fly; the moment they lose contact with the ground, their power is gone.) Then Shimon ben Shatakh went to the entrance of the cave and yelled, "Open, open; I am one of you." From inside, astonished voices were heard: "How did you manage to stay dry in such a rain?" "I am telling you, I am one of you," he replied. "I walked between the drops." "What do you want?" "I want to learn and to teach; show me your power and I'll show you mine." A witch uttered a word and fresh bread appeared out of nowhere; another one used the same magic to produce meat, a third one procured vegetables, and a fourth one was responsible for wine. "And you?" they asked. "What can you do?" "I can whistle," he said. "I will whistle twice and I'll show you eighty young men with dry gowns; they'll dance with you, they'll entertain you." The plan worked. All eighty witches were judged, sentenced, and executed the same day—even though the Law forbids two executions to take place on the same day. But, says the Talmud and explains Maimonides, Shimon ben Shatakh had to show an example.

Examples mattered to him. After this event, his enemies used two false witnesses who accused his son of a capital crime. He was condemned. And the father, as president of the Sanhedrin, had to confirm the verdict. His son did not protest: "Father," he said, "if I am guilty, may my sins survive me; if I am not, may my death erase all my sins, and let the crime fall on the heads of the false witnesses." Thereupon the two witnesses confessed that they had lied. "Father," said the son, "if their change of heart is due only to your intervention, I prefer death." Like father, like son: they sought to serve both justice and truth.

A story: a servant-slave of King Yannai (or, according to another source, a servant of King Herod) was accused of murder. He appeared before the Sanhedrin alone. Since the Law stipulates that a slave must be accompanied by his owner, who becomes his codefendant, the king was summoned to appear before the court. He came and sat down. "Stand up," said Shimon ben Shatakh. "A defendant must stand when answering the court's questions." "It's not you but the court that I shall obey," answered the king. "Let the court tell me whether I ought to stand or not." Thus the president turned to his right and saw all his colleagues with their heads lowered; he turned to his left and saw his other colleagues with their lips sealed. "You all pretend to be thinking of something else," Shimon admonished them. "But you very well know that He who reads all secret thoughts will punish you." Shimon ben Shatakh was right. King Yannai soon had them all slain.

So feared and hated was the king that the day of his death was declared a national holiday. Yannai was afraid that that was about to happen. That's why . . . Listen: when Yannai fell ill, he ordered the imprisonment of seventy spiritual leaders and told the warden: "When I die, they must follow me in death; thus the population will not be in a mood of rejoicing." But his wife, Queen Shlomit, prevented the massacre. As soon as her royal husband passed away (at the age of forty-nine), she sent his ring with a message to the prison warden: "Your king had a dream, and because of it, he decided to free all the imprisoned sages." It was only after their liberation that she announced the king's death.

A MAN OF indomitable character, Shimon ben Shatakh seems to have encountered difficulties with nearly everybody: with his king, the Saducees, the frightened judges of the Sanhedrin, and even with a mysterious sage who was known for his piety and modesty, Honi Hama'agal. He enjoyed a unique reputation as someone whose human compassion resulted in God's.

When things went badly, in periods of drought, for instance, people turned to Honi Hama'agal, asking for his intercession in heaven. Once he drew a circle around himself and declared: "Master of the universe, I shall not move until You help Your children." And drops of rain fell from the sky. Thinking that God had merely wanted to get rid of the sage with a token gesture, his pupils exclaimed: "That's all?" When Honi Hama'agal said, "It's not for my sake but for the sake of Your children that I am addressing my plea to You," it began to rain. No: to pour. Indeed, Palestine was threatened with floods. "Master, do something!" the pupils pleaded with Honi Hama'agal, who in turn pleaded with God to show some restraint.

Everybody was happy—everybody but Shimon ben Shatakh. He was angry at Honi Hama'agal for having disturbed God and for forcing His hand: "Actually," Shimon told him, "I should have excommunicated you, but I could not. Aren't you God's spoiled child? He refuses you nothing."

Nothing? Honi Hama'agal's future proved that God could be harsh even to one of His favorite children.

Two versions of his death exist. The first links it to a power struggle between two brothers: Hyrcanus and Aristobolus. At one point, Hyrcanus's soldiers seized Honi Hama'agal and tried to force him to pray for them. He consented but in his own manner: "Master of the universe," he said, "have pity on Your children. When some curse the others, do not listen." Incensed, the soldiers killed him.

The other version is more lyrical. Commenting on the verse from Psalms, "When we shall return—or when we have returned—from exile to Zion, it shall be—it has been—as if in a dream," Honi Hama'agal wondered: since the exile lasted seventy years, how was it possible for a man to sleep all that time and have only one dream? He then took a walk and saw a man who was planting a carob tree: "How long will it take for this tree to bear fruit?" "Seventy years," answered the man. "Are you sure you'll still be here in seventy years?" "No, I am not," answered the man. "I am planting this tree not for myself but for my children." While meditating on the meaning of this encounter—can one dream so far ahead?—Honi Hama'agal fell asleep under a tree. When he awoke—seventy years later—he saw a man picking the tree's fruit. "Did *you* plant it?" he asked the man. "No, that was my grandfather," said the man. Only then did the sage understand what waiting really means.

The story is beautiful, but it does not stop there. Now it becomes funny. And tragic. Honi Hama'agal returned home and asked for . . . Honi Hama'agal. "Honi—who?" people answered. "Honi Hama'agal? He died long ago . . . His son, too, passed away some time back." "But I am Honi Hama'agal," exclaimed Honi Hama'agal. People looked at him with disbelief. So he went to the House of Study. There he heard sages quoting his own sayings. He even heard one of them say: "If only we could find Honi Hama'agal, who knew the solutions to all problems." Unable to contain himself, Honi Hama'agal said: "I am Honi Hama'agal." The scholars must have thought something was wrong with a man who made such strange claims. It's then that he responded bitterly, *"O havruta o mituta"*—better to die than to live without friends. Incidentally, this saying—also attributed to Rava—is the only one of his that has been recorded.

More is to be found in Talmudic literature about his long sleep. He is supposed to have slept through the destruction of the Temple in Jerusalem. When he awoke, he knew nothing of the tragedy that had befallen our nation. When he introduced himself to people, they shook their heads and said, "You, Honi Hama'agal? Impossible! When Honi entered the Temple, it would instantly illuminate itself." To prove his identity, he went to the place where the Temple stood—or to the Temple itself—which would once again become flooded with heavenly light.

OTHER TALES about other masters are waiting to be told . . .

Take Rabbi Yossi ben Halafta and visions. Ordained by the old

Rabbi Yehuda ben Baba, he inspired his generation with his judicial and esoteric knowledge. Often, the prophet Elijah would come to visit with him. He taught his pupils the art of seeing what is beyond reality: "Men look and look and do not know what they see. For instance, the planet earth. It stands on columns. The columns stand on water. The water is in the mountains. The mountains are sustained by air. The air is inside a storm. And God is holding all of them in His arms."

Rabbi Hiya the Great, Rabbi Yehuda's mischievous disciple. When he exaggerated, Rabbi Yehuda would send him outside: "Go, I think you have been called." The disciple and future co-editor of the Tosefta would then know not to reappear for thirty days. We are told that his powers were so great that the Angel of Death could not take him. Disguised as a beggar, the Angel knocked at his door. "Open," said Rabbi Hiya to his servant. "It's a beggar. Feed him. He is hungry." Whereupon the Angel of Death cried out: "You feel sorry for a beggar but not for me? Don't you know what my mission is? Give me your soul, so I don't have to take it against your will!" When Rabbi Hiya died, fiery stones fell from heaven.

Rabbi Eleazar ben Shamua, Rabbi Eleazar ben Arrakh, Rav Hisda, Rav Huna, and hundreds and hundreds of other names. Each master is singular, enriching, in his own manner, the Talmudic universe. Sometimes without knowing one another, except through their learning, they challenged and defied one another, contradicted one another, only to find themselves reconciled, appeased in the end.

How did they manage to make abstractions out of all that happened around them? The destruction of the Temple, the sacking of Jerusalem, the massacres, the individual and national humiliations, the deportations, the executions under the Greeks and the Romans and the Persians, none of these tragedies impeded their work. For Rabbi Yehuda and his colleagues who edited the Mishna, for Rav Ashi and Ravina, who did the same thing for the Gemara, nothing could insinuate itself between them and their mission, which involved collecting arguments, apprehensions, conclusions, and more conclusions: anything that would contribute to our people's collective memory.

Attitudes toward women and children, madmen and heretics, dreamers and their dreams, past and future: everything is there. Even sex. And humor. And fantasy. To read Rabbah bar bar Hanna's incredible adventures is to admit that literature's Oriental storytellers have had predecessors. Have you heard of the place "where heaven and earth catch fire"? Rabbah bar bar Hanna knew it; he describes it as he describes, in full detail, a fish so big that to walk on it from end to end would take you three days and three nights.

To follow these masters is to love them. It is to provoke in us a taste and a passion for study. And study is everlasting. The Torah has no beginning and the Talmud has no end. Rav Ashi and Ravina—the fifth-century Amoraim—concluded the compiling of the Talmud (Rav Ashi was then ninety-two) but did not seal it. Enriched by new volumes that are being published to this day, the living Talmud keeps many of us alive.

Written in the present—Rabbi Yitzhak says . . . Rabbi Yohanan declares . . . Shimon bar Lakish responds—the Talmudic discourse becomes a constant appeal for personal involvement. The rabbis did not speak to each other alone; they spoke to us—they speak to us.

Talmud means exchange and mutual respect, that is, respect for the other. Talmud means dialogue with the living and the dead. All are our interlocutors, our companions, our friends. They involve themselves in our affairs, just as they did in those of their contemporaries. Everything was of interest to them; nothing left them indifferent. I would venture to say that the essence of Talmud is to fight indifference.

In Hasidism

Zanz and Sadigur

Z ANZ AND SADIGUR: two small towns, shtetlach, one in Bu-kovina and the other in Poland, where Jewish life flourished for three centuries until it was stifled by the enemy of the Jewish people—the enemy of humankind—one long generation ago.

Zanz and Sadigur: two capitals of a kingdom created by the Besht and his companions to the glory of God and the honor of His people. Two concepts, two paths, two systems, both meant to bring Jews closer to one another and to their Creator. They had so much in common. And yet, and yet . . . Rivers of hate and mountains of anger separated them. What they said about one another has been said about all of us, by the worst of our enemies.

Zanz and Sadigur: a story of jealousy, of ideological clashes? Of personal conflicts? Zanz and Sadigur: a sad story indeed. I feel embarrassed as I retell it. As God is my witness, I have always tried to show the beauty of the Hasidic experience. I may even have been guilty of glorifying it. Starting with the Besht, I have described the movement's luminous and inspiring aspects. Though I have great admiration for the scholarship of the "Mitnagdim," the learned opponents of Hasidism, I feel a profound affection for its persecuted masters. I have seen myself on their side, always. Still, sometimes when they quarreled among themselves, I empathized with both sides. Lublin against Lizensk, Pshiske against Lublin, Medzebozh against everybody—I tried anxiously to understand and defend all sides in the heated disputes. Some were tragic but not serious, others were serious but not tragic. The benefit of the arguments was that both camps felt compelled to study harder, to improve their ways, and to analyze their own world and their relationship to it.

But in the dispute between Zanz and Sadigur, the quarrel brought honor neither to Hasidism nor to the Jewish people. Participants on both sides claimed that the dispute was *"le'shem shamayim,"* for the sake of heaven. I know that it did not bring *me* closer to heaven.

And yet, and yet . . . There were astonishing figures on both sides. Great masters whose charismatic powers influenced thousands and thousands of followers found themselves in the midst of a battle that shook the Jewish world, both in Europe and Palestine. Rabbi Hayim of Zanz and Rabbi Avraham-Yoseph of Sadigur were, each in his own way, renowned leaders of their respective schools. Both commanded authority and respect. Both were pious and learned. Both remain pillars of Hasidism. What could have provoked the tragic split between them? What turned them into enemies? Personal considerations? Hurt feelings? A clash of ambitions?

A story:

Rabbi Hayim of Zanz once visited the city of Ungvar, where Reb Menahem, a great scholar, had invited him to deliver a discourse. The whole community came. Rabbi Hayim spoke and everybody was enchanted. Then Reb Menahem responded, taking the speech apart. Such was the custom among scholars: their disagreements served to enhance the beauty of Torah. But, to everyone's surprise, Rabbi Hayim did not answer. What was supposed to be a lengthy dialogue remained two long monologues. When Rabbi Hayim left town, he told Rabbi Menahem's son, who had accompanied him to the station, "Tell your father to look in such and such a place—he will see that I was right."

Do you know many scholars who would set aside their pride and opt not to display their erudition publicly to prove their point? Rabbi Hayim chose to be considered the loser rather than to hurt another scholar's position in his community. How then is one to understand his subsequent appeals to his followers to shame and defeat their opponents—and his?

Incidentally, the Ungvar story has an appealing sequel. It is told that as soon as Reb Menahem received Rabbi Hayim's message, he hastened to invite his entire community to his House of Study: "I wanted you to come," he told them, "because I want you to know the truth. And the truth is that Rabbi Hayim is more learned than I. He knew all the answers but he chose not to embarrass me."

A second story:

Rabbi Avraham-Yoseph of Sadigur once praised progress to his followers. One can learn from everything, he said. From God's creation and from man's invention. "Really?" a Hasid asked. "What can one learn from a train?" "Not to be late," answered the rabbi. "One minute can make a difference." "What about the telegraph?" another Hasid wanted to know. "What can one learn from the telegraph?" "That every word counts," answered the rabbi. "And what about the telephone?" a third Hasid wondered aloud. "From the telephone we learn to be careful," said the rabbi. "What you say here can be heard there."

Both anecdotes are characteristic. Rabbi Hayim was concerned with erudition, Rabbi Avraham-Yoseph with modern discoveries. The first was pious, the second had a practical side as well. Both worked for the welfare of their followers. Both quoted the same sources and followed the teachings of the Besht. Both sought to help people in distress. Both believed in *ahavat Yisrael*. Why then did they allow a fire of unprecedented violence to rage in their own ranks? Why didn't they teach tolerance and compassion to their own disciples?

Of course, disputes are not new in Jewish history. They existed even before history. When God asked the angels whether He ought to create man, they quarreled. As did the higher waters and the lower waters. And the sun and the moon. And Cain and Abel, Isaac and Ishmael, Jacob and Esau, Joseph and his brothers, Saul and David, Hillel and Shammai. If a Jew has no one to quarrel with, he quarrels with God, and we call it theology; or he quarrels with himself, and we call it psychology. Or he quarrels with the psychoanalyst, and we call it literature. But please, do not read into my words an apology for quarrels, for then I would quarrel with you. All I mean to say is that Jews have never been afraid of quarrels. Two Jews and three opinions are better than three Jews with no opinions. Passionate arguments are better than passionless acceptance. Remember the definition of a Hasid? A Hasid does what other Jews do, says what other Jews say, prays when other Jews pray—but he does so with a defining passion. If that results in conflict, so what? Quarrels come and go, disputes flare up and die: doesn't the *Ethics of Our Fathers* teach us that certain quarrels are destined to be eternal?

So let us not be excessively afraid of Hasidic disputations and disputes. They were bitter while they lasted, but they did not last too long. The fight between Mitnagdim and Hasidism, a century earlier, lasted longer—and the Jewish people survived.

Zanz and Sadigur differ in many respects. Each is a world in itself. Their leaders' outlook on Jewish life and survival is different. Furthermore, Rabbi Hayim built a dynasty, whereas Rabbi Avraham-Yoseph inherited one. The father of the first was a rabbi; that of the second, a rebbe. Rabbi Hayim emphasized study and prayer, whereas Rabbi Avraham-Yoseph . . . where did he place the emphasis? Neither on study nor on prayer. Is it conceivable that Sadigur neglected *ahavat Torah* and *yirat shamayim*, love of God and fear of heaven?

Who was Rabbi Hayim? His file is rich with biographical data. Born in Tarnograd in the year of Poland's second partition in 1783, he quickly acquired a reputation as a child prodigy. His father, a renowned scholar, had served as rabbi in Pzemizsl. The Seer of Lublin's brother, Reb Yossele, who had also lived in Tarnograd, excited the young boy's interest in Hasidism, which led to a singular situation: the father—who opposed Hasidism—gave into his son's pleas and took him to Lublin. The Seer made a profound impression on the young visitor, who joined the movement right then and there, becoming its youngest member. Until the Seer's death he considered himself his disciple. Then he belonged to Rabbi Naphtali of Rop-shitz, and later to Rabbi Zvi-Hersh of Ziditchoiv.

But insofar as pure learning was concerned, he recognized mainly the authority of his father-in-law, Reb Baroukh Frenkel. Rabbi Hayim was seventeen when he married Rachel. Many legends circulate in Hasidic chronicles about his wedding. Apparently, Rachel was not too happy about marrying him. Granted, he was a brilliant scholar, but . . . he limped badly. According to one version, Reb Hayim asked her father for permission to speak to her alone. What he told her we do not know. But we do know that he convinced her. As for her father, he simply commented, "My future son-in-law does indeed have a crooked foot, oh but his mind is straight."

Was he born like that? One Hasidic source tells us that his leg was injured by an unnamed tutor while he was still in *kheider* and that he cursed this tutor for years. More likely it was a birth defect. Reb Hayim suffered from it his entire life. But it did not stop him from learning.

He stayed one year in Rudnik, spent some time in the Hungarian town of Kalev—whose rebbe was famous for his miracles and for his Hungarian songs—and then accepted the position in Zanz. We have before us the text of the contract offered to him, the *ktav ha'rabanut*:

On this Friday the seventh day in Shvat 1828 a full assembly was held with the participation of community leaders, spiri-tual personalities and certain wealthy members. It was unani-mously agreed to hire the great light and sharp minded Rabbi Hayim Halberstam, the head of the Rabbinical Tribunal in Rudnik, as a true and just guide for our community so that he may decide what is and what is not allowed to be preached in the Synagogue on Shabbat, and establish regular Torah les-sons, especially for young students. He will deliver his own sermons in the principal shul. For his sustenance—in great dignity—he will receive four Reinish a week, in addition to other income befitting a Rabbi.

Possibly because of the low salary, or for other reasons, Reb Hayim hesitated. He accepted the position only in 1830. But he kept it until he died in 1876.

Was he happy there? Not in his family life. He became a widower several times. Some of his children died at a young age. Two sons lived long enough to be killed by the Germans. When, at the age of seventy, he announced his decision to marry for the fourth time, his son Reb Baroukh tried to dissuade him: "Father," he said, "when your rebbe, Reb Zvi-Hersh of Ziditchoiv, became a widower, he refused to remarry, explaining: I am married—to the Torah!" Reb Hayim understood the hint and replied, "If so, the Torah is already married to someone else: how could I marry her?" From this anecdote we learn several things: that he was definitely stubborn, that he probably enjoyed married life, and that most certainly he had a sense of humor.

Thanks to him, Zanz became a new center of Hasidic communal life. His disciple Reb Yossele Neustadt was asked, "What can you possibly see in Zanz that you have not seen in Lublin?" "Zanz was in Lublin," answered Reb Yossele Neustadt, "but Zanz is more than Lublin." He taught Talmud using the rationalist Lithuanian methods but practiced Hasidism. Even though he immersed himself totally in his studies, he still ran once or several times a day to the *mikvah* to purify himself. Scholars from all over Poland and Russia solicited his views in matters of Responsa; at the same time, Hasidic rebbes and followers came to join him in prayer. The Rabbi of Radomsk, at times, left his own followers and went to spend Shavuot, the holiday of Kabalat-Torah, with the old master of Zanz. When asked for a reason, he said, "Only in Zanz do I feel what our ancestors felt when they stood at Sinai, ready to receive the Law." It was said that Rabbi Akiba's soul resided in Rabbi Hayim's soul. And Rabbi Levi Yitzhak's too.

Sometimes Rabbi Hayim would run from one corner of the room

to the other shouting, weeping, attaining ecstasy with those sacred words in which the higher and the lower spheres are united. A disciple asked him respectfully, in the third person: "What is the Rebbe doing before davening?" And he answered, in Yiddish: *"Farn davenen, daven ich"*—Before praying, I pray. And another time: "I am davening, I am praying, to be worthy of praying." When Rabbi Hayim prayed, he forgot his own body. His wife, the rebbetzin, pleaded with his old master Rabbi Naphtali of Ropshitz: "Why do you allow him to hit his wounded leg during services? Tell him, at least, to hit his healthy one!" "Do you really think," answered the Ropshitzer Rebbe, "that when he worships, he knows the difference?" Apparently he was capable of such concentration that when physicians performed surgery on his leg, he refused anesthesia. All his thoughts were in God, for God. Already as a child he would go around whispering to himself: "There is no one but You, no one but You." He kept on repeating this until his last day. He would also whisper: "I want to burn, to die for Your sake, and for the sake of Thy people." In his prayers, he would enumerate the four ways of dying: "For Your sake, and for the sake of Thy people."

Constantly on the go, he slept two to three hours a day. When questioned about this, he would quote Napoleon, who didn't want to "sleep away an empire." "And I," said he, "refuse to sleep away Torah."

"Actually," he said, "it is easy to sleep little. Some people eat fast, learn fast, get wealthy fast: I sleep fast." But he prayed slowly, concentrating on every word, on every syllable. He was so slow that, at times, the cantor would continue the services without him. Concentration, *dveikut,* was a consuming preoccupation for Rabbi Hayim of Zanz. Once, during Rosh Hashanah services, a huge portion of the ceiling crumbled. The worshipers fled in panic; the rabbi alone remained inside the House of Prayer, oblivious to the danger. On another occasion, the table at which he was studying caught fire; he went on studying until a disciple pulled him away. As he clung to God, he forgot himself. Listen to his statement: "Whoever so much as blinks without *kavanah,* without concentration on its meaning, is not human." It is said that whenever the "Yetev Lev," Rabbi Yekutiel Yehuda Teitelbaum of Sighet, returned from Zanz, he would refrain from talking for thirty days.

Rabbi Hayim was also known for his love of singing. He had learned the importance of singing from his teacher, the Ropshitzer. In Zanz, Shabbat meant a seamless song of joy and peace. Composers had a special place at the court of Zanz. *Ba'alei tefila* and a chorus would provide highlights during services and festive meals. Rabbi Hayim loved the Kalever Rebbe because of his beautiful melodies. Of the Kalever Rebbe, Rabbi Hayim said, "He is humbler than grass and quieter than water."

But what was most defining of Zanz was the rabbi's total commitment to the *mitzvah* of charity. Whatever he received he gave away. His house was forever crowded with beggars, wanderers, and others in need of financial support. No one was sent away empty-handed. He deprived his own household in order to help strangers. When his own money ran out, he took loans. Once, during the Shavuot holiday, he summoned three of his rich followers—one of them was Reb Kalman Kahan from Sighet—and told them, "When I was young I used to deliver long sermons; today I will give you a short one. I need money for my poor people. If you do not pledge it to me as soon as the holiday is over, I shall not say *kiddush* today." The three Hasidim assured the rabbi that he would get what he wanted.

"I love the poor," he would say. "Do you know why? Because God loves them." His son asked for financial assistance to marry off his daughter; Rabbi Hayim refused. Minutes later, he offered support to a poor man who had come to him with a similar request. "Why him and not me?" the son wondered. "You are my son, others will help you. Who will help him?" answered the rabbi.

A man came to see him, weeping: his daughter was walking around barefoot. "Give him some money to buy her shoes," said the rabbi to his servant. Later, his daughter came into his study, crying: she too was walking around barefoot. "I cannot help you," answered the rabbi. His servant couldn't help wondering aloud, "Why did the rabbi help the other girl and not his own daughter?" "Because that girl is the daughter of a scholar," said the rabbi. "Some people say that this one is also the daughter of a scholar," remarked the servant. "All right," said the rabbi. "You win. Give her what she needs to buy a pair of shoes."

Hasidic chronicles say that he would receive around a hundred thousand guldens from his followers each year. He did not keep a penny. Naturally, he was admired and loved by the poor. He was their best ally, their protector, their spokesman, their hope.

One day he saw a woman crying. "Why do you cry?" "I am a merchant," she answered. "I sell apples. That's my livelihood. But today people refuse to buy my apples. They say that my apples are not good." "Come," said Rabbi Hayim of Zanz. "I will help you." He went with her to the marketplace, took a position behind her barrel, and began yelling: "Who wants to buy good apples, beautiful apples, splendid apples?" The woman never had so many customers in her life.

But then we are back to our first question. If the man was so charitable, so compassionate, so kind, why did he provoke so many other Jews, especially Hasidim? If Zanz was so generous, why did it persecute Sadigur?

Sadigur was the place where the Maggid's grandson, the celebrated Rabbi Israel of Rizhin, established his kingdom. And what a kingdom it was. The rabbi dressed like a king and behaved like a king. He readily spoke of his royal descent, of his ancestor King David. There were many legends about his wealth. It was said that he ate only out of golden bowls, that he wore only golden sandals. That his carriage was drawn by six white horses. And that an entourage of a hundred servants, cooks, and musicians followed him in his travels. The rumors were extravagant, and yet, strangely enough, no one was offended. Most masters worked with the poor and were themselves poor—and yet even they viewed the Rizhiner with pride. None of them considered Hasidic luxury a contradiction in terms or Hasidic wealth a scandal. The Rabbi of Rizhin was above reproach. The greatest of the great would come to visit him—and leave deeply impressed. Was it because the Rizhiner represented a living link with the Maggid of Mezeritch? Or because he had endured jail and persecution? He was unanimously loved and respected.

Rabbi Hayim of Zanz himself came to Sadigur and was won over by Rabbi Israel's sense of grandeur. When asked why he went to Sadigur, Reb Hayim answered, "Why was the temple built on Mount Moriah and not on Mount Sinai? Because a place where a man is willing to sacrifice himself for the sake of heaven is more important to the Almighty than a place where the Law was given. And I am ready to testify to the Rizhiner's willingness to sacrifice himself for the sake of heaven at every minute of his life."

As long as the Rizhiner was alive, Sadigur enjoyed a spotless reputation everywhere in the Hasidic world, including Zanz. He was quoted in every court; his comments were brilliant, penetrating. "How is one to distinguish the silent sage from the silent fool? The sage doesn't mind being silent." And this one: "Look around you. Works of art are cherished and honored, while man—God's masterpiece—lies in the dust." And this prediction: "A day will come when all nations will begin hating Jews; they will hate them with such passion and violence, that the Jews will have no choice but to go to the land of their ancestors. And then, woe unto us and woe unto them, for it will be the beginning of redemption." And this one: "A day will come when man will stop hating others and hate himself; a day will come when all things will lose their coherence, when there will be no relation between man and his face, desire and its object, people and their appearance; a day will come when there will be no connection between question and answer, between parables and the meaning of the parables."

Rabbi Israel was a great master, and Sadigur, during his reign, was a unique center of attraction in the Hasidic universe. After his death, things changed. At least as far as Zanz was concerned, Sadigur no longer represented sublimation in Hasidic life but came to represent degradation instead. A seven-year feud began in 1869; it ended only with the passing of Rabbi Hayim of Zanz. What motivated it? A story goes that Rabbi Hayim came to visit the Rizhiner's youngest son, Reb Mordekhai-Feivish, who, for some unexplained reason, did not rise to welcome him. Others lay the blame on Sadigur's "modern" ways. Conservative, even ultraconservative in his views, Rabbi Hayim radically and vehemently rejected anything that evoked the winds of emancipation and reform that were blowing across Europe at the time. Women were forbidden to wear hairpieces and hats; only kerchiefs were allowed. Children were forbidden to study secular languages and sciences. Jews, according to Zanz, were duty-bound to follow in the footsteps of their fathers and forefathers. Times had changed? So what? Jews must remain faithful to their tradition and not succumb to the temptations and seductions of their surroundings.

Sadigur did not reject modernism. As befitted the members of a royal family, the rebbe's children dressed elegantly. Unlike other Hasidic masters, the Rebbe of Sadigur did not daven together with his followers; he worshiped in an adjacent room. Only on special occasions would he mingle with the crowd. One of the rebbe's brothers, Reb Berenyu of Lowe—to whom we shall return later—wore gloves when greeting his Hasidim.

Wild rumors began spreading about Sadigur. That the rebbe denigrated study. That his daughters engaged in indecent exposure by dressing in the latest fashion, riding horses, smoking in public, and going to the theater. Fact or fiction, genuine concern or gossip, these rumors lit a fire that eventually split the Hasidic movement in Galicia and shook the Jewish world from Russia all the way to Jerusalem.

To understand the situation better, let us look at the state of Hasidism in the world of the nineteenth century. It seemed to reflect the overall state of the world at the time. Political upheavals, social revolutions, and military adventures had marked the century. Kingdoms were rising and falling. Napoleon's astonishing conquests were matched only by his no less astonishing defeats. In philosophy, metaphysics had given way to economics; in literature, the romanticists were taking over from the classicists. Emancipation was the key word among intellectuals, both non-Jewish and Jewish. Enlightenment had become both goal and way of life.

For a while, the Hasidic world was quiet. Gone were the quarrels between Lublin and Lizensk, the disputes between Lublin and Pshiske, the bitter fights of a century earlier between Hasidim and Mitnag-dim. Gone was the visionary of Kotzk; his celebrated outbursts against complacency, self-righteousness, and serenity no longer aroused fear and trembling in the thousands of Hasidim whose thirst for knowledge and truth, whose total opposition to compromise gave the entire movement new intensity and meaning. Now, in the second half of the century, there were still Hasidic masters, some of them endowed with greatness, but there were too many centers, too many leaders, too many opportunities for conflict.

When the Rizhiner died, he left six sons and three daughters. The oldest, Reb Sholem Yoseph, died soon after. Of the surviving five, four established courts in Galicia, Moldavia, and Bukovina, creating new dynasties. One, Rabbi Avraham-Yoseph, stayed in Sadigur. Rabbi David-Moshe went to Potok and then to Chortkov. Reb Berenyu became Rebbe of Lowe (in Moldavia), Reb Nakhum settled in Stefan-est, and Reb Mordekhai-Feivish in Husiatin.

But the war between Zanz and Sadigur did not start in any of those towns; it erupted in Reisha, where, in 1869, followers of Zanz and of Sadigur began to feud to such an extent that they eventually attended two different Houses of Study and prayer. The Hasidim of Zanz sent a complaint to their master, urging him to speak up against their opponents. The letter, signed by two rabbis and several other prominent members of the community, was answered by Rabbi Hayim in person.

What were the accusations? The same ones that, a century earlier, the Mitnagdim leveled against Hasidim. That the followers of Sadigur constituted a sect apart. That they spent too much time drinking and rejoicing. That they showed disrespect toward learned men. And that they were doing "hair-raising" things during nights of festivities. The Zanzer Hasidim, therefore, requested their rabbi's permission to take measures against the Sadigur followers, including denunciation to local authorities.

At first, there were people at Sadigur who urged the rebbe to answer the attacks. One version has it that the Rebbe of Husiatin himself advocated counteroffensives. However, the Rebbe of Sadigur and his brother, the Rebbe of Tchortkov, refused to go along. "Yelling wears one out; silence does not," they said.

The Zanzer camp was not monolithic either. Of course, the majority followed the rabbi and even tried to outdo him. But here and there some voices of moderation were heard. At least one source tells us that the rabbi's eldest son, Reb Yekhezkel of Shinive, himself was not happy with the situation. He disagreed with the smear tactics so many of his father's followers used against another rebbe in whose greatness he believed. A pro-Sadigur text affirms that, as a result of the son's disagreement with the general Zanz position, Reb Yekhezkel stayed away—or was pushed away—from his father for several years.

Soon the war spread beyond Reisha, and even Galicia. A new scandal—the Reb Berenyu affair—added fuel to the fire.

Listen: Reb Berenyu—the Rizhiner's fourth son—was, according to many sources, the most erudite, refined, and intellectually curious of the brothers. At the age of fourteen, he wed Sheindel, the daughter of Rabbi Motel of Chernobyl, but theirs was not a happy marriage. Perhaps as a result of this, Reb Berenyu devoted more time and more passion to study. Some adversaries of Sadigur maintained that he had befriended Jewish and Christian freethinkers, and even met with and discussed philosophy and science with a telegraphist who had left Judaism and converted to Christianity.

The year 1869 was a sad one for Reb Berenyu: his beloved brother, Reb Nakhum of Stefanest, died, and Reb Berenyu, at fifty-two, fell into a deep depression. Had he spent too much time with proselytizing elements in his town? Was he really in danger of falling prey to missionaries? His wife and brothers decided to take action: a physician was called who put Reb Berenyu to sleep. When the young rebbe awoke, he found himself in his brother's house in Sadigur. Somehow the story of the kidnapping reached "*haskala* circles," the emancipated intellectuals, who alerted the authorities. The affair escalated when the police came to the court of Sadigur and freed the prisoner. He was transported to Chernovitz, where he stayed with the deputy leader of the community, a certain Dr. Yehuda-Leib Reitman. The Rizhiner's son among the *maskilim,* the emancipated? You can imagine the storm! Hasidic communities everywhere gathered to pray for his return to sanity. In Berditchev, a day of fasting was proclaimed. But in Zanz, people were jubilant. Reb Berenyu's behavior corroborated their charges—especially since the court of Sadigur officially refused to turn against Reb Berenyu. Worse, soon after Reb Berenyu arrived in Chernovitz, the *maskilim* in Kishinev published a letter praising him for his move: "Our heart is glad that you tore the rabbinic mask off your face which now radiates wisdom and knowledge. . . . You have cast away the throne of the rebbe and removed the Hasidic crown from your head. . . . You have said: Let truth reign over us. . . . We thank you for coming to help your brothers who are sinking in mud and dirt. . . . We thank you for fighting fanaticism."

The reaction in Hasidic circles? Pain, embarrassment, and confusion. Their only explanation: Reb Berenyu must have lost his mind. To counteract this accusation, the Chernovitz *maskilim* published an open letter, allegedly signed by Reb Berenyu, in which he explained what had happened to him: "In my heart I kept my faith in God and will always keep it alive; I remain faithful to the Torah and to the Sages of Israel who go forward and not backward. . . . I have not ceased fearing God, but I have separated myself from the crowd of silly people who observe false stupidities and who turn darkness into light and light into darkness. . . ."

This letter—advocating progress at the expense of tradition—provoked anger in all Orthodox circles. Protests were organized, with Zanz leading the way. The attacks were directed not only against Reb Berenyu but against Sadigur itself. Still, Sadigur chose not to respond. Meanwhile, the rabbi kept his dignity, wrapping himself in silence. He and his family, though hurt, ignored the barrage of insults.

Reb Berenyu did not remain with his emancipated friends very long. Fourteen days after publishing his letter, he returned to his family, published a retraction of his earlier views, and embarked on an existence of total seclusion and meditation. Followers of Sadigur celebrated the event with their customary exuberance, hoping that the chapter had been closed for good.

Reb Berenyu's prestige grew immeasurably among his followers. They besieged his door, waiting to be admitted to receive his blessing. But he refused to be rebbe. He sought solitude and, after a while, he found it. His wife left him and returned to her family in Chernobyl. He stayed with his brother in Sadigur, isolated in his room, while he searched day and night for answers to eternal questions. Perhaps he realized that the search itself contained an element of eternity. He passed away five months before Rabbi Hayim of Zanz.

But let's not get ahead of ourselves. Let's see what was happening in Zanz while Sadigur was celebrating Reb Berenyu's return.

In his letter to his followers in Reisha, Rabbi Hayim had openly stated that "the wicked sect ought to be expelled and chased away from our community with the help of the laws of the land." He classified Reb Berenyu as a "convert" and "atheist." Therefore, in the words of Rabbi Hayim, "The scribes of Sadigur are renegades: their mezuzot and *tefillin* are impure. Their teachers ought not to teach Jewish children. Their ritual slaughterers are unworthy." Rabbi Hayim continued: "Separate yourselves from the tents of the wicked; do not talk to them; humiliate them in public, uncover their shame. And if, like the mute, they come silently into our House of Study and prayer, stay as far away from them as possible." Why such harshness? Rabbi Hayim explains: "They are to be compared to the Sabateans and the other false prophets. It is absolutely essential not to feel pity for them." Were it not for the Austro-Hungarian law forbidding excommunication, Zanz surely would have excommunicated Sadigur and all its members. Still, upon hearing Rabbi Hayim's orders, a collective hysteria swept through the Hasidic communities. Families were divided. Fathers rejected sons, husbands left their wives; friendships were broken, partnerships betrayed. There were homes where parents mourned—sat shiva—for their children, if they belonged to the opposing camp.

One could reasonably expect that Zanz and Sadigur would never unite again, never again recognize each other as sons and daughters of the same people. Their fight lasted seven years—with Rabbi Hayim always attacking, while the rebbes of Sadigur showed restraint and silence. As for the other Hasidic rebbes and non-Hasidic scholars, most preferred to stay on the sidelines. The rare exception was Rabbi Aharon of Chernobyl, who wrote to Rabbi Hayim of Zanz: "I am ninety-three years old. I am feared both in heaven and below. Were it not for your learning, I would do things to you. . . ." Other masters said nothing. Evidently, Rabbi Hayim was shielded by his scholarship and piety. After all, he *was* the *gadol ha'dor*, the greatest Halakhic authority of his generation. Even the Sadigur Hasidim refrained from attacking him; they attacked his followers, but not him.

That was the situation in Europe. In Palestine, things were different. Tempers ran higher there. The Sadigur Hasidim in Jerusalem, Safed, and Tiberias were less tolerant, and surely less passive than their co-disciples in Galicia. Upon hearing the news of the persecutions Sadigur Hasidim were subject to in Poland, they decided to respond in kind. Sadigur Hasidim were beaten up in Galicia? Zanzer Hasidim would be beaten up in Palestine. Jewish blood was shed in Poland? Jewish blood would be shed in the Holy Land too. Sadigur followers were discriminated against in Poland? Only one thing to do: Zanz would be excommunicated in Palestine.

The ceremony took place in the old city of David, near the Western Wall. A few days later, similar ceremonies were held in Tiberias and Safed. The synagogues were draped in black. Black candles were lit. The shofar was blown. Ancient maledictions were invoked against the Rabbi of Zanz, whom the participants formally expelled from the house of Israel.

These events took place two weeks after Passover 1869. When the news reached Europe, it stunned its Jewish communities. This time even neutral rabbis felt the need to intervene on behalf of Rabbi Hayim Zanzer. This time the Palestinian Hasidim had gone too far: one does not excommunicate a man like Rabbi Hayim. Four weeks later, during the holy day of Shavuot, hundreds of Hasidic leaders and some two thousand of their disciples gathered at the Zanz synagogue, where the secretary of the rabbinic tribunal read the text of excommunication against all those who, in Palestine, had insulted Rabbi

Hayim and all their fellow Hasidim who, in Poland, had betrayed the Hasidic ideal with their words and deeds.

Thus, the war between Zanz and Sadigur acquired new impetus. Now the two camps were enemies for life and death. What they had in common was their hatred for one another. The violence subsided only when Zanz lost its leader in 1876. Reb Berenyu had died five months earlier. Eventually, the hatred turned into mere animosity, the animosity into mild antagonism, the antagonism into criticism, the criticism into "difference." Today Zanz and Sadigur have made peace; their children even marry each other.

At this point I suggest we return to Rabbi Hayim. I don't want to leave him on an angry note. What about his intolerance? His fanaticism? They surprise me, for he also had a marvelous sense of humor; people who know how to laugh tend to be more tolerant toward their fellow men.

A story:

One day he could not control his cough, so his son Reb Barukh offered him a cup of tea. "Don't you see I am studying?" said the father. "My mind roams the higher spheres of *atzilut,* nobility; and I can tell you, my son, that in the sphere of *atzilut,* one does not drink tea." "May I humbly draw your attention, Father," said Reb Barukh, "to the fact that in the *olam ha'atzilut* one does not cough either?" And Rabbi Hayim accepted the tea.

Another story. Once, on Yom Kippur afternoon, a wealthy man, known for his greed, could not take the fast; he fainted. Rabbi Hayim was asked what to do. "Give him water," said the rebbe, "and tell him that for each time he swallows, he will have to give charity tomorrow." The man barely touched the water.

He once sat with Reb Hersh of Dinev and talked about Hasidism and Torah. In honor of his distinguished guest, he asked for drinks to be served. "Hasn't the doctor forbidden you to drink?" wondered the Rebbe of Dinev. "Yes," answered Rabbi Hayim, "but he is asleep now."

The older he grew, the more stories he told. Listen: A man was lost in the forest. After many days he encountered another man. He ran toward him and shouted with joy: "Thank God you are here. Now you will show me the way out." "I am sorry," answered the second man, "I too am lost. All I can tell you is—come with me, I will show you where not to go." After a long silence, Rabbi Hayim commented, "Let us find a new way together; the road we have taken until now leads nowhere."

Another of his parables. There was a widow with many small children; they were hungry and she had nowhere to turn. One morning she found an egg. "Children," she cried, "we are saved. See this egg? We shall not cook it. Instead, I will ask a neighbor to allow me to use one of her chickens. And so our egg will become a chicken. But we must remember not to eat the chicken. Instead, we must wait until the chicken will lay eggs; they, in turn will become chickens who will lay more eggs. Remember: let us eat neither the chickens nor the eggs. Let us sell the chickens and use the money to buy a cow. We will have milk—but do not drink it; we will sell the milk and buy more cows, then we will sell a few cows and buy a piece of land, and then we will be rich and know no more hunger." As she spoke, the egg fell from her hand and broke. Her intentions were good; what she forgot was that hunger must be dealt with in the present.

A third story. In a faraway kingdom, a prince sinned against his father, the king, who exiled him from the palace. As long as the prince was near his city, people treated him well, for they knew who he was. But as he wandered farther away, people mistook him for a beggar and treated him accordingly. Since he had to work for his living, he eventually became a shepherd. And he had forgotten that once upon a time he had been a prince. He ate and drank and sang like all the other shepherds. And he was happy—except for the fact that all the other shepherds had their own huts, and he had none. Soon, he heard that the king had arrived in the region. Thousands of peasants flocked into the city to greet him, to assure him of their loyalty. The king saw fit to reward them. They all filed by the throne asking for favors. When the prince's turn came, he simply asked for money to build himself a hut. "Woe unto us," concluded Rabbi

Hayim, "when we forget where we come from and who we are. We are princes, we are all princes."

Rabbi Hayim of Zanz's faith in the Almighty God and in His compassion was absolute. A man once complained to him, "Rabbi, I am a father and my children are hungry!" "You are not the only father I know," said the rabbi. "God is our father, he knows that we are hungry."

Did he believe in miracles? "If I really try, I could prevail in heaven," he once remarked. "But one must be clever about it." Occasionally he would say: "I never said that those stories about miracles are true; all I said was that it is important to tell those stories."

He often referred to himself with a kind of self-deprecating humor. "When I was young," he said, "I decided to improve the world. But then I discovered that the world is so big, so vast, I had better begin somewhere. Where? I decided to improve the country I lived in. But then I realized the country is so huge. I decided to improve the city I dwelt in. But the city itself is so large. I decided to improve the street I lived on, but there are so many houses on it. So I decided to improve the house I lived in, then the members of my community, then the members of my family. Then I decided I had better begin with myself." And Rabbi Hayim sighed, "When will I begin to improve myself?"

Did the quarrel have a lasting effect on him? Of course, he had won the battle—but what about the scars? Granted, most rabbis and leaders had taken his side against the radicals of Sadigur in Palestine—but had the victory improved the image and the fate of future Hasidim and his spiritual message?

Talmudic debates rarely degenerated into personal disputes. Rav and Shmuel had felt a profound respect and affection for one another. The same was true of all the masters who illuminated the Talmudic universe, in Palestine and Babylonia. *Talmidei hakhamim marbim shalom ba'olam*, we are told. Learned men increase peace—or at least the chances for peace—in the world. Ideological opponents found a way to transcend themselves and lift their discussion to higher levels. Reb Yohanan and Resh Lakish, Abbaye and Rava, Shammai and

Hillel, could all serve as examples of tolerance. What made Zanz and Sadigur different? How could they remember their Talmudic studies—as they did—and deny their ethical and social implications?

I still fail to understand the deep motivation for the dispute. More precisely, I fail to comprehend its violence. What was it about Sadigur that infuriated Rabbi Hayim to such a degree? The status accorded to wealth? The exhibitionism of certain dignitaries?

What is amazing about this dispute is not that it occurred but that it ended so quickly—and that it left no lasting bitterness in either camp. Obviously, great scholars and rebbes of the time intervened and saw to it that the episode would be concluded without blaming or shaming either side. They succeeded. Today, one can tell the painful story of that quarrel without risking the fury of Zanz or Sadigur.

Zanz loved the poor—did that mean that Sadigur did not? There are documents proving that in Sadigur, as in Zanz, the poor were looked after by the rebbe's court—in fact, by the rebbetzin herself. The difference between Zanz and Sadigur? In Zanz everything was public, whereas in Sadigur everything was discreet. Didn't Rabbi Hayim know that? Didn't he know that *tzedakah*, charity, is fundamental to Hasidism, for it is fundamental to Judaism? Why then was he so angry? Because of the craving for luxury he thought he detected in Sadigur's rabbinic homes? Did he fear that this might be imitated by the ordinary Hasidim as well? It hardly seems a good enough reason to wage such a war.

More than a hundred years later, I confess that I like both masters—although I am closer to Sadigur's silence than to the Zanzer thunder. Both reflect moods and passions of our people. Both find their place in our history, and certainly our contemporary history.

I prefer to remember Zanz not as a center of warfare but as a center of *ahavat Yisrael* and a source of purity. I prefer to remember it as a *heikhal ha'negina*, a place where words turn into melodies and melodies into prayers, and prayers into human offerings of friendship.

Hasidic chronicles tell us that the famous author of "Kol Aryeh" used to spend Shavuot in Zanz. One day, on the eve of the holiday, he went to the House of Study. Since it was too early for services, he opened a Talmudic treatise and began studying. An hour later he was joined by the wealthy Hasid, Reb Yoseph-Leib Kahana from Sighet, who looked at him and looked and looked, and all of a sudden began to dance and sing in ecstasy. "What's the matter with you?" asked the author of "Kol Aryeh," surprised. "Why such rejoicing?" Answered Reb Yoseph-Leib Kahana: "As I was looking at you I said to myself, 'Had God Almighty not given us His Torah, where would we be today?' You would be holding some position of honor in some important community, and I would have been a peasant who wouldn't even have known what he was missing. So how can I not rejoice?" At that point, his friend was so moved that he closed the treatise of Talmud and started dancing too. By that time, services were about to begin. Hundreds of worshipers appeared in the synagogue. As they saw the two friends dancing, they joined them without asking why. Then Rabbi Hayim Zanzer appeared. Without a word, he entered the circle and danced with the others—and when Rabbi Hayim of Zanz danced, the gates of heaven opened, so that all prayers were received, all favors granted, and all perils vanished.

At the same time, the Hasidim and their rebbe danced in Sadigur, too. After all, once upon a time, they all stood at Sinai, together, to receive the same Law.

They? They alone? No: all of us.

The World of the Shtetl

WHENEVER I THINK of the shtetl, the small colorful Jewish kingdom so rich in memories, I am invaded by an emotion mixed with pity and sadness.

I think of those men and women who created it, nourished it, and kept it alive. The known and the unknown, the sacred and the profane, the impoverished tutors and their mischievous pupils, the joyous innkeepers and their tired customers, the beggars and their songs, as well as the princes in disguise, carriers of ancient melodies and eternally renewed dreams of hope and redemption: how have they managed for such a lengthy period in history to overcome so many threats and perils from a world that could not understand them?

In my mind, I see them again, defenseless citizens, living on love and faith, in the streets and roads of the shtetl somewhere in Poland, Romania, Hungary, the Ukraine—in short in all the regions of Eastern and Central Europe where the turbulent winds of history brought them, often by force, as if to plant there a variety of aspirations and regrets without which no culture could ever exist.

When did the shtetl originate, at least under this name? Whose idea was it? Who was its first builder? Heaven knows, history does not. In those times of ancient calendars, kings and rulers who could no longer dwell in boredom found both pleasure and interest in chasing their Jews from one province to another, from one country to another, only to invite them back to help rebuild their national economy and, at the same time, to divert the anger of the population toward them.

I hope you will not mind my dealing with this theme neither from the sociological nor from the anthropological viewpoint. My goal is to evoke and meditate on memory.

The reason is a simple one. Though buried in the ashes of recent history, the shtetl remains very much alive to some of us whose numbers are dwindling steadily. Yes, we are the last remnants of these Jewish communities that the cruelties of the twentieth century destroyed forever but whose traces can still be found strangely dispersed here and there, as if determined to go on haunting a world that wants to forget.

Like most survivors, I live in fear. What will happen when the last witness will no longer be here to testify, or simply to tell the tale? Who will the witness be? What will happen to that final testimony with its burning images, tears, and whispers? What will happen when there will no longer be a man or a woman who will say, "The shtetl? You want to know what it was like living and dying there? Listen, I come from a shtetl . . ."?

But then, what makes a place inhabited by Jews a shtetl? The word means "a small town." Would a town of ten or fifteen thousand Jews be a shtetl? What about a village of only two thousand? Or a hamlet numbering no more than 120? How is a shtetl to be measured, how is it recognized? By what features is it to be defined? Only by its picturesque or exotic aspects? Why is Chagall's Vitebsk a shtetl, whereas Saloniki with its exiled Jews from Spain and Portugal is not? The fact is that the shtetl belongs to the Ashkenazi world in Eastern Europe. But what about its beginnings? Again, no precise date seems to be available. All we know is that a Jewish presence in Western Europe can be traced back to the destruction of Jerusalem by the Romans, who sent many of its Jews to Italy, France, and Germany. As for Eastern Europe, chronicles tell of Jews, during the persecutions linked to the First Crusade in 1096, fleeing Prague for Cracow. Since then, Jews came to, left, and returned again to Poland, where they knew periods of both happiness and distress. In 1261, King Boleslav the Pious published his Statute of Kalisz guaranteeing Jews many important rights. For example, it prohibited Christians from using false accusations of blood libel against Jews. The king went so far as to threaten transgressors with the same punishment Jews would have received, had the accusations been well founded.

Another Polish king known for his kindness toward Jews was Casimir the Great, in the middle of the fourteenth century. He protected them, and some people think they know why: he had a Jewish mistress, Estherke. Just like her namesake in the Megilla, she had a strong and beneficial influence on him.

In general terms, the living conditions of Jews depended on the mood, the capriciousness, and the good will of kings, and of the economic situation in the land. In other words, dwelling in constant uncertainty, Jews never knew what tomorrow would bring. They endured many pogroms, some worse than others. Take the massacres conducted by the bloodthirsty mobs under Hetman Bogdan Khmelnicky in 1648, when most Jewish communities were decimated. At least seventy thousand Jews were murdered. In the chronicles of the time, one reads with horror scenes of such brutality that, in Sholem Ash's words, one would lose faith in the humanity of man. They also raise Halakhic questions based on historical events. For example, in a shtetl ravaged by a tempest of fire and blood, the few survivors are confronted by a heartbreaking dilemma: what should the orphaned community rebuild first, the house of prayer and study or the cemetery?

That was the fate of hundreds of communities. The enemy would suddenly emerge with sword and dagger in his hands, in a frenzy of violence and hatred, beheading men, women, and children in the streets, in poorly barricaded homes, caves, and attics. The murderers left only when they thought the last Jew was dead. Then, as if out of nowhere, a man, a woman, an adolescent appeared, haggard, all in mourning, orienting themselves with great difficulty among the ruins. They immediately began digging graves. They buried the dead, said Kaddish, and life again began flowing, binding the abandoned individual souls into a community. They rebuilt their homes, opened schools, arranged weddings and circumcisions, celebrated holidays, fasted on Tisha b'Av and Yom Kippur, danced on Simhat Torah, and made their children study Talmud: all that while waiting for the next catastrophe. That was life in the shtetl: a parenthesis. While the calm period lasted, and even during the storm, great books were written, important lessons offered. At one point, the Va'ad Arba Ha'aratzot, the Committee of the Four Lands, was established. As the highest authority, it dealt with urgent issues in organized Jewish life that were not covered by tradition and ancient Law. Its so-called heter iska, authorizing Jewish bankers to ask for interest on loans (which is forbidden in the Bible), is still displayed in every bank in Israel.

Then the brackets of temporary respite and renewal closed definitively, irrevocably, in the middle of the last century, because the fiercest and bloodiest of our enemies wanted them closed. Of all Hitler's pledges to his bewitched nation, the only one he almost fulfilled was the one to annihilate the Jewish people and erase it from the surface of the earth. I say "almost" for, thanks to the Allied armies and their bravery, he lost the war. But I think when we evoke the shtetl, we may omit the "almost." There, Hitler's victory sadly and tragically seems total. The shtetl is gone. For good. Granted, Jewish life can be found elsewhere, and it fills us with pride and joy. In Europe, the United States, and the former Soviet Union, but especially in Israel, it welcomes us with a face shining with hope. Oh yes, Jewish life is again flourishing, vibrating with impressive creativity. But that of the shtetl belongs to the past.

Need I say that I miss it? Must I say aloud what, in many of my writings, I repeat in whispers? The shtetl is my childhood. I remain attached to it and faithful.

Let us try to revisit it together. No matter where it is located on the map, the shtetl has no fixed geographical features. Nestled in the Carpathians or situated on the plains, dominated by Polish princes or governed by Romanian landowners, it is built on the same social structures, contains the same pulsations, the same human resources, the same attachment to a collective destiny both dark and glorious. In other words, in its broad outlines, the shtetl is one and the same everywhere.

In Yitzhak Leiboush Peretz's Hasidic tales as well as in I. J. Singer's novels, the same characters are plagued by the same worries, stifle the same outcries, and pray the same prayers composed in ecstasy. No need to question them: young and old, rich and poor, satisfied and dissatisfied, what they all have in common is their Jewishness. When asked to identify themselves, a Jew in Hungary, Poland, or Romania will not say "I am a Hungarian, Romanian, or Pole of Jewish origin or faith" but "I am Jewish." How did they create a Jewish life apart, a Jewish identity in itself? Was it part, the essential part, of their heritage? Of their collective consciousness perhaps? Their Jewishness was their principal commitment to both religion and history. When a son or a daughter left home for study or work in the great city or abroad, the parents would always give their benediction accompanied by an earnest plea: "Do not forget that you are Jewish!" Being Jewish, to them, also had an ethical imperative. It meant: there are things a Jew cannot, must not do. *S'past nisht* is a common Jewish expression from the shtetl: it is not nice. Not nice for a Jew to say or do certain things, in certain ways. And then, also, whatever a Jew did implicated other Jews. That is why the need not to bring shame on Jews, not to endanger them, was a frequent argument governing Jewish behavior in the shtetl. A Jew from the shtetl thought of other Jews even after leaving the shtetl—and even when the shtetl ceased to exist. In the shtetl, the Jews felt that the entire world was looking upon them and passing judgment on their actions.

Hence the key word would be solidarity. In the shtetl, it was all-important. Was it because they were all threatened by the same peril? Probably. For the anti-Semite, too, every Jew was responsible for all Jews. When accusing a Jew of cheating, the anti-Semite indicts all Jews as scoundrels. When accusing a Jew of being a bad citizen, the anti-Semite shouts: all Jews are traitors. Needless to stress a known fact: all these accusations were and remain baseless, pure or impure inventions of poisoned minds and tongues.

Does it mean that the shtetl was an Anti-Sodom, a city of no evil? Does it mean that all its inhabitants were saints? Nonsense. Since 1516 we know that Utopia is a place that does not exist. The absolute is a divine attribute, not a human one. As everywhere else, among the inhabitants of the shtetl, good *and* wretched men could be found. Some were pure, others were not. Some were innocent, others guilty. However, contrary to large cities, in the shtetl people knew one another's virtues and shortcomings. Speaking of Yankel, they would say, "Ah, you mean Yankel the thief"? or "Ourke the liar"? or "Shmulik the cheat"? I remember: in my little town there was an informer. That must have been his profession. He had red hair and wore brown leather boots. Whenever he appeared in shul, people would lower their voices. He did not mind. He knew that we knew. Somehow he was not ostracized. Not a single person was hurt because of him. Why the leniency? Was it because the overwhelming majority of Jews in my town were Hasidim? And that Hasidism teaches us compassion for the sinner?

Since we mention Hasidism, let us seize this opportunity to elaborate, for the last time, on this movement, which had grown to become symbolic of the spiritual richness of the shtetl for nearly two centuries.

On more than one level one could say that Hasidism was born in the shtetl, for the shtetl, and could not have been born anywhere else. It is in isolated and impoverished villages and hamlets that Rabbi Israel Baal Shem Tov, the Master of the Good Name, known by his initials as the Besht, gathered his first friends, allies, disciples, and followers: it is said that he personally visited more than 280 villages, attracting by his mere presence simple men and women in need of strength as well as scholars in quest of transcendence. In big cities, people were too busy and perhaps too lethargic to go and hear a wandering preacher, a teller of tales, who came not to reprimand but to reassure. The Besht, in the beginning, took children to school and addressed women in marketplaces, neglecting no occasion to create and broaden his network of solidarity and companionship and thus save thousands of families and hundreds of small communities from going under. One must remember: for the Jewish villagers and inhabitants of small forsaken agglomerations, exile had become unbearable, and their separation from large Jewish centers of learning too painful. Their resignation would have made the cut-off irrevocable, had it not been for the Besht.

It is in the shtetl that Hasidism flourished. Elsewhere, in the big cities, the establishment exerted its powerful influence in matters of economic welfare and intellectual development to such a degree that it gave villagers the feeling of being pushed away, despised. For them, for their survival, the Hasidic message was essential, even vital. What was its content? It said that God listens even to those men and women who do not know the mysteries of Kabbala. That God is present everywhere, in all our endeavors, in all our aspirations, not only in study but also in prayer: both lead to God. One may attain truth by way of the heart as well as the mind. The illiterate shepherd with a warm heart is for God as important as the learned man whose knowledge is rooted in books.

A Rabbi Moshe-Leib Sassover, a Rabbi Zousia of Onipol, a Rabbi Levi-Yitzhak Berditchever could not have emerged in Troyes, Odessa, or Vilno, where biblical study and Talmudic research enveloped a dazzling elite, itself dazzled by inspired teachers endowed with charismatic powers. There, Hasidic masters were not needed.

They were needed in the shtetl, where tired and sad Jews had to be told, and were told, that what a Talmudic scholar accomplishes in a thousand pages of commentary, a devout Hasid can gain by reciting with fervor one prayer alone, the simplest of all: the Shema. What matters is the intent, the *kavanah,* the purity of intent.

A story. One day, the Besht summoned his close disciples and told them that it was time to do what was necessary to hasten redemption. One must not wait any longer. They had better be ready to knock at the highest and most secret gates, all inaccessible to the common mortal, break the locks, and allow the Messiah to come and save those who believed in him. The Besht knew what had to be done: he knew the place, the time, and the words. The disciples received precise instructions for the days and nights ahead, and the date of their next meeting—the first day of the first week of the month of Elul—somewhere in the forest. Burning with enthusiasm, barely controlling their impatience, the disciples followed his instructions to the letter. They fasted from Sunday to Friday, prayed with particular *kavanah,* and at midnight recited the appropriate litanies known only to the initiated. They spent hours concentrating on certain combinations of divine names, careful not to allow any impure thought, and invoking memories of ancestors.

At last the day arrived for the disciples' final meeting. From near and far they converged upon the secret place in the forest. But the Besht was not there. Precious moments turned into anguished hours. Silently, not daring to look at one another, the disciples wondered whether they had done something wrong. Were they unworthy of their sacred task? Perhaps they misunderstood or misinterpreted some of the master's directions: were they responsible for the failure of the entire undertaking? They were close to despair when the Besht appeared, breathless: "Do not feel guilty," he told them. "You have done nothing wrong. This morning, as I left the village on my way to you, I was already at the outskirts when I heard a child crying in a house nearby. I opened the door. The room was empty. I looked to my right, to my left: nobody. Only the child, in his cradle. He was weeping, weeping: his mother must have gone to do some errands. His tears broke my heart. So I stayed a while to calm him. I sang for him. When I stopped, he cried again. So I went on singing. Oh, I knew, with all my heart and soul I knew that you were waiting for me, and that the Messiah himself was waiting, but what could I do? I thought, when a Jewish child cries, one must not leave him; when a lonely Jewish child is so unhappy that he is shedding bitter tears, the Messiah himself will have to wait."

Another tale. It happened on Rosh Hashanah, the Day of the New Year, before or during the *mussaf* service. The hour was near for Reb Mendel, the appointed man, to blow the shofar which would permit the holy community of Israel to plead before the celestial tribunal. He was waiting for the rabbi's order. But the rabbi could not give it; he was sadly perplexed, because Satan, in heaven, had erected obstacles to interfere with the prayers. So the rabbi used all his inner resources, he appealed to his ancestors, imploring them to come and help him vanquish Satan. In vain. Satan remained vigorous and his barricade unmovable. The rabbi made an even greater effort, reciting prayers used for emergencies only. Still nothing. As for the faithful, they felt the gravity of the situation. They were about to burst into tears when, all of a sudden, the delicate sound of a flute pierced the silence: it was a young shepherd who wanted to play something. Naturally, after the shock subsided, he was swiftly silenced and reprimanded: didn't he know that it is forbidden to play musical instruments on such a holy day? But the rabbi quieted them down. "Why did you want to play?" he asked the flutist. "I don't know how to pray," answered the young shepherd, "I don't even know how to read. But like everybody here, I wanted to do something for God, and tell Him that I love Him, that's why I played a tune for Him." Then, the rabbi, his perplexity gone, spoke to his faithful of his joy: "What I couldn't do with my prayers, this young shepherd did with his tune. He vanquished Satan. Now let us proceed with the sacred service. Blow the shofar, Reb Mendel!"

Adversaries of Hasidism would disparage such tales, describing them as anti-intellectual, unworthy of the Jewish tradition, which emphasizes learning. That was, by the way, the initial major reproach leveled at the Beshtian movement: too much prayer, not enough study; it was thought to appeal to simplistic ways and methods, thus encouraging complacency and ignorance. Unfair criticism, to say the least, is the answer given by supporters of Hasidism. All of the Besht's closest disciples and friends—the Maggid of Mezeritch and Rebbe Pinhas the Kotitzer, among others—were recognized scholars with high standing in the scholarly community. How could they have despised learning and celebrated ignorance?

In truth, the Besht had one goal alone: use all means possible to maintain the Jewishness of Jews by showing them that their links to the great community of Israel have always been and will remain forever indestructible. And that they too, each in his or her own way, have a part to play in its destiny. As Rabbi Aharon of Karlin used to say: "If you don't know the Zohar, study Talmud. You don't know the Talmud? Open the Bible. You don't know the Bible? Say Psalms. You don't know Psalms? Do you know the Shema Israel? No? Then just think of our people and love one another. That will be sufficient."

Well, you may ask, is that really sufficient? Correction: as a beginning, that will be sufficient. After all, to love one's fellow man is a biblical commandment. That would lead the Hasid to look for it in the text. And study its commentaries. And climb the ladder of knowledge higher and higher. What was important was not to give up.

In the shtetl, one would often have enough reasons to indulge in doubting one's own chances and possibilities to the point of giving up. Came the Besht and declared: Stop! Take hold of yourselves! The people of Israel need each and everyone of you—and so does the God of Israel.

A Hasidic master would never say to his follower: You study too much, you spend too much time buried in books. Quite the contrary, he would say to him: You have not studied enough yet, continue; learn more, always more; but remember: study alone is not enough: it must bring you closer to others.

That is why, until the very last day of the shtetl, Hasidic *shtiblekh* existed in every small city, in every village, even in places where there was no local rebbe. In my little town, there were Hasidim belonging to many rebbes who would, on occasion, come to spend a few days and evenings with them. And then the entire town would join them for services, or for a *tish* on Shabbat. To be together, that was what Hasidism wanted. To be able to evoke common experiences and events one or the other has witnessed at the court of his master. *Dibuk Haveirim*, the obligation to be attached to friends, was—and still is—to Hasidim as important a principle as *Emunat Tzadikkim*, faith in the just teacher.

At this point, let us be frank: when we speak of the shtetl and its Hasidim's boundless faith in the *Tzaddik*, we must not fail to recall that it also had those who believed in the occult. People believed not only in the intercession of rebbes but also in the evil activities of Satan's envoys and various representatives. They were feared for their malevolent tricks and deeds. They were supposed to curse specific homes, turn friends into enemies, steal newborn babies. People also believed in virgins' being possessed by dead souls, or dybbukim, that very few rebbes could exorcise. Ah, all those legends of the powers of King Ashmedai's wife, Lilith; and of the little devils luring nocturnal travelers into the woods; and of the dead who rise from their graves at midnight, go to the synagogue, and read from Scripture: woe to the passerby who, if summoned by them, does not enter backwards. I myself, I remember how I used to tremble when I had to use the sidewalk near the cemetery.

But though terrified, we did not let it interfere with our studies. A shtetl without its schools—or the *kheider*—was inconceivable. The poorest of the poor saved enough, or nearly enough, to pay his children's tutor. The learning process began at age three, when his father would envelop him in his *tallit* and bring him to *kheider*. For the little boy, the *kheider* did not represent a kindergarten where he could play with his peers, but the first alien and probably hostile environment, far from his parents. There he would face a teacher with a long beard and, at times, a nasty look in his eyes if a pupil could not repeat after him the alphabet: this is an aleph, this a beth, this a gimel . . .

Usually, in spite of the honey candy given to him for every letter, as a kind of promise that the Torah is sweet, at that point, the little boy would begin to cry, unwilling to continue, afraid that once he is through with the alphabet, he will have to open the Five Books of Moses, then Rashi's commentaries, then the Talmud and multitudes of commentaries on commentaries—in other words, once he begins, there will be no end to study! Well, little boy from the shtetl, that's how it is, that's how it has always been; ask your father and his, and their grandfathers, ask thirty centuries of fathers, and they will tell you: the study of Torah has a beginning but no end!

The passion for learning, which is an essential part of the Jewish tradition, did not begin in the shtetl, but it existed there too. I never saw my father or any of my uncles go anywhere without a book under his arm. What was the worst insult thrown at a person? That he is an *am ha'aretz*, an ignoramus. Who is respected? A *talmid hakham*, a scholar. To describe him, we make use of several words: *Ben Torah*, son or man of Torah; *ilui*, someone with an oceanic memory; *harif*, someone with a sharp mind and penetrating intelligence; and, of course, *ga'on*—a genius.

Again, here too, we ought to recognize reality: not all children aspired to dedicate their lives to study. Some became merchants, others shoemakers, tailors, woodcutters, barbers, or . . . beggars. There were those who, fed up with the difficulties at home or anti-Semitic provocations in the street, responded to the call of an easier life in the Western world. Some went to study medicine in France or join an enterprise with an uncle in America. A few doctors came back and stayed in my town until the end. Then there were those youngsters who, influenced by communist agitators, ran away to Russia or stayed home to work clandestinely for the communist revolution aimed at transforming society by destroying its structures (at that time few people were aware of Stalin's cruelty and deep anti-Semitism). How many future intellectual leaders of various communist parties actually came from the world of the shtetl, and even from the world of the yeshiva? At the origin of their political commitment was the misery of their communities. Was it a rebellion on their part against their parents? Possibly. But not always. It may also have been *for* their parents—wishing to spare them an existence of more anguish, suffering, and humiliation. This point must always be remembered: life in the shtetl that we so love to celebrate was, from the economic viewpoint, far from being easy or pleasant.

I remember my first return to my little town twenty years after I had left it. I remember the shock I felt when discovering how poor the Jews of my town had been. I walked around familiar streets and squares, entering homes of friends I remembered from my childhood. What had transformed them into stifling, miserable dwelling places? Oh, I knew there had been poor people in our midst, but not that there were that many. Nor did I know that even people who were thought to be wealthy were in fact poor. For instance, my own family. In my childish perception, I thought we were not poor. Well, we were not. We owned our own house, we had a store. True, we had no running water, no bathroom, no toilet—so what! One could live very well without them. Still, we were properly dressed. On Wednesdays all the beggars would be fed in the courtyard. Why complain? But two or three generations later, I understood how mistaken I had been. Certain images resurfaced: my parents, on a long winter night, discussing whether we could afford to buy new clothes for the children, ordering a new stove, planning a trip to the mountains . . . Well, as in everything in life, wealth in the shtetl was relative; only the poverty of the poor was not.

And yet . . . on Shabbat, if poverty did not vanish altogether, it was attenuated. One can never speak enough of what Shabbat was like in the shtetl—and what it did for its inhabitants. The Shabbat helped people endure the other six days of the week, often gray and dark, heavy with sorrow and anxiety. Hence the waiting for Shabbat, which actually began much earlier. Thursday evening or early Friday morning, the housewife would already be busy preparing the hallah, gefilte fish, and cholent, the traditional elements of a Shabbat meal in the shtetl. The white tablecloth, the white shirt: everything had to be ready, and everything was the housewife's responsibility. One easily forgets that we owe the gift of Shabbat to the queen of the home, *Shabbat malka*, the Shabbat queen. We couldn't wait for her arrival.

In the stores, business was conducted with haste. Sellers and customers were equally in a hurry to go home. Men would go to the ritual bath, the *mikvah*, then dress and prepare to be worthy of welcoming the Shabbat, already on the horizon. The first to spot her would be the beadle, the shammash: he would go around stores and homes shouting *"Yidden, greit zicht tzu Shabbes!"*—Jews, ready yourselves for the Sabbath! Or a variation on the same theme: *"Yidden, s'is bald Shabbes oif der velt!"*—Jews, it's almost Sabbath in the world! At home, one did not need these reminders: the mother, mine too, lit the candles honoring Shabbat, one for each member of the family, and blessed them silently, with gestures of grace and tenderness.

Suddenly, her face would be illuminated by a light coming from another world, from another time, a light at once frail and eternal. And her beauty was multiplied sevenfold, so that even now as I am writing these words, the tears well up in my throat.

In the shul also, everything seemed different. More luminous, the candelabras. More serene, the faces. More melodious, the prayers. The Talmud is right: on Shabbat, one gains an added soul, the *neshama yeteira.*

Then, at the end of the service, many worshipers began running toward the visitors in shul. If there were none, the shammash would yell aloud, "Are there strangers here?" It was forbidden, absolutely forbidden, to allow anyone to be without an invitation to partake with some family in a Shabbat meal. Frequently people would fight over a visitor. It was an honor to invite him or her to their table. I myself can hardly remember a Shabbat without an honored guest in our home.

Whenever my maternal grandfather, Reb Dodye, was with us, we would feel doubly honored. And I was three times as happy. I have sworn never to forget him, nor his return from the Shabbat-eve office. He would stop at the threshold, kiss the mezuzah, and, his face burning with delight, start the Wizsnitzer *"Sholem aleikhem malakhei ha'shareit"*—Be blessed, angels in the service of peace. And it was as if peace now reigned over heaven and earth, a peace that brought together men and women of all nations, of all ages, a dream of which Shabbat remains the uplifting and inspiring symbol.

The end of Shabbat was signaled by mother and grandmother. Shortly before the Havdalah ceremony, which separates light from darkness and the sacred from the profane, the Shabbat from the weekdays, both women, like all mothers, would recite the special prayer attributed to the great Rebbe Levi-Yitzhak of Berditchev: *"Gott fun Avrohom, Yitzhok un Yankev . . ."* God of Abraham, Isaac, and Jacob, extend your protection over Thy children and ours . . . When the prayer ends, the Havdalah begins.

Whereupon another song takes hold of my memory: *"Bobeshi, zog nokh nit God fun Avrohom . . ."* It's a little child pleading with his grandmother not to recite her prayer, not yet, let her wait a bit longer, the sun hasn't set yet in the west, let Shabbat last a while longer . . . The little child loves the Shabbat and refuses to leave it behind—or to be left behind.

Which, of course, recalls an old Hasid or rebbe who, during the mystical Third Meal, is doing in his way what the grandmother could have done in hers. He sings a song: *"Ven ich volt ge'hat koi'ekh,"* if I had the strength, *"volt ich in di gassen gelofen,"* I would run through the streets, *"un ich volt geshre'in hoikh,"* and I would yell with all my might, *"Shabess, heiliger shabess,"* Holy, holy Sabbath . . . And legend has it that as long as he sang, the Shabbat would remain with him and his followers. So he sang and he sang . . .

This is perhaps the moment to remind you that Yiddish was the language of the shtetl, a language that dates back to the High Middle Ages. Feverish, rich in meaning and fantasy, it carries better than any other tongue the life and dreams of the shtetl. There are Yiddish words that have no equivalent in any other language: cholent is something other than a beef stew; a yarmulke is not quite a *kippah;* a *yossem* is different from an orphan, and *rahmones* is something more than *rahmanut,* or compassion. (By the way, "cholent" is French; during Napoleon's invasion of Russia, the troops used ways of keeping food warm on a slow fire: *chaud-lent.* In the same vein, the Yiddish *yente* comes from the Spanish name *Gentila* and Yiddish *Beile* from French *Belle.*)

I have said it often, let me repeat it: I love speaking Yiddish. There are songs and lullabies that can be sung only in Yiddish: prayers that only Jewish grandmothers can whisper at dusk, stories whose charm and secrets, sadness and nostalgia, can be conveyed in Yiddish alone—though I imagine Sephardic Jews could offer Ladino the same praise. I love Yiddish because it has been with me from the cradle. It was in Yiddish that I spoke my first words and expressed my first fears. It was in Yiddish that I greeted the Shabbat. I did not say *"Shabbat shalom"* but *"a gut Shabess."*

This immense love for Shabbat in the shtetl has often inspired Yiddish literature—and some anecdotes as well. Listen to one:

It is Friday afternoon. An old villager returns home from the *mik-vah*. It is snowing, but he doesn't mind it. Soon it will be Shabbes. He will rest, eat well, meet friends in shul. Suddenly he notices Ivan, freezing while pushing his sleigh with heavy sacks of coal on it. So he thinks to himself: ah, how clever of Uncle Jacob, and how silly of Uncle Esau. The Talmud says they decided to divide among themselves both worlds created for man. Jacob got the world to come, whereas Esau chose the world below. And look at Esau! What did he get? He works hard day after day, endures the bitterness of a laborious existence, whereas I am given to savor the joy and serenity of Shabbat. Well, who of the two brothers made a better deal? Sometime afterward, the old villager has to travel to Vienna, either on business or for medical reasons. He is put up at one of the good hotels. And for the first in his life he discovers luxury: big halls with flowers on every table, well-heated rooms, golden chandeliers, the most expensive fruits available, decorated bathrooms with showers and bathtubs . . . So he examines the material aspects of non-Jewish life and thinks to himself: Well, well, now, having seen Esau's world, I think I can say that Uncle Esau was not such an idiot after all.

This is a good transition to still another facet of shtetl life: humor. You may ask, isn't Jewish humor everywhere the same? It is. But in the shtetl it was funnier. Sharp yet never offensive, it displayed a taste for self-ridicule. One laughed at oneself more than at others.

Listen, for instance, to a brief dialogue by Sholem Aleichem, between a father and his little son:

"Moishele, be nice; close the window; it is cold outside."

"Dad, if I close the window, will it be warmer outside?"

A Hasidic anecdote: A future rebbe is received by an illustrious master, who asks him: "I hear that you are a great scholar. You are supposed to know the entire Talmud by heart. Is it true?"

"No, it is not."

"What! What people say is not true?"

"Not really. I do not know the entire Talmud; I only know half of it."

"Half? Which half?"

"Any half," answers the scholar, shyly lowering his head.

A peasant visits the big city and witnesses a grandiose funeral. The coffin is carried by horse and carriage draped in black; five cantors sing the appropriate chants; a crowd of hundreds accompanies the deceased to his resting place.

"Who is he?" asks the peasant.

Someone tells him: it is a very wealthy man who served as president of the community.

"Ah," exclaims the visiting peasant. *"Dos heist gelebt!"*—That's called living!

And another story. A cantor came home for his Shabbat luncheon; he looked depressed. "What is troubling you?" his wife asked.

"Can you imagine?" said the cantor. "I worked hard, so hard, on today's service. Then, as we left the synagogue, Yankel the shoemaker said to me: 'Well, Hazzen, today you were not aie-aie-aie: you could have been better.' How can I not be upset?"

"What does a Yankel know about cantorial music? He just repeats what everybody else says."

Still another anecdote, titled *"Eins fun di beide."* An unhappy man tells his friend his troubles—more precisely, his son's troubles. "He has been drafted to serve in the Czar's army, which is anti-Semitic, as everyone knows. I am at a loss: what should I do?"

"Don't worry," says his friend. *"Eins fun di beide,* it's either-or: either he passes the medical exam or he doesn't. If he fails, why worry? If he passes, *eins fun di beide,* either-or: either he is sent to the front or he isn't. If he isn't, then everything is OK. If he is, either-or: either he is wounded or he isn't. If he isn't, why be upset? If he is, either-or: either he lives or he dies. If he lives, all is perfect; if he dies, *eins fun di beide,* he goes either to paradise or to hell. If he goes to hell, *eins fun di beide:* either he manages to bribe the guard or . . . well, don't worry. Knowing him, he will."

Naturally, laughter in the shtetl is a remedy for misfortune, fear, and despair. In a way, it reflects the shtetl's generosity. We have already commented on this theme—yet not enough. For its magnitude and depth, it deserves a closer appreciation.

In spite of the religious dissensions, political splits, and social conflicts that can be found in every community, the shtetl's spirit of generosity cannot but move the reader. Numerous groups, committees, and associations covered well-defined sectors: the poor, the aged, the sick, the prisoners, the widows and orphans, the dead—and even the rich who were no longer rich. The latter were taken care of by a select committee whose members remained secret. It was called *matan be'seiser*: the clandestine charity. It had at its disposal special funds that were sneaked under the doors of the recipients at night.

Even nobler was the way some communities dealt with *tzedakah*: every year, before Passover, people would line up at the entrance of the community offices. Inside, in an empty room, there was a table and on it a plate with money. Each person would enter alone. If he or she was rich, they left money; if they were poor, they took money. And no one ever knew how much was taken or given.

And this custom, which reflects the way the shtetl was sensitive to people's pain and sorrow: At funerals, the beadle would precede or follow the coffin with a black charity box in his hands, saying in singsong: *"Tzedokoh tatzil mi'moves"*—Charity saves from death. Question: is it true? True forever? But then wouldn't a rich person live to 120 years, or longer? It would be enough for them to give charity every week, and why not, every day, every hour. But it is not that simple. Listen to the superb commentary, which I heard from an American rabbi: What is charity? It is for the living to be concerned with someone else's sadness or sickness. One who is not concerned is in fact not sensitive; one who is not sensitive is not really alive. And this is the meaning of the beadle's appeal: charity saves us from dying while we are still alive.

In the shtetl people lived—well or badly—but people lived before dying. And that was so until the day when the cruelest of our enemies emerged victorious over the shtetl, which they reduced to ashes.

May I, in conclusion, now speak of all that remains of the shtetl: its memory.

Long ago, I wrote a plea for the dead; then I composed a plea for the survivors. And then, as we entered a new century and millennium, I felt the need to write a new plea, a plea for the survivors' right to be remembered.

I confess: in spite of my growing pessimism concerning the memory of Auschwitz and Treblinka, I did not anticipate the recent insults and attacks from various quarters that their survivors have had to endure. Relentless, obscene, and ugly, they reflect a total absence of sensitivity toward them. As if they were to be hated for having suffered and for remembering, and above all, for still being alive.

Their desire to bear witness is being questioned, as is the veracity of their testimony. Unworthy motives are being attributed to them, their suffering is being transformed into farce and entertainment in films, plays, docudramas, and musicals. At best, they are being used in pseudo-scientific studies so as to prove a thousand and one scholarly theories—and they, the survivors, are not allowed even to protest.

My friend and companion Primo Levi called these malevolent critics and commentators "thieves of time . . . who infiltrate themselves through keyholes and cracks and cart out our memories without leaving a trace."

It is a painful subject to deal with, for it is a sad phenomenon. Is it new? Was it better in the beginning when there were no such thieves at all, when few writers dared to approach the theme itself? When survivors themselves preferred to be mute, since no one was willing to hear their tales, which were felt to be too morbid? Good-hearted people would interrupt them, giving them soothing counsel: "The past is past. Forget it. Better look to the future." Anyway, survivors forced themselves or were forced into silence, thinking: "What's the use? What we have to say, nobody would understand." Was Carlyle right in claiming that language belongs to time and silence to eternity? Must the ineffable remain outside the realm of words, simply because there are no words? Can Auschwitz be understood by anyone who wasn't there? An Israeli historian claims to be able to explain, and in doing so he proves how far he is from understanding it. Between facts and truth there is an abyss one may not cross with impunity. Only those who were there know what it meant to be there.

And yet . . . at one point, we all felt the imperative to listen to Shimon Dubnov's last desperate appeal as he was led to his execution by a Gestapo chief, his former pupil: *"Yiden, shreibt unfarshreibt"*—Jews, write, write down everything. We decided to open up our memory, and within the framework of what is possible, to do the impossible. Is it because of the Holocaust deniers who dominate so many Websites with their repulsive stories and articles? No. They do not deserve such credit. We must never grant them the dignity of a debate. What they say is indecent and is to be ignored with disdain.

But lately the attacks come from another direction—from Jews. Motivated by a senseless hatred of Israel, they try to delegitimate its sovereignty by depriving it of its memory. Then they slander those who defend it. One of them went so far as to write a preface for a book by Robert Faurisson, the principal denier in Europe. His disciple and ally published a frivolous pamphlet which became a bestseller in German-speaking countries because of its vicious attacks on Zionists and survivors; he calls them liars, profiteers, manipulators. In Germany, Martin Walser, seen as the old man of letters, declared publicly that he is fed up with being reminded of Auschwitz. Ernest Nolte, who acquired notoriety by relativizing the Holocaust, received an important award that provoked shock on both sides of the ocean.

In many academic and literary circles, a kind of taboo has been broken. Now everything goes. Nothing is off-limits any more. What used to be sacred is being commercialized, trivialized. Receiving a Tony award on television, watched by millions all over the world, a talented comedian found it possible to say, "Thank you, Adolf Hitler," then added, "for being so funny on stage." Well, to his victims, Hitler may have been many things but surely not funny.

What then could the very last survivors do now except persevere? The task of remembering is getting harder and harder, more and more discouraging, we all are aware of that. But to choose oblivion would be worse. It would be treason.

Acknowledgments

This volume is the written version of lectures given in recent years at the 92nd Street Y in New York and at Boston University, where I have been teaching since 1976.

The editing was superbly done by Ileene Smith and Altie Karper: I owe them my gratitude.

E.W.